Harvard East Asian Series 25

CHINA'S STRUGGLE
FOR NAVAL DEVELOPMENT
1839–1895

The East Asian Research Center
at Harvard University administers
research projects designed
to further scholarly understanding
of China, Korea, Japan, and adjacent areas.

CHINA'S STRUGGLE FOR NAVAL DEVELOPMENT

1839-1895

John L. Rawlinson

HARVARD UNIVERSITY PRESS
CAMBRIDGE, MASSACHUSETTS
1967

© Copyright 1967 by the President and Fellows of Harvard College. All rights reserved. Distributed in Great Britain by Oxford University Press, London. Library of Congress Catalog Card Number 66-10127. Printed in the United States of America.

Preparation of this volume was aided by a grant from the Ford Foundation.

To Margaret Alexandra

FOREWORD

China's struggle for naval development was confined to the early period of her unhappy contact with the modern world, from the Opium War of 1840 to the year 1895. The Chinese navy of the 1880's and 1890's, a front line of defense against foreign aggression, was one of China's first modern achievements. But it came to an abrupt end and its history was all but lost to view in the confusion attending the collapse of the imperial order. While China's military development continued steadily, through successive phases marked by the Hunan army, the Peiyang army, the Whampoa cadets, and the People's Liberation Army, naval development came to a halt as if the Peiyang fleet had been sunk without trace or survivors. This story has the fascination of high tragedy. Professor Rawlinson's analysis in this volume puts it also in the perspective of China's problem of modernization.

The late-Ch'ing attempt to modernize included an extensive and costly effort to build a navy because in the nineteenth century naval power was a chief index of great power status. When the war with Japan over Korea grew imminent in 1894, British naval officers who had been assisting Li Hung-chang in building the Peiyang fleet hoped that it could give a good account of itself against the modern fleet which other British officers had been helping the Japanese to develop. But by the end of the war in 1895 the Japanese fleet had destroyed the Peiyang fleet. More than anything else, this defeat dramatized imperial China's tragic failure. For half a century afterward China's international fortunes tended on the whole to decline, notably without any attempt again to develop significant naval power.

John Rawlinson is well equipped to tell this important story. He began his experience of things Chinese as the son of a distinguished American missionary editor in Shanghai. After graduation from Oberlin in 1942, he studied Chinese in the United States Navy, and after World War II he served under the American Embassy in China, becoming vice-consul at Tientsin. He then took his M.A. and Ph.D. at Harvard and is now associate professor of history and chairman of the Asian Studies Program at Hofstra University, Hempstead, Long Island.

East Asian Research Center
Harvard University

ACKNOWLEDGMENTS

In gathering the information for this book, I have tried insofar as possible to do my own translating from Chinese sources, but so great was the bulk of material that I have had to rely on expert assistance. In this connection, I deeply appreciate the careful work done by Immanuel C. Y. Hsü, Wai-kam Ho, Kwang-chih Chang, and John B. Liu. Mr. Te-kong Tong also made helpful suggestions. I am especially indebted to my friend Hsin-pao Chang, whose untimely death is a loss not only to me but to the community of scholars.

At the East Asian Research Center, Kwang-Ching Liu, Elizabeth M. Matheson, and Olive Holmes have made most valuable suggestions, Mrs. Matheson in particular helping me to overcome many stylistic grotesqueries. Over many years I have been indebted to John K. Fairbank, scholar, mentor, gentle but persistent critic, and friend.

My departmental chairman, Dr. Gerrit P. Judd, painstakingly read the manuscript and excised many cumbersome passages to the profit of the reader.

Thanks for further helpful suggestions made by Francelia Mason of Harvard University Press are also most appropriate, and they should include the work of Marjorie Lawlor, who typed the manuscript.

Permission from Constable and Company Limited, London, to quote material from *Pulling Strings in China* by W. F. Tyler (1929) is gratefully acknowledged.

Since this volume is dedicated to my wife, I need not reiterate here the great importance of her contribution.

June 1, 1966   J.L.R.
Hofstra University

CONTENTS

I	The Traditional Chinese Water Force and Its Failure in the Opium War	1
II	China's Delayed Response to the Western Naval Challenge	19
III	The Military Self-Strengthening Movement, to 1875	41
IV	Li Hung-chang and Naval Development, 1875–1885	63
V	Achievements and Problems in the Military Building Effort, 1875–1884	96
VI	Disaster in the South: The Chinese Navy in the Sino-French War, 1884–1885	109
VII	Naval Developments after 1885: the Emergence of the Peiyang Fleet	129
VIII	Naval Training, 1885–1894	154
IX	Disaster in the North: Naval Aspects of the Sino-Japanese War, 1894–1895	167
X	Conclusions	198
	NOTES	207
	APPENDICES	
A	Table of Organization	243
B	Table of Officer Ranks	244
C	Ships, 1860–1894	246

CONTENTS

D	List of Chinese Personal Names	262
	BIBLIOGRAPHY	292
	GLOSSARY	306
	INDEX	307

CHINA'S STRUGGLE
FOR NAVAL DEVELOPMENT

1839–1895

I

THE TRADITIONAL CHINESE WATER FORCE AND ITS FAILURE IN THE OPIUM WAR

China was soundly defeated by Britain in the Opium War of 1839–1842. The Treaty of Nanking in 1842, the first of the "unequal treaties," opened a new phase of the Western impact on China; ultimately, the Confucian system proved to be incapable of adjustment to this impact. China's defeat in 1842 may be called the start of a revolutionary process which is still under way.

Since the modern challenge to China has come almost entirely from the sea, it follows that the old China was not able, from 1839 at least, to defend her coast, whether with forts and troops ashore, or with a navy. This failure — in particular, the failure of the Ch'ing dynasty (1644–1911) to create an adequate modern naval defense — is the subject of this book. It is one of history's important failures.

Why did the dynasty fail to defend itself on the sea? It is not enough to say that the dynasty was weak, or in decline. It mustered enough strength to put down the terrible Taiping Rebellion (1850–1864) and the associated rebellions elsewhere in China which lasted well into the 1870's. The idea of "dynastic decline," although it touches on morale and the quality of leadership, seems to be on close examination a question-begging convention rather than a sufficient explanation.[1] In this case, at least, a modern navy was built (or bought) and manned, and it went into two modern naval wars, one with France in 1884–85, and one with Japan a decade later. It was both times defeated, but the dynasty's maritime defense was modernized despite the "decline" of the Manchus, and modernized enough to ensure that the contemptuous Western references of the 1830's to the traditional Chinese water force (one Briton dismissed it as a "monstrous burlesque" which could be defeated by a handful of New Zealand

1

war canoes) were in the 1880's replaced by professional Western praise of China's modern steam fleet.²

New ships were assembled, but the dynasty did not use them effectively. Leadership was of course involved in this inefficiency, but there were able as well as inept men in the hierarchy. Ability is conditioned by attitudes and organization; that is, by institutions. Hence the explanation of the dynasty's nineteenth-century failure to defend itself on the sea must involve the institutional structure of Confucian China. The term "institution" will here include such phenomena as the political organization of the empire and the civil service examination system; and the major thesis of this book is that traditional China's institutions worked against effective naval modernization.

China's traditional water force had its first sustained modern encounter in the Opium War. Britain fought the war in the name of freer trade, diplomatic equality with China, and extraterritoriality, and also for compensation for the opium which Commissioner Lin Tse-hsü confiscated and destroyed in 1839, in his root-and-branch extirpation of the smuggling which had long strained Anglo-Chinese relations. In general, Britain sought to destroy the age-old Confucian tribute system, by which China had subordinated trade to a ritual supposed to demonstrate barbarian veneration of the Son of Heaven.

Naval fighting began in the Chuenpi battle of November 1839, in which the war junks of Admiral Kuan T'ien-p'ei were defeated. After several intermissions, Britain terminated the war on her own terms, in August 1842 at Nanking. The first phase of the fighting took the British in the summer of 1840 (their fleet of nearly fifty ships included four steamers) up to the mouth of the Pei-ho, near the capital, Peking. In this first northern naval expedition, Britain entered and blockaded several coastal ports, and took strategic Tinghai on Chusan Island (July 5, 1840). Britain's object was to present her demands to China's highest officials. Ch'i-shan, governor-general of Chihli, interviewed Captain Charles Elliot and persuaded him to return his fleet to Canton. Extended talks were promised. In December 1840, Ch'i-shan and Elliot started their negotiations near Canton. Elliot reinforced his demands by taking the Chuenpi forts, which guarded the estuary of the Pearl River. In February 1841, the so-called Chuenpi Convention was drawn up. Britain was given some of her demands, and Elliot returned the Chuenpi forts and Tinghai. To the Tao-kuang emperor, who discovered that Ch'i-shan had been dishonest in reporting the convention, it gave far too much. In any event, the agreement was repudiated by both sides.

The second phase of the Opium War began under new leadership on both sides. Ch'i-shan, who had replaced the disgraced Lin Tse-hsü, was himself replaced as military commander by I-shan and as governor-general by Ch'i-kung (note the division of power). The British leader, Captain Elliot, was succeeded by Sir Henry Pottinger. In February 1841 the British advanced on Canton, taking all the river forts and forcing the Canton officials to ransom the city — which the helpless I-shan financed with the aid of Canton merchants. This second truce lasted until Pottinger arrived with instructions to retake Tinghai and present British demands in the north. A second northern expedition started in August 1841; Tinghai was reoccupied on October 1. A winter hiatus followed, and then Pottinger, reinforced, resumed hostilities in the spring of 1842. He advanced up the forbidden but largely undefended Yangtze in June 1842, and finally forced China, now represented by a new imperial commissioner, Ch'i-ying, to sign a treaty at Nanking.

So China was propelled into a new era. Her water force had not defended her against this latest "barbarian" thrust. It had not really been an "opium war"; it was a clash between cultures. In the following pages we shall make a systematic survey of the traditional water force. Much of the illustrative material will be taken from the Opium War. It will not be necessary to review all of the battles, even those which were primarily naval ones; there are already many accounts of them.[3] That China's traditional water force was in need of drastic reform will be clear enough.

In the early nineteenth century, the average Chinese war junk was a small vessel, displacing at the most between 250 and 300 tons. Speed and handiness aside, such craft were of about half the displacement of American China packets built in the 1830's, and were smaller than a sixth-rate battleship of Nelson's day, which had twenty to twenty-eight guns, a 120-foot lower gun deck, and displaced about 600 tons.[4] Traditional Chinese sketches show war junks of perhaps 100 feet in length, with two or three masts, an unprotected deck, a few pieces of ordnance, and perhaps one or two fighting tops. Chinese shipyards could build junks of upwards of 1000 tons (still much smaller than a British first-rate sailing battleship, which displaced from 2000 to 2600 tons, and carried 100 or more guns), but this size was not the war junk standard.[5]

Such central direction of war junk building as there was lay in the Board of Works in Peking, but this agency was mainly concerned with civilian works. In the provinces, there had been, since 1732, a fairly elaborate system of water force construction. Each province with a water force yard had a superintendent of repair, acting through junior military and civilian officers.[6] A mid-nineteenth-century listing shows eighteen shipyards: five in Kwangtung, four in Fukien, three in Chekiang, five in the Kiangnan provinces of Kiangsu and Anhwei, and one in Shantung.[7] Repair regulations stipulated that minor repairs could be made to ocean war junks every three years; major repairs were allowed only in the fifth year. The system was not completely rigid, for there were some exceptions, but apparently it was designed to prevent peculation.[8] War junks were divided into classes, based on construction costs, and were assigned a ten-year life — about the same longevity estimated for eighteenth-century British wooden warships.[9]

That all was not always well in these shipyards is shown by several sharp eighteenth-century edicts demanding efficiency. At times repairs immobilized too many war junks, so that the pirates had a free run; or there were delays; or too much expenditure. Whether or not the yards were periodically brought back to peak efficiency, at the time of the Opium War the estimate longevity of ocean war junks had dropped to seven years.[10]

The nineteenth-century war junk was not a clearly specialized instrument of war. In the West, the introduction of heavy naval ordnance had forced changes in hull and rig design for fighting ships, and merchant vessels followed this lead. Whatever the efficiency of those Chinese junks which amazed Marco Polo, or of those which later bore the eunuch-admiral Cheng Ho to Africa's east coast, by late Ming times China's commercial junks were bigger and faster than her war junks. To control the pirates, who used commercial junks, the Ming tried to limit the size of such vessels, rather than increasing war junk size. Failing in this, the government (the Manchus, in this case) ordered that its war junks should be disguised as merchantmen, so that capture might be effected by guile.[11] But the pirates were not checked, and merchants often voluntarily built their own protective fleets, or hired protection. In 1809, for example, Canton merchants bought a 108-ton British brig. Later they tried to charter a 350-tonner, at the direction of the Canton prefect, "to stiffen the Chinese Navy." [12] As late as 1857, British witnesses wrote that imperial war junks were indistinguishable from commercial junks, save for the guns on the war junks. Bulwarks and gunports were not used, although some of the junks met by the British during the Opium War attempted to protect their crews with rattan shields.[13] In the heyday of Ming naval power, 400-man crews were usual on war junks, but in the Opium War, the average was closer to 100.[14]

As a result of this regression, the early nineteenth-century Chinese water force was a mélange of types. According to a Board of Works list, there were twenty-seven types of ocean war junks in random disposition (five of these types were used on inland waterways as well). The list is not discernibly ordered by size, number of masts, or the like. Some of the type names cannot be translated, being entirely of local currency, and seemingly nonsensical. The designation "grain boat" appears frequently in this list of war junk types. Although the weirdness of some of the names can be perhaps matched by that of the American terms "pinkie" and "bug-eye," which refer to fishing vessels, the point remains that China's traditional naval lists showed little standardization.[15]

Although many contemporary Westerners admitted that Chinese junks had fine sailing qualities, the prevailing Western opinion of them as war vessels was unflattering. One Briton in the 1830's wrote that traditional war junks were

large unwieldy-looking masses of timber, with mat sails, wooden anchors, rattan cables, a considerable sheer, flat upright stems, no stern posts, enormously high sterns, ornamented with gold and paintings, considerably weakened too by a large hole in which the monstrous rudder can be hoisted up and housed in bad weather, immense quarter galleries, and look-out houses on the deck; generally drawing but little water, flat-floored, painted red and black with large goggle eyes in the bows . . . few are over two hundred and fifty to three hundred tons.[16]

These war junks were armed in haphazard fashion. In the Opium War, the number of guns, as noted by foreigners, varied from four to fourteen per ship. As a rule, these guns threw a ball of less than ten pounds. Foreign guns of uncertain vintage were seen, in one case guns so big relative to the junk across whose deck they were lashed that a foreigner was sure that if they were actually fired they would either sink the junk or be flung by their own recoil into the water.[17] Guns were mounted on solid beds or crude swivels. A coarse, uneven gunpowder was used. War junks also carried assortments of traditional small arms: lances, pikes, swords, gingals, and even "plenty of good stones." [18] To compare such vessels to a British seventy-four-gun third-rate, or, worse, to an armed steamer like the experimental iron *Nemesis*, which with a few others of her kind wreaked havoc among Chinese fleets during the Opium War, would be absurd. In some cases, British tars using mere ship's boats, armed with swivel guns or rockets, triumphed over as many as fifteen or twenty war junks.[19]

If individual Chinese war junks were weak and ineffective against nineteenth-century British sailing and steam ships, the organization of the Chinese water force made the contrast all the more dramatic, for it worked against any concerted military effort. Most of the old water force was part of the Chinese Green Banner land force, which was established by the Manchus, apart from their centralized Manchu Banner units, as a kind of provincial constabulary. The Board of War in Peking did not have real power.[20] The Chün-chi ch'u, or Grand Council, could issue imperial military directives without using the Board. A strong emperor could coordinate all of his military forces; even a weak one had the power to punish his officers. Since military officers down through the second grade were directly linked to the emperor by the right of direct memorial, we can hardly say that the fault of the Green Banner system was that it could not be centralized.

Green Banner units, land and sea, were organized by province. Provinces in Manchu China were grouped by two's, as a rule, and placed under governors-general. In maritime China Proper there were four such pairs or regions: Liang-Kwang, the linked provinces of Kwangtung and Kwangsi; Min-Che, or Fukien and Chekiang; Liang-Kiang, or Kiangsu, Kiangsi, and Anhwei; and Chihli, the single province in which the capital was located. Shantung stood alone under its governor. Governors-general, and below them the provincial governors, stood at the head of the provincial chains of command. These civilians held military authority by concurrent appointment, ex-officio, as presidents or vice-presidents of the Board of War.[21] Under them, in each province, came Green Banner generals and admirals, for the land and water forces respectively.

There were, however, many breaks in this chain of command. The officials mentioned commanded the Chinese land and sea forces. Manchu troops in provincial garrisons were under their own generals (the so-called Tartar generals), who were not subordinated to provincial authorities. The Tartar general in a given region usually outranked the governor-general, and his military unit was always the larger. In five of the costal provinces (Manchuria was administered purely by Manchus), the Tartar general also had water forces, that is, in Kwangtung, Fukien, Chekiang, Kiangsu, and Fengtien.[22]

Furthermore, governors-general and governors were often at odds. The former had no control over provincial officials directly below each governor, for example, lieutenant-governor, finance commissioner, salt controller, and so on. These provincial officials were appointed directly from Peking, and had to do with revenues and in some cases with military duties. All of these high officials enjoyed the right of direct memorial. Here was the Manchu system of checks and balances, in which high Manchu and Chinese officials watched one another. Governors-general and governors alone had the right to impeach subordinates, but this provision did not make for a single, strong chain of command in each region or province.[23]

Below these high officials were others with both civil and military authority — for example, the taotais. In each region there was a blurring of responsibility, which was exemplified in Chekiang in 1840. Hearing that British forces were near Tinghai, the Chekiang admiral, Chu T'ing-piao, led his force to sea; at the same time, Li Shao-fang, the Ning-shao-t'ai taotai, led water forces to Chenhai; a little later, the Ningpo prefect (chih-fu) was ordered to build a boom of boats and chains to keep the enemy out.[24] In addition, each of the highest officials had his own command. In the coastal Manchu and Green Banner establishments, there were twenty-four of these commands, not uniformly established: the distribution was such that in Kwangtung and Fukien each there were five commands, those of the governor-general, governor, admiral, general, and Tartar general, but in Chihli only two, for the governor-general and admiral.[25] These so-called "direct commands" were nominally of brigade strength (those under the military men were larger than those under the civilian officials), and were largely independent. Other Green Banner forces in each province not in direct commands were "indirectly" commanded by the named officials. Some brigadier-generals had more strength than their superiors in this system; some district civilian officials with military concurrencies could be nearly independent, acting only in response to a "direct" command; in some cases, local officers had to answer to three or four chiefs, as did the senior post captain of a water force unit on Formosa who corresponded with the Board of War about the Formosan aborigines, and was also beholden to the Tartar general *and* the admiral at Foochow, as well as to the Min-Che governor-general.[26]

In this elaborate system, the Green Banner table of organization for land and water forces (brigade, regiment, battalion, squadron, and post) almost disappears from view. Yet the disarray was not a function of dynastic decline. The system had been largely created by the K'ang-hsi Emperor, to ensure stability.[27]

Comment on the personnel system of the traditional water force must be based largely on material directly pertinent to the parent Green Banner land force. There were nine Green Banner officer ranks in each of the provincial forces. The water force designations, in approximate English equivalent, were admiral, senior post captain, junior post captain, commander, lieutenant commanding, senior lieutenant, junior lieutenant, sub-lieutenant, and ensign. These nine ranks corresponded to the nine basic civilian official grades, save that admiral did not rank in the top half of the opposite civilian grade (each of these being divided into an upper and lower half), but only in the lower. Military service did not have the prestige of the civil service.[28]

Officer recruits came from the civil service, the ranks of hereditary nobles, officers' sons, the land military, successful candidates in the military examination system, and the rank and file. Some water force officers were ex-pirates who had been lured from their old calling by the offer of rank.[29] There were minute regulations governing promotion, in which the accumulation of seniority and merit were nominally basic. However, the emperor could set aside the regulations, and not all officers were experts. Imperial interference was most notable in the higher ranks; below junior lieutenant, provincial authorities had the say, for officers and enlisted men. They preferred men of the sea, fishermen or ex-pirates, or men of martial accomplishment as shown in the land military. Fukien was a favored source of seafaring men; it was said that the Fukien pirates included the "flower" of the nation, whereas the imperial fleet had chiefly the "dregs."[30]

There were detailed provisions for rewards, honors, and superannuation. Green Banner punishments were drawn from a basic code dating from 1731, which had been slightly amended. Officers and men were not subject to the same penalties. For the former, a greater emphasis was laid on corrective humiliation (one Westerner in the 1830's noticed a water force officer near Shanghai with an arrow thrust through his ear, captioned with a statement of the culprit's disregard of a military law),[31] which included degrading them but keeping them on at their posts. For cowardice or treason, the code uniformly prescribed death. The operation of the code depended on the will of the emperor. There was no provision for the investigation of a charge by a military court, and the criteria were ultimately moral, so that ultimate judgment could be exercised only by the Son of Heaven. Uncertainty about condignity of punishment, or the imperial mood, must have been familiar to men in action, certainly to the higher officers.[32]

Most training took place in prescribed coastal patrols. These patrols were not always properly made, for an edict of 1806 referred to standing orders about coastal training and warned officers to select good men, and to go to sea themselves. Just before the Opium War, annual examinations were specified for water force officers, who again were ordered to go to sea in person.[33] In 1840, an imperial commissioner expressed concern about personnel shortages and the failure of the routine provincial examinations, and called for a special system to cull men of the sea for the water force.[34] The military examinations were farcical, and probably most officers did not hold degrees in any event. A Western eyewitness of the 1830's wrote that Chinese sailors were proficient in "mere coasting"; the coasts were known, with harbor directories which were "pretty correct," but clearly the typical water force officer was not expert in open-water navigation. Not even dead reckoning was used.[35]

There were formal provisions for coordinating the efforts of the provincial Green Banner water force units. The provincial "posts" had interlocking patrol areas; in season at least, the coast was covered by cruising vessels, with penalties fixed for nonperformance. Sometimes special arrangements were made, as in 1750, when the heavily-traveled Min-Che coast was given a special coverage, involving three governors-general and a variety of local officials. Manchu water force units were not involved in such patrols.[36] It has already been noted, however, that merchants often hired their own protection against pirates. In 1800, the cruise system was reorganized (yet another example of an order including an imperial injunction that officers actually go to sea).[37] In 1831, a censor asked that admirals not be limited to fixed areas for cruising. His request was refused, on the ground that if this were done, there would be no clear definition of responsibility. Everything considered, we may wonder about how well or regularly the cruise system was carried out.[38]

Military leaders were not in a formless situation. Each was tied to the center by appointment, by memorial, by required periodic audiences, and by the threat of punishment. But the organization of the military was, in the words of one recent student of the subject, "almost usless in time of war."[39] It was further complicated by the designation, during emergencies, of special imperial commissioners, whose surrogate powers could supposedly move the ancient mechanism quickly.

As for the number of war junks which could be gathered in a threatened zone, either there were too few vessels in the nineteenth century, or there was too little coordination to make even an impressive show. Thomas F. Wade, in his excellent study of China's mid-nineteenth-century armed forces, listed these fleet strengths: Kwangtung, 159 vessels; Fukien, 272; Chekiang, 302; Kiangnan, 108; Shantung, 12; and Fengtien, 10.[40] In early Ming days, the guard stations had 2700 war junks. Evidently there had been a decline.[41] Furthermore, the vessels were too different to have made much of a joint effort, even if the organizational scheme had facilitated such an effort. In practice, only a few junks were as a rule present in one spot. In 1833, the missionary Charles Gutzlaff, who was a passenger on an armed British merchant vessel which was illegally exploring China's coasts, noted seven or eight vessels at Namoa, although this was the admiral's headquarters, and the admiral supposedly mustered 5237 men.[42] Admiral Kuan T'ien-p'ei mustered twenty-nine war junks off Canton in the first clash of the Opium War, in November 1839. When they took Woosung in June 1842, the British encountered an outer fleet of 100 junks, but most of them were fishing boats pressed into official service.

A concrete example of the lack of coordination is the organizational situation on the Min-Che coast in summer and early fall of 1840. The British, then on their first naval expedition to the north, took Tinghai (on Chushan Island, off the Chekiang coast, near Ningpo) on July 5. A few war junks made a feeble resistance, of which a cynical British observer wrote that "they had no mercy to expect from the emperor, if they had not waited for the effects of our attack . . . which they did in the most devoted manner, and were almost immediately destroyed." [43] The governor-general of Min-Che was Teng T'ing-chen. One of his "direct" commands was a naval battalion. The Fukien admiral was based at Futsing. At Foochow there was a Manchu water force battalion under the Tartar general, who was the best-paid of his kind in the empire. Amoy was considered to be a strong water force station, with huge granite-faced batteries.[44] None of these places made any floating resistance. In Chekiang, Wu-er-kung-o was governor, but he did not directly command the provincial admiral, with his three water force brigades at Hwangyen, Wenchow, and Chushan. There was also a Manchu water force unit at Chapu.

The fall of Tinghai brought punishments. Wu-er-kung-o was cashiered and replaced by Liu Yün-k'o in August. The Chekiang general was also removed, to be replaced by Yu Pu-yun, the Fukien general. In addition, I-li-pu, who was the governor-general at Nanking, was sent to Chekiang as imperial commissioner with orders to retake Tinghai.[45]

Before learning of his demotion, Wu-er-kung-o asked the emperor to order Teng T'ing-chen to send Fukien troops into Chekiang, and to order I-li-pu (still at Nanking) to send water force units. Teng replied to the emperor's order that he could spare no troops, but had ordered recruitment of 1000 "water-braves" for Chekiang's relief. After Wu-er-kung-o was removed, Teng again memorialized that he could not meet the ex-governor's request for 2000 Fukien mariners.[46] In September, Yu Pu-yun, now in Chekiang, asked for naval reinforcements from Kwangtung and Fukien. This request the emperor referred to I-li-pu, who was now at Ningpo. I-li-pu himself asked for troops, and Yu Pu-yun, seeing no result to his earlier request, repeated his plea.[47]

Tinghai was not retaken by force, but was returned to China in connection with the abortive Chuenpi Convention of January 1841 (it was retaken by the British on their second northern expedition in 1842). The interesting thing about the requests and orders noted above is that they reveal a command situation in which the governor approached his own governor-general only by way of the emperor, and a general on special assignment bypassed not only both of these superior civilian officials, but also the Chekiang admiral, under whose orders the Chekiang general was supposedly placed,[48] and all of this was to request military reinforcements for Chekiang which were to come at least in part from the paired province of Fukien. Even I-li-pu, an imperial commissioner with rank of governor-general, did not move troops on his own authority, even though the emperor sought his opinion on troop movements undertaken by the Min-Che governor-general. Evidently the designation of an imperial commissioner did no more than open another channel of communications to the emperor, where there were already too many. No water force concentration was produced.

Further evidence of the prevalent disorganization is the fact that the British usually left only one ship, and not more than two, to blockade the ports they entered and reduced on their northern expeditions. In their final thrust up the forbidden Yangtze in the summer of 1842 they left the guarding of the lower estuary to the solitary *North Star*, which bore twenty-six guns.⁴⁹ The invaders feared no grand cooperation between the scattered parts of the traditional water force.

The organizational fragmentation of the traditional water force suggests a further problem: the force had no over-all strategy, or tradition of far-ranging, purposive missions. In Ch'ing times, the water force was strictly an antipiratical force. Some very impressive antipiratical missions were led by Shih Lang (1621–1696) and his son Shih Shih-p'iao (d. 1721), and also by Li Ch'ang-keng (1750–1808). In 1721, Shih Shih-p'iao, as Fukien admiral, led 600 ships to defeat rebels on Taiwan. Li Ch'ang-keng, as Chekiang admiral, persistently fought Annamese and Chinese pirates around the turn of the nineteenth century, although his ships were usually smaller than those of the pirates, and he sometimes had to build his own larger vessels with special funds which he persuaded provincial authorities to give him.⁵⁰ On the other hand, pirates were often merely ignored, or they were bought over. What was lacking was a tradition of meeting an enemy far offshore. Perhaps antipiratical activity can produce no blue-water strategy — although in early Ming times, when the pirates were Japanese, it was said that "the Wako come by sea and should be fought at sea," for "to repel them at sea is easy, [but] to repel them after they are ashore is hard." ⁵¹ The Ch'ing dynasty in the 1660's, however, deemed it more prudent to parry the Taiwan-based Ming loyalist Coxinga by clearing the coasts of population than by meeting the raider at sea.

After the founding of the Ch'ing dynasty, the maritime challenge came predominantly from the West. In the eighteenth century occasional armed foreign ships appeared. British warships were among them, and they were not always heedful of the imperial exclusion of foreign men-of-war from the inner waterways of Canton, which after 1757 was the only port open to Western trade. We may see the Chinese naval strategy by looking at the Chinese responses to these thrusts. There was no massive effort made to exclude the intruder, or to improve Chinese war junks so that they could match the obstreperous foreigners' ships. The five volumes of H. B. Morse, *The Chronicles of the East India Company Trading to China*, contain but a dozen or so references to the water force, none of which show the water force in a favorable light as an enforcer of imperial regulations.⁵² Often the principal weapon used to bring the "barbarians" into line was the suspension of the trade which brought them to China's waters. For example, in response to the blatant violation of China's neutrality in the War of 1812 by the H.M.S. *Doris*, which seized an American prize ship right at Canton itself, local authorities cut off the trade.[53] It was the tribute-system mentality of official China, with its condescension toward all non-Chinese, which set the pattern of enforcement.

Since British naval policy in the nineteenth century generally showed a considerable respect for China's regulations, this non-martial approach worked fairly well. Even after the abolition in 1834 of the East India Company's monopoly — which brought more friction, as thereafter many more British ships entered the Canton trade and were no longer subject to Company restraint — British navy ships were ordered to show "great caution and discretion" in their "occasional" visits to Canton.[54] On no account were they to force the guarding forts. With few exceptions, the British navy did not challenge the Chinese water force until the Opium War itself. But the choice always lay in the hands of the British. In 1834, when Lord Napier called two Royal Navy vessels to Canton to support his efforts to regularize Anglo-Chinese relations after abolition of the Company's monopoly, the ships fought their way in through the Bogue forts and found that defending cannon balls merely bounced off their sides and at times hardly tumbled from the forts' guns.[55] Gutzlaff's account of the illegal cruise of the *Amherst* in the mid-1830's is full of comic-opera references to war junks at the various ports, which fled at the lifting of a British spy-glass (mistaken for the lifting of a gun), or dispersed from a close watch of the intruder when the irritated British command sent a long-boat to cut the cable of the Chinese flagship, or contented themselves with setting off firecrackers.[56]

Probably the explanation for the absence of a clear-cut strategic tradition in the Chinese water forces was that China had no wide-flung maritime colonial system. In the fifteenth century the Ming admiral Cheng Ho took ships of great size repeatedly into the Indian Ocean and as far as Africa, long before Europe entered her Age of Discovery. But he was not searching for a New World, or spices, or colonies. After the capturing of a few petty rulers en route and the exaction of tribute missions, these deep expeditions were cut off. Various explanations of this curious lapse have been advanced, and the Confucian mentality of the Ming officialdom figures largely in them, along with economic troubles and the revival of a threat on the inner Asian frontiers.[57] Cheng Ho did not lay down a strategy. In the nineteenth century, China's water force men had only a certain tactical sense, which was invoked when a maritime enemy came within sight of the home ports of China. For this kind of activity, no "far-distant, storm-beaten ships" (to use Mahan's description of the British fleet which defeated Napoleon) were needed. Forts and guns ashore better symbolized China's defenses than did the war junk itself.

The forts at Canton were an example of the best Chinese river and shore fortifications. The Bogue (the Bocca Tigris, or Tiger's Mouth) was the primary fortified area, about twenty-five miles below Canton on the Pearl estuary. Outside of this narrow pass lay Chuenpi and Tycocktow Islands, both fortified. The three-quarter-mile Bogue channel was braced by heavy forts on Anunghoy and Wantung Islands. Inside were Little Tycocktow and Tiger Islands, with minor works. Between the Bogue and Canton were numerous other forts, some on remote deltaic side passages and very old. Guns were of various descriptions, some being of Ming Jesuit provenance. Lin Tse-hsü made great efforts to strengthen the whole system during his tenure at Canton in 1839 and 1840, as did his successor, Ch'i-shan. Early in 1841 the British confiscated about 1200 guns from the whole river system — although some of this number were still unmounted, so hasty had been the preparation, and some were by Chinese admission liable to overheat and blow up.[58] Canton's granite-faced forts were not typical. In many ports taken by the British up the coast, the forts were decayed, or consisted of sandbags, mud, and overturned boats, whose slimy bottoms, it was held, would cause the enemy's shots to slip harmlessly away.[59] Amoy had a well-built battery, and in August 1841, when the British re-entered the port, one of them wrote that "every island, every projecting headland, whence guns could be made to bear, was occupied and strongly armed." The Chinese admiral, however, the writer went on, had "suddenly been seized with a burning zeal to cruise after pirates elsewhere." After a fruitless bombardment of the massive fort, the British simply landed and walked into the keep, some troops entering through the very embrasures.[60] It was not always so easy, and at Chapu in the spring of 1842, the British found stiff resistance on the land.[61] This was characteristic. What real resistance there was, was fort-to-ship, or ashore.

Forts were supplemented by other defenses. One of these was the fire raft, of great antiquity in China. Fire rafts, designed to drift aflame down through enemy fleets, were used during the Opium War, and were sometimes elaborately prepared. In 1842, the British seized thirty-seven of them near Ningpo, each filled with combustibles and powder, and fitted with "leather caps and fire-proof dresses for the men," whose escape was ensured by sampans.[62]

Other supplements were fixed. In 1839, two massive chains were trussed across the Bogue channel, so floated as to permit them to be winched up or down. Some 120 swimmers were assigned to man this water-gate. Unfortunately, these chains gave way easily under the weight of advancing British men-of-war (the defenders claimed that they were unlinked by enemy "water-devils").[63] Canton's approaches were also in places blocked by stakes, which caused some delay. At Chenhai the British simply landed to one side of the stakes at that Chekiang port. River approaches might also be choked by sunken junks, boulders, or by shore-to-shore rafts or booms.[64]

China's defenders had implicit faith in these defenses. In 1839 a Canton official confidently memorialized:

When the several gates are installed, additional war junks and fireboats will be despatched to the upper stream at critical times. Although the barbarians are extremely stubborn, we don't think they will put themselves into the trap . . . Once they get in, the chains and stakes will impede them if they seek to advance; wind and water will check them if they seek to retreat. Meanwhile guns from our forts will fire at them from all directions, one after another. Our fireboats will push at them, and our war boats will follow suit. Even though the barbarian ships are as sturdy as iron and rocks, they will become ashes at once.[65]

A significant feature of this tactical formula is the secondary role assigned to war junks. They were to be used upriver, as an adjunct to fixed defenses. This paralyzing passivity is illustrated by the tale of the *Cambridge*. Early in 1841, after the breakdown of the Chuenpi talks, the British retook the river defenses of Canton. On their way upstream beyond the Bogue, they were blocked by an immense raft, stretching about 500 yards from bank to bank. Behind this barrier they found the *Cambridge*, a large Western merchantman, well armed, which had been purchased by Lin Tse-hsü from American owners early in 1840. Lin might have put the 1080-ton craft to good use, but she was moored behind the raft, and at that in such a way that only her bow guns could be brought into play. She mounted thirty-four English guns; her decks were clean and orderly; fire buckets were in orthodox array. There were a number of war junks moving about behind the barrier also. There was an exchange of fire, but when the steamer *Nemesis* was reinforced by the British Light Division (six unrated armed sailing vessels), resistance ceased. The British boarded the *Cambridge* by her starboard ladder as the Chinese crew exited by way of the larboard one. The Englishman W. D. Bernard, an eyewitness, wrote that "the Chinese are not sufficiently acquainted with naval tactics to be able to make the best use even of the resources at their command." [66]

Given their outmoded equipment, disorganization, haphazard personnel system, and passive defense concepts, it is no wonder that the Chinese were massively defeated by Britain in the Opium War. Imperial vacillation and frequent changes in leadership worsened the situation. An inadequate financing system was another factor. In imperial China there was no real central budget. The provincial officials collected the revenues, sending quotas to the capital and retaining the rest for their accustomed expenses. Much of this money was diverted to personal use. Green Banner units were financed by the provinces. On occasion, the central government ordered special subsidies for certain shipyards.[67] Once for economy the entire Tientsin water force unit was eliminated.[68] But the court had little influence in determining priorities within the provinces. Most of the defense problems had to be worked out on the spot, at the expense of local merchants, who suffered numerous special levies. The Canton hong merchants had raised most of the money for the forts and chains described; in January 1840 Lin Tse-hsü reported gathering a volunteer fleet supported by funds raised by merchants; later in 1840 Lin, I-liang, and Yu-k'un (the Hoppo) memorialized that the hong merchants had volunteered heavy sums for three years.[69] On occasion, an official might even meet some cost from his own purse, as did Canton admiral Kuan T'ien-p'ei in 1839 when he pawned personal effects to make up back pay due to his men.[70]

If China was to defend itself against the West, it had to make radical changes in the equipment, organization, training, and underlying concepts of the old water force. This, however, was to be more than a technical problem.

II

CHINA'S DELAYED RESPONSE TO THE WESTERN NAVAL CHALLENGE

A defeat in war can serve as a stimulus to reform. China did not begin a real naval reform, however, until twenty years after the Opium War. Given the organization and values of the Confucian political system, it took repeated shocks and some fortuitous changes in leadership to bring some officials to a realization of the need.

There was some activity during and immediately after the Opium War which may be variably linked to a discussion of naval reform. It has been noted that Commissioner Lin Tse-hsü bought the *Cambridge* in 1840. He also bought two twenty-five-ton sailing vessels, and a small paddle ship. In the eyes of some Westerners, Lin was planning a new navy to drive out the invaders. In any event, all of his ships were captured.[1]

Of greater interest are the Chinese wartime experiments in the building of improved ships and guns. These efforts were fairly widespread, ranging through Kwangtung, Chekiang, and Kiangsu. Apart from the improvement of ordnance, much of this interest centered on the building of "wheel-boats," or man-powered paddle vessels, which resembled the *Nemesis* and her kind at least in that they could be independent of the wind.

One wheel-boat builder was Kung Ch'en-lin, who in the year 1840 was appointed magistrate at Ningpo. It is not clear when he began his experiments. Possibly it was not until the arrival in Chekiang of Lin Tse-hsü in the spring of 1841, after Lin had been removed from his position as Canton governor-general for failure to cope with the British. Lin in his turn may have been influenced by the experiments at Canton with a wheel-boat of Ch'ang Ch'ing, a petty official in the salt administration of Kwangtung. In any event, Lin, who was interested in naval reform and not deterred by his disgrace, brought with him to Chekiang pictures of eight fighting ship types. Most were pictures of traditional small vessels, but one was of a two-decked, three-masted, thirty-four-gun Western vessel, and one was of a wheel-boat. He talked with Kung Ch'en-lin, and possibly enlisted the support of the Chekiang governor Liu Yün-k'o. Yü-ch'ien, imperial commissioner for the retaking of Tinghai in the spring of 1841, was also interested. However, Lin Tse-hsü was sent to Ili after about a month in Chekiang, in punishment for his original dereliction. Whether for lack of sustained support or lack of time, the wheel-boats were not completed, and when the British took Ningpo in October 1841, they found interesting but unassembled cogs, shafts, and water-wheels.[2]

Kung Ch'en-lin was also interested in guns, and evolved an iron-molding technique which was more advanced than that found in the contemporary West.[3] At Ningpo in 1841 the British also found new brass tube guns, of about three-pound caliber, each fitted with handles for two men and "curiously bound with catgut." [4]

Canton also saw experimentation. Ch'ang Ch'ing worked with Yi Ch'ang-hua, a prefect at Canton, and Hsü Hsiang-kuang, a member of the Canton gentry, although largely with small craft of traditional type, so that perhaps the efforts of these men show more public spirit than real experimentation.[5] P'an Shih-ch'eng, also of the Canton gentry, was more of an innovator. Besides being interested in Ch'ang Ch'ing's wheel-boat, he cast guns "somewhat in imitation of the foreign style" in 1841, and in 1842 created his "water-thunder," an underwater explosive with which he hoped to rip open foreign warships.[6] P'an also built a warship with native rig but with a foreign-style coppered hull, with two gun decks and "regular port-holes," and thirty-six Liverpool-made guns. Although Bernard called this ship a coppered junk, he still concluded that China had taken "the grand step of beginning a change of some sort or other." [7]

Another Canton innovator was Ting Kung-ch'en, a Fukien businessman in Canton. With P'an Shih-ch'eng he worked with guns and sights, and in 1841 became interested in steam propulsion, building working models of a paddle ship and a railroad engine.

The lack of machine tools at Canton forced him to drop this promising work.[8]

That this most significant kind of experimentation — with steam power — was not general is shown by the fact that when the British took Woosung in June 1842, the *Nemesis* easily captured five man-powered wheel boats. These new traditionally-armed vessels developed only about three knots, but at least the hard-working human "engines" were below deck and protected. Behind this Kiangsu building effort stood Niu Chien, the Nanking governor-general.[9]

Late in 1842, after the end of the war, there were other promising experiments. In Canton, P'an Shih-yung hired foreign workers and built a small steamer. At about the same time Kung Ch'en-lin and two colleagues, Ting Shou-ts'un and Cheng Fu-kuang, had started work on a steam engine, writing a detailed description of their progress.[10] Another ambitious but perhaps not so farsighted post-war experimenter was Admiral Wu Chien-hsün at Canton, who took the lines of an American three-master and caused to be built a ship of about 150 feet over all, with foreign rig as well as foreign hull, mounting fifty guns.[11]

Yet all of this work, whether new or traditional, remained only a collection of largely isolated incidents. The explanation is not that China did not have enough money to sustain experimentation; nor is it that China lacked skills, although, relatively speaking, she was not well equipped with steamer-builders.[12] The main problem was that official attitudes militated against experimentation. Most of the recommendations of China's high officials during the Opium War indicated no awareness of the need for naval reform. Wartime memorials were in the main florid elaborations on traditional themes: the weapon of trade suspension might be advantageously used; the bestial barbarians, although bold, could be defeated by China's existing weapons and moral superiority; the barbarians should be wiped out on land after having come ashore; more forts should be built, or junks sunk in harbors, or troops gathered; fishermen should infiltrate enemy fleets to spy, or to sabotage them; divers might bore holes in the bottoms of enemy ships, and so on.[13]

A few exceptions do appear in the record, all before the removal of Lin from Canton in the spring of 1841. The names of Lin Tse-hsü, Teng T'ing-chen, Ch'i Chün-tsao, Huang Chüeh-tzu, Wu Yen-yung, and I-li-pu are attached to these recommendations (sometimes in a joint memorial, as with Teng, Ch'i, Huang, and Wu in July 1840), but Lin Tse-hsü and Teng T'ing-chen were the only two who made more than one recommendation.[14] These recommendations were usually rather general, calling only for larger vessels without further specification. Teng and his fellow memorialists called for sixty larger vessels in July 1840, large enough to mount thirty or forty guns. In October 1840, Lin called for larger ships in a long-range plan, suggesting that they be financed from customs receipts.[15] In 1841, after his removal from office but before his departure from Canton, Lin suggested to I-shan (who had just arrived to replace Lin's immediate successor, Ch'i-shan) that China make long-range plans, involving the building of large ships at the rate of five per month for four months, and then at a diminishing rate until 100 were built.[16] Since Lin could not memorialize directly, perhaps this last item should not be included in a list of recommendations to the throne. It does not add much to the list in any event, for not even Lin went so far as to openly espouse the building of military steamers by China.

Even these few recommendations, vague as they were, were only part of a stream of memorials passing to Peking, most of which were of the traditional kind already suggested, or like that of Yü-ch'ien, who in September 1840 assured the emperor that British naval guns could not shoot high enough to destroy the Woosung forts, for "if they shoot upward, the bullets will go down and consequently lose the force of shooting." [17] Even while calling for larger ships, Teng T'ing-chen laid his emphasis on beating the enemy ashore, and Lin himself, in a recommendation in August 1840, could in the same memorial call for a sea battle of annihilation while later pointing out that "it is not worth our while to embark on a combat at sea." [18] The emperor in any event was not interested in fighting at sea, and when he did not ignore the recommendations for larger ships he was likely to dismiss them, as he did Lin's of October 1840, as "foolish talk." [19]

That so few of China's officials saw what in retrospect seems to be an obvious need — naval reform — was a product of their education and political situation. Ignorance of the enemy was widespread, and is exemplified by the serious report that British uniforms were so tight that once the British were knocked down, they could not regain their feet.[20] Intelligence was gathered by fishermen or similarly inexpert observers. Lin Tse-hsü fostered the early idea that China had rendered "Six Smashing Blows" to the British just after the Chuenpi battle of November 1839 because he accepted reports of fishermen who occasionally hooked British naval hats out of the water and construed from such bits of evidence the proof of Chinese victories.[21] One version of the British withdrawal from Canton in 1841 (after the city in fact had been ransomed) was that they left upon seeing the Goddess of Mercy hovering over the town.[22]

Some officials learned. Lin Tse-hsü gathered Western information. Ch'i-shan, who replaced Lin Tse-hsü late in 1840 in order to "soothe" the barbarians, came to talk with some appreciation about explosive projectiles and armed fighting tops.[23] But there was such a high rate of turnover among these high officials, as they were successively punished, that their fragmentary knowledge served little purpose. Lin's power passed to Ch'i-shan, who in turn lost some of it to I-shan (who was one of a trio of emergency trouble shooters who could do no more than arrange for the ransoming of Canton in the late spring of 1841), and I-shan himself was shortly punished. Another example of high turnover — in Chekiang — has been noted in the first chapter. There were many others. On the other hand, even if the few "experts" had not been removed, their knowledge might just as well have served as a basis for appeasement. Niu Chien, Nanking governor-general in 1842, late in the war saw a steamer's engine room and so was finally convinced that such ships were not driven by hidden oxen — and he prudently attached his name to a plea for peace.[24]

The high rate of turnover in office was a function of the political situation of the high officials. In the absence of a clear line of command, these officials (with the right of direct memorial) all stood at the ends of separate lines to the throne. This may have been excellent for checks and balances, but it was not good for the emergency sponsorship of naval experimentation. Naval reform would have required full official sponsorship. Yet even well-informed officials in that Manchu-Chinese Confucian system were as a rule too preoccupied to give it. They had to watch out for their individual careers; the emperor could always punish his officials. Confucian values furthermore did not admit the possibility that failure might lie outside of the moral control of the upright official. Alien technical considerations such as were involved in military steamships were looked down upon, while wheel-boats, which had a long history in China, did not involve such considerations.[25] Censors in the distant capital were not likely to weigh technical considerations in the impeachments which they wrote following news of China's defeats. It was safer to hide behind the accepted stereotypes, or, at the most, to write vaguely of "large ships." There was no protection for the true innovator.

If the gestures were orthodox, even punishment might be eased. The ritual self-abasements, the excoriations of the "rebellious barbarians," the "wild scramble" for favorable mention in reports which Waley notes in the Opium War documents [26] — all sprang from the Confucian world view in which all men had a fixed place in a moral order centered on the Son of Heaven. To report defeat at the hands of mere barbarians was doubly hard. Some quite genuinely found the new situation hard to believe. In 1840 Lin Tse-hsü did not want to believe reliable advice that a British fleet was en route to blockade Canton. Such a thing was an impertinence! [27]

Officials resorted extensively to falsification in reporting the course of the war. This may have been partly because the officials, moving often from unfamiliar place to place, were forced to court the cooperation of the established local interests and clerks and so were reluctant to be over-meticulous in checking reports handed to them for transmission to the throne. There was in any event a consistent effort to gloss over defeat. Naval warfare, involving foreign ships whose classifications were exotic and whose actions were remote and intricate, lent itself to vagueness and carelessness about evidence. The emperor could not always be fooled, however; he had many sources of information. When a massive fire-raft attack on the British at Canton (May 1841) was falsely reported as a victory, he angrily retorted that he knew better, and issued stern warnings. On the other hand, a similar lie about a later fire-raft attack at Tinghai (March 1842) was accepted, even after investigation.[28]

Despite their many precautions, practically every one of the high officials in the war period was degraded or removed from office. A few escaped disgrace. Yang Fang, one of the trio of officials who replaced Ch'i-shan in 1841, was allowed to withdraw into private life after a brief tour — "a rare act of clemency for one who had failed." [29] Ch'i-ying also survived, but this man, who was the Manchu negotiator at Nanking in the summer of 1842, entered the struggle late and had many friends at court.

That innovation was discouraged by the official system and its values is further shown by the fact that nearly all of the innovations noted above were initiated by men outside of the official system, or with only subordinate places in it. Hsü Hsiang-kuang, Ting Kung-ch'en, P'an Shih-ch'eng, and P'an Shih-yung (the only one to complete a steamer) were all Canton gentry or merchants. Yi Ch'ang-hua and Ch'ang Ch'ing, who were not really innovators, were minor officials at Canton. Kung Ch'en-lin was a magistrate at Ningpo, and although he, with two non-official collaborators, did interest himself in steamers, he did not have the right of direct memorial, nor did Yi and Ch'ang at Canton. The list includes an admiral and Lin Tse-hsü, but the latter was politically discredited during his advocacy of "large ships." The fate of Admiral Wu Chien-hsün will be noted shortly.

The personality of the Tao-kuang Emperor was an important element in this political situation. His long insistence that all fighting should be on the land, his distrusts, his vacillations, and his impulsiveness all added to the burdens borne by his officials.[30] It was only when the British had deeply penetrated the Yangtze in the summer of 1842 that he came to express an interest, urgent if vague, in larger ships, although at the time there was a rising official clamor for peace.[31] From the start of this interest until its end, early in 1843, the emperor issued about thirty edicts on the subject, full of phrases such as "it is necessary to change," and "we must not follow old methods." [32] Yet very little came of these commands.

Perhaps the most interesting exchange was between Peking

and Kwangtung. In September 1842 the emperor ordered the Kwangtung officials, as he had others, to build large ships, and asked for plans. He also asked the Kwangtung officials for more information on what Ting Kung-ch'en had been doing — although this postwar request came, apparently, about thirty months after Ting had first submitted a report on his work to the Canton officials early in the war.[33] At about the same time the emperor asked the Chekiang officials what they knew of one Ho Li-kuei, a Cantonese with about twenty years' overseas experience in foreign shipyards.[34]

The reply from Kwangtung was written by I-shan, and it was received late in October. His detailed report covered the work of Hsü Hsiang-kuang, Ch'ang Ch'ing, P'an Shih-ch'eng, and Admiral Wu Chien-hsün. As for Wu's imitation of an American vessel, I-shan recommended that it be of a medium-sized one, rather than the largest. He attached plans for five types of war-vessels (those of Wu Chien-hsün, Yi Ch'ang-hua, Ch'ang Ch'ing, P'an Shih-ch'eng, and Hsü Hsiang-kuang), and recommended that a suitable naval program should include thirty "large war vessels" served by thirty or forty smaller vessels. Although the emperor had shown an interest in "fire-wheel boats" in his inquiry about Ting Kung-ch'en, and I-shan's report did not include plans for a steamer, the emperor was nonetheless pleased, and decreed that P'an Shih-ch'eng should be placed over a ship-building program which would be centered at Canton and extend through Min-Che and Kiangsu. Provincial authorities were to study the five vessel types to determine which would be best. Money was to be diverted from the repair of old-style vessels to this new construction.[35]

By the end of October 1842, then, the emperor, now "converted" to naval reform, had linked himself with a high provincial official (who was also an imperial clansman) in a plan to create a large-scale naval innovation. But it was not to be. The fate of I-shan is instructive. Although still at his Canton post, he had for about a year been stripped of his rank for his failures in 1841, and after the Nanking Treaty of August 1842, he was ordered to return to Peking for punishment. He lingered at Canton long enough to make a negative report in December on P'an Shih-yung's steamer,[36] and did not arrive at the capital for imprisonment until early in 1843. The Kwangtung shipbuilding project was taken over by his successor, Governor-General Ch'i-kung. Late in 1842 Ch'i-kung reported that P'an Shih-ch'eng had started, and needed money. As for raising money, Ch'i-kung pointed out that total suspension of repairs on traditional vessels would be wasteful. Subscriptions might be realized, but in general Ch'i-kung's report stressed the problems involved in such a peacetime effort.[37] One may doubt that P'an Shih-ch'eng had really started. In any event, the only concrete steps taken involved the purchasing by two merchants, P'an Cheng-wei and Wu Ping-chien, of two foreign sailing vessels, the 108-ton *Ramiro* and the 317-ton *Lintin*. Bernard acknowledged that these had been bought "at considerable cost," but wrote further that they were "rather the worse for wear."[38] With this, naval innovation at Canton came to an end.

Ch'i-kung may very well have been aware of I-shan's fate, which had been in no way ameliorated by his support of the emperor's ideas on naval change. He was not alone in his lack of enthusiasm. At the end of 1842, the Nanking governor-general, Ch'i-ying, reported negatively on the five types of war vessels (some of which were traditional), and proposed a building program which would center around the T'ung-an (Fukien) traditional war vessel. This was granted, and a program established which overlapped P'an Shih-ch'eng's supposed authority.[39] In the spring of 1843, Ch'i-ying was sent to Canton as imperial commissioner. Other provincial authorities had also taken a dim view of the use of P'an Shih-ch'eng's vessel; for example, the Chihli authorities had argued that "the sea by Tientsin is too narrow and shallow for . . . [P'an's ship], and merchant ships will be used instead." Shantung, Kiangsu, and Chekiang (the last two by the end of 1842 committed to the T'ung-an type) offered nothing more edifying by way of excuse.[40] The emperor's passing enthusiasm for a little-understood naval reform accomplished no more than to persuade a few officials that it would be tactful for them to pay a visit to a foreign war vessel, which several did.[41]

Ting Kung-ch'en's drawings of guns were finally placed before the throne, and the provinces here and there did adopt improved sighting devices, but without further experimentation. P'an Shih-ch'eng's "water-thunder" never got an official test.[42] The war had no more effect on strategic thinking. Although Wei Yuan, in his much-quoted *Hai-kuo t'u-chih* of 1842, did advocate naval strengthening, he still argued confidently that "to defend the open sea is not so good as to defend the ports, and this is not as good as to defend the inland rivers." [43]

The Opium War only weakened the traditional water force. And in 1844, the *Chinese Repository* advised its readers that "the late Admiral Wu has recently been deprived of official rank . . . On his first degradation he was sent to sea, on the coast of this province, to retrieve his character, by the eradication of piracy. After cruzing [*sic*] five months, and spending several thousands from the Imperial Treasury, he reported the capture of three pirates." [44] Here was the fate of another innovator.

Also in 1844, Caleb Cushing, whose presence as treaty negotiator for the Unted States symbolized the new era, came to China. He brought with him technical works on guns, ships, forts, and military and naval strategy, for presentation to the Chinese government. But they were not used. China was not yet ready for naval innovation.

China's next challenge came from within. The devastating Taiping Rebellion (1850–1864) was rooted in popular grievances against an officialdom which was increasingly corrupt and inept; it was also directed against agrarian and social inequities. Indeed, it was only the greatest of a series of uprisings that had scarred the earlier decades of the nineteenth century in China. Here were the signs, unmistakable to China's Confucian officials, of dynastic decline. But the Taiping Rebellion also symbolized the Western impact, for the ideology of the movement was a pseudo-Christianity, originally propagated by the leader of the rebellion, Hung Hsiu-ch'uan. In its later phase the rebellion also brought foreign intervention on behalf of the dynasty — that is, on behalf of a dynasty which in 1860 had been forced by the West to make additional concessions to Western commerce and diplomacy. Dynastic decline in the nineteenth century was like no other phase of the dynastic cycle in China's long history — although, as we shall see, China's officials were ready to explain it in the old way.

The Taiping Rebellion was a far more serious threat to the existence of the dynasty than the Opium War had been, but during this struggle there was only a sporadic official interest in the use of steam war vessels. There was a much greater official interest in enlarging and improving the supply of ordnance. Tseng Kuo-fan and Tso Tsung-t'ang, the great Chinese scholar-generals who did so much to save the Manchu Confucian dynasty, set up ordnance plants in Hunan. Tseng sought foreign guns. Tso tried unsuccessfully to bring Kung Ch'en-lin to his arsenal in 1854. In 1855, Governor-General Yeh Ming-ch'en at Canton employed P'an Shih-ch'eng to set up a cannon factory. The need for guns and ammunition in the struggle against the rebels was obvious to all officials engaged.[45]

One official who did try to buy or rent foreign ships, including steamers, was the Shanghai taotai, Wu Chien-chang. In 1853–54, when Shanghai was besieged by imperial forces, he was active in buying ships for defense of the city, although he was unable to obtain steamers. In 1856 the Shanghai authorities purchased a 430-ton ex-Russell and Company steamer, the *Confucius*.[46] Shanghai and Ningpo merchants also bought two steamers to clear the interport route of pirates. Yet when these two steamers were sent in 1856 to Hsiang Jung, the imperial commissioner directing the war against the Taipings, he said he did not need them and that they would only bring foreign influence into the interior.[47] There was no policy aimed at the use of steamers in the river water force; instead, there were only personal reactions to the exigencies of battle. In 1856 Horatio Nelson Lay, the chief of the infant Imperial Maritime Customs service, proposed that China buy steamers to crush the rebels. Money was placed in his hands for this ostensible purpose, but the ulterior objective of the officials dealing with Lay was to test his honesty. Nothing came of the episode.[48] Ho Kuei-ch'ing, governor of Chekiang from 1854 to 1857, urged naval reform, but was discredited.[49]

The disinterest in steamers may have been caused in large part by the fact that the rebels themselves fought with traditional river water forces. In the mid-1850's, Tseng Kuo-fan's naval commanders Yang Yüeh-pin and P'eng Yü-lin gained important victories by combined land-water efforts on the Yangtze and on Poyang Lake. In one victory of December 1854 these commanders broke through strong rebel river and land lines about forty miles above Kiukiang on the Yangtze, and the emperor used the account of this traditional battle as a model which naval officials throughout the empire were to emulate.⁵⁰

If the rebels provided no stimulus to naval reform in the early 1850's, neither did the treaty powers. Relations were nominally peaceful until 1856, and the fact that Britain took an active part in the suppression of coastal piracy further encouraged a comfortable passivity about naval reform on China's part.

By the late 1850's, however, China found herself once again at war with Britain, and this time the British were militarily supported by France and receiving varying degrees of diplomatic support as well from the United States and Russia. The Sino-American treaty of Wanghsia (1844) had provided for revision in twelve years, or 1856; by the most-favored-nation clause, the other treaty powers were similarly entitled to revisions. There had been Western dissatisfaction with the Nanking treaties. American attempts at revision had been ignored. Then Britain and France joined in the revision effort. The British were further angered when at Canton in 1856 Chinese officials seized the crew of the lorcha *Arrow* on suspicion of piracy, though the *Arrow* was registered at Hong Kong and flew the British flag. The French, on their part, charged that certain Chinese provincial officials, who had executed a French missionary illegally traveling in the interior, had perpetrated a "judicial murder." From these combined irritations the so-called "Second China War" (1856–1860) broke out. But the dynasty, facing attacks from within and without, was no more prepared to offer naval resistance than it had been at the end of the 1830's. Indeed, it was less prepared, for its principal Western antagonists in the Second China War, Britain and France, had since the Opium War embarked on a competitive naval revolution which was taking them from sail to steam, from wood to iron, and from muzzle-loading single-cast ordnance throwing solid shot to breech-loading, built-up naval rifled guns using explosive shells.⁵¹

A careful examination of the battles of the Second China War, at both Canton and Taku, shows that China's naval defenses were unchanged.⁵² Canton was finally opened in December 1857 (the British insisted that they had a right to enter the city after the Opium War, but had been excluded nonetheless). The fighting which opened the city was all in the city's river approaches. The

Fatshan Creek engagement of June 2, 1857, in which seven British ships' boats did most of the fighting against twenty war junks, brought some losses to the British. In commenting on this engagement, the British Admiral Seymour wrote that it had opened "a new era in Chinese naval warfare."[53] He may have been referring to the number of junks involved, or to the determination of the defenders; for technical improvements in the Canton area were limited to improvements in fire rafts (they were packed with explosives, not merely with combustibles) and in the defensive arts of mining.[54] It has already been noted that many imperial war junks were in fact only armed merchant junks.[55] At one point in the fighting near Canton, imperial forces seized a foreign steam-packet, the *Thistle* (this they did by the strategem of disguising troops as passengers), but they then burned the ship.[56] No one thought of using her steam engines in the imperial cause, either against the British, or against the Taiping rebels in the vicinity. Strategy was unchanged. This was no "new era."

The most famous of the Second China War battles was the repulse of the Anglo-French force at Taku in 1859. In 1858, bent on treaty revision, a Western fleet of thirty ships (twenty-four were steamers) came to Taku. Chinese defenses were massive and traditional, although some of the ammunition for the 140-odd guns in the great shore emplacements which guarded the approaches to Tientsin and the capital was cannister and hollow eight-inch shot like that used in the Royal Navy. After taking the Taku forts in 1858 in a severe fight, the allies moved on to Tientsin and dictated the Tientsin treaties. Ratifications were to be exchanged in 1859 in Peking itself.[57]

China made a vigorous but traditional response to this invasion. The Tientsin water force, disbanded in 1767, was reactivated; the Taku forts were rebuilt and extended, and supplemented by stakes, a chain, a timber boom, and solid shore-to-shore raft.[58] When the allies returned to Taku in 1859 to advance to Peking for the exchange of treaty ratifications, they were repulsed. The steamers *Lee* and *Kestrel* were sunk; their mates *Plover* and *Cormorant* were abandoned aground. About 100 of the attackers were killed, and 350 wounded.[59] This sharp victory for China seemed to vindicate the traditional defense system.

In 1860 the allies returned with about 100 ships and close to

20,000 men. They retook the Taku forts from the rear. The British used the built-up, rifled Armstrong naval gun for the first time in this engagement. Chinese ordnance was varied. Some of the captured guns had been taken from the *Plover, Lee,* and *Cormorant.* Some guns were of brass, in some cases double-mounted on strong wooden carriages "after the fashion of double-barrelled fowling pieces," in the words of a British report. Other guns were made "of wood, bound round with leather, hooped with iron." The invaders also found a kind of land mine, made of a thirteen-inch shell and a trip-string. There was stiff resistance on the land as the allies advanced to Peking, but it gave way, and the Tientsin treaties were forcibly ratified in the capital itself (after the looting and destruction of the Summer Palace by the allies) in the summer of 1860.[60] Save for the fact that the final action took place in the capital, and that China scored one signal victory, the Second China War was substantially only a re-enactment of the Opium War, so far as the student of China's naval response is concerned.

That some Chinese and Manchu leaders in the 1860's began to think of naval modernization, and that their proposals were implemented, was the product of a fortuitous concatenation of domestic and foreign pressures, changes in court leadership, and changes in the pattern of relationship between certain provincial officials and the court.

The West had finally succeeded in breaking down the tribute mechanism whereby aliens had been kept on China's periphery in a few trading centers and admitted to the capital only under an ancient ritual with its kowtow, which clearly marked the visitors as subordinates. The Tientsin treaties gave further advantages to the west; they provided for the residence of foreign ministers in Peking, for many more treaty ports, and for the opening of the interior to foreign travel and the propagation of Christianity. The approach of the allied forces to Peking had caused the Hsien-feng Emperor to flee and hastened his death; this in turn led to the *coup d'état* of 1861 that ushered in the reign of the T'ung-chih Emperor, who was controlled by a relatively progressive group of Manchus, most notably Prince Kung, half-brother of the deceased Hsien-feng Emperor. Prince Kung led the Grand Council and also the new Tsungli Yamen, which latter office, although a temporary concession in Manchu eyes, was a kind of foreign office to meet Western demands for proper diplomatic relations. In fact, the Tsungli Yamen lasted past the turn of the century, and came to be involved in reforms which included naval innovation.[61]

Changes in the pattern of the Taiping Rebellion were also important in this concatenation of events. After 1860 the rebellion reached into the lower Yangtze valley, where foreign ships were better known. The dynasty also perforce relied more on the efforts of Chinese officials to defeat the rebels, since Manchu forces had proved to be worthless.[62] Tseng Kuo-fan, who since the early 1850's had been forming, training, and using his personally-organized Hunan militia force, was in 1860 made governor-general of Kiangnan and Kiangsi and imperial commissioner for the suppression of the Taipings in all of South China. This linkage of formal central appointment with significant regional military power was what the dynasty had long sought to avoid. Tseng sent subordinates into certain areas to pacify them. These appointments by him were confirmed by substantive appointments by the throne. Thus, early in 1862 Tso Tsung-t'ang was appointed governor of Chekiang, and shortly became Min-Che governor-general. By this time, Li Hung-chang, another of Tseng's lieutenants, was acting governor of Kiangsu. These three loyal Chinese officials symbolized the so-called T'ung-chih Restoration, which sought to revive the dynasty after the devastating Taiping attack — a revival which had supposed historical precedents, and so had profound ideological as well as practical concomitants.[63] Each of the three men commanded armies, and enjoyed a power usually not exercised by provincial leaders. Each, after his individual fashion, came to advocate reform, including naval and military reform.

In the early 1860's, a complicated political situation, which involved foreign and native interests, developed at Shanghai. Trade continued at the port, with important revenues and profits. When the Taiping rebels in 1860 started to fight in the lower Yangtze, the Chinese at Shanghai had already organized a volunteer mercenary force, the so-called "Ever-Victorious Army," commanded by F. T. Ward, an adventurous American who had been an officer on the *Confucius*. Britain was officially neutral with regard to the Taiping Rebellion, but early in 1861 Admiral Hope made an agreement with the Taipings that only if the rebels stayed at least thirty miles from Shanghai would Britain continue to be neutral.[64]

At about this time Peking was advised by Yüan Chia-san, imperial commissioner in Anhwei, that Russia and France had offered ships and men to the dynasty. Peking's reaction to these offers was a suspicious one, particularly when it developed that Britain might make a similar offer.[65] The foreigners should be played off against each other — a real possibility, since Britain profoundly mistrusted Russia, and was in a naval race with France. Britain also bore the principal burden of clearing the China coast of pirates; strengthening the dynasty would shift this burden, and (in the eyes of Frederick Bruce, H. M. Minister at Peking) would also necessitate a centralization of power in China which would simplify the problems of diplomacy.[66]

The presence of foreigners in the capital was a factor working for naval reform, for they could communicate with Prince Kung directly and were not subject to the elaborate forms of address that typified the official Confucian communications; they also had nothing to fear. In June 1861 Robert Hart, a British subject employed by China in the newly-organized Imperial Maritime Customs, proposed to Prince Kung that China purchase from England a steam flotilla to strengthen the imperial naval forces. Bruce, as minister of a still-neutral Britain, did not at the time officially involve himself. Here was the origin of the unfortunate Lay-Osborn scheme — so called because Horatio Nelson Lay, then inspector-general of the Imperial Maritime Customs, was on leave in England and was authorized by Prince Kung to buy the actual ships, and Lay, in his turn, appointed Sherard Osborn, a Royal Navy captain, to command the purchased flotilla.[67]

The Lay-Osborn scheme is called unfortunate because the eight ships which were purchased by China were returned at the end of 1863, without making any contribution to the ending of the rebellion or the reduction of piracy. The affair is instructive, nonetheless. Tseng Kuo-fan, when consulted about the French and Russian offers noted above, had replied that China had no need for steamers, as they were too clumsy for upriver fighting.[68] After the taking of Anking from the rebels in September 1861, Tseng established his headquarters there, with a shipyard and an arsenal. His reply to imperial inquiries about Hart's proposal was no more enthusiastic about the immediate benefits to China of acquiring steamers, but he did see that China might buy the ships and study them, so as to strengthen herself in the future. He recommended that the ships be bought and staffed with foreign officers, but that their crews should consist of Tseng's own men, drawn from his Hsiang-chün, or Hunan "braves." Tseng's long-range interest in steamers was shown by his purchase of one locally, the first he had ever seen. His proposals for the manning of the Lay-Osborn fleet showed that he intended these ships also to be "his." [69]

In England, Lay was engaged in protracted negotiations with the British government for permission to buy ships on China's account and for authority to enlist British naval officers and men to serve in them (Britain was neutral until an Order-in-Council of January 9, 1863, permitted British military and naval personnel on half-pay to serve in the imperial forces in China). He purchased eight ships and engaged Osborn. With Osborn he drew up a secret personal agreement providing that Osborn would command the eight ships and all other foreign-built ships purchased by China, and that this imperial steam fleet would be subject only to the orders of the emperor — save that Lay alone would transmit the imperial orders, *if he held them to be reasonable*. When this agreement became known to Prince Kung, he of course flatly rejected it. Not only would it have made of Lay — about thirty years of age, and to Prince Kung a mere employee of the emperor — an admiralissimo; it would also have disrupted the time-tested decentralization of power in China, which was now even more pronounced. Even Bruce, with his hopes for a strengthened "Chinese Executive," had to back off from Lay's position. The complicated negotiations in Peking involved Anson Burlingame, the American minister (who feared that if the fleet was disbanded the ships would pass into the possession of the Confederate States of America and so hurt the Union cause in the American Civil War), and it was finally decided that there was nothing for it but to return the ships, as Osborn adamantly refused to depart from his agreement with Lay. The ships, by the end of 1863, had been in Chinese waters only about three months.

Before the Lay-Osborn agreement was known to Prince Kung

or the ships came to China, the court had been corresponding with Tseng Kuo-fan about their use. Tseng's purchased steamer had broken down, but he had another one built at his Anking shipyard by his aide Ts'ai Kuo-hsiang. Early in 1862 he had ridden in this little launch, the *Wang Kao*, and was very proud of it. Hsü Shou, who had built the engine, had only once before seen a steamer's engine, and had built this one largely from a description he read in a translation of Hobson's *Natural Philosophy*.[70] Tseng now had a steamer built in his own shipyard, and he planned to reward Ts'ai Kuo-hsiang by making him commander of the Lay-Osborn fleet. The crews would of course be Hunanese, and Tseng furthermore had definite ideas about where the ships would be used. He was getting used to having steamers at his own disposal; the Shanghai merchants, anxious to have Tseng send Li Hung-chang to protect the city, had rented ten foreign steamers and sent them to Anking to transport Li's troops down river, which was done in April 1862. But if the court was later to insist inflexibly to Bruce, Lay, and Osborn that Tseng alone should take direction of the Lay-Osborn ships, it was at the same time concerned lest Tseng's control over the ships be too great. The correspondence between the court and Tseng included successive proposals from the court about the manning of the ships with Manchus, Filipinos, and other provincials including *some* Hunanese, and suggestions that the ships be used in campaigns far from Tseng's native Hunan province — even to protect the northern maritime approaches to Peking. Tseng politely clung to his own ideas. When the final break came, he was still arguing about crews, and he made no powerful attempt to have the ships kept although they had already been partly paid for and could certainly have given his shipbuilders excellent prototypes for study and imitation. As for Li Hung-chang, one of his efforts during the short period when the ships were at Shanghai was to entice Osborn's British tars into his own service.[71]

Naval modernization, as espoused by Tseng Kuo-fan, was subject to political considerations. One informed contemporary Westerner had this to say:

> The Chinese Government . . . never displayed any wish to advance beyond the point of having a certain number of its troops accustomed to foreign drill and the use of foreign arms. And even if the Govern-

ment had been exceedingly desirous of making a change in its military system, by establishing a small efficient army which it could employ in any part of the Empire, it could not have done so in the face of the opposition of Tseng Kuo-fan and the other generals who had for so many years been successfully opposed to the Rebels. I daresay the Tartar section of Peking officialdom would have been not averse to a military reform which would have been a formidable counterbalance to the growing influence and power of Tseng Kuo-fan, Tseng Kuo-ch'uan, Li and other purely Chinese mandarins in the south and centre of the country; but these latter would have had the support of the people in their opposition to such an innovation.[72]

Apart from the overambitiousness of Lay and Osborn, and the issue of Peking versus Tseng Kuo-fan, there was another cause of the Lay-Osborn fiasco. Tseng Kuo-ch'uan, Tseng Kuo-fan's brother, wanted to retake Nanking by himself, without foreign help, all the more because Prince Kung had made an agreement with Lay in regard to the distribution of the expected plunder of Nanking which would have given Osborn's fleet at least one third, and in the event that the fleet took Nanking by itself, seven tenths of it.[73]

The Lay-Osborn affair illustrates some of the complexities which will figure in various forms later in this story of naval modernization, but there was one aspect of it that augured well for that modernization. Britain's own naval revolution, spurred on by French competition, was full of experiment, and a high rate of obsolescence. China was able to acquire some of the vessels in which Britain had a passing interest. The London *Times* of May 8, 1863, noted of one of the Lay-Osborn ships, the *Kiangsi* ("one of the handsomest models ever seen") that this 241-foot vessel, capable of eighteen knots, had produced such "extraordinary" results on her test runs that she was "unanimously pronounced by all the naval scientific authorities to be one of the fastest vessels afloat." However, she was made of wood. In 1860, Britain's navy had received the *Warrior*, an armor-plated iron ship-rigged steam frigate, 380 feet overall. The *Kiangsi* was outdated.[74]

Li Hung-chang appreciated the value of steamers, having moved his troops to Shanghai on some, as noted. In February 1863 he commented to Tseng on the "excellent" ships of the West, with their "ingenious and uniform" cannon. He doubted that the West ever let its best ships and cannon go to China; he also remarked that certain Chinese were unwilling to learn.[75] Li was willing to learn.

Li, however, seemed to be most interested in ordance and the trappings of land power. In August 1863 he saw the Ever-Victorious Army (now reorganized under the command of Charles Gordon of the British Army, who was subordinate to Li) make victorious use of ammunition manufactured at Li's Sungkiang arsenal.[76] Early in 1864 Li moved this Sunkiang arsenal to Soochow, and his British arsenal director, Halliday Macartney (a former British army surgeon), bought for it some machinery that the canny Osborn had brought to China in his flotilla for private sale. Li was at first irritated at the cost of these "bits of iron," but was delighted when Macartney dramatically started the machinery for Li's inspection.[77] Li did not like to rely entirely on a foreigner, so he set up two more arms plants in Soochow, one under Han T'ien-chia, a military man, and the other under Ting Jih-ch'ang, the taotai at Shanghai. Han's plant was run entirely by Chinese. After the recapture of Nanking from the rebels in 1864 by Tseng Kuo-ch'uan, Tseng Kuo-fan moved his Anking facilities to Nanking, and in the spring of 1865, when Li Hung-chang became governor-general at Nanking, Li moved part of his Soochow plants to Nanking, shifting the rest to Shanghai. Li's machinery, in combination with other equipment bought in America by Yung Wing for Tseng Kuo-fan, was the nucleus for the Shanghai Kiangnan Arsenal.[78]

Of Tseng Kuo-fan's subordinates, it was Tso Tsung-t'ang who expressed the clearest interest in steamers. In 1862, when Tso was governor of Chekiang, one of his subordinates used a steamer for military inspections and to facilitate tax collection. Tso made increasing use of steamers in the years 1862–1865, as his responsibilities increased. One of these responsibilities, apart from suppression of the rebellion, was to cope with piracy. He had some reservations about steamers, for running costs were high, and he was aware that experts were needed to get the right ships and make a proper use of them. Although he did not dream of a radical elimination of all traditional naval vessels, he looked to the naval use of steamers, and wrote in 1864: "We must imitate the steamers in order to deprive the foreigners of the superiority through the very weapon they depend upon. We should not be embarrassed at the time of treaty revision which is now drawing very close." [79]

Of the leaders Tseng, Li, and Tso, Tso alone expressed indebtedness to the ideas of Lin Tse-hsü.[80] He distrusted the practice of leasing steamers, for the foreigners involved might have aims other than the serving of Chinese interests. He tried building a steamer, but was disappointed in it. The disappointment inclined him toward a major building effort. His official advocacy of a shipbuilding program was precipitated by British insistence upon an improvement in antipirate protection. After the failure of the Lay-Osborn scheme, the British finally hit upon a scheme of international patrol, in which China and the treaty powers would cooperate. The plan was complex. In April 1865 Prince Kung consulted the provinces about the desirability of China's buying steamers to do China's share of the proposed antipiratical work. Tso was opposed to the buying of steamers, and in June of 1865, having already consulted foreign engineers about the building of a shipyard, he made his official proposal for the establishment of a modern dockyard. Out of his advocacy there came the Foochow dockyard.[81]

From a combination of domestic and foreign pressures, these men, each in his own way, advocated military and naval reform. Their names are associated with the launching of the so-called "self-strengthening" movement, which did not appear until twenty years after the Opium War — a crucial wastage of years.[82] These "self-strengtheners" were, however, high officials, whose power and influence had been enhanced by their roles in the suppression of the Taiping Rebellion. It had been minor officials and merchants who had initiated the sporadic naval experiments of the Opium War period.

Yet these great reformers were tremendously busy men, who were not solely interested in military matters. They had some curious reservations about naval change; for example, Tso Tsung-t'ang, the father of the Foochow dockyard, never used a steamer himself, and sought to prevent his relatives from doing so.[83] But the greatest reservation of these men, idiosyncracies aside, was commitment to the preservation of the Confucian order, which they had just saved from the pseudo-Christianity of the Taiping Rebellion. The T'ung-chih Restoration idea, which largely molded their thinking, was in essence conservative; indeed, a penetrating modern study of it is entitled *The Last Stand of Chinese Conservatism*.[84] Their hope was to preserve Confucian institutions by the limited use of foreign military techniques — a hope cogently expounded by the essayist Feng Kuei-fen in the early 1860's — but the combination was to generate contradictions that were to hamper the naval reforms which they finally initiated.[85]

III

THE MILITARY SELF-STRENGTHENING MOVEMENT, TO 1875

By 1875 the principal modern arms plants had been set up in China, and despite many problems they were an impressive achievement. These principal plants were near the coast, and were the Kiangnan arsenal at Shanghai, the Foochow dockyard (actually at Ma-wei, near Foochow), and the Tientsin arsenal.[1]

We have seen that the Kiangnan arsenal was set up when Li Hung-chang broke up his Soochow arsenal in 1865. He sent Han T'ien-chia and Ting Jih-ch'ang to this new plant in Shanghai. The machine tools that Yung Wing had purchased for Tseng Kuo-fan in the United States were delivered to Shanghai in the spring of 1865, to the newly designated Kiangnan arsenal, which was the combined plants of Han and Ting and an ironworks earlier established by Li Hung-chang under the direction of the prefects Feng Chün-kuang and Shen Pao-ching. The Kiangnan arsenal was placed under Ting Jih-ch'ang, then the Shanghai taotai, and Ying Pao-shih, the Shanghai customs intendant.[2]

In the fall of 1865 the arsenal acquired the largest foreign shipyard in the area and added shipbuilding to its operations. Two years later it added more land, partly because it needed space, and partly to get away from close foreign neighbors. In 1867, Tseng Kuo-fan asked that twenty percent of the Shanghai customs income be assigned to the arsenal, with half of this reserved for steamer building. At the time, even foreign shipbuilders at Shanghai had to import engines for their completed hulls.[3]

Late in 1868 the 185-foot *T'ien Chi*, Kiangnan's first ship, was tested at Nanking. Boiler and hull were made at the arsenal, and with a used foreign engine she was driven by her paddle wheels at twelve miles an hour upstream.[4] Although they did not come into full operation at once, the various shops started at Kiangnan in 1867 performed many functions. The machine shop built large and small military engines, machinery, dock pumps, and lifts; the carpenter shop made all patterns for machinery; the casting shop housed molding equipment; the wrought iron shop made parts for the plant and the ships; the steamer yard turned out parts for warships and provincial steamers; the boiler shop produced machine parts in addition to boilers, and later added armor plate and bars; there was a gun factory (at first over the machine shop), and an engineering bureau that did the necessary bridging, ditching, and housing.[5]

By 1872, the year of Tseng Kuo-fan's death, the Kiangnan arsenal had produced six ships. After the *T'ien Chi* came the *Hui Chi*, built also in 1868, and she was followed in 1869–1870 by the *Ts'ao Chiang*, *Ts'e Hai*, and *Wei Ching*. These ships were in approximately the same class, being about 200 feet in length, with engines not exceeding 600 horsepower. The *T'ien Chi* and *Ts'e Hai* mounted fifteen twenty-four-pound howitzers apiece, all made at the arsenal. One specification of the *Hui Chi*, probably common to all of these ships, was a cargo capacity, in the *Hui Chi's* case 600 tons. In 1872 a foreigner observed that the Kiangnan ships had "for some time past" been used to move government stores and personnel. These ships, designed to pay their own way, were not exclusively military.[6]

The sixth Kiangnan steamer was the *Hai An* of 1871. This 1800-horsepower, 3000-ton vessel carried twenty-six guns, and was described by a British consul as a "most creditable specimen of naval architecture." Save for her propeller shaft and cranks, she had been built entirely at the arsenal. The *Hai An* and another much like her, the *Yu An* of 1873, were powerful ships by Chinese standards, but since they played no part in the 1874 Liuchiu crisis with Japan, when naval transport was badly needed, we may wonder about how well constructed they were. In 1875 the arsenal launched the 1800-horsepower, 2800-ton *Yu Yüan*, but after this it virtually ceased to build ships, concentrating on ordnance and ammunition.[7]

The change to ordnance might have been foreshadowed by the comment in 1868 by Tseng Kuo-fan that although shipbuilding had high promise, the immediate need was for guns. At that time certain rearrangements were made so that "by combination and division" of existing machinery and plant, more than thirty machines for armament manufacture were improvised. The upstairs arms shop acquired its own building in 1868. Tseng said its product was as good as any, and in his enthusiastic description of gunmaking talked of bores "as smooth as lard." But he was not content with simile, and talked knowledgeably of needing barrel makers, polishers, bore drillers, threading machines, and so on. In 1872 the Shanghai British consul wrote of 1300 workmen at Kiangnan laboring with "remarkable efficiency" to make Remington rifles, shot, shell (smooth bore and rifled), iron gun carriages, and the like, using a "vast variety of . . . articles of a complex character."[8]

During these years improvements in the Kiangnan ships were introduced or contemplated. The *Ts'ao Chiang* had iron armor, and the yard's administration was contemplating building composite ships (iron frames and wooden skin) in 1872. There were problems, however. The ships were expensive to maintain, and in 1872 Ho Ching, who became southern commissioner after the death of Tseng Kuo-fan, was uncertain that he could rent out the Kiangnan ships, and became less active in support of the shipbuilding program. In 1872 there came an attack by the conservative Sung Chin on the self-strengthening program, and this, coupled with the death of the arsenal's mentor Tseng Kuo-fan and the doubts of Ho Ching, probably encouraged the officials in charge of the arsenal to shift to the less controversial emphasis on ordnance and ammunition.[9]

After 1874 plant expansion at Kiangnan favored ordnance and ammunition. A powder works at Lunghwa, outside the city, was added in 1874, which was soon turning out a ton of powder daily. In 1875 a small-arms plant was put up at Lunghwa. On the other hand, Li Hung-chang, who was one of the directors of the Kiangnan arsenal, observed that attempts to imitate steel breech-loading Krupp rifles at the plant were frustrated by insufficient machinery. He recognized that it was difficult to keep up with foreign prototypes, and that complete retooling would require about 300,000 taels, even if the right machines were available, which they were not. The Lunghwa works, he added, were behind in the supply of ammunition.[10]

In the 1870's, Li Hung-chang came to be more immediately interested in the Tientsin arsenal. In 1866, Ch'ung-hou, then northern commissioner, set up an arsenal at the "Tientsin josshouse," under British guidance. When Li Hung-chang became Chihli governor-general in 1870, this modest plant was producing a few cannon "with fair merit." Li sent for Shen Pao-ching of the Kiangnan arsenal and made him director of the Tientsin plant. Shen was also made Tientsin customs intendant, and placed over coastal defense as well; thus this new man of Li's controlled money, arms, and troops. Li asserted that his reorganized Tientsin arsenal, now without foreign direction, would be superior to the Foochow dockyard, which was under foreigners. Two branches of the arsenal were developed. One, the "eastern branch," made guns for Li's own water and land forces; the other, the "southern branch," made cannon and small arms for Honan and Kirin and "other provincial units." [11]

In some ways, the early product at the Tientsin arsenal was not impressive. Halliday Macartney, director of the Nanking arsenal, in which Li was also interested, visited Li in 1872 to get support for adding rockets and torpedoes to the Nanking products. Macartney watched a demonstration of a Tientsin-made rocket, but the test missile failed to leave the stand, and proved to be made of bits of tin and similar substances. On the other hand, at the same time Macartney saw experiments at Tientsin with electric torpedoes.[12]

Li continued to buy foreign arms, and learned about them. In 1874 he memorialized on muzzleloaders and breechloaders, muskets and rifles, cataloguing Martini-Henrys, Sniders, needleguns, Chassepots, Remingtons, and others. The best artillery, he wrote, came from England and Germany. He was using Krupp ordnance to refit the Taku forts; Armstrong, Whitworth, or Woolich ordnance was also good. He wrote of contact, friction, and electric mines and torpedoes. China could make at Shanghai and Nanking many of the smaller cannon, but not so well as the foreigners. He hoped that China would buy furnaces, steam hammers, hydraulic presses, and that mines would be opened.[13] Thus, by 1875, the Tientsin arsenal was well established and under the direction of one of China's chief "self-strengtheners."

In establishing the Foochow dockyard, Tso Tsung-t'ang had the help of the French Foochow customs commissioner De Meritens, and more importantly the help of two other Frenchmen, Prosper Giquel, also of the customs service, and Paul d'Aiguebelle, a *lt. de vaisseau* who (with the Chinese rank of brigade general) had been a member of the mixed force which retook Hangchow from the Taiping rebels. Tso sent D'Aiguebelle to France to gather plans for a shipyard while Tso consulted Giquel. In his memorial of June 25, 1866, already referred to, Tso proposed the construction of a shipyard. The year was one of excitement; the Wade-Hart proposals about the internationalizing of piracy suppression off the China coast, proposals which had precipitated Tso's own proposal to the court, were taken by the Chinese to presage Western demands for the revision of the Tientsin treaties. Peking interested itself all the more in the *lien-chün*, a Western-trained land force under central officials, and once again strengthened the Taku forts. Tso's shipyard proposal was approved on July 14. The yard was to be built at Ma-wei, on the Min river below Foochow. Tso wanted not only to build ships, but also to train shipbuilders and naval personnel.[14]

Late in the summer of 1866, Tso and Giquel drew up a building contract. On D'Aiguebelle's return, the two Frenchmen signed it, over the seal of the French consul at Shanghai. Tso was disturbed by an edict of September 25 transferring him to the Shensi-Kansu region as governor-general to suppress the Mohammedan revolt, but managed to have the order stayed until he got the dockyard started. He arranged that Shen Pao-chen, the son-in-law of Tso's old mentor Lin Tse-hsü, and a man trusted in foreign and native circles, be made superintendent of the dockyard. In mid-December 1866 Tso left. Shen was then in mourning, and did not take over at once; Ying-kuei, the Tartar general at Foochow, acted for him during the first winter.[15]

Giquel believed that the dockyard would succeed because it would enjoy Tso Tsung-t'ang's sponsorship, and that Tso would be near it, in his capacity as Min-Che governor-general. When Tso knew that he could not be personally present, he tried to arrange for local official and gentry support for the dockyard. There was sure to be opposition, from conservatives fighting modernization, or from political opponents, or even from progressives who desired naval modernization but preferred to buy foreign ships rather than build modern naval vessels in China. He tried to meet some of the opposition by arguing in his original dockyard memorial that the new ships could carry cargoes in peacetime, and so pay their own way. He could also rely on his great prestige. The local gentry wanted him to stay at Foochow, and no official could ignore the local gentry. Tso established a committee of 100 local officials and gentry to keep accounts and discipline in the dockyard. One of Shen Pao-chen's prime qualifications for his new post — apart from his having served as governor of Kiangsi — was that he himself was from the Fukien gentry. As superintendent, Shen held an imperial commission, with a governor's rank. He was to be aided by a permanent high official group consisting of the Min-Che governor-general, the Fukien governor, and the Foochow Tartar general.[16]

Despite his precautions, when Tso finally left on his Shen-Kan assignment in December 1866, he warned Peking that *in absentia* he could not prevent trouble. Giquel said that if political pressures closed the dockyard he would refund all advances on the building of the plant. Shen had no illusions; the officials in the dockyard bureaucracy might be "worse than merchants" — a Confucian slur. Local prejudice against the yard was so great that apprentices had to be paid as much as government clerks. Giquel and D'Aiguebelle suggested that the yard's administrators use Tso's name in their reports. Although the court tried to reassure Shen that his fears were groundless, it was arranged that the name of the absent great founder of the dockyard, Tso Tsung-t'ang, would be affixed to dockyard reports, and this was done until 1875 and occasionally thereafter.[17]

Trouble did come soon. Ying-kuei, while acting for Shen Pao-chen, had been told by De Meritens that Giquel had duped Tso with his talk of building ships. De Meritens believed that China should buy her navy, as Hart was urging. Aside from De Meriten's pressure, Shen feared that Giquel and D'Aiguebelle would be loyal only to Tso, and not to himself.[18] There were other problems as well. Wu T'ang replaced Tso as Min-Che governor-general, and in 1867 Shen reported that Wu T'ang was "prejudiced against the shipyard." Wu had tried to intimidate Shen's aides (save for Hu Kuang-yung, who was Tso's personal agent) by keeping them from their posts, by stirring up litigation against them, or by open removal. This trouble coincided with the court's inquiries to the provincial officials about the pending revision of the Tientsin treaties, and Tso Tsung-t'ang, in his response to the court's questions about the treaty question, inserted his counterattack on Wu T'ang. Tso learned that men were trying to leave the dockyard and that funds were being misused, but Wu T'ang had evaded his questions about these matters. Tso charged that everything had changed.[19] Still, his intervention saved the yard, although the Wu T'ang trouble had been intensified by unfriendly agitation in Peking by French consular authorities. De Meritens was at least able to set Giquel and D'Aiguebelle against each other, so that in 1870 the latter left the yard and went to Kansu to see Tso. Even if Hart was correct in saying that D'Aiguebelle was "of no account," this was troublesome. It is small wonder that Shen Pao-chen had been reluctant to accept Tso Tsung-t'ang's invitation to take the superintendency of the dockyard.[20]

By their contract, the two European directors had a fivefold task: to establish workshops and building yards; to set up schools of navigation and naval construction and to train foremen; to engage such European staff as was needed; to build a side-launch slip of French type; and to set up a metal forge capable of rolling iron into bars and plates. The contract ran for five years; thereafter the entire dockyard operation was to be in native hands.

The contract called for building sixteen ships. Of these, eleven would have 150-horsepower engines, and the remainder, eighty-horsepower ones. Two ready-made French engines would be bought as a start on the bigger ships. Since local construction of the other nine 150-horsepower engines was expected to fall behind the building of the appropriate hulls, it was decided to maintain full operation of the yard by building, during anticipated slack periods, five hulls for the smaller ships, for which five eighty-horsepower engines were to be purchased from France.[21]

The first machinery arrived from France on December 13, 1867 — the paddy fields on which the plant was to be built having been raised five feet in the meantime. The first keel was laid in January 1868. The opening of the engine shop, which legally started the contract period, did not come until early in 1869.[22]

Although a foreign visitor in the summer of 1868 contemptuously dismissed the "quarter-section of a gunboat" and the "feeble school," a great change had transpired by the end of the contract period in 1874. Permanent buildings housed heavy forges and rolling mills, a boiler shop, an engine shop, a foundry, and supporting shops. Seven 150-horsepower engines had been locally built, with two others "well advanced," even though the plant was not complete. The smaller shops were also impressive. The compass shop had supplied all but two ships with "compasses, operaglasses, barometers, steam gauges, axiometers, graduated measures, sights for cannon, etc." Even chronometers had been made. All of this exacting work was entirely in Chinese hands when the contract ended.[23]

Three sets of stocks and sheds formed the building yard. There was an "immense" molding loft, and the launching slip could handle a 2500-ton ship. Outside an encircling brick wall there was a brick field for ordinary and fire brick and most of the personnel quarters. Plant area had tripled over the first "feeble" days. The number of foreign experts had increased over the contract period from the stipulated thirty-eight to forty-five. The yard was not independent, but ships were built in China.[24]

Foochow's first ship, launched on June 10, 1869, was the *Wan Nien Ch'ing*. This six-gun, screw-driven 238-footer was longer than Kiangnan's *T'ien Chi*, but her carrying capacity of 466 tons was smaller, and her engine was only about half as powerful. Tso Tsung-t'ang received many congratulations on the *Wan Nien Ch'ing*, including one from Ch'ung-hou, the northern commissioner, who inspected her on her trial run to the north. (Unfortunately Shen Pao-chen was seasick when he rode the ship.)[25]

The next two ships were of the eighty-horsepower type. These were the sister ships *Mei Yün* and *Fu Hsing*, with three guns each, launched on December 6, 1869. Like the first ship, they were designed at the dockyard. A third type, the *Fu Po,* a five-gun, 1258-ton transport, was launched on December 22, 1870. About six months later came a real triumph: the 1005-ton *An Lan* contained a 150-horsepower engine built, over a ten-month period, entirely at the yard. The *Chen Hai,* another of the smaller ships, followed.[26]

The yard's training program was in full operation during the contract years. In view of the Confucian heritage of the students, the task of training shipbuilders was not merely routine. Of the School of Naval Construction, one of the three branches in the

French-language shipbuilders school, which branch was organized with twelve students in February 1867, Giquel wrote (as it appears in English translation):

The object sought in this school has been to put it in the power of the pupils to explain to themselves, by the aid of reasoning and calculation, the functions, the dimensions, and the parts played by the different parts of an engine, in such a way as to be able to design and reproduce one of its detached members; and in regard to the hulls, to calculate, to design, and to trace in the molding hall, the hull of a wooden ship not differing much as regards size from those which the Arsenal had to build. This course of study was amply sufficient to occupy them to the limit fixed by our contract, as it is easy for me to demonstrate. Thus, in order to calculate the dimensions of a piece of machinery or a hull, it is necessary to know arithmetic and geometry; in order to reproduce that object on a plan, it is necessary to understand the science of perspective, which is descriptive geometry; in order to explain the pressures exerted on engines and ships, as well as on all bodies, by gravity, heat, and other phenomena of nature, it is necessary to understand the laws of physics. Next in order come the movements a body undergoes under the impulse of the forces to which it is subjected; the resistance which it will need to overcome, the strain which it is able, or ought to bear, which is the science of statics and mechanics; and for these the calculations of ordinary arithmetic and geometry no longer suffice; it is necessary also to possess the knowledge of trigonometry, or analytical geometry, or the infinitesimal calculus, so as not to be any longer bound down to reason as to objects of determined form and size, but to be able to arrive at general formulae applicable to all the details of construction. The preliminary studies were complicated in the case of the pupils at our schools, by the learning of the French language, of the first word of which they were ignorant when they were handed over to us.

After about five years of this curriculum, the surviving students entered the shops for practical work, which totaled fourteen months by the end of the contract in February 1874. Giquel's talk of this practical work bristled with talk of "tooth and pinion wheels," the determination of "the respective positions of the piston rod which moves the crank shafts, and the eccentrics which set in motion the valves for the distribution of steam," and so on. Late in 1873, there were fourteen graduates of the School of Naval Construction, veterans of the first two classes.[27] These graduates were prepared to manage a shipyard, but Giquel still recommended four years of advanced study in Europe, with more practical work. "China," he wrote, "does not offer at the present time a field of industrial manufacture sufficient for the forming of engineers." [28]

The French language school also included a School and Office of Design, for the study of geometry, arithmetic, descriptive geometry, and "a very complete course in a marine engine of one hundred and fifty horse-power." This curriculum evidently required only three years, since ten students admitted in 1868 entered the School of Naval Construction in 1871 apparently as graduates of the design course.

The third branch of the technical school was the School of Apprentices, started in the summer of 1868 largely because on-the-job training of dockyard workers held out little hope of producing good foremen. In this school workmen in their teens received attention, and by the end of the contract period these apprentices were having three hours daily of classes, in day and evening sessions, to enable them to read plans, and calculate bulks, weights of engine parts and hull members. This course, taught also in French, took at least three years. Some forty students had completed it in 1874, although in Giquel's opinion they were still too young and inexperienced to become foremen. For these students also he recommended further work in Europe.[29]

While this training effort, which Shen Pao-chen thought to be more important than the actual shipbuilding, was in progress, ships were continually launched. The twelve-gun, 1393-ton, 250-horsepower corvette *Yang Wu* was the seventh ship, launched in 1872. She was, it was said, "completely copied from foreign war vessels," with her engine below the waterline. She was followed by a transport of similar displacement, the *Fei Yün*, launched June 3, 1872. This six-gun ship had the standard 150-horsepower engine. After her came two small gunboats, the *Ching Yüan* and *Chen Wei*, launched in August and December 1872, both of the *Chen Hai* class.[30]

On January 2, 1873, the *Chi An*, of the *Fei Yün* class, was launched. This year an agreement was reached which slightly changed the contract terms. Whereas it had been originally agreed to build eleven 150-horsepower and five eighty-horsepower ships, it was now agreed that the added power of the *Yang Wu*'s 250-horsepower engine justified the elimination of one of the smaller gunboats.[31]

Another agreement reached in 1873 was to convert the dockyard for a time to the building of merchant ships. Money was short. The first ship affected was the *Yung Pao,* the dockyard's twelfth vessel. Before her launching on August 10, 1873, her 1391-ton hull was respaced for passengers and freight. The *Hai Ching, Ch'en Hang,* and *Ta Ya* (1873–1874) were also merchant ships, to be delivered to Li Hung-chang's newly established China Merchants Steam Navigation Company. However, in the Formosa crisis with Japan in 1874, Shen Pao-chen, who was placed in charge of the relief of Formosa, managed to keep the *Ch'en Hang,* and she and *Yung Pao* and *Ta Ya* carried Li Hung-chang's Anhwei Army troops to Formosa, so that the shift to merchant ships was not a total loss to the defense effort. Significantly, the Chinese at the yard completely built and installed the engines of two of these ships.[32]

By the end of the contract period in 1874, the Foochow dockyard had built fifteen ships. Giquel reported to Shen Pao-chen that as of the expiration date — February 12, 1874 — the yard would be ready for independent operation. The fourteen Construction School graduates would superintend the building of engines, the plans office, the fitting and setting-up shops, the foundry, and the boiler shops. Students had produced seven ship designs, along with plans for two engines. Starting with the *Yung Pao,* hulls were entirely native-built. Although Giquel asked for advanced work in Europe for his best students, most of the foreigners did depart from the Foochow dockyard, and Shen reported that the contract was fulfilled.[33]

During the contract years, there had been a solid achievement at the Foochow dockyard. Giquel was about forty years of age when the term ended, and had started with no more than a lieutenancy in the French navy by way of professional background. His old chief in the Imperial Maritime Customs, Robert Hart, wrote that Giquel was clever, fluent in Chinese, "a Frenchman and mad for glory, and also attached to sycee." Giquel was rewarded with the Yellow Riding Jacket and a large sum of money — but on the other hand was to be made a scapegoat for future troubles at the yard, of which there were to be many.[34]

Shen Pao-chen left the superintendency in 1875. His administration was probably the most productive the dockyard had. To be sure, the ships were wooden, most with paddle drive, at a time when iron and screw propulsion predominated in the West. The *Wan Nien Ch'ing* displaced about 1500 tons; in 1874, H.M.S. *Thunderer* displaced almost 10,000. But, in Chinese perspective, these ships were impressive.[35]

That the contract was fulfilled is also impressive, in view of the constant shortage of funds that marked the contract period. The expense of building and running such an undertaking brought political opposition. Five years after the Wu T'ang trouble, there came an all-out assault on the Foochow dockyard, this time from Peking. Early in 1872 Sung Chin, of the Grand Secretariat, charged that although more than five million taels had been spent, the dockyard could show nothing comparable to Western warships. The yard was furthermore a bother to the people in its locality, he charged, and in any event war junks were adequate. The situation at the Kiangnan arsenal, Sung Chin added, was just as bad. All such work should stop, and the funds be diverted to conservancy works.[36]

The throne consulted with Tso Tsung-t'ang and Li Hung-chang, and asked if the Foochow dockyard should not be converted to making ammunition. Tso in his reply summarized some of the arguments which had been advanced in the controversy, including those of Wen Yu, acting Min-Che governor-general, and Wang K'ai-t'ai, the governor of Fukien, who seemed to support the Sung Chin line. Tso's own argument was that although initial costs were high and the product inferior to Europe's best, the yard was improving and the investment should not be wasted by closing the yard.[37] Li Hung-chang replied that China was in an unprecedented situation, in which the old war junks were inadequate. He made ominous reference to Japan. Initial costs were high, and although there was room for economy, and although China still could not equal Western ships (for example, he wrote, steel-armored ships with metal-turreted guns fired simultaneously by electricity), the yard should be kept open. Shen Pao-chen, Prince Kung, and Ho Ching, the southern commissioner, also defended the Foochow dockyard. Once again, it was saved.[38]

Many people had joined in the attack, however, and not only on conservative principles. Tso Tsung-t'ang felt that the Fukien provincial officials had not been fair. His belief suggests that intramural jealousy had not ended with the Wu T'ang trouble. Sung

Chin, Tso wrote, was a spokesman for "the Chekiang people." Perhaps these "Chekiang people" felt left out of an activity concentrated entirely in Fukien, Chekiang's paired province. Li Hung-chang preferred the Kiangnan to the Foochow establishment, and had himself discreetly criticized the southern yard as too expensive. Li was a rival of Tso Tsung-t'ang, but he was not a reactionary like Sung Chin, and he urged decommissioning old-style war junks to save money for the building of modern vessels.[39]

Actually, the money problem at the Foochow dockyard was acute during these contract years. Tso Tsung-t'ang, who expected help from other provinces, had originally planned an investment of 300,000 taels, plus a monthly operating budget of 50,000 taels. By the end of 1866, he had to increase his investment estimate by about one third, but then hoped that monthly costs might come only to 40,000 taels. But the payments from the Fukien maritime customs would not cover monthly costs, and revenues from the likin tax were already committed to other uses. Furthermore, Tso by the end of 1866 hoped to rely entirely on Fukien revenues. Consequently he suggested that Peking allow him to borrow from the forty percent of the foreign customs receipts which the maritime provinces usually remitted to Peking (the remaining sixty percent of the foreign customs revenues being kept by the collecting provinces for local uses). Tso also asked that certain subsidies assigned to the troops of other provinces stationed in Fukien be diverted to the dockyard; this would bring in 50,000 taels per month. Early in 1867, the court allowed Tso to borrow for the dockyard from the forty percent of the customs revenues reserved for Peking, but it also instructed Tso to take 30,000 taels monthly from Fukien to subsidize Tso's new Kansu campaign, although Fukien provincial authorities had already asked to be excused from such a contribution.[40] Here is early evidence of the insufficiency of funds, and of the competition over them.

Another problem that soon arose for the dockyard was that of paying for the maintenance of finished ships. Ying-kuei reported on this as early as mid-1869. He used opium revenues, hitherto allocated for guns, to maintain the new Foochow-built ships, which displeased the Board of Revenue. By the end of 1871 it was clear that the opium tax would not support the five completed ships, so it was proposed to distribute them among the coastal provinces to spread the maintenance burden. But the designated provinces objected, either because they were short of funds themselves, or because they were doubtful of the quality of the ships, or of the reception that would be given to the Fukienese in the crews. Li Hung-chang, for one, was not eager to take Foochow ships. Four ships were sent to various ports in 1872, and the unwilling provincial hosts maintained them from the court's forty-percent share of their maritime customs revenues. This controversy was in progress when Sung Chin attacked the naval program. Evidently these provincial raids on Peking's funds contributed to his conservative rejection of naval modernization.[41]

During the Sung Chin debate in 1872, Prince Kung, in defending the "self-strengthening" movement, suggested that the Foochow dockyard build merchant ships for a while rather than be closed. This Sung Chin controversy was the immediate background to the decision at the Foochow dockyard, already noted, to convert some of the ships to a commercial use. Although Tso Tsung-t'ang at the outset knew that warships were lower in the water and faster than merchant ships, he himself had initially eased in his shipbuilding program by saying that the new ships could earn their way. We have seen that ships' specifications, at Kiangnan and Foochow, included varying cargo capacities. In 1870, the British consul at Foochow observed that Foochow ships were used more to carry tribute rice than to chase pirates.[42] It might be argued that the 1872 conversion to merchant ships involved little more than a verbal concession to the conservatives.

Nonetheless, there had been an increasing concern with making the Foochow ships more martial before the Sung Chin attack. In 1871, Wen Yu urged making them better fitted for war. Hsia Hsien-lun, one of Shen Pao-chen's principal aides, and Li Ch'eng-mo, commander of the Fukien squadron, agreed. Hence ship number seven, the *Yang Wu*, had a 250-horsepower engine that took up possible cargo space, and ships numbered eight and nine, the *Fei Yün* and *Ching Yüan*, were described as warships, without cargo space, and were evidently not so "high and deep" as earlier models refused by Li Hung-chang because of the shallow waters in his area. Although the conversion to merchant ships called for little more than omitting guns, adding more deck houses, and using the standard 150-horsepower engine, the change did involve a serious reversal of intent.[43]

The change affected ships numbered twelve through fifteen. Prince Kung assured the advocates of "self-strengthening" that only these ships would be converted, and the yard would then return to its original function. The return was aided by a suggestion of Tso Tsung-t'ang that 20,000 taels from his Kansu military budget be returned to Fukien for the use of the yard. Shen Pao-chen and the Fukien provincial leaders supported the proposal. These men reported that the basic investment for plant at the dockyard had come to over one million taels, and that it had been necessary to use operating funds to complete the basic plant. Maintenance and the cost of training men destined to serve elsewhere also cut into the construction budget, which showed a monthly deficit of 20,000 taels. Tso's suggestion was approved by the court, although it did not take effect until mid-1873.[44] In 1874, with the crisis with Japan over the Liuchiu Islands and Formosa deepening, it was decided to increase the number of gunners on the existing ships. It is symptomatic that Shen bought two American gunboats during the 1874 crisis. And when he summed up the five-year contract period and recommended that the shipbuilding program at Foochow be continued "forever," he also proposed building only two ships a year in the future, which could be done within the 50,000-tael monthly budget. Prince Kung suggested that these future ships be transferable to Li Hung-chang's new steamship company.[45]

Prince Kung's politic suggestion was of little value. Li Hung-chang was willing to defend the yard in theory, but in practice felt that foreign competition to his steamers, the uncertain demand for China Merchants Company stock, and the patent superiority of foreign-built ships made it unwise for him to commit himself to take two Foochow-built ships every year. Li Tsung-hsi, the southern commissioner, favored the two-ship-a-year proposal, but did not know how to apportion this output between warships and merchant ships, and assigned no clear mission to the Foochow dockyard. Although Li Hung-chang was gratified that ship number sixteen was a "warship," he did not show any more interest in the matter. The coincidental conclusion of the contract and conversion to merchant ships did little to give later administrators of the yard a clear sense of purpose. The financial problem was still unsolved.[46]

In the middle of 1874 Shen Pao-chen submitted an accounting

for the first seven and one-half years of operations at the Foochow dockyard. From December 1866 to August 1874 the yard's income had been 5,360,588 taels, while expenditures had been 5,356,948 taels. Some 621,831 taels from the opium tax had also been used for ship maintenance.[47] There was a small surplus, but Tso Tsung-t'ang, who had originally estimated that five millions would be enough for only five years, had evidently imagined a greater future for his dockyard.

Although money problems hampered the shipbuilding effort down to 1875, there was at Foochow during Shen Pao-chen's administration an important naval training program. During these years, the principal naval academy was at Foochow. The Taiping Rebellion had produced an interest in Western-trained land (not sea) forces. The central government had feared foreign influence in troop training; it tried to limit Western training to Peking-controlled troops rather than allowing it for provincial "irregulars"; money shortages had constricted even this limited effort; and the training had been largely a matter of marching drill. Entrenched scholarly objection to any kind of Western curriculum existed, as instanced by Wo-jen's Confucian rejection of the proposal to strengthen the Peking T'ung-wen kuan, or interpreter's school, in the mid-1860's. No naval officer was free from this kind of opposition.[48]

It is likely that Tso Tsung-t'ang was even more interested in the long-run training program at Foochow than he was in the immediate acquisition of China-built ships. By the original contract with Giquel and D'Aiguebelle, two schools were established. One was the French-language construction school already discussed. The other was a naval academy, with instruction in English, for naval officers in deck and engine divisions. The contractors agreed to present the "studies essential to the commanding of ships" in a five-year curriculum. To prepare graduates for the immediate assumption of command was ambitious. The French contractors made an interesting qualification. They guaranteed that in five years they would train cadets to navigate within sight of land, but "as to the navigation on the high seas, in which the ship has for her guidance only the compass, the chronometers, calculation, the aspect of the sky and sea — five years cannot be sufficient to learn it." Their statement is reminiscent of an earlier one made by Tseng Kuo-fan, touching on the tradition of the water force, to the effect that "a single glance" was enough for maneuver on the rivers, but at sea, "one cannot fix the points of the four directions and fathom the depths without years of training and practice."[49]

Each school in the academy had its chief instructor and his aides, including men who could use Chinese. James Carroll was master of the English school, with an assistant to teach physics and chemistry, and later assistants drawn from the graduates of the academy. The engineering department had a staff of about five men. All teachers had three-year contracts, an odd situation in view of the five-year curriculum. There is little information on the selection of students. Tso Tsung-t'ang knew that naval studies would lack prestige, and that handsome stipends and commissions as military or civil officials would be necessary to attract candidates. According to one later student of the subject, the "best" students entered the English school; those not so good entered the French school.[50]

Cadets were to be under sixteen, and family and student had to promise in writing that the candidate would not quit the school, even for a long leave. Room and board were provided, with a stipend of from four to nine taels monthly — probably enough to maintain a "moderate-sized family."[51] The rigorous daily class schedule allowed vacations only on May 5, August 15, and the New Year. Quarterly examinations were set, with three grades, linked to rewards and punishments: a "first" merited a reward of about eight taels; a "second" sufficed for passing; and a "third" brought demerits, with two "thirds" bringing a warning, and three, dismissal from the school. More than one "first" would entitle the scholar to additional clothing. Following theoretical training, there was to be a trip on a training ship, after which graduates were eligible for low-ranking naval commissions.[52]

The shore curriculum included arithmetic, rectilinear and spherical geometry, astronomy, navigation, and geography. Early in 1870, Shen Pao-chen asked Wu Ta-t'ing, one of his assistants, to compile his coastal observations for academy use. For engine men, there was steam engine theory, and later the dry-land assembly of engines. All cadets had to study English. To keep his scholars from becoming Westernized, Shen Pao-chen reported in 1867 that they would study the eighteenth-century imperial maxims in the *Sheng-yü kuang-hsün*, the Book of Filial Piety, and the *lun-ti*, or topical questions on political and financial matters.[53]

The school was made up of southerners, with students coming

from "the best families" in Hong Kong, Canton, and Foochow. Some could already use English; if anything, the greater handicap among the students was a general unfamiliarity with the standard "mandarin" pronunciation used for Chinese instruction. The cadets had their own schoolboy codes, and Canton and Foochow boys lived apart.[54]

In 1869 the dockyard administration purchased a Prussian sailing ship for a trainer, naming it the *Chien Wei*. Early in 1871 eighteen cadets boarded her for a cruise from Liaotung Bay to Singapore. In May, Giquel reported to Shen Pao-chen that twenty-three students had finished their course, and had mastered the art of *open-water navigation* as well. We may wonder. Later in 1871 Carroll complained concerning many prolonged absences among the cadets, contrary to the regulations, for family ceremonial occasions. Also, in a final examination given to this group of cadets, the poorest performance was in arithmetic and navigation.[55]

While cadets were being trained, the modern fleet was growing. It needed organization and officers. The first senior officer for the modern fleet was Admiral Li Ch'eng-mo, imported in 1871 from the traditional water force of Fukien. He was assisted by Yang Yüeh-pin, a river force officer who had become famous in anti-Taiping upriver naval operations. The organizational scheme called for squadrons of three or four modern ships each, with a squadron leader for each, and provision for drills, joint action, supply, repair and the like. Crews were to come from the Kwangtung and Min-Che water forces. The modern fleet was under the ultimate command of the dockyard superintendent.[56] The first captains were taken from the old water force. Shen Pao-chen in 1870 listed Huang Lien-k'ai, Pei Chin-ch'uan, Wu Hsi-ch'ang, Wu Shih-chung, and Chang Sze-kuang as able and loyal transferees of this kind. Pei Chin-ch'uan and Huang Wei-hsuan had compiled coastal charts which were being checked in use.[57]

In the summer of 1873 the *Chien Wei* spent seventy-five days at sea under Captain Tracey, R. N. The cadets made daily observations and took the helm in all seas and weathers. Shen Pao-chen was proud of them, and the achievement was marked in Peking by an edict relieving naval cadets of the traditional study of archery![58]

Shen was convinced that two of his new officers, Chang Ch'eng and Lu Han, were ready for command, and he assigned these

Kwangtung men to the *Hai Tung Yün,* a ship purchased by Wu T'ang in 1869, and the *Ch'ang Sheng,* purchased by Tso Tsung-t'ang in 1865. He still preferred the old water force men for the newer, bigger Foochow-built ships, and so planned to give the 1200-ton *Chi An* to Wu Shih-chung. In 1873 Wu was master of the new *Fei Yün,* and Shen planned to replace him with the *Fei Yün's* first officer, Lin Wen-ho, also of the old force. But it did not so happen. The *Fei Yün* had been "distributed" to Shantung, and that province refused to let Wu Shih-chung be reassigned. Shen then tried to get Lu Wen-ch'ing, expectant senior lieutenant, old force, then captain of the *An Lan,* for the unfinished *Chi An.* But the *An Lan* had been sent to Kwangtung, and the same obstruction was met. Finally Shen made shift for the *Chi An* with another old force man, Cheng Yü, whom he took from the much smaller *Ching Yüan.* This last ship he gave to Chang Ch'eng. To another graduate, Yeh Fu, he gave the old *Hai Tung Yün.* Evidently Lu Han got the *Ch'ang Sheng,* and to Lin Wen-ho Shen assigned the command of the *Yung Pao,* one of the merchant ships, apparently with no demur from Shantung.[59] It is a paradox that the very shortage of captains, given China's provincial organization, interfered with even these modest plans for the placement of the academy graduates. Shen was more modest than Giquel, since he originally selected only two of the four cadets whom Giquel declared to be ready for command in July 1873.[60]

Later in 1873 Carroll took another contingent of cadets, who had had three-and-one-half years of theory, on another cruise, leaving fifteen cadets who had only thirty months of theory in the school. There were then fourteen graduate engineers at sea, with seven awaiting berths. Giquel asked that the education of these men be continued, so that they not be "scattered to the winds." This suggests that the graduates were tempted to leave their careers, or that they were either unready for a command or unable to get one. Shen Pao-chen was planning to send students to Europe for further work, and Prince Kung and Tso Tsung-t'ang lent support to the plan. There was a precedent in the China Educational Mission (C.E.M.) to the United States of 1870. In 1874, Shen prepared elaborate regulations for students who were to be sent to both England and France, providing even that they should have Sunday afternoons for sightseeing, and that they should write home every week, postage to be paid by the dockyard.⁶¹ By the end of the contract period, then, the Foochow dockyard had a well-established naval academy.

Despite these significant advances in naval materiel and training, the political organization of the empire showed no formal adjustment to the needs of a modern navy. The new ships, whether bought or built at Shanghai and Foochow, were not organized into a single national fleet. The Tsungli Yamen did not emerge as a new directorate, as the Lay-Osborn fiasco demonstrated, although it was much involved in naval as well as diplomatic matters. The Yamen and the Grand Council were identical in membership until 1884. Until his death in 1876, Wen-hsiang, who was greatly respected by foreigners, was a member of the Yamen, and may have been more influential than Prince Kung, who stood at the head of both agencies.⁶² The Lay-Osborn affair, in the words of the British minister at Peking, Rutherford Alcock, "left deep traces of discouragement in the official mind, and paralyzed the most advanced and progressive among the leaders of the Yamen and the Grand Secretariat. It went so far as to destroy . . . . [Wen-hsiang's] influence, especially in regard to progress or reforms by foreign agencies." ⁶³

There were some informal organizational changes of importance to the new navy, however, and these may be observed in the Sino-Japanese tension in 1874 over the Liuchiu Islands. The trouble over the Liuchiu Islands began in 1871. In that year some shipwrecked Liuchiu sailors were killed by aboriginals on Formosa. The Japanese government, using the argument that the Liuchiu islands acknowledged Japanese suzerainty (actually, the king of the islands sent tribute to both China and Japan), and thence that the murdered sailors were Japanese subjects, demanded redress from China. The matter dragged on for some years. Finally, in 1874, faced with vacillation in Peking (and faced also with the adventurous schemes of dispossessed samurai in Japan, who were reacting angrily to the strains of Japan's own modernization program), the Japanese government sent a naval expedition to Formosa to chastise the murderers.⁶⁴

Although in 1874 neither the southern commissioner of trade at Nanking nor his northern counterpart at Tientsin had been given the added responsibility of coastal defense, one might assume that these new regional officials, with positions created, as was that of the Tsungli Yamen itself, to cope with the new problems of foreign relations after the Tientsin treaties, would be involved in any crisis. Furthermore, the location of Formosa would seem primarily to involve the southern commissioner, Li Tsung-hsi, in this crisis.[65] Both Li Hung-chang and Li Tsung-hsi were instructed to concern themselves with the threat. However, it was Li Hung-chang, Chihli governor-general and commissioner of trade for the northern ports since 1870, who on May 10, 1874, recommended that Shen Pao-chen, still superintendent of the Foochow dockyard, be sent to Formosa with troops.

Only three Japanese ships and about 3600 men were involved in the Japanese expedition to Formosa. The Japanese naval ministry had been established only in 1872 and disposed of only seventeen indifferent ships, aggregating about 14,000 tons. Alarmist Chinese officials warned Peking of a large invading steam armada, but foreign observers expected that China's twenty-one steamers, mostly in the 1000-ton class — "all [are] new and steam well" — would be "well able" to cope with the Japanese.[66]

China's ships, however, were not in a unified fleet. Kwangtung had some modern ships, purchased by governor-general Jui-lin in 1868; there was the Foochow modern fleet; the southern commissioner had the Kiangnan-built steamers; and there were other provincial fleets, with a few steamers. The Foochow fleet was probably the most modern. Shen Pao-chen commanded it, through Li Ch'eng-mo. But in 1874, the Foochow dockyard fleet was partly scattered along the coast — a dispersal, as has been mentioned, effected to spread maintenance costs. Shen had once proposed keeping some control by sending a Fukien official to keep track of the distributed ships, but this had not been done. Although Shen's emergency powers in 1874 were impressive, and included the right to commandeer steamers from Kiangsu and Kwangtung, it took time to gather a fleet.[67]

Shen was alarmed. Japan reportedly had two ironclads. (In fact, one was "old and completely unseaworthy" and the other was undergoing boiler repairs at the time.) Shen negotiated for two American gunboats to offset the Japanese advantage, although they were not delivered until 1876.[68] All of the Foochow-built ships were of wood. Shen had four ships in and about Formosa, one at Amoy, one at sea en route to Shanghai, one each in Chekiang and Shantung, and three at Tientsin. In asking for troops from the southern and northern commissioners in July, he also sought naval support. In all, Shen mentioned nineteen ships, and planned to use sixteen, including two from the southern commissioner's fleet. Yet only in late September was he able to report that seven steamers had brought 6500 of Li Hung-chang's Anhwei Army troops to the Pescadores, with another steamer en route with a battalion of Hupei men. Since he then had six ships already at P'eng-hu, and had borrowed one from the Customs, he almost realized his plans to use sixteen vessels. In November, some 10,000 Chinese troops had been landed, but the operation had taken about half a year — and no one, evidently, had thought of using warships to make a direct interception of the Japanese ships on their way to Formosa.[69]

The Formosa crisis of 1874 was peaceably ended with a money payment to Japan which in effect recognized the Japanese claim to sovereignty over the Liuchiu Islands. Throughout the crisis, initiative rested with the northern commissioner. Li Hung-chang determined policy, was involved in ship movements, got his own troops first to Formosa, and was closely involved in the *détente*. The southern commissioner did not become so involved.

Not surprisingly, the Tsungli Yamen deferred to Li Hung-chang when Shen Pao-chen suggested that China buy ships. Inspector-General Robert Hart of the customs in 1874 thought of providing gunboats for China through himself as agent, to avoid disordered provincial steamer-buying, which was secured on customs revenues. Hart was sent by the Tsungli Yamen to Li Hung-chang. The Yamen stipulated that any ships acquired would be under the direction of some designated governor-general. In the event of war, these governors-general would consult with Peking as to the use of the ships. No coordinating role was suggested for the northern and southern commissioners. Shortly after Hart's visit to Li, both northern and southern commissioners initiated ambitious ship-buying programs, which conflicted with the build-at-home program and were not unified efforts. Li Hung-chang was to become pre-eminent in such buying, but not even he could effect a real centralization of the navy.[70]

IV

LI HUNG-CHANG AND NAVAL DEVELOPMENT, 1875-1885

In 1874, the position of Empress Dowager Tz'u-hsi was strengthened when she forced the succession of her nephew to the throne, although this succession violated the rules of the ruling Manchu clan. She retained power in the court from this time until her death in 1908. Li Hung-chang, already started on an unprecedented tenure of office — that of commissioner of trade for the northern ports and Chihli governor-general from 1870 to 1895 — also gained in power in the 1870's. Li's emergence is attributable to his combination of political adroitness, personal military power, progressive ideas, and the wealth accumulated from his offices and his modernizing ventures. He became interested in building a naval force under his command. Although his power never sufficed to unify the navy-building process, he became an increasingly important competitor to all other sponsors of it. Given the political and institutional situation that obtained in China in the post-Taiping period, the impact of this powerful person was probably more deleterious than advantageous to the naval effort.

Li Hung-chang, as northern commissioner, had considerable influence in the territory of the southern commissioner, where he had served in several high positions before 1870. At times this influence was exerted through the southern commissioner himself. In the north Li enhanced his power in 1870 by arranging for the merging of the offices of northern commissioner and Chihli governor-general, and through manipulation of the subordinate office of Tientsin maritime customs intendant drew into his own hands the direction of customs funds, coastal defense, and the Tientsin arsenal. The central government in the 1860's had organized the Peking Field Force (*lien-chün*), and planned to absorb into this foreign-trained unit such personal armies as Li Hung-chang's

Anhwei army, while retaining the old Manchu Banner and Chinese provincial troops. Li could not eliminate the rival *lien-chün* in Chihli, but he infiltrated it with men loyal to himself, and units of his Anhwei army largely replaced the established Manchu and Chinese military units in Chihli. Yet Li was loyal to the dynasty. His chief rival was Tso Tsung-t'ang, the founder of the Foochow dockyard.[1]

During and after the 1874 Formosa crisis further attempts were made to unify China's navy, which now included the purchased ships of the northern and southern commissioners as well as the Foochow China-built ships and the mixed fleets of other provinces. Late in 1874 Ting Jih-ch'ang, long associated with Li Hung-chang, urged formation of a tripartite system, having a northern admiral at Tientsin overseeing Shantung and Chihli, a central admiral at Woosung for Chekiang and Kiangsu, and a southern admiral at Amoy for Kwangtung and Fukien. Each admiral should command six large and ten small modern ships, so that in annual joint maneuvers there would be assembled a fleet of forty-eight ships. Wen Pin, acting governor of Shantung, suggested that the three admirals be respectively Li Hung-chang, P'eng Yü-lin (Tseng Kuo-fan's associate in anti-Taiping river naval campaigns), and Shen Pao-chen, with all three subordinated to an all-China naval chief.[2]

Although Li Hung-chang preferred a single national naval command, he supported Ting's three-part system. He could not be sure that he would be the single naval chief, but he did enjoy influence in Kiangsu (having been Kiangsu governor in 1862–1865, Nanking governor-general in 1865–1867, and being at the time one of the directors of the Kiangnan arsenal), and since the Ting plan called for splitting the Min-Che region and joining Chekiang to Kiangsu for naval purposes, he might have dominated the system, if only unofficially.[3] Ting's scheme was not adopted, although in 1875 the northern commissioner was given the added responsibility for the defense of the northern coast. It is interesting that the southern commissioner did not receive a similar concurrency until 1879, when the incumbent was Ting Jih-ch'ang, a "Li man."

In the spring of 1875, Peking established a Sea Defense Fund, to be made up of one half of the forty-percent remissions from the maritime customs receipts. This *hai-fang* fund was to be divided between the northern and southern commissioners.[4] In the late

1870's Shen Pao-chen recommended that the northern commissioner be allowed to purchase a naval fleet before the southern commissioner; that is, that the entire Sea Defense Fund should be sent for the time being to Li Hung-chang. This priority was not allowed.[5]

The coastal fleets continued to be poorly organized. In 1879 — Japan occupied the Liuchiu Islands in that year — there was talk of setting up a national naval command at Woosung. Robert Hart of the customs was to be the naval chief, but Li Hung-chang and Shen Pao-chen blocked the proposal.[6] In 1881, the problem of naval disunity was reflected in advice given to Li Hung-chang by "Chinese" Gordon (Charles Gordon of the "Ever-Victorious Army"). Gordon suggested that a naval ministry be created (which would supposedly be under Li Hung-chang), but concerned himself primarily with land military matters.[7] Nothing came of the suggestion.

In 1883, the central government offered the post of naval director once again to Robert Hart. Hart wrote:

They have hinted to me at the Yamen that if I will decide not to quit China at all, or at least stay five years longer without moving, they will take the advice I gave them seven or eight years ago and establish a Hai-fang Yamen, or Admiralty, and make me Naval Inspector-General. Of course if they did this, I'd make their navy really respectable in five years time; it would be a great pity to let slip such a chance of doing something big, and it would be a greater pity still to see the work drift into —— or —— hands, which it is likely to do if I don't hold on.

This court offer to Hart was probably designed to check the strength of Li Hung-chang, with whom Hart was increasingly at odds. Hart feared that Li was too much influenced by Gustav Detring, the German customs commissioner at Tientsin, and no doubt one of the blanks in Hart's statement was intended for the word "German." The other blank was probably reserved for the word "American." At the time, Li Hung-chang was trying to interest Commodore Robert Shufeldt of the United States Navy, who was in Tientsin to negotiate a Korean-American treaty, in training Li's Peiyang fleet.[8]

Hart at least endorsed the idea of an admiralty, nominating Prince Ch'un, the father of the Kuang-hsü Emperor, as its chief. Meanwhile, Li Hung-chang received an imperial commission to go to Kwangtung to deal with the growing crisis with France in Annam. All troops in Yunnan and the Liang-Kwang region were to be under his command.[9] In making this assignment, the court bypassed Tso Tsung-t'ang, although Tso had recently returned from victories in Turkestan.

Early in 1884 Li Hung-chang once again urged the Tsungli Yamen to establish a single coastal defense command. Although he admitted that such a position would give too much power to a provincial official, he proposed himself as a candidate, resolving the contradiction by proposing that the new naval office be located in Peking, on the premises of the Tsungli Yamen. As northern commissioner Li was a member of the Yamen in any event, and his provincial base at Tientsin was close enough to Peking to allow him to meet his regional responsibilities. This was a realistic proposal in the eyes of Kuo Sung-t'ao, a prominent and progressive Chinese, who held that any fleet director based in Peking alone would be isolated. Still, no admiralty was established.[10]

There was one more attempt along this line before the Sino-French War. Chang P'ei-lun, a member of the Tsungli Yamen, had studied Western naval systems, and asked for a single naval minister, so that the Chinese navy could be "like one family." Chang had recently been Li's private secretary, and probably hoped his old chief would be the new navy minister. Prince Kung favored the idea, and hinted at court that Li was available. But the prince was soon cashiered for supposed ineptitude in the trouble with France, and this last project also collapsed.[11]

Although neither Li nor the court were able to unify the fleets, some simplification did take place. Commodore Shufeldt counted four "distinct" fleets, nominally under the two coastal defense commissioners; we might, in our turn, say that on the eve of the war with France there were *only* four modern fleets. The Nanking flotilla was larger than Li's, but Li had influence in the south.[12] When the war came, Tso was no longer at Nanking. Li had his own sources of information along the southern coasts, and the wartime superintendent of Fukien coastal defense was Chang P'ei-lun. Li might have effected an informal coordination between China's modern fleets.

Had there been a strong emperor in 1884, naval unification might have been realized. But the Empress Dowager was not a great leader. Prince Kung was replaced as the throne's chief adviser by Prince Ch'un, who was inexperienced and too dependent on the Empress Dowager in any event.

Still, the empire had not broken down into a mere cluster of regional autonomies. Too much can be made of post-Taiping decentralization. Loyalty to the throne remained — and the emperor had not lost his power to punish. Negative sanctions, however, do not constitute leadership. The political structure of the empire was strained; there was more room for competition between China's regional and provincial leaders.

There were many ways in which these leaders could compete with each other in this period. The purchasing of naval ships and materiel was one. Tseng Kuo-fan and Tso Tsung-t'ang wanted China to build her own ships, but others disagreed. Jui-lin, the Canton governor-general, although aware that foreign agents might cheat him, bought six small gunboats from France and England in the late 1860's. Even Ting Jih-ch'ang, who followed Shen Pao-chen as the Foochow dockyard superintendent, agreed that foreign-built ships were better and cheaper.[13]

Whether China should buy or build her navy was an important question. China should certainly have worked toward eventual naval independence; but she did not need to rely at once entirely on her own shipyards, particularly to create a defensive fleet. A judicious mixture of buying and building would have been quite possible. But the court laid down no policy, and the decisions were made by men whose ideas, locations, and interests varied. Decisions were conditioned by the prevalent rivalry. Fleet unification and standardization could not be achieved.

Before the 1870's, Li Hung-chang was preoccupied with land military strength, and his strategic ideas were so traditional that he advocated building a wall along the Grand Canal at Tientsin during the Tientsin Massacre crisis of 1870, to strengthen coastal defense.[14] His interest in foreign-built ships arose when he founded the China Merchants Company in 1872, for which he used British ships. Even Shen Pao-chen, as we have seen, bought two American gunboats during the 1874 crisis, although at the time foreign arms hucksters were tripling prices, and the vessels were not delivered until 1876. Robert Hart was concerned about piecemeal charges against the customs revenues of this or that province for foreign arms, and tried to centralize the buying of military goods. He encouraged buying, rather than building, ships and arms, no doubt assuming that the process could be controlled.

The 1874 Formosa crisis brought a spate of defense recommendations, mostly traditional in their emphasis on harbor works, but with a few suggestions for large ships. The emphasis was on the buying of foreign-built materiel. Wen-hsiang, depressed by the Formosa affair, also urged buying ships. The emperor called on the southern and northern commissioners, Li Tsung-hsi and Li Hung-chang, to raise funds quickly and buy armored ships, monitors, and other weapons. The gesture was a grand one, but showed little understanding.[15]

Li Hung-chang wanted six cruisers and some smaller ships, as prescribed in the three-sector, forty-eight-ship navy scheme mentioned above. He urged that funds be taken from the western regions (where Tso Tsung-t'ang was then stationed), that troops raise their own food on good coastal lands to save money, that the forty-percent customs remissions to Peking, along with forty percent of the income of the Board of Revenue, be assigned to the Tsungli Yamen and coastal officials for maritime defense, and that traditional land and water forces be eliminated.[16]

Whatever Li's motives, there was a need to rationalize the finances of the empire. At the height of the 1874 crisis, Peking was distracted by plans for rebuilding the Summer Palace. Prince Kung protested against the enormous graft involved and was dismissed for a token period (September 10–11, 1874). He complained:

Since I took over the Tsungli Yamen, I have tried to train troops and raise funds and teach the building of machinery and ships. In several of these matters, I have asked for authority, but differences of opinion have militated against realization. In some cases, we lacked funds; in some, we had money, but not enough; in some others, we had a good start, but couldn't continue. Of agreement there has been little; of disagreement, much. The difficulties we have experienced in the Tsungli Yamen can't be known by others.

The problem also alarmed Wen-hsiang, but he too was unable to correct it.[17]

Li Hung-chang and Robert Hart both sought changes in the buying of weapons. Although Li complained of factions, and wrote that the recent invasions of China's coast were "the greatest change in Chinese history," he did not become a convert to sea power. He believed that the land forces must bear the brunt of any attack. When a navy was built, it should best be used off China's ports (he cited a Prussian strategy manual), but the present Chinese navy, "with its handful of ships," could not be so bold. It should concentrate at the important ports of Taku, Pei-t'ang, Shanhaikuan, and at the Yangtze estuary. Of China's twenty-one modern ships in 1874, Li felt that only two, both built at the Kiangnan arsenal, were usable.[18]

Late in 1874, British naval experts were arguing about a new Armstrong gunboat which might be the answer to a problem then agitating the rapidly changing navies of the West — the problem of whether a sufficiently heavy armor protection could be devised to protect naval vessels from the ever-increasing power of rifled naval guns. The new Armstrong gunboat, the *Staunch*, had a single large gun mounted on an unarmored hull, and it was said that she was too small to be hit save well within the radius of her own powerful offensive fire. Hart wanted China to buy ships of the *Staunch* type, and was sent by the Tsungli Yamen to see Li Hung-chang, as noted above. In April of 1875 Li placed with Hart an order for four of the experimental gunboats.

By that time, the *Staunch* had been improved upon, so that two of Li's gunboats were to have twenty-six-and-one-half-ton guns, for 536-pound projectiles, and the other two, thirty-eight-ton guns for 800-pound shells. These rifled guns were elevated and served hydraulically, and with 100 rounds each, ready for sea, these nine-knot vessels, two of 300 and two of 400 tons displacement, were to cost £112,800 sterling, with a total cost to China of 450,000 taels. Of this sum, 130,000 taels were to come from the Shanghai customs; 40,000 each from Hankow, Kiukiang, and Ningpo; and the balance from the Kwangtung customs.[19]

One wonders what happened to Li Hung-chang's desire for cruisers. These Armstrong vessels, despite their impressive voyage from England with such heavy ordnance mounted on such low hulls, were gunboats. Li was an opportunist rather than a strategist, but by 1875 he had commenced his naval purchasing, and in the next few years he was to buy no less than ten ships through Hart. But he did not always deal with Hart; nor was he China's only purchaser of naval materiel. The buying of ships and arms was decentralized and confused, as the following pages will show.

In 1875, the Kiangnan arsenal built the twenty-six-gun *Yu Yüan*, its last major vessel, and the Foochow dockyard started on a decline. Even without uncoordinated buying, it would have been hard to expand shipbuilding facilities. Competition was rife, and Li Hung-chang, partly by trying to become the coordinator of purchasing, added to it.

The southern commissioner, Li Tsung-hsi, also ordered four Armstrong gunboats, of steel rather than iron, and with lighter eleven-inch guns. Li Hung-chang's best boats, with the builder's type-designation of "gamma," with their thirty-eight-ton, twelve-and-one-half-inch guns, had elicited a British comment that China in buying them had "by a sudden and adventurous leap placed herself abreast of ourselves"; of the Nanking boats, called "epsilon" types by the builder, it was remarked that they carried "the most formidable weapon which the English Navy possess at the present moment." [20]

Li Hung-chang was cautious. He asked Shen Pao-chen to direct Giquel, then buying iron ship-frames in Europe for the Foochow dockyard, to check Hart's prices for the "gammas." He also consulted Shen on the number of ships that would be needed. He feared that the new annual Sea Defense Fund of four million taels would be drawn from provincial defense accounts already charged against the forty-percent customs remissions, so that anything he planned for the "new" fund would compete with his current defense activities (for Li, these included financing the China Merchants Company). He wanted the Sea Defense Fund to be really new; that is, drawn from hitherto uncommitted portions of the forty-percent customs remissions.[21] Li would shift the defense burden still farther in the direction of Peking.

Li trusted no one entirely. He wanted to have Li Feng-pao (who was to be sent by the Foochow yard to supervise a student training mission in Europe) check on Giquel, who was checking on Hart. Li also offered to have naval plans which Giquel had obtained for the Foochow dockyard checked by German naval experts in Tientsin. Giquel was under a cloud for alleged "squeezing" by the use of old machinery at Foochow. Yet Li could still cite Giquel in urging Wu Ts'an-ch'eng (the new superintendent at the Foochow dockyard) to build faster ships in future at the Foochow yard. Li had some interest in Foochow ships. Although he said that the *I Hsin* was unstable, and that the *Ch'en Hang* and *Chen Hai* were slower than British ships, he wondered if Foochow might design an economical power plant. Li still had no modern ships in a fleet of his own; in 1876 his new Armstrong gunboats had not yet arrived.[22]

In the Sino-British Margary affair in 1876, there were official recommendations for improved coastal defenses. Some officials, like Hsüeh Fu-ch'eng, urged more naval strength.[23] At the Chefoo negotiations over the Margary affair, Li invited an American, Major Manneck (or Mannix) to direct his electric torpedo works at Tientsin, which he added to his arsenal in 1876.[24] In talking to foreign admirals, Li became interested in ironclad vessels, and wrote to Shen Pao-chen, then southern commissioner and working through Giquel in naval matters, that he had asked Li Feng-pao to make secret inquiries in Europe about ironclads. He also suggested to Wu Ts'an-ch'eng at Foochow that the addition of plate might convert Foochow's planned iron-framed composite ships into fast armored ships. He vacillated on whether Foochow could imitate the Armstrong gunboats, with their hydraulic gear and all-metal construction. Probably Li was less interested in supplying his own naval needs from the Foochow dockyard than he was in having that yard meet the gunboat needs of other provinces, thus easing pressure on the Sea Defense Fund — which was supposed to yield two million taels annually to Li, but in 1877 produced only one tenth of that for him.[25]

German vessels were not inferior to British ones, Li had learned, and so in 1877 he moved some of his overseas students to a German yard. But he was not done with Hart, and in the same year he ordered four more Armstrong gunboats through him, at a time when Hart had heard that Shen Pao-chen had just ordered two Armstrong cruisers through Giquel.[26] Hart's dislike of competition may have made him more persuasive with Li, whose strategic ideas were flexible.

It was at about this time that Shen Pao-chen urged that the four millions of taels supposedly accruing annually in the Sea Defense Fund go entirely to the northern commissioner, to be sent entirely to the southern commissioner after a northern fleet had been built up. Although this was not done, Li continued to seek primacy. When he heard that Ho Ching, Ting Jih-ch'ang's successor as governor of Fukien, was trying to buy vessels through Hart, Li discouraged the attempt. The Foochow dockyard itself also wanted to buy an ironclad through Hart, and Li similarly discouraged Wu Ts'an-ch'eng, saying that Hart was not to be trusted, that China had no dockyards deep enough for the repair of such heavy ships, that the conversion of composite ships was best, and that there were not enough captains for so many additions to China's ships. A little later he did suggest that the Foochow dockyard buy a foreign dock in the Min River which was for sale, but apparently Li imagined that such a yard would accommodate ironclads that Li himself or Shen Pao-chen would purchase.[27] He wanted to protect the Sea Defense Fund for the southern commissioner and himself, and to monopolize the contact with Hart.

On the other hand, Li Hung-chang kept in close touch with Li Feng-pao, who in 1877 was made China's minister to France, Germany, Italy, Holland, and Austria. Li Feng-pao reported on armored cruisers and gunboats — the one too deep, the other too slow. Li Hung-chang began to think of building a repair yard of his own, even though it would cost three or four million taels. Since the armored-ship class was fast developing, he thought China should have some built abroad and build a dockyard for them at home, as he wrote to Kuo Sung-t'ao late in 1877. Perhaps this desire for a yard of his own was enhanced by his concern that his Armstrong gunboats, then manned by Foochow men and training in southern waters, might remain permanently attached to the Foochow dockyard.[28]

Early in 1878, despite Li Hung-chang's belief that China should buy armored vessels rather than try to build them, Wu Ts'an-ch'eng of the Foochow dockyard decided to build a 2600 horse-power cruiser. After some correspondence with Li Feng-pao, Wu decided to send Foochow dockyard observers to a Glasgow building firm, and asked the Tsungli Yamen for money.[29] In that year, famine ravaged Honan and Shansi, and money was needed for famine relief. Even the coffers of the China Merchants Company were opened for famine relief. Shen Pao-chen wrote to Li Hung-chang that he preferred to spend money for defense to spending it on the famine.[30] When Governor Ho Ching of Fukien planned to send Fukien's contribution to the Sea Defense Fund to Li Hung-chang to be used for famine relief, Li stopped him, evidently because he preferred that relief funds come from uncommitted parts of the Fukien customs forty-percent. Li wrote that the Sea Defense Fund was a central government trick to protect its revenues. At the same time, Li suggested to Wu Ts'an-ch'eng that Li Feng-pao's advice about the future of the Foochow dockyard was better than Giquel's, or, that British models would be best for the imitation attempts at Foochow.[31] In this reversal of his earlier discouragement of the dockyard's plans for building large ships, Li was advancing the use of Li Feng-pao as an agent; it might also be said that in encouraging the yard to build more expensive vessels, which would take money from Fukien sources, he was striking a blow for the provincial cause versus that of Peking in the matter of the disbursement of revenues. At the time, Li was not thinking of keeping Foochow-built ships for his own use.[32]

Whatever plans he might have had, Wu Ts'an-ch'eng had to see the third composite built at the Foochow dockyard, the *K'ang Chi*, altered for commerce. He wanted to resign.[33] As for Li Hung-chang, his naval buying program was threatened in 1878 not only by the famine, but also by renewed court interest in rebuilding the Summer Palace. Li undoubtedly noticed too that in 1878 the governor of Kiangsu used some of the money supposedly earmarked for the southern commissioner's Sea Defense Fund for river conservancy projects.[34] Shen Pao-chen was interested in acquiring Foochow ships, if only to take them off the Foochow dockyard maintenance account so as to keep intact the Fukien contribution to his Sea Defense account.[35] Nothing, it seems, was more vulnerable than the Sea Defense Fund.

In 1879, with Japan taking over the Liuchiu Islands, Li Hung-chang was even more interested in buying armored ships and in building a dockyard for himself. But money and trained men were in short supply. He considered a foreign loan, but rejected the idea.[36] Although Li was discouraged, Shen Pao-chen still wanted to buy ships, through Hart. Li countered Shen's proposal by questioning Hart's reliability, since Hart was still urging gunboat types on China. Li even suggested that Shen interest himself again in the Foochow dockyard, from which Wu Ts'an-ch'eng had resigned. To Li Feng-pao, who was his purchasing agent, Li Hung-chang wrote that both he and Shen opposed Hart, both in strategy and as a candidate for a proposed naval directorate. Li also asked Shen Pao-chen about armored ships, saying that even one would do (although he had earlier discouraged Shen's buying projects with the argument that only two would be useless). Hart should not be the buyer. In his search for ironclads, Li also sought advice from Tseng Chi-tse, China's minister to Britain, and was sufficiently aware of current naval developments to specify an interest in ram-equipped ships. Li wanted to buy through his own channels, and to dissociate himself both from Hart and the Tsungli Yamen, which had apparently accepted Hart's ideas about gunboats. In his relations with Shen Pao-chen, Li was flexible. He disagreed with Shen's desire to fight Japan in 1879, and in matters of ship buying, evidently regarded the southern commissioner as a rival.[37]

An ingenious swap made by Li in 1879 reveals this rivalry. The four improved "epsilon" gunboats, ordered by the southern commissioner in 1875, had arrived. Through Hart (who still had his uses), Li arranged to have them delivered to Tientsin. There he wanted to keep them. After all, Li argued to Shen, Li's responsibility embraced the stormy northern seas, while Shen's responsibility for the quiet Yangtze was not so demanding. Therefore, Li's original "gammas," although pitted, barnacled, and in need of a refit at the Kiangnan yard, would be adequate for Shen. Further, although he again discouraged Shen from buying armored ships, citing money shortages and Tsungli Yamen opposition, Li stated that he had asked Hart to order two new ram cruisers. Even though Li asked Tseng Chi-tse in London to check on Hart's latest reports, it seems that as long as Li Hung-chang did the buying, Hart might be used.[38]

As for the Japanese taking of the Liuchiu Islands, the only concrete action was taken by the Foochow dockyard, which increased the number of gunners on its ships.[39] Shen Pao-chen's death late in 1879 removed him from the many tribulations and intricacies of the "self-strengthening movement." At the turn of the decade, then, Li Hung-chang became probably the most important spokesman for naval development.

Li's orders for cruisers involved ships not much bigger than the unarmored Armstrong gunboats, and no faster. But the steel ram cruisers mounted two ten-inch Armstrong guns, fore and aft, as well as four of the new quick-firers, and each had two auxiliary steam cutters with spar torpedoes.[40] As for the older gunboats, other provinces might buy them, thought Li. In 1880, when Li was already worried that Russia might occupy Korean ports to support her claims in Ili, Hart made the ominous report that Japan had just bought fifteen of these gunboats.[41] Consequently Li surveyed the need of the provinces for gunboats, which he hoped to order for them through Hart. Li stipulated that money from the provinces for such gunboats should not come from their forty-percent contributions to the Sea Defense Fund, which he should continue to receive. He found that Shantung wanted two gunboats, as did Fukien; Chekiang sought one. Kwangtung did not propose to work through Li. In the end Li ordered through Hart only two gunboats for Shantung. The Canton governor-general bought one, but not through Li.[42] After these disappointments, Hart no longer served Li as ship broker.

Li Hung-chang did not stop trying to buy ships for other provinces. In the spring of 1880, he wrote to Li Feng-pao, seeking two British ships, one for Fukien province, which province would remit directly, and the other for either himself or the southern commissioner, then Ting Jih-ch'ang. Hart should be kept out, and Li Feng-pao, Li Hung-chang wrote, should disprove the late Shen Pao-chen's warning that Chinese could not handle matters of this kind. Li had another concern, which was that the Foochow dockyard might not cooperate with him in the matter of supplying trained personnel.[43]

The Fukien provincial administration planned to pay for its new ship with funds marked for new construction at the Foochow dockyard, a sign of the old Fukien intramural competition as well as of the immiscibility of simultaneous buying and building programs as they were being conducted in China. Li Hung-chang planned to pay for the second ship partly with Sea Defense Funds assigned to the southern commissioner.[44] He did not mention the source of these latest orders when he wrote to the Foochow dockyard superintendent, Li Chao-t'ang. Nor did he mention the financial arrangements, although he mentioned the ships and also that he had been ordered to establish a naval shipyard on the Sungari in Kirin, for which he might need supervisory personnel trained at the Foochow dockyard.[45] His encouragement of shipbuilding improvement at Foochow seems to have been perfunctory.

This latest ship-buying project collapsed when the British admiralty objected to selling finished naval units to China during China's trouble with Russia. Li Feng-pao thought that if orders were placed for new construction, which would of course take time to finish, the difficulty might be surmounted. Li Hung-chang obtained court approval for new-construction orders, but suggested that French ships might be just as good; for that matter, Krupp breech-loading naval ordnance was the best, and China's arsenals could make the ammunition they needed. Accordingly Li asked Li Feng-pao to inquire about German torpedo boats. The English orders were rescinded, and in any event Li no longer tried to buy for Fukien.[46]

Li Hung-chang's strategic notions, never clear-cut, seemed to be changing. In September 1880 he wrote to a friend that he wanted four fast armored ships and ten torpedo and mine ships, to operate from Talienwan and Port Arthur. Still, he did not regard the navy as the most important element in China's defense. Li Feng-pao in the meantime was coming to prefer the German market. Li Hung-chang asked him if the types involved might not be ordered in British or French yards; if the orders were for new construction, one might ignore Tseng Chi-tse's mumblings about diplomatic repercussions.[47] But Li Hung-chang was also coming to favor German yards, possibly because of the diplomatic impasse, and possibly because of some estrangement from Tseng Chi-tse. Hart would have argued that Li was showing a German preference because of the sinister influence on him of Detring.

Li had to watch in many directions. Some officials wanted to send ships to the Liuchiu Islands in 1880, to force tribute payments, but not Li. There was also growing opposition to Li from Chang Chih-tung, then a tutor in the Imperial Academy and identified with the militant party at court. While Tso Tsung-t'ang was receiving six or seven million taels annually for his western campaign against Russia, Li was falling behind in his expected defense receipts. He was bitter about Tso, who was urging a strong navy. Tso was a hypocrite, said Li.[48]

German yards became more interesting to Li, and he argued with Tseng Chi-tse about using Giquel. From the Foochow dockyard he wanted personnel. Early in 1881, via Li Feng-pao, he placed an order in a German shipyard, although he was still making inquiries about British ships through Tseng Chi-tse, sometimes using such technical language that Tseng's legation staff had trouble with the questions. Tseng was piqued at the "German shift," as it undercut the role of his London legation.[49]

Li's order in Germany was for a 7500-ton battleship, of which he ultimately wanted three, for an integrated north-south defense of the China coast. He wrote to Li Chao-t'ang at the Foochow dockyard about the possibility of building such large ships at home, but without conviction. He wanted some Foochow dockyard men to observe the building of his German battleship, and also others for his proposed Kirin dockyard. He hoped the "fast ships" being planned at Foochow would turn out well, but his real expectations of the Foochow dockyard seemed to lie in the field of ordnance, hand arms, and supporting equipment. Since Li Hung-chang made a contemptuous reference to Tso Tsung-t'ang's idea that Foochow-built ships could cope with the Russian threat, and was busily buying foreign ships, Li Chao-t'ang probably wondered about the future which Li Hung-chang envisioned for the Foochow dockyard.[50]

The northern commissioner did plan a future for the Foochow dockyard. In the spring of 1881 he talked of using the *Wei Yüan* and the *Chi An,* built respectively in 1877 and 1873 at the Foochow yard. He was arranging for payments on his German battleships (by then he had ordered two). He was later concerned because subsidies promised to the Foochow dockyard from the southern commissioner had not been paid, but since at the time Tso Tsung-t'ang was southern commissioner. Li's interest may not have come entirely from partiality for the dockyard.[51] Although he had often called for the disbanding of traditional water forces to save money for the building of modern ships, he kept his own Anhwei water force at Port Arthur, where in 1881 he started the construction of a naval base, and there was a great deal of corruption in this lingering force.[52] Whatever Li Hung-chang planned for the Foochow dockyard, when Li Chao-t'ang reported the start of a new fast cruiser at the Foochow dockyard he also reported that some of his yard space was devoted to the commercial conversion of the old *Wan Nien Ch'ing*.[53]

In 1882 Hart tried to resume his old agency with Li Hung-chang, sending him specifications for a new Armstrong ship somewhat like Li's German battleships, then being built. Li passed these specifications on to Li Feng-pao, but decided to continue dealing with Germany, while keeping the line to Hart open, since China might profit by generating a British-German rivalry. As Li Feng-pao had been criticized, Li Hung-chang warned him that a great deal depended on the correct execution of the orders.⁵⁴ Another of Li's problems was that Li Chao-t'ang wanted to keep the Foochow dockyard construction-school graduates in Foochow, to supervise new building, while Li wanted them in Germany to observe the building of his new battleships — and presumably to ready themselves for later service with Li Hung-chang. Here is another example of the clash between the buying and building programs. Li Chao-t'ang sought to resign, pleading insomnia.⁵⁵

In 1882, when Chang P'ei-lun argued that China should attack Japan because of Japanese interference in Korea, Li Hung-chang parried, saying China was unprepared: the planned delivery of the annual two million taels of Sea Defense money to each of the northern and southern commissioners had gone astray; some provinces, including Fukien, were in arrears. In fact, the domestic building program was in difficulties; even Tso Tsung-t'ang was unable to get an order for gunboats filled at the Foochow dockyard. Li himself was ordered to cut back his Anhwei Army by 10,000 men — although the order was undoubtedly as much aimed at curbing Li's power as it was at economy.⁵⁶

Toward the end of 1882, Li approached Hart for advice on faster vessels, and then turned the blueprints he received over to Li Feng-pao to be checked in British and German yards. Li Hung-chang wondered if these ram vessels could be used with armored ones, which suggests a growing tactical sophistication. He also asked Li Chao-t'ang at the Foochow dockyard if he could build ships like those advocated by Hart — of 5000 horsepower, developing seventeen knots. In addition he asked for the *Yung Pao* and *Ch'en Hang*, which he needed for transports; and he observed to Li Chao-t'ang that a fleet should be sent to Saigon, India, Japan, and Korea to make an impressive show. Li Chao-t'ang still sought to resign.⁵⁷

Even Tso Tsung-t'ang, when advised that Germany could supply large ships more quickly and cheaply than they could be built in China, ordered two German cruisers. He was still buying ships from his old yard at Foochow — and, for the first time in the yard's history, paying half of the building costs — but he complained that the Foochow dockyard had deteriorated. Li Chao-t'ang reported to Peking that the fast ship *K'ai Chi*, of 2400 horsepower, was to be delivered to Tso, adding that Tso (still the southern commissioner) wanted five of these vessels, and the northern commissioner, two. Li Chao-t'ang asked for plant expansion, but shortly thereafter, on March 23, 1883, Chang Meng-yüan was ordered to replace him as the dockyard superintendent.[58]

During these years tension with France was mounting. When Chang Meng-yüan took over at the dockyard, he urged support for shipbuilding, for China could not rely on foreigners. The dockyard was behind the times. In the early 1880's it came under attack by conservatives who charged that its ships were unstable or outmoded. Li Hung-chang was not as positive in his defense of the dockyard as he had been in 1872; he had long been going his own way, and the yard's administration was not sufficiently cooperative in supplying personnel to him.[59]

This account of the buy-versus-build problems has stressed the role of Li Hung-chang, although it has shown that others also preferred to buy ships. Ordnance and ammunition for land and sea units were also purchased in the foreign market. As early as 1871, Tseng Kuo-fan was concerned with unregulated buying by provincial officials, often for profitable resale.[60] There was no coordination of expenditure or strategic thinking. It might have been a good thing if Li Hung-chang had succeeded in centralizing all arms purchasing. A strong leader might have achieved standardization of materiel, ashore and afloat. As it was, the Chinese fleets on the eve of the Sino-French War were far from standardized.

China's modern fleets were described by Shufeldt in 1882 as four "distinct" units. Li Hung-chang had about a dozen modern ships, including, in Shufeldt's phrase, "unique" gunboats with very heavy guns. While cataloguing large caliber, hydraulically-served guns, machine guns, electric lights, and so on, Shufeldt still observed a lack of "intelligent personnel and thorough organization." He might also have wondered about the tactical or strategic integrity of Li's assorted vessels. The gunboats were rated at nine knots, the cruisers at sixteen, and the Foochow ships at perhaps ten. Even if these speeds had been reduced to a low common figure by hard use and indifferent maintenance, it does not seem likely that the assortment could have been used as a fleet on some common mission other than harbor defense. Li sensed the problem in 1882, when he cautioned Li Feng-pao not to buy vessels of apparently the same class from both Germany and Britain, but he made the warning only once.[61]

Other modern fleets were no more standardized. In 1883 the Kwangtung fleet, consisting partly of torpedo boats, was ordered by the court to reconnoiter the French in Annamese waters, but Tseng Kuo-ch'uan, then the Canton governor-general, refused, partly because his ships were "not of a class" and needed repair anyway. In that year the governor of Kwangsi, Hsü T'ing-hsu, asked the Foochow dockyard to send ten large steamers to protect the southern coast, saying that the Kwangtung ships were useful for enclosed maneuver only, and those of Liu Ming-ch'uan "small and weak." Hsü's own plans for defense included fire rafts — a reminder to the modern reader that the old water force fleets had not been disbanded.[62]

There was even less standardization in the bores and makes of the armament of the ships and forts. In 1875 Li Hung-chang urged Shen Pao-chen to make standard use of Krupp heavy pieces and Snider and Remington hand arms, adding that the Foochow ships mounted too many different makes. Yet in 1879 an English observer in Li's own territory remarked: "Not long ago, the present writer saw in the course of a few hours trip from the Taku forts to the city of Tientsin, guards of soldiers with Remington breech-loaders, match-lock men, archers, river junks carrying smooth bores, and trim gunboats mounting Krupp breech-loading cannon."[63]

Li had been right about the Foochow gunboats, nonetheless. The *Yang Wu* in her terrible hour in the Ma-wei battle in 1884 mounted thirteen British muzzle-loaders; the *Fu Po*, five French Vavasseurs; the *Fei Yün*, five Prussian breech-loaders; the merchantman *Yung Pao* (destroyed on the ways by the French, evidently in the midst of a hasty reconversion) had three eight-inch, ten-ton Krupps. In 1876, the British naval observer Shore saw at the Foochow yard a dump with shot and shell for Whitworth, Krupp, and Blakely ordnance, with some of these pieces together with old smooth bores. Chang P'ei-lun's reports on the Ma-wei shore fortifications mentioned many gun types, including Tso Tsung-t'ang's *p'i-shan-p'ao,* or "mountain-splitting gun," invented by him during the Taiping rebellion.[64]

Quality of ammunition was not high. Some of the *Yang Wu* duds after the Ma-wei battle were found to be charged with coal or charcoal. Foreign supply carried no guarantee; at about this time Tseng Chi-tse warned that ammunition bought by China did not fit the intended ordnance, and that the powder was too old.[65]

In that disordered buy-and-build situation, there was no plan, no grasp of the problem. There were only varying degrees of hostility to China's several external foes. Much money was spent, but with little effect. The variety of equipment, which reflected the political compartmentalization of the coast, contributed to the lack of coordinated action and grand strategy. Li Hung-chang only added confusion with his wily and opportunistic purchasing of ships and arms.

Li's growing preference for purchasing naval materiel may be explained not only by the pressure of time and the superiority of the foreign product. It was also partly a matter of personal influence. The several arms-building plants, created by highly-placed officials, were too dependent on the careers of their founders. The works at Tientsin, Shanghai, Nanking, and Foochow were implicitly associated with personal names. A man like Li Hung-chang could have influence in Tso Tsung-t'ang's dockyard, but although Li was a shrewd player of the political game, he did not "win" it, and the Foochow yard remained not "his." As Li's tenure of his northern offices lengthened, he lost influence in the south, where most of the plants were. His maneuvers to reorganize the coasts and centralize purchasing were in part his response to this situation. He was encouraged to seek as much independence as possible, beginning with his "own" Peiyang fleet. The personal element affected the quality of the arms produced in China and complicated the "buy-build" problem.

Halliday Macartney, who was so instrumental in establishing Li Hung-chang's arsenals, wrote in 1876 that there were four dockyards and arsenals in China: Tientsin's plants, under the governor-general of Chihli; the Shanghai arsenal, under the taotai and the governor of Kiangsu; the Nanking arsenal (although it was dependent on Kiangsu funds), which "acknowledges only the Viceroy of Chihli"; and the Foochow arsenal, under an imperial commissioner.[66]

Li closely guarded the output of the Tientsin arsenal, which went to the Peking *lien-chün*, to northern Manchu and Green Banner forces, and of course to Li's Anhwei Army. During the Sino-French war he felt no obligation to supply forces in the Kiangnan area with his torpedoes and mines.[67]

At Nanking, Li remained influential long after his removal to Chihli. Both Shen Pao-chen and Tso Tsung-t'ang, during their incumbencies at Nanking, had to build other plants to provide their own ammunition needs. But Li's influence at Nanking was limited. After his departure, there were schemes by successive taotais against the plant's director, who was Macartney. They filled the shop with idle "foremen," winked at stealing, talked covertly to Li about Macartney, and so on. On his part, Li was once disappointed by the failure of a 260-part Gatling gun made in Nanking and tested before Li at Tientsin. As a result of many exasperations, Macartney offered to resign, and Li finally released him in 1875. The Nanking arsenal lost a good man in a time of rapid technological development. Macartney left mainly because Li, although still "boss" at Nanking, could not protect him from afar.[68]

Although Li was a director of the Kiangnan arsenal until 1896, his influence there declined, particularly after Tso Tsung-t'ang's incumbency at Nanking in the early 1880's. Li did not exert a marked control over the distribution of the Kiangnan output or ordnance and ammunition. The arsenal's records include a ninety-five-page chart of arms deliveries from 1868 to 1904, and in this chart the northern commissioner appears as consignee through some twelve organizations, but the southern commissioner appears as recipient much more frequently, mainly through units in Kiangsi and Kiangsu, including some old water force units. At that, Li Hung-chang tended to get more of the Kiangnan output than did the Foochow squadron of China-built ships. Of the twenty-five modern ships supplied by Kiangnan during the period, nearly all were in the fleet of the Nanking governor-general; only one was in the Ma-wei battle in August 1884.[69]

Li's relation to the Foochow dockyard, which was founded by a rival and was physically most distant from Tientsin, is most interesting. He kept up an extended correspondence with men at the dockyard, and no doubt enjoyed a considerable influence. For example, Li was usually involved in the selection of dockyard superintendents after Shen Pao-chen. In his correspondence the names of Kuo Sung-t'ao, Ting Jih-ch'ang, Wu Ts'an-ch'eng, Li Chao-t'ang, and Chang Meng-yüan were mentioned as candidates. Save for Kuo, all became superintendents, although the appointment of Chang followed a brief re-entry by Tso Tsung-t'ang (as Nanking governor-general) into the selection of a superintendent, and Chang occasionally used Tso's signature on his reports, after a lapse of this practice going back to the days of Ting Jih-ch'ang in 1875. Chang P'ei-lun was also a superintendent of the dockyard in the 1880's, but Li's collected letters stop short of this appointment. It is noteworthy that Li's interest does not appear in the formal documentary collections, such as the *I-wu shih-mo* or the *Ch'uan-cheng tso-yi*. He worked informally. Occasionally he felt isolated from a superintendent, since he sometimes worked indirectly to achieve some goal at the dockyard, for example by writing to Shen Pao-chen when he was at Nanking, or even to Li Feng-pao, overseas.[70]

Usually Li Hung-chang suggested a candidate for superintendent on the grounds of competence, but one incident suggests that in his mind competence had political as well as technical dimensions. When Wu Ts'an-ch'eng was appointed governor of Fukien, Li was consulted as to a successor at the dockyard. He mentioned Li Chao-t'ang, who, with Wu Ts'an-ch'eng, was a Tientsin associate of Li Hung-chang's; in fact, when he recommended Wu Ts'an-ch'eng for the superintendency, Li Hung-chang had suggested Li Chao-t'ang as an alternative. But in 1878, when the question of Wu's resignation came up, Li Hung-chang wondered if Li Chao-t'ang, who been Tientsin customs intendant, knew enough about steamships to replace Wu. Li Hung-chang wanted Wu to stay on as superintendent, and tried to encourage him by writing to Ho Ching, the Min-Che governor-general, to ask that payments to the yard be facilitated. But Wu was still not content, and recommended as his successor either Wu Chung-hsiang or Hsia Hsien-lun, both men with long experience in the supervision of the yard's work. The matter of Wu's resignation dragged on, and in September 1879 Li Hung-chang observed to Ho Ching that Chang Mengyüan might take over; Li also suggested to Shen Pao-chen at Nanking that Shen might once again interest himself in the direction of the dockyard. Li did not endorse the experts recommended by Wu Ts'an-ch'eng himself, however, and when Wu's resignation was finally accepted in October 1879, Li did not object when the post passed to Li Chao-t'ang, whatever his competence.[71]

For some time thereafter, Li's correspondence with the Foochow dockyard was indirect. One of his respondents was Ho Ching, and he and Li Hung-chang were involved in the attempts to purchase a ship for Fukien province, as we have seen. In March 1880, Li Hung-chang wrote to Li Feng-pao that Wu Chung-hsiang (who had stayed on at the yard as an assistant to the superintendent) would not cooperate in certain of Li Hung-chang's plans for the use of Foochow-trained men. Li Hung-chang expressed dislike of the man. At the end of the year, during a conservative attack on the dockyard, an edict specifically charged Wu Chung-hsiang with ineptitude and peculation. Li Hung-chang, Ch'en Lan-pin, and others sat in judgment and heard the defense. In this case, Superintendent Li Chao-t'ang urged that Wu Chung-hsiang — whom he praised — be sent to the Board of Civil office for a special interview, with a view to a possible appointment as a taotai.[72]

The decision seems like a compromise, in which the offending man was "kicked upstairs." It becomes more interesting in view of the fact that Li Hung-chang soon took Wu Chung-hsiang into his own naval establishment at Tientsin. Evidently Li did not so much dislike the man as he disliked his independence of Li; if Wu were in Li's direct employ, his competence would be useful. Wu's place at the Foochow yard was filled by Lü T'ung-chih, who was recommended by Li Hung-chang. Of Lü's competence, Li said only that he had come to Chihli in 1880, that he, Li, had been unable to give him proper employment, and that Tso Tsung-t'ang had once wanted him. If anyone benefited from these shifts, it was Li Hung-chang.[73]

It is apparent that what Li Hung-chang wanted from the Foochow dockyard was trained men. He was seldom interested in using the ships; in all of his letters between 1875 and 1883 there are hardly half a dozen references to his use of Foochow-built ships. Occasionally he urged the yard to improve its product, and some fourteen references in his letters are of this kind, but of these fourteen, about a third deal with guns, torpedoes, and the like, and the rest seem to be perfunctory suggestions rather than expressions of a strong interest in home-built ships.[74]

First, Li wanted from Foochow a stream of trained men for his purchased ships and his plants. From 1875 to 1883, some sixty letters deal with his need for men, his disposition of Foochow graduates among his purchased ships or to overseas yards where his ships were being built. Foochow was the best source for such trained personnel. There was some shipboard training at the Kiangnan arsenal, but evidently Li preferred the more thorough ship-and-shore training at Foochow.[75]

Over half of these sixty letters show Li's interest in captains and officers. Over the seven years included in his collected letters between 1875 and 1883, some sixteen names of officers appear, and of these, nine — more than half — fought in Li's Peiyang fleet in the battle off the Yalu River in the Sino-Japanese War of 1894–1895. Trained officers were few, and Li's interest was keen, even though in the case of two of the Foochow-trained men who came into his service, Liu Pu-ch'an and Ch'iu Pao-jen, Li had once had some reservations about their personal character.[76] Some of the Foochow dockyard academy graduates served in the Foochow steam squadron, of course, but since only four of the nine captains involved in the 1884 Ma-wei battle with France were Foochow graduates, it would seem that Li Hung-chang triumphed.

Li also wanted Foochow construction-school graduates to observe the building of his German battleships, although the same men were in demand to supervise Foochow's own building program. Three such students were Wei Han, Ch'en Ch'ao-ao, and Cheng Ch'ing-lien, who at the end of 1880 were back in Foochow after advanced study in Europe. Li himself had called them outstanding in a memorial recommending certain returned Foochow graduates.[77] The first two had once complained to Cheng Ch'ing-lien that they had small prospects in the Foochow building program — or so Li Hung-chang heard from Li Feng-pao. Li Hung-chang wanted these three to go to Germany, but was not sure that Superintendent Li Chao-t'ang (whom he lectured on over-ambition and bad habits among returned students) would cooperate.

But when Li Chao-t'ang reported the launching of the composite *K'ai Chi* in 1883, he gave credit to Yang Lien-ch'en, Li Shou-t'ien, and Wu Te-chang, three men who had the same training as Wei, Ch'en, and Cheng, but who had not been rated so highly by Li Hung-chang on their return from Europe. Li got the best men. The return of Cheng Ch'ing-lien to Foochow, and plans for Wei Han's return, were not announced until November 1883, in a memorial from Superintendent Chang Meng-yuan which carried the signature of Tso Tsung-t'ang.[78]

Li Hung-chang also sought men from the Foochow dockyard for his own naval academy, which he founded in 1881. In that year, he removed from the roster of Foochow graduates about to be sent overseas for advanced training four men whom he took into his academy as instructors. He wanted men too for his proposed shipyard in Kirin, although when Wu Ta-ch'eng in 1882 did establish a Kirin plant for Li, it was an arsenal. Li did set up a small dockyard at Taku in 1881, which built small craft and included a mine base.[79]

Li thus imagined a subordinate role for the Foochow dockyard. Yet he could defend the Foochow training program when it was attacked by conservatives.[80] He needed it, but was generally unwilling to help the dockyard when it, in its turn, needed men. Once, for example, Li indicated that he would not separate from the Tientsin arsenal a man wanted by Wu Ts'an-ch'eng as a general foreman. When in 1880 Li Chao-t'ang, in an attempt to improve the dockyard's administration during a severe criticism of it, fired some of the local gentry on the supervisory committee set up by Tso Tsung-t'ang, Li sought to hire one of the men who was affected. Li Hung-chang was also periodically concerned lest his Foochow-manned gunboats be kept in the south, where they wintered, and even when he sent his lesser "gammas" to Shen Pao-chen in the 1879 he was careful to provide for the return of the Foochow-trained officers who had sailed them down to Shen's "quiet waters."[81]

There were continued training efforts at Foochow in 1875–1885, including overseas missions, but the context of these efforts has been suggested above. Shen Pao-chen worked with Li Hung-chang in planning for the overseas training called for by Giquel. In 1877 Shen and Li, as southern and northern commissioners, submitted a joint memorial urging the necessity of such advanced training in view of rapid technological advances. Construction school graduates should go to France; navigation school students, to England. They planned to send thirty in all, under a Chinese and a European supervisor, who, as equals, would report to the dockyard superintendent and the two regional commissioners. A three-year curriculum in both fields would include theory and practice, with regular examinations. The students would return as fully fledged shipbuilders or naval commanders — although it was acknowledged that some might take up other lines of study, such as chemistry, international law, or diplomacy. The proposal received imperial approval.[82]

There had already been a training mission of sorts. Giquel, in the winter of 1875 (after the contract period he was retained by the dockyard as an aide and advisor) had gone to Europe to purchase material for shipbuilding and had taken five graduates with him. Wei Han and Ch'en Ch'ao-ao, the construction graduates sought by Li Hung-chang in 1881, were in the first group, and stayed on in Europe to join the mission of 1877.[83]

Although Shen Pao-chen had already given commands to some of his navigation school graduates, there was need for this further training overseas. By 1876, command of the growing dockyard steam fleet had passed from Li Ch'eng-mo (who returned to the Yangtze traditional water force) to Lo Ta-ch'un, of the Fukien Green Banner land force, and then on to Tsai Kuo-hsiang, Tseng Kuo-fan's early steamer-builder. Perhaps some improvement was shown in these changes, but the turnover had still been high. The *Yang Wu* was being used as a trainer, but the English instructor observed that there were factions among the trainees (Cantonese as opposed to Fukienese), and that midshipmen were loath to soil their hands in ship's work. Henry Shore of the HMS *Lapwing*, who in 1876 criticized the condition of the ships, which were mostly used for hauling coolies, wood, coal, and general stores, also remarked on the lack of a naval tradition and doubted that any of the trainees could assume command.[84] No Foochow student was ready for the post of *t'ung-ling*, or fleet commander. In the spring of 1876 Wu Shih-chung, a man from the old water force, was being considered for the post, evidently as a replacement for Tsai Kuo-hsiang. On the other hand, there were some who felt that too much time overseas would be bad for China's naval and construction cadets.[85]

At the end of March 1877, Giquel and Li Feng-pao, the two directors, took twenty-six students and three apprentices to Europe. Of the total, twelve were naval officers, and went to England. Half of these were sent at once to British naval ships which later cruised in the Indian Ocean or to the United States. These students later had instruction ashore with guns and torpedoes, and visited shipyards and plants. In 1874 Giquel had judged three of these men, Liu Pu-ch'an, Lin T'ai-tseng, and Chiang Ch'ao-ying, to be ready for command, although Shen Pao-chen had then not assigned commands to them. On the other hand, the graduates who had been assigned to command by Shen were not included in the 1877 overseas mission. The other six navigation students entered shore training first, principally at the Royal Naval College at Greenwich, and then went to sea in British naval units. One of this group, Yen Tsung-kwang (Yen Fu), was recalled to teach at the Foochow dockyard academy before getting British sea duty. Of the fourteen construction men, five entered upon a study of mining and metallurgy, and the rest entered either the Toulon Navy Yard or the Ecole de Construction Navale in Cherbourg, and then visited arms plants in France, Germany, and England. The apprentices, who were joined by six more in 1878, studied in similar establishments, with some entering foreman-training programs.[86]

At the Foochow dockyard meanwhile other academy graduates were getting commands. The *Wei Yüan* (1877) was first given to the water force man Chou Feng-chien, but his place in the old *Wan Nien Ch'ing* was taken by Ch'eng Pu-ch'uan, of the same class as Liu Pu-ch'an. Within four months, the *Wei Yüan* passed to Lü Han, and the vacancy left by him in the *Chien Sheng* went to another academy graduate. At least one of the old water force men, Ch'eng Yü, was taken by Shen Pao-chen to Nanking when he went there as southern commissioner, but the old days were passing. Training afloat at the dockyard continued, sometimes involving trips to Japan.[87]

There were disagreements about the value of overseas training. Kuo Sung-t'ao felt that it should not concentrate entirely on military skills, and Li Hung-chang agreed that a study of industrialization was also needed, but pointed out that China had few students for study abroad. Tseng Chi-tse argued outright that overseas naval training was of no benefit to China. Tseng's criticism came in 1879, and Li, who was aware of growing opposition to the civilian Chinese Educational Mission in the United States, was worried. Perhaps Minister Tseng was trying to bring the naval training effort then going on in England under the control of his London legation (Ho Ching and Li Ch'ao-t'ang thought that this was the basis of his critical comments).[88] Li Hung-chang was thinking of starting his own northern naval academy, which might be set up for him by Chang Ch'eng, a Foochow-trained captain of one of Li's gunboats.[89]

Opposition to overseas training continued. In 1880 conservatives declared that the naval students then overseas were being Christianized, and a committee was designated to investigate. Li Hung-chang was on this committee, along with Ch'en Lan-pin, that conservative who, despite his earlier experience in the Kiangnan arsenal, helped to wreck the Yung Wing educational mission to the United States. In 1881, conservatives attacked the training program at the Foochow dockyard itself, charging that the cadets were merely singing and drawing. Governor-General Ho Ching replied that they were really studying language and draftting.[90] Li Hung-chang did not enter prominently into the yard's defense, possibly because he was planning an academy of his own, or because the Foochow dockyard administration was not sufficiently cooperative in supplying trained men to him.

No doubt there were many who preferred the traditional training methods. The old water force fleets were still in existence, their training methods made the more ludicrous in contrast with those of the Foochow academy. In 1876 Shore observed an official water force visit to the *Lapwing*, and wrote of dirty official war junks with guns decorated with pink calico, whose bumbling crews made a fiasco of the supposedly solemn occasion. The crews, he said, were "absolutely killing, and if a London stage manager could only get hold of a score or so of them for the pantomime season — billhooks and tridents of course included — they would bring the house down." [91]

Despite the conservative attacks, Li Hung-chang in 1881 urged the sending of a second Foochow dockyard mission to Europe.

But since he took four of the candidates for teachers in his own new academy, only two naval officers were included in the mission. The other seven members of this smaller second overseas group were in the construction field, and only one of these concentrated on shipbuilding. This three-year effort contributed little to the naval self-strengthening effort.[92]

Chang P'ei-lun, as Foochow dockyard superintendent just before the Sino-French War, memorialized on degeneration at the dockyard's academy, which he hoped to check by drawing in competent English instructors. In 1873 there had been over 300 students in the dockyard's schools, but in 1884, there were only 188, mostly in the construction school. A new school building was put up during the war, and Li Hung-chang called for another overseas mission, but the record shows a decline.[93]

Li Hung-chang, prior to founding his own naval academy, had long been aware of the need for training, as well as of some of the institutional problems involved in such an effort. In the 1860's, he had written about the traditional separation of fighting man and scholar in China, whereas in the West, a technically competent man could become "an official." In 1867 he observed that the "dwarf pirates" — the Japanese — had dispensed with foreign personnel on their naval ships, and his support of the China Educational Mission of 1870 was based partly on the expectation that it would produce military and naval men.[94] His interests favored the land military, but he knew that training must be more than mere drill, and that the civil service examinations must be adjusted to test Western subjects. He also sought to gain admission for Chinese to West Point.[95]

When Li ordered gunboats from Hart in 1875, his interest in trained naval officers became active. His torpedo factory (1876) at Tientsin was a training center. In 1878 he took delivery of his first four Armstrong "gammas," which were brought to him by Foochow dockyard academy graduates, under the taotai Hsü Ch'ien-shen, Li's marine training director. In that year, he set up at Tientsin an Office of Naval Affairs, paralleling one of his water force establishments; he also brought in as his fleet commander Ting Ju-ch'ang, the provincial land commander-in-chief. In 1880, Li established his naval academy at Tientsin.[96]

At first, Li wanted Wu Ts'an-ch'eng as director of the academy. Wu had been associated with Li in the China Merchants Company, and had since been Foochow dockyard superintendent. However, Wu took over the direction of the Tientsin arsenal, and Li's first academy director was Yen Fu, who brought with him from Foochow a copy of the Foochow academy regulations. At first, Yen Fu served as an aide to the taotai Wu Chung-hsiang, who was at this time in Chihli.[97]

Li also borrowed for his academy three foreign officials from the customs service, by commissioning them into his Peiyang flotilla. Another of his aides was a young American, L. C. Arlington, a drill instructor, who claimed to have surprised Li by reporting early each day. The daily work took only two hours. Arlington said his students were "bright and clever men."[98] In 1880 Li acquired, along with the superior "epsilon" gunboats he got from Shen Pao-chen, more Foochow-trained officers, and in 1881 he retained the above-noted four Foochow graduates who had been listed for the second oversease mission which Li himself had sponsored.

In 1881, the Tientsin academy buildings were completed. Li's first students were "returned men," evidently some of the C.E.M. students who had just been recalled from America. Later he organized his mine and torpedo schools to provide naval engineering courses. These older schools had trained men from as far away as Kwangtung and Fukien, with classes of about twenty. In this way Li developed a complete academy, with deck and engineer branches, each with "inner" and "outer" departments. The "inner" deck department offered English, the Chinese classics, geography, astronomy, navigation, and other theoretical subjects like those offered at the Foochow academy; the "outer" deck department dealt with signaling, gunnery, group drilling, and so on, with some subjects taught on training cruises.[99]

Li's regulations called for entrants under the age of seventeen, capable of writing an ordinary composition, equipped with statements of paternal descent for four generations and written guarantees from parents and "the gentry of Tientsin." During the five-year curriculum, the cadets might not marry, nor could they take the literary examinations, "for fear that these might obstruct their proper studies." After a three-month probation, candidates would be paid four taels monthly. For two out of the seven weekly school days, the cadets must study Chinese. Li's deputies would give examinations each spring, summer, and winter, and Li himself would sit on examination boards each autumn. Superior students would get commissions, and those of "lower standards" a money reward, with clothing and brevet rank. Holidays were as infrequent as at the Foochow academy.

The foregoing program was published in Tientsin in 1882, in what amounted to a public-relations campaign. Either because of "the dull abilities of the scholars," some of whom were too old, or because the stipened at first had been only one tael per month, the school had had a bad first year. Li in 1882 advertised grand possibilities, as exemplified at the Foochow academy, where "scions of respectable families . . . have studied . . . and on finishing were made captains. Some are now second and third rank officials, and have been decorated." [100] Li promised to ask the throne for honors for his own graduates. Evidently he was competing with the civil service. In mid-1882, he wrote to a personal friend advising him to enter his son in the Tientsin naval academy, since Western studies were of great importance. In the West, he wrote, a navy man ranked high, as would be the case in China as more ships were acquired.[101]

Li's academy could not break his dependence on the Foochow dockyard schools for a number of years. His first attempt to bring back purchased ships from Europe with his own crews came late in 1880, when he sent Ting Ju-ch'ang to England to take delivery of the Armstrong cruisers *Yang Wei* and *Ch'ao Yung*. Tseng Chi-tse attended the ceremonious flag-raising, and on August 9, 1881, the two ships bravely cleared Newcastle for home. Unhappily, Ting later shoaled his ship, and the *Yang Wei* ran out of coal and drifted about the Mediterranean for two days. Li had somewhat overextended his men in this assignment. When the ships arrived, they were entrusted to Lin T'ai-tseng and Teng Shih-ch'ang, Foochow academy classmates, although Li on an earlier occasion had temporarily relieved Teng of command after a grounding incident.[102]

It might be imagined that Li's forced reliance on southerners might have had the effect of eroding the old provincial loyalty of these southern men making their careers in the north. But in

1882 Shufeldt remarked of Li's navy: "The absence of naval rank and consequently of esprit de corps — of maritime experience and knowledge of the outside world among the officers — incongruous crews from different provinces, wanting in that pluck and dash which national feeling and a national flag only can create — deep-seated and ineradicable financial corruption — all these combine to neutralize the qualities of the ships and render them valueless as a fighting force." Still, trained men were scarce. It was later remarked of this period that "graduated students all returned to China; the Superintendents of Trade of the Northern and Southern Oceans fought to be the first in employing them." [103]

Political considerations affected Li's search for a director for his naval establishment. Early in 1880, Hart was asked to engage British officers for Li's fleet, at a time when a relative of U. S. Grant was a candidate for an army post with Li, as was a brother-in-law of the German minister to Peking. Britain particularly wanted the naval directorate, but Li was willing to find men wherever he might, and in August 1880, Robert W. Shufeldt of the United States Navy was present in Tientsin, at Li's invitation, on a diplomatic mission. Li asked if Shufeldt would care to organize his Peiyang fleet. Secret negotiations ensued for a year, and Shufeldt was so frequent a visitor to Li's ships that other foreigners were convinced that the American had secured the prize. But, perhaps because China's situation eased after the Russian withdrawal from Ili, Li became evasive, and finally Shufeldt left in disgust. Tientsin, he said, was a sink of intrigue; the Inspector-General of Customs (Hart) and Gustav Detring were competing with each other over the navy; three English customs men, "quasi-officers" of the Royal Navy, were even then afloat in Li's fleet; two ex-officers of the French navy were highly paid by Li for "unspecified purposes." Shufeldt added that "the viceroy, astute in all things but in the wisdom of the outside world, is more or less a victim of the flatterers or the arts of these ambitious men, who persuade him that he has a navy." [104]

Hart triumphed after all, in arranging to have Li hire W. M. Lang of the Royal Navy. Lang had brought Li's first "gamma" gunboats to China, and Li had been interested in him since 1879. Hart urgently wired to Campbell, his London agent, in April, 1882: "I have secured for Commander Lang the highest naval position possible in Tientsin. He hesitated, fearing damaging naval career. Please beg Rendel move Dilke move Admiralty allow Lang if serving China to count service as sea time. From naval, national, and political standpoint it is important to induce Lang to accept." [105]

Although Lang was "induced," he had little time to work before the Sino-French hostilities forced his recall. Li then turned to Li Feng-pao, and through him hired a German with supposed naval experience, reportedly even in the American Civil War. It developed that Li Feng-pao had been misled about this man, Siebelin, who was intended to be the captain of one of the new German battleships, the *Chen Yüan*, whereas previously he had only been the captain of a small vessel, and was not a naval professional. Li did not give him the battleship when it was delivered, with its sister ship, after the Sino-French War. During the war itself, Siebelin played a minor role. He knew no Chinese; his students called him one "whose body is full of swords, but none of them sharp." [106]

The Sino-French War was full of calls for Li's ships, but the war was not a test of his own men — largely because Li withheld his ships, which must have been officered by some of the approximately three dozen graduates of his Tientsin academy, including eight who had been C.E.M. "boys." Except during this brief prewar period, naval training was a southern monopoly. Foochow trainees were slowly replacing old water force men as captains. But of the fourteen captains in the war records, for the northern as well as the southern ships, only eight had modern training. Of these, five had been declared ready for command by Giquel in 1873, but only two had had actual command before the war. It does not appear that any of the captains were former C.E.M. students. The former water force captains are largely nameless in the record, although there is a note that one of the Foochow captains had been a water force lieutenant on Lake T'ai, with some experience at sea.[107]

Naval training was hampered by institutional frictions. The problem was to create and maintain an incentive for cadets and officers in a society oriented to the civil service examinations. How the social isolation of naval officers bore on their attitudes and aptitudes can only be indirectly suggested. One anecdote may be indicative. In 1876 Shore walked around Amoy and came upon a party of half-pay naval officers picnicking on Bass beer, porter, and vermouth. One was an ex-captain of a gunboat wrecked off the Formosa coast in a typhoon; the loss was not his fault, said Shore, but he had nearly lost his head over it. This picture seems to show enforced idleness which apparently came somewhat earlier in the career of a Chinese naval officer than did the standard half-pay hiatus in the career of a British naval captain waiting for advancement. It also suggests a politically hazardous occupation (and rather strange drinking tastes for Chinese).[108]

V

ACHIEVEMENTS AND PROBLEMS IN THE MILITARY BUILDING EFFORT, 1875–1884

During the decade between Li Hung-chang's first order for Armstrong gunboats in 1875 and the Sino-French War of 1884–1885, although there was heavy and uncoordinated purchasing of foreign military and naval materiel, the building or manufacturing of ships and arms in China continued. This effort was subject to numerous difficulties, some of which we have discussed. Other troubles which beset the building effort will be presented in the present chapter.

The shift from shipbuilding to ordnance and ammunition at the Kiangnan arsenal was underlined by the 1878 conversion of a plant originally designed to build heavy internal parts for steamers to the manufacture of nine-pound muzzle loaders, Armstrong-type 800-pound pieces, and later, quick-firers up to 380-pounders. In 1879 another Kiangnan factory started on twelve-pound and twenty-four-pound explosive shot, Krupp-type lead-wrapped explosive and solid projectiles, and Lee magazine rifles (patented in 1879). In 1881, a mine shop started making underwater explosives. The Kiangnan plant continued under foreign direction. There was some training activity. In the 1880's a small group of students and shop apprentices took courses in mathematics, drawing, a foreign language, and Chinese. There was also training for artillerymen. Some foreign observers were impressed by the plant; in 1877 Cyprian Bridge, a British admiral, observed great activity there, including the production of breech-loading Remingtons and small arms "of all descriptions." Bridge also saw machinery for making armor plate.[1]

Shipbuilding continued at Foochow, although between the end of the first contract (1874) and the Sino-French War only seven ships were launched. There were some innovations which partly

THE MILITARY BUILDING EFFORT

account for this halved rate of production. In 1875 Ting Jih-ch'ang, while he was briefly superintendent of the Foochow dockyard, reported a new plant for making composite ships (iron frames with wooden skins). We know that Giquel, after the contract period was retained by the dockyard as a purchasing agent, and was in 1875 in Europe ordering ship frames and recent engine models. The first composite ship was the 1350-ton, 240-foot *Wei Yüan*, whose late-model English horizontal engine developed 750 horsepower.[2]

While this ship was being built, older-style wooden steam vessels were produced. The *Yuan K'ai*, of the same hull class with the *Yang Wu* but with a more powerful engine, was launched on June 4, 1875. The next ship, the *I Hsin*, was hardly more than an armed launch. In 1877 the *Wei Yüan* was tried out, and in that year two more all-wood ships of the same size were launched, *the Teng Ying Chou* and the *T'ai An*.[3]

Henry Shore of the H.M.S. *Lapwing* praised the yard in 1876. He was told by M. Segonzac, "the engineer," that native foremen were thoroughly trustworthy. Shore saw Foochow-built 150-horsepower engines "equal to anything turned out in our engineering establishments." He visited a 1300-ton vessel in the fitting-out slip (he disliked the slip, since it was of French design) and reported that the vessel had "clean and businesslike" engines. The Chinese, he remarked, had mastered the art of building wooden hulls, in this case using Siamese teak.[4]

After the 1877 launchings at the Foochow dockyard there came a two-year hiatus. On July 21, 1879, the *K'ang Chi*, the second composite, with a 750-horsepower vertical compound engine purchased by Giquel, was launched. The year also brought trouble, in the form of a complaint by the Board of Revenue that Foochow-built ships were being repaired too often. The Board sought to go back to the traditional three-and-five-year minor-and-major repair system that had been used in the old water force yards, and to charge repairs coming too early to the individuals responsible. Wu Ts'an-ch'eng, then superintendent, fought the suggestion. He admitted that hulls wore out before engines, but knew of no way to predict repairs. In the end the Board retreated.[5]

In October 1880, the *Teng Ch'ing*, a 750-horsepower composite built entirely at the yard, was launched. But there was more

97

trouble. Early in the year Robert Hart of the maritime customs passed on to the Tsungli Yamen a report from his Fukien customs commissioner that the *K'ang Chi*, which was destined for the China Merchants Company, was unstable. Hart argued that his customs service should inspect Foochow-built ships. Native ranks closed to repel this alien thrust. Li Hung-chang reported that the ship was stable (although he also reported that she had a 150-horsepower engine, rather than the specified 750-horsepower plant). Li Chao-t'ang, then superintendent at the dockyard, charged that Hart was trying to bring native-built ships into disrepute, in order to encourage the sale to China of foreign-built ships. Li Chao-t'ang cited Giquel for support in this argument, although elsewhere he blamed Giquel for most of the yard's troubles.[6] His blaming of Giquel came in the course of a conservative attack on the yard in 1880 already noted. Li Chao-t'ang then charged Giquel with the fact that Foochow-built ships were outmoded. Furthermore, the original foreign staff recruited by Giquel under his contract with Tso Tsung-t'ang had deliberately slowed down production by demanding refabrication of perfectly good parts; this they had done so that the contract quota of ships might not be finished before the termination of the full — and profitable — five contract years. This evil precedent had encouraged slow-down practices among the native workmen as well. The Chinese bureaucracy was inefficient, some of its members having purchased their jobs; there would have to be some dismissals (we have already seen that Li Hung-chang tried to get one of these dismissed men for his own staff). Li Chao-t'ang defended the building effort by arguing that the trained men should not be wasted, and since he was also dubious about the practicality of opening a shipyard at Kirin, as Li Hung-chang planned to do, it is clear that he did not see an exodus of his men to the north as the way to save their talents.[7] Later, in connection with the conservative charge that Foochow cadets were merely singing and drawing, Governor-General Ho Ching (who had himself brought financial woe to the dockyard) admitted in his defense of the yard that the Foochow ships were not completely military, and blamed Giquel.[8]

In 1883 and 1884 the composites *K'ai Chi* and *Ching Ch'ing* were launched. The first mounted Krupps, and this 2000-ton ship was designed and built by Foochow dockyard construction school graduates who had returned from further training in France. Save for her iron plate and some of her machinery, she was entirely China-built.[9]

There were still complaints that the dockyard was behind the times. When Chang Meng-yüan took over the superintendency in the fall of 1883, he urged greater support for native shipbuilding. The dockyard was still using foreign frames for the composites. Tso Tsung-t'ang, then southern commissioner, had ordered two "fast" vessels at his old dockyard, and consulted Li Feng-pao in the matter. He was advised that Giquel had supplied plans dated in 1872. Tso consulted engineers, and then reported to the Tsungli Yamen that the new unarmored composites were not outmoded after all, were less expensive than the foreign types purchased by Li Hung-chang, and were also able to carry freight. Tso evidently still did not believe that the dockyard should build ships which were entirely specialized for war.[10]

Other complaints dealt with the slowness of the yard's work. Tso himself complained of a tardy fitting-out for the *K'ai Chi* of 1883. The problem was inherited by Ho Ju-chang, Chang Meng-yüan's successor as superintendent, who stated that the northern commissioner had sent two ships to the dockyard for repair, and the southern commissioner one, while the yard already had four ships scheduled for repair. These repairs had taken 36,700 labor days. It was true that the lengthening roster of Foochow ships had to be repaired somewhere, and evidently the mother yard was preferred to the Kiangnan arsenal.[11]

In sum, it would seem that during the period 1875–1885, the self-strengthening movement could show more advances in the field of ordnance manufacture, as exemplified by the Kiangnan arsenal, than in the field of shipbuilding.

Financial troubles at the Foochow dockyard were no less acute in this decade than in Shen Pao-chen's administration. Shen did not leave the yard immediately after the termination of Giquel's contract, early in 1874. His last months were marked by financial troubles, particularly with the Fukien provincial administration. The yard depended on customs revenues gathered in the province; that is, on the sixty percent of these revenues retained by the province. These funds were already overcommitted. For example, in 1875 it was hoped that the sixty percent would yield a million taels, but only 820,000 were realized, and from this sum had to come payments for Manchu troops in the province, bandit suppression, administrative expenses, and many other items, including remittance charges on the forty percent sent to Peking — in all, the demands totaled 1,070,000 taels. The stipulated payment to the dockyard, in the mind of Wen Yu, who was Tartar general and administrator of the customs receipts, was far down on the list. In the spring of 1875, Shen, using Tso's name as well as his own, asked Peking that neighboring provinces send help from their retained customs sixty percents, arguing that the warship program was at stake. The Board of Revenue ruled that Shen must rely on Fukien funds. Consequently, in July Shen made another sally on Peking's forty percent. Other demands on this reserved portion had already been allowed; 10,000 taels went each month to Tso Tsung-t'ang in the Shen-Kan region, and each year 300,000 and 173,000 taels went from the forty percent to Taiwan defense and foreign indemnification respectively. These demands took about half of the expected forty-percent yield for 1875.[12] It is not surprising that Li Hung-chang regarded the Sea Defense Fund of 1875 as a central government trick, intended to reclassify and limit provincial demands on the Peking portion of the customs yield.

Shen's move of July exemplified the prevailing competition, in that he attempted to shift defense burdens to the central government. In August 1875, the Board of Revenue instructed the Tsungli Yamen to let Shen and Wen Yu borrow from the forty percent from Fukien for the first six months of each year. By October, the Board had allowed an outright six-month grant from the forty percent, with part of the earlier indebtedness forgiven.[13]

When Ting Jih-ch'ang took over the superintendency late in 1875, he was soon deeply involved in money problems. Maintenance charges were piling up, and opium revenues would not cover them and the costs of the Chenhai traditional water force battalion (which was carried on the Foochow dockyard account), plus the cost of sending students overseas. The Formosa defense fund was exhausted, but the fleet could not be decommissioned, for it was supplying the island. He soon offered his resignation. The court's indirect reply was another manipulation of the forty percent, so as to provide 20,000 taels from it each month to the dockyard, with the remaining 30,000 of monthly costs to come from Fukien's sixty percent. In the spring of 1876, still another arrangement was for the yard to use the forty percent — apparently the balance from the Sea Defense Fund — for four months every year, with full remission stipulated for the rest of each annual accounting.[14] Since only 35,000 taels a month were left in the forty-percent fund after other deductions, this latest arrangement would net the yard only a little more than half of the 240,000 taels annually promised under the plan immediately preceding it.

Yet when Wu Ts'an-ch'eng in 1879 submitted accounts for the period from July 1874 to February 1, 1878, he showed a small surplus, even from an average annual income of 485,000 taels, or about seventy percent of the annual average during Shen Pao-chen's incumbency. Five ships had been built, and a sixth well started, showing a construction rate of less than two ships per year. Cost of new construction was about half of Wu's expenditures. The next largest expenditure item was that of maintenance. Cost of repair, in the period between February 15, 1875, and February 1, 1878, came only to 65,342 taels. Obviously the yard had operated on a narrow margin, and had apparently used construction funds for maintenance. In 1885, when Chang P'ei-lun was superintendent, he regretted that between 1869 and 1885 over a million taels had been so diverted.[15]

The arrangements for the support of the dockyard had evidently returned to that whereby the yard was to collect 20,000 taels from the Fukien forty percent and 30,000 taels from the Fukien sixty percent each month. In 1879 Wu reported heavy arrears, all in funds supposed to come from the sixty percent. From the forty percent, there had been a slight overpayment (in 1878 Wu had asked for special help from Peking's fund, and had received it).[16] The provincial administration had more successfully protected its share of the customs revenue than had Peking.

Even Tso Tsung-t'ang may be seen as a competitor of the dockyard for Fukien funds. Early in 1877 Wen Yu had asked that the Fukien sixty percent be freed of the dockyard expense, arguing that Tso had to be supported by the province. Evidently with the Sea Defense Fund reclassification and manipulation of the forty-percent portion, he had been forced to include the provincial contribution to Tso in his retained funds. Shen Pao-chen also was a competitor for funds. In 1879, as southern commissioner, Shen charged that Wu Ts'an-ch'eng was using Sea Defense Fund money for ship maintenance. Shen argued that the dockyard should no longer rely in part on the Fukien forty percent, and that its ships should be sent to him so that he could maintain them out of Sea Defense funds, which were supposed to be disbursed by the two great regional commissioners. Other provinces, he said, followed the Fukien lead and were dipping into Sea Defense Fund sums before remitting them.[17]

These classifications and assignments of funds were largely nominal, but behind them lay a competition between the central government, which sought to protect its revenues, and the provinces, which were trying to shift the modern defense burden to Peking. Control of the modernization effort was not involved; even if the provinces had managed to charge all such costs to the forty percent, they would still have retained local control, for it would have required a revolution to effect any radical change in China's old system of provincial autonomy, particularly after the relatively greater decentralization which came about during the Taiping Rebellion.

There is little point in pursuing the story of the dockyard's financial woes in detail. Complaints, imperial exhortation, and competition over the sixty percent and the forty percent were continual. The accounts of Li Chao-t'ang again showed a small surplus, as well as a slightly lower annual average annual income over the period from February 2, 1878, to February 9, 1880. Only the composite *K'ang Chi* was launched during this period, and nearly 100,000 taels of her cost had appeared in the previous accounting. Late in 1880 Li Chao-t'ang proposed a six-month construction holiday at the yard.[18]

Enforced parsimony characterized the Foochow operations in the 1880's. Chang Meng-yüan, who followed Li Chao-t'ang, attacked the maintenance problem by suggesting a cutback in crews. But he did more than ask Peking for the usual order to the delinquent Fukien customs administration. He asked that in the future all provinces ordering ships at the dockyard pay for half of the construction costs, instead of receiving the ships free. He also wanted to decommission Foochow's ships, but with training still to be carried on. Chang could show a small surplus, and report the launching of two ships, the *Teng Ch'ing* and *K'ai Chi*, but the construction of the vessels was not wholly his work, and they were in any case launched more than two years apart.[19]

Ho Ju-chang, Chang's successor, reported on the familiar money shortages. Tso Tsung-t'ang, as Nanking governor-general in the early 1880's, initiated the practice of recipient provinces paying half the cost of ships delivered from the Foochow dockyard. He also sent a small official subsidy of 40,000 taels to the dockyard, and a few other officials in the early 1880's did the same, although the total of these subsidies covered only about three months' operating costs.[20] Some provinces maintained their delivered vessels, and the yard was at least relieved of having to support the old water force battalion at Chenhai. On the other hand, the ugly maintenance problem entered even the national famine crisis of 1878, in which the dockyard administration stipulated that it would pay the crews but would not pay for fuel consumed by ships it sent to relieve the famine. And if some provinces maintained their ships, others returned ships to the dockyard to avoid this expense.[21]

Financial considerations hampered even the limited strategic thinking that was manifested. In the summer of 1881, Tso Tsung-t'ang, P'eng Yü-lin, and others conferred on naval matters, and agreed that China should build small gunboats for harbor defense. P'eng wished to have ten such gunboats built at the Foochow dockyard, but the order was not filled for lack of funds. The order dragged on for two years, while France increased her agression, by which time Tso considered having them built at the Kiangnan yard, even though the responsible official there, Li Hsing-jui, quoted a higher price. Tso complained of deterioration at "his" dockyard in the seventeen years since his departure from the Min-Che governor-generalship. Of necessity he changed his plans and sought five new larger "fast ships," in addition to the gunboats. He ordered two of the larger ships in Germany, as we have seen, and took delivery of one of the Foochow composites.[22] There is no evidence that the ten gunboats were ever built.

We may wonder how much of the financial problem arose from an absolute national poverty, or how much it came from the organization of the empire, and from its leadership. It cannot have been entirely a matter of national poverty, for there was heavy purchasing of foreign military products during this decade before the Sino-French War. There was also much peculation. Li Feng-pao was removed from his ministerial post in 1884 for squeezing over a million taels on ship orders.[23] The real problem was institutional. Mary Wright, in discussing central military administration during the T'ung-chih Restoration, mentions "insuperable difficulties," mainly that of "China's economy, which Restoration leaders did their best to keep stable, stagnant, and incapable of expansion." She adds: "The radical concepts of an expanding economy with expanding revenues, of a national military budget and a centralized administration were as necessary to China as they were repugnant to China's leaders." [24]

The decline of the dynasty heightened the competition over available revenues. But the arms effort remained economically isolated. For example, Macartney had to use iron ballast-pigs from the Shanghai shipping to make his complicated guns at Nanking. Gideon Chen concluded his study of the Foochow dockyard by remarking that it was always an isolated activity, dependent on imports, with no effect on the life of the country surrounding it. Some of China's leaders had a sense of this problem, but they could not remake the economy overnight, even in accordance with their limited concepts.[25]

One of the institutional factors that inhibited the arms modernization effort was the preference of able Chinese for the civil service over any permanent association with a technical arms or shipbuilding career. Wright and Biggerstaff have concluded that official Chinese Western-subject schools set up during the T'ung-chih period failed because of conservative preference for a Confucian curriculum, which was the traditional road to power and recognition. The arms-building effort was also affected by a preference for a traditional civil service career.[26]

Since civil-service officials could best cope with opposition coming from others of their kind, the Foochow dockyard was directed by such officials. The ultimate objectives of the superintendents therefore lay beyond the confines of the dockyard itself, or the career it represented. From its inception to the Sino-French War, there were eight superintendents at the Foochow dockyard. This was a very high turnover, yielding an average tour of duty at the dockyard of about two years. Only the first incumbent, Shen Pao-chen, served long enough to get real experience, and he moved on to the Liang-Kiang governor-generalship. All of the superintendents were civil officials, and if they did not "succeed" as well as Shen in later official life, we may guess that their ambitions lay in this direction.[27]

Furthermore, after Shen's time superintendents often had other concurrent official duties in the Fukien provincial administration. Perhaps these concurrencies were designed to ensure greater cooperation from the province in the delivery of the dockyard's revenues. Ting Jih-ch'ang was concurrently governor of the province, and he soon dropped the dockyard post; Wu Ts'an-ch'eng also was both governor and superintendent; and in 1884 Chang P'ei-lun was concurrently Fukien commander-in-chief.[28]

The qualifications for the superintendent were political rather than technical. Shen had risen to be governor of Kiangsi before going to the dockyard; Kuo Sung-t'ao, who was briefly a candidate, had been governor of Kwangtung; Ting Jih-ch'ang, for all of his Kiangnan arsenal experience, had in the interim been governor of Kiangsu. After Ting, the superintendents were lesser men. Wu Ts'an-ch'eng had been metropolitan prefect; Li Chao-t'ang, Tientsin customs intendant; Chang Meng-yüan, judicial commissioner of Fukien; Chang P'ei-lun had been briefly in the Tsungli Yamen (but seems to have achieved distinction primarily through his close association with Li Hung-chang). Necessarily the first superintendents had to be selected from the body of officialdom, but there was no progress in the direction of creating technical criteria for selection. After Shen's long and successful administration, a decline set in, and the rate of turnover increased.

The assistants to the superintendent (*t'i-tiao*) were undoubtedly in closer contact with the daily technical work of the dockyard. On this level, there was some advance towards professionalization. Originally, there were three of these officers, simultaneously holding office; these men were Chou K'ai-hsi, Hu Kuang-yung, and Yeh Wen-lan, all in the civil service. In 1868 Shen complained that Hu and Yeh (the latter was under attack by Wu T'ang) were inactive, and replaced them with Hsia Hsien-lun and Wu Ta-t'ing, respectively Fukien financial commissioner and Taiwan taotai. Hsia complained in turn that he did not have time to do two jobs, but apparently did both of them nonetheless. By the end of the 1860's Chou's name disappears and Wu Ta-t'ing was transferred to the Kiangnan plant to do training work.[29] The records mention two other *t'i-tiao* in 1875: Wu Chung-hsiang and Liang Ming-ch'ien. Wu Chung-hsiang had been with the dockyard from the first, and, there being no reference to any prior official occupation of his, he appears to have been a professional dockyard man.[30]

On the other hand, even with the sponsorship in the late 1870's of the outgoing superintendent, Wu Ts'an-ch'eng, Wu Chung-hsiang could not rise to the superintendency; the top position went to Li Chao-t'ang of the Tientsin customs, even though Li Hung-chang had wondered if he had the necessary experience.[31] Yeh Wen-lan continued at the dockyard as *tsung chien-kung*, or general foreman, but in the mid-1870's went to Taiwan to supervise coal mining. His replacement at the yard was Yeh T'ing-ch'uan, Kwangtung taotai. It is interesting that the Board of Civil Office asked if the latter's familiarity with foreigners was sufficient qualification for shipyard work. The Tsungli Yamen replied that it was. Yeh T'ing-ch'uan never came to the dockyard, and there is no further information on Yeh Wen-lan's replacement.[32] But at least the question of professional competence had been raised.

The conflict between civilian and technical values at the dockyard appears clearly in the periodic recommendations for rewards. As an inducement to enrollment it was originally stipulated that Foochow graduates, if from the civil service, should advance as civil officials, even if they were in the navy.[33] When Shen left the dockyard, he recommended some ninety persons for reward; for each, he proposed an advance in civilian official rank. Likewise in 1879 Wu Ts'an-ch'eng sponsored sixty-seven gentry members and seventy students and technicians. All were promised titular civil advancement, and the students were eligible for official employment in any month, rather than only in alternate months, as was customary. How many moved *out* when they moved *up* is unknown, but Biggerstaff's comment that about two thirds of the students enrolled in the construction school dropped out during the contract period indicates that this new career had formidable outside competition.[34]

The political-technical ambivalence was no less marked at the Kiangnan arsenal.[35] The directorate there was a committee of

THE MILITARY BUILDING EFFORT

four high civil servants: the governor-generals of Chihli, Liang-Kiang, and Hu-Kuang, and the governor of Kiangsu. High turnover at this level may not have been critical, yet Li Hung-chang was the only official to serve during the entire period 1865–1895.

Undoubtedly the second, or general-manager (*tsung-pan*) level, had more day-to-day importance. The Su-sung-t'ai taotai had the *tsung-pan* position as a concurrency. These men were hardly specialists. Down to the Sino-French War, thirteen men served in this post, usually for the standard two-year official tour, although four served for only one year. Only two, Feng Chün-kuang and Nieh Ch'i-kuei, had any prior experience, both having been assistants to other *tsung-pan*. Some had brilliant later careers in the civil service: Ting Jih-ch'ang, after his Foochow dockyard tour, advanced from the governorship of Fukien to the post of governor-general to take charge of the defenses of the southern coast and foreign affairs in 1879; Shen Ping-ch'eng became southern commissioner seventeen years after he quit the Kiangnan arsenal; Liu Jui-fen became minister to Britain and Russia in 1885, some eight years after he left the arsenal; and Shao Yu-lien (who served an unusual term of four years as *tsung-pan*, 1882–1885), in eleven years became governor of Taiwan. Although there was less turnover here than at the top, there was still too little stability.

Assistants to the *tsung-pan* were almost all aspirants for civil office.[36] Of the twenty names listed in arsenal records down to the Sino-French War, only three are of men known to have had previous arsenal experience: Han T'ien-chia, Ting Jih-ch'ang, and Huang En-ch'ao. Ting and Han have been mentioned earlier; Huang had served briefly in the fourth and lowest level of the arsenal's management. Of the twenty, twelve served less than a year, and only Nieh Ch'i-kuei and Feng Chün-kuang moved on to the *tsung-pan* level. One, Li Hsing-jui, served for five years, but under three chiefs; another, Ts'ai Hui-ts'ang, served from 1878 to 1881; but apparently neither continued at the arsenal. Some of the names listed at this level appear later in more distinguished contexts: Ch'en Lan-pin, "a conservative official known for his devotion to learning," as La Fargue describes him in his Hummel biography of Jung Hung, went to America with Yung Wing in the educational mission of 1870; Chen Tsao-ju in the 1880's became Minister to the United States over a decade after leaving Kiangnan. Nieh Ch'i-kuei, who in the early 1890's was *tsung-pan* for three years (after having been away from his assistant's position since 1883), seems to have distinguished himself chiefly by marrying one of Tseng Kuo-fan's daughters.

The Kiangnan arsenal records include a fourth level in the management, although no title was assigned to it. The post was vacant until 1873, when three men held it successively. These men were not officials, and few served for long. Hsü Chien-yen, son of Tseng Kuo-fan's steamer builder Hsü Shou, held the position from 1874 to 1877, then studied in European arsenals from 1879 to 1884, and later directed arsenal work at Tientsin, Tsinan, Foochow, and Hanyang. He and Wu Chung-hsiang, who served at Foochow and Tientsin, seem to have been the only "professional dockyarders" that the records clearly show.

Employees at the Kiangnan arsenal, who had to be paid from four to eight times the prevailing labor wage, had leaders who were preoccupied with other careers and moved out rapidly. Possibly it was one of these employees who said that at the arsenal things "were merely copied, and not made from the heart."[37] Perhaps the wonder is that these plants produced any usable armaments.

China's self-strengthening plants were hedged about not only with political opposition, conservative objections, and financial troubles; they also had to operate in a climate of values which was not benign. In other words, there were arms plants, but no arms-building institutions. The civil service was the towering institution in China, and duty in the arsenals was only a steppingstone for civil servants.[38]

VI

DISASTER IN THE SOUTH: THE CHINESE NAVY IN THE SINO-FRENCH WAR, 1884–1885

French imperialism had been increasingly manifest in Annam from the late eighteenth century onward. During the Taiping Rebellion, France seized parts of Cochin China and Saigon, and later took the Red River delta and Hanoi. In 1874 France signed a treaty with the Annamite emperor at Saigon which made his realm into a protectorate of France. China, involved with Japan, denounced the treaty, claiming Annam as a tributary of China, but took no action. In 1880, indeed, Annam sent tribute to China. French shipping on the upper Red River was harassed by the troops of Liu Yung-fu, a former Taiping rebel who had moved his troops to China's southern border. Regular troops of the dynasty were moved to the south in 1882 after France proclaimed Annam to be independent. By 1884 Liu Yung-fu's Black Flag troops had been made part of China's regular armed forces, and hostilities had commenced. The court still vacillated; on the one hand, it dismissed Prince Kung and the Grand Council for incompetence; on the other, it ordered Li Hung-chang to negotiate. The Li-Fournier agreement of May 1884 recognized the 1874 treaty while stipulating vaguely that China's suzerainty continued; Chinese troops were to withdraw. However, the Chinese won a battle – at Baclé, June 23, 1884 – and France returned to her demand for an indemnity, which China had previously rejected. The French began a naval buildup along the China coast, and several naval (sometimes ship-to-shore) engagements followed. France did not win all of these engagements, but she won the war.

The resulting loss of Annam was a serious blow to the Confucian monarchy of China, for it further weakened the tributary system, which Japan had already damaged by taking the Liuchiu islands. Morse and MacNair wrote about the Sino-French War in a chapter entitled "The Weakening of the Empire." Actually, since China won diplomatic victories over Russia in Ili, and military ones over France in Annam, the explanation for China's defeat cannot be simply that she was weak. Li Chien-nung stated that the French won by "sheer luck," while China lost through "indecision." [1] Indecision there was, but it was only part of the problem. This chapter will concentrate on the two principal naval episodes of the war — the Ma-wei battle of August 23, 1884, and the Chinese attempt to break the French blockade of Formosa in 1884–1885 — in an attempt to set forth in greater detail the reasons for China's defeat in her modern naval war.

China had over fifty modern naval ships in 1884, more than half of them home-built. Of the rest, some thirteen were Armstrong gunboats;[2] two were Armstrong cruisers and two were German ships, the pairs displacing respectively about 1300 and 2300 tons for each ship, with the German pair mounting two eight-inch guns apiece. These two pairs, the *Ch'ao Yung* and *Yang Wei* and the *Nan Ch'en* and *Nan Shui*, were respectively in the northern commissioner's Peiyang and the southern commissioner's Nanyang fleets.

There was still no single "national" fleet. If the gunboats and torpedo boats at Canton are counted, China still had four modern fleets. The Canton and Peiyang fleets (respectively fourth and second in order of size) were hardly involved in the war; the southern commissioner, with the largest fleet, and, presumably, direct responsibility for a naval war which was fought off the southern coasts, participated only grudgingly and late. In the Ma-wei battle, fought in the anchorage of the Foochow dockyard, it was the Foochow modern flotilla which fought, almost alone — and in about a quarter of an hour was almost totally destroyed.[3]

In the north, Li Hung-chang was building his great Port Arthur fortifications, which will be described in a later chapter. The growing French menace produced a flurry of new fortifying along the coasts. Not all of the defense works were of steel and concrete; some Chinese provincial officials supplemented their forts with that most modern of devices, international law. Chang Chih-tung, Canton governor-general, built forts and blocked the river early in 1884, and tried to justify the blockade in legal terms. Since the foreign consular objections were not unified, Chang almost achieved his aim. The American minister Young was particularly upset because Chang had disrupted peaceful neutral trade, and without authorization from Peking.[4]

International law was also involved in the defenses of the Foochow dockyard. There was no shortage of forts, on the Fukien coast and at the mouth of the Min River.[5] Many had modern foreign guns, supplemented by mines, sunken junks, land troops, and water force units. There was also a heavy investment of steel and concrete along the approaches to the dockyard, about twelve miles upriver. Just inside the main channel entry was the Chin-p'ai fort, the Tartar general's headquarters; the fort had been recently strengthened, and presented eight-and-one-half-inch Krupps mounted in barbettes of six-inch plate. Opposite was the Ch'ang-men fort. Farther up the river were other emplacements, with Armstrong ordnance and heavy iron casemates — it took the French two days to take the Min-an Pass forts (about nine miles below the dockyard) from the rear, after the Ma-wei battle of August 23. At the dockyard itself and in the surrounding hills were other positions, recently strengthened.[6] Many guns were old muzzle-loaders, and the court itself later acknowledged that the preparations were inadequate.[7] However, since the action in the Ma-wei battle took place upriver, *behind* most of these forts, most of this strength was utterly wasted. The anomaly is partly explained by uncertainty among China's leaders about the bearing of international law on the relations between France and China after France repudiated the Li-Fournier agreement.

In 1884, the structure of command in China at large and in the Foochow dockyard area in particular was confused. After a defeat in the spring, Prince Kung and his colleagues (who made up the Tsungli Yamen as well as the Grand Council) were dismissed. The new chief adviser at court was Prince Ch'un, with Prince Ch'ing at the head of the Tsungli Yamen. Hart feared the rise of these inexperienced men. Li Hung-chang was northern commissioner; his counterpart at Nanking was Tseng Kuo-ch'uan.[8] Ho Ching was Min-Che governor-general; the governor of Fukien (for part of the year) was Liu Ming-ch'uan; that of Chekiang was Liu Ping-chang; the Foochow Tartar general was Mu T'u-shan; the deputy for Fukien coastal defense was Chang P'ei-lun; and the dockyard superintendent, responsible for the Foochow fleet, was Ho Ju-chang. Chang Ch'eng, a Foochow academy graduate of about ten years, was captain of the flagship *Yang Wu* and in charge of the tactical disposition of the ships.

Nationally or locally, there was no clear-cut chain of command. Neither Li Hung-chang nor Tseng Kuo-ch'uan served as a regular channel for imperial orders or for reports to Peking. Even the Shanghai taotai sent direct reports to the Tsungli Yamen, and Chang Chih-tung once reported on the movement of ships nominally under Tseng Kuo-ch'uan's command.[9]

Confusion in the chain of command compounded the indecisiveness about the legal situation. China did not declare war on France until after the Ma-wei battle; France never did declare war. Hence French ships were allowed to pass by the forts protecting the dockyard, although Li Hung-chang warned the court on July 11, 1884, that the French intended to take the dockyard to support their renewed indemnity demands.[10]

On July 13, the Foochow authorities refused repairs to a damaged French vessel. The "army people" (Mu T'u-shan?) wanted to block the river, but could not obtain agreement from the other leaders in the area. China and France, it was argued, were not at war.[11]

On the same day, Chang P'ei-lun wired to the capital a report from the French consul that two French warships would soon come upriver to the Foochow dockyard, under cover of an international practice allowing two warships of a given power to enter the ports of other powers with whom no hostilities existed. Chang sought instructions from the Tsungli Yamen.[12] On July 17, Admiral Courbet in his flagship *Volta* came up the river, followed shortly by three more French warships, *d'Estaing, Duguay Trouin,* and *Villars.* Mu T'u-shan called these entries illegal, but the governor-general would not let him use his forts.[13]

Other French warships, including the 4727-ton *Triomphante,* so heavy that she had to lighten herself before she could come upriver, were converging on the Min. July 21 was the supposed deadline for the renewed indemnity talks; on that day there were four French warships to four of China's in the Ma-wei anchorage.[14] Still, Chang Ch'eng was told that he must give proper notice before opening hostilities. On July 22 Courbet withdrew two of his ships; Chang P'ei-lun claimed that this withdrawal was the result of his militant preparations, which included shifting troops ashore in plain view, with a great deal of drumming and flaunting of banners, but Courbet had withdrawn the ships for his own reasons (one of them blocked relief supplies bound for Keelung) and the advantage of the French was soon restored.[15]

Early in August, Chang P'ei-lun could still talk of a stalemate, and advise the Tsungli Yamen that he would block the river if the French sought to bring up more ships. Unlike Chang Chih-tung at Canton, he asked for permission to block the channel, but the Yamen prudently replied that other foreign ships were in the Min River and their interest must be consulted. At this time, international law seemed to be still working in favor of France. Indeed, the Yamen authorized Chang to destroy the dockyard rather than agree to a blockage.[16]

During all of this while there had been attempts to move in Chinese modern naval reinforcements, but difficulties were encountered even when the local leaders sought the return of "distributed" ships from the Foochow modern fleet. Mu T'u-shan was the first to ask for help, even before Courbet came upriver on July 17, but after Li Hung-chang's warning of July 11. The court replied with soothing words, promising that Tseng Kuo-ch'uan and Li Hung-chang would send ships of they were needed.[17] On July 19 Ho Ju-chang also asked for aid, reporting the arrival of the first four hostile warships, to which he could only oppose a weaker force consisting of the *Yang Wu, Fu Hsing, Fu Sheng*, and *Chien Sheng*. After the July 21 indemnity-talk deadline, he issued instructions to his captains to prepare for war, although Chang P'ei-lun had been told by the Tsungli Yamen that "a little defeat" might later be recouped. Ho appealed directly to the emperor and the Empress Dowager for aid, but received the flat reply that the northern and southern commissioners could do nothing, and Ho must do his best. Mu T'u-shan was ordered to resist if attacked, but promised no reinforcements. Ho and Chang asked for help again.[18]

On July 24, Governor Liu Ping-chang of Chekiang wired the Grand Council that Chang P'ei-lun had asked him to send the *Ch'ao Wu* to Ma-wei. Liu could not spare the ship; he suggested that others help instead. The court ordered Li Hung-chang to send two ships to the dockyard. Chang P'ei-lun reported that at Shanghai a single French warship was being watched by six Nanyang ships, whereas the Foochow authorities, with a much greater need for ships, were even being asked to send ships to help meet the Japanese menace in Korea. Li Hung-chang shortly replied to the order to him that he could spare no ships for the dockyard; indeed, the north was more important than the south. Chang P'ei-lun tactfully agreed with this, and turned to Nanking for help for the dockyard. The court could only state that negotiations were still in progress; if a break came, instructions for the assistance of the dockyard would be issued. These requests, orders, and replies took place between July 24 and 29, long after the supposed deadline.[19]

Chang P'ei-lun was not without ambivalence. He wrote reports on his weakness and on his efforts to mobilize the gentry and *pao-chia* to aid morale; even fishermen were to do their bit. He argued against a final break. Yet he also opposed continued negotiations, arguing that the French were bluffing, and that China might take advantage of the Min River's swift tides to make a strike. While his written reports were in transit, he wired on July 27, urging the advantage of taking the initiative, but still seeking advice.[20]

Some help did come. Chang Chih-tung sent in the *Fei Yün* and *Chi An*, Foochow ships which in 1882 had been sent to Kwangtung supposedly to make feints in Annamese waters and had stayed on to become Kwangtung ships, although maintained by Foochow.[21] Still, as late as August 7 Li Hung-chang argued against sending any of his Peiyang ships, saying that surely his ships (described as weak) would be intercepted by the French before they could get to the dockyard.[22]

On August 12, Chang P'ei-lun, Ho Ching, and Mu T'u-shan jointly memorialized for instructions. Their ships were surrounded, they said, and more enemy ships were en route. If action came, let the orders be secret, so that China might take the initiative. The reply from Peking exhorted them to prepare "so that nothing unforeseen may arise." [23] On August 14 the court ordered Tseng Kuo-ch'uan to send the *K'ai Chi* to the dockyard. Tseng demurred, even asking for leniency for captains who might balk at orders of this kind. Although some officials had evidently urged decapitation for captains caught in such insubordination (which would seem to be routine, under wartime discipline regulations), the court agreed with Tseng, acknowledging that beheading would be bad for discipline. Furthermore, Chang P'ei-lun was accused of "wrangling," and had to take time to defend himself.[24]

On the other hand, an edict of August 18 declared that war was to be expected, and that the several generals, governor-generals, and governors were to attack at will in case of enemy aggression. No imperial delineation of strategy was given. Mu T'u-shan was told that war was inevitable, and that he should keep *in* those French ships that were already upriver at Ma-wei, and keep *out* those that were not.[25]

The Foochow authorities feared that the local gentry would burn foreign warehouses and so invite a terrible vengeance. Other fleets were not cooperating. Surely defeat would bring rebellion; let the southern and northern fleets come! Still, on August 20 the court asked Li Hung-chang and Tseng Kuo-ch'uan if it was advisable to raise more troops. Chang P'ei-lun was told that talks were still going on, and that he should hold off and continue "secret preparations." Tientsin and Nanking, said the court, had been ordered to help. The next day, Tseng Kuo-ch'uan was put in sole charge of the Kiangnan regional defenses, and Li Hung-chang was ordered to buy large German guns and send them to Foochow.[26] The "indecision" referred to by Li Chien-nung in his explanation of China's defeat is well illustrated in these late actions of the court.

On August 22 Ho Ju-chang believed that negotiations had collapsed, yet was against breaking relations with France. He preferred to "stand firm" while getting in more ships. Other Foochow leaders reported on that day that war seemed inevitable. British and American ships hitherto anchored near the French and Chinese warships had moved off on the 21st. Help was needed. These last requests elicited the usual imperial nod, and a "firm" order to Li Hung-chang and Tseng Kuo-ch'uan to send ships, and not to be "province-minded." This order was useless; the battle came the next day.[27]

Although the telegraph was extensively used in this correspondence, it did not centralize the empire, as some have argued. Regional and provincial officials may have relied formerly on the passage of time between the receipt of written edicts and registering of their fluent objections, but even over the wire they still seemed more ready to argue than to comply.[28]

The modern Chinese fleet at the Ma-wei anchorage on August 23, 1884, numbered eleven ships. All were at least nine years old, made of wood, and "of elegant appearance, but light build." The flagship *Yang Wu* displaced about 1400 tons, and was matched in size by the *Ch'en Hang* and *Yung Pao* — although the last was destroyed on the dockyard ways and made no contribution to the battle. The *Fu Po, Fei Yün,* and *Chi An* were in the 1300-ton class; the *Chen Wei* and *Fu Hsing* were about half as large, and the *I Hsin* was even smaller. The *Fu Sheng* and *Chien Sheng*, the American gunboats bought by Shen Pao-chen and delivered in 1876 were in the 250-ton class. Watertight bulkheads "more or less" protected these ships. There were also seven "ordinary steam launches," equipped with spar torpedoes, and three or four "rowboats" carrying the same weapon. Some twelve "very large" war junks were also on hand, manned by 1190 men whose fortitude, as they lay for weeks under the "ready-slotted" French guns, was "simply marvellous." Of the steamships, only five got under way, so that their speeds were not a factor in the battle.[29]

The eight French ships anchored in the Ma-wei roads were on the whole superior to the Chinese ships. The lightened *Triomphante* was rated at 4727 tons; the smallest French ships were the *Lynx* and *Aspic*, of about 470 tons each. The *Yang Wu* was outclassed by the *Triomphante, Duguay-Trouin, Villars,* and *d'Estaing*. All of the French ships were armor-clad, although some were composite in hull construction. The French had two torpedo launches of sixteen knots speed, with spar torpedoes. One Westerner called the French ships "models of naval architecture," with guns which were "triumphs of mechanical skill." [30]

China's ships had a respectable if unstandardized armament. Of the fifty-six major pieces of ordnance on the eleven ships at the anchorage, two were eight-inchers, throwing 411-pound projectiles. Some thirty pieces were French Vavasseurs of just under six-inch bore. The total weight of simultaneous salvo was 4500 pounds. The French, whose six largest pieces measured nearly ten inches, could simultaneously fire 6000 pounds. The French advantage was not overwhelming; these calculations show theoretical maxima. There was room for maneuver, for stealth or guile.[31]

Had they been decisive, the Chinese might have seized a last opportunity. Last-minute timing in the Ma-wei anchorage could have been important, for time meant tide, and the tide was fast. Shen Pao-chen had remarked on the speed of the tides as early as 1867.[32] Captain Chang Ch'eng deployed his ships before the Ma-wei battle in a way that was not so "stupid" as some later charged.[33] The flagship *Yang Wu* was centered in one squadron above Pagoda Point, off the dockyard, close to three small French gunboats, the *Aspic, Vipere,* and *Lynx,* and the French flagship, the *Volta*. Distinctly removed, downstream, were the heavier French units, and in this area were the *Chen Wei, Fei Yün,* and *Chi An,* outclassed where they were, but not by the smaller French ships at Pagoda Point.

The tide ran at almost four knots — about half the average speed of the Chinese flotilla. It was in flood until about two p.m. on the day of battle. In a secret move, the downstream Chinese vessels could have been drifted up on the same flood tide that was bringing up the lightened *Triomphante*. They could have thus gone beyond the point where the heavier French ships could pursue them, and then all of the Chinese ships could have disposed of the lighter French ships upstream, including Admiral Courbet's flagship. On the other hand, the ebbing tide would leave the outclassed downstream vessels (if unmoved) close to their opponents, who would also be reinforced by the *Triomphante*; furthermore, the two Chinese detachments would be stern-to relative to the French clusters, affording enemy torpedo craft the advantage of attacking under blind counters. Admiral Courbet was well aware of these alternatives, and relied heavily on Chinese hestitation.[34]

How that hesitation came about will never be exactly known; there are several accounts of the forty-eight hours immediately preceding the battle. Foreign commercial ships withdrew on the 21st of August, as has been mentioned. According to one of the accounts, a "declaration" (of intent to fight?) was handed by the French on that day to Ho Ju-chang via Chang Ch'eng, but Ho kept it secret.[35] According to another, the restless gentry sought out Chang P'ei-lun on the 22nd, although he avoided or ignored them. Wei Han had it from a French shipyard instructor that a fight was coming when the French chose the proper moment.[36] Li Hung-chang was advised by wire from Foochow that the attack would come on the 24th, and he so informed Peking.[37] Chang P'ei-lun was confident that the French would wait until the current heavy weather lifted, and predicted to Chinese captains that this change would come on the 23rd.[38] Actually, Courbet instructed his captains on the night of the 22nd, assigning objectives and arranging action signals, which would be displayed when the *Triomphante* came up the river.[39]

As for the day of battle, the 23rd, one report said that the French sent a Catholic priest to Governor Ho Ching with a declaration of war. This report stated that Ho kept the matter quiet, despite gentry insistence on warning the dockyard by telegraph, which was not done. Chang P'ei-lun had only the starting gun as his warning. Ho Ju-chang supposedly quieted Wei Han's doubts by talk of continued negotiations. Wei Han then received Chang P'ei-lun's instructions to seek a delay from the enemy, but the fight started while Wei Han was in transit.[40] It was later reported that Ho Ju-chang was first told at noon on the 23rd of a battle which would start at 2:00 p.m., and that he advised Chang P'ei-lun and Ho Ching and sent Wei Han on his futile mission.[41] Ho Ju-chang also later reported on this warning at noon, saying that he tried to wire the news to Mu T'u-shan at Ch'ang-men (to stop the *Triomphante?*) but that the wire was cut.[42] Ho Ching similarly recalled a noon warning, saying that as soon as the dockyard and Ch'ang-men were notified (how, if the wire was cut?), the shooting started.[43]

Different men, different recollections. If we accept the noon warning of the 23rd, there were about two hours of tidal advantage for China still remaining. France started the action, when she was ready, with the Chinese ships still at their moorings, stern-to and divided. The contradictory Chinese accounts of what happened reveal the lack of Chinese communications, both physical and organizational. They also reveal that information was probably suppressed. There was no unity among the leaders.

The French faced steamers, fire raft, forts, troops ashore, and even a contingent of 100 "swimming braves." But the invader had taken advantage of Chinese delay, and a few minutes before 2:00

p.m. the French torpedo boats were sent into action. One Chinese historian wrote that "the Chinese fleet, clumped, in great urgency cut its cables and with drums sounding turned to meet the enemy." [44] Only five Chinese ships moved far, and all were hampered by a lack of signaling devices. An American observer put a twelve-minute limit on the action, which sank, burned, or dispersed the Chinese ships, only two of which managed to escape.[45] Then the French turned to the destruction of the dockyard. That night, according to a French report, the *Vipere* and *Triomphante* frustrated "in the twinkling of an eye" an attack by two Chinese torpedo boats (Chang P'ei-lun later reported that China had no torpedoes), thanks to French "photo-electric apparati" (searchlights). The French ships sustained only two minor hits, and on the 24th, "playing songs of triumph" and with Courbet grandly surveying the carnage from his conning-tower, they made their exit. They took the river forts from behind on the way out, in ship-to-shore encounters as noted briefly above. Erroneously, the Chinese reported that Courbet had been killed.[46]

There was individual heroism as well as cowardice among the men who fought for China. Of the nine ships in action on that doomed afternoon, only four were commanded by Foochow graduates. These men had no monopoly on the courage of the day, although save for Chang Ch'eng, who seems to have thought mainly of escaping from the first-stricken *Yang Wu,* the more distinguished men were from the dockyard's academy.[47]

The Foochow captains, of whatever background, were under the orders of men of questionable fitness. Chang P'ei-lun "directed" the battle from a mountain eyrie to which he prudently moved; Ho Ju-chang also decamped. Mu T'u-shan stayed at his post; the governor and governor-general were not at the scene. There were too many leaders. Although Chang P'ei-lun had much to apologize for, he spoke truly enough when he later wrote: "In one province to have four military leaders is not as good as to have an army under one's self, when things can be done quickly, and without irregularity and delay." [48]

Who was to blame? After the battle was over, Peking, in characteristically punitive mood, appointed a special commissioner to investigate the fiasco. The commissioner, Tso Tsung-t'ang, was to be assisted by Mu T'u-shan and, at first, Chang P'ei-lun.⁴⁹ There had been many reports about what happened at the Ma-wei battle, and in them the French reportedly suffered many losses. But no one tried to say that China had won the battle. And the war was not over. For China, which finally declared war on August 26, 1884, it had just legally begun.⁵⁰

As for Courbet, he took his fleet back to Formosa, and although he was unable to effect a landing, on October 23 he threw a blockade along the island's west coast, which remained in effect until April 23, 1885. By then negotiations had been resumed, spurred by another Chinese land victory over France, at Langson. While in effect, the Formosa blockade — although it was indifferently enforced — raised the problem of relieving the island.

The Nanyang fleet was under the command of Li Ch'eng-mo, who had done another tour with the traditional Yangtze water force after his service with the modern Foochow flotilla.⁵¹ Thirteen ships were at his disposal. The ships that finally comprised the relief expedition were the Nanyang ships *Nan Ch'en* and *Nan Shui*, the two sixteen-knot German ships ordered by Tso Tsung-t'ang, with eight-inch guns in their main batteries; the Kiangnan-built *Yu Yüan*; and the Foochow-built ships *Teng Ch'ing* and *K'ai Chi*.

It had not been intended that only Nanyang ships would be involved. After the Formosa blockade was announced, the court ordered Li Hung-chang and Tseng Kuo-ch'uan to send "six or seven" ships each to the island's relief. Many orders ensued, interspersed with the evasions of these officials. At one time, after Tso Tsung-t'ang, then specially commissioned to defend Formosa, entered the correspondence about relief ships, Li Hung-chang took the part of Tseng Kuo-ch'uan, arguing that Tseng could only supply three ships, not the five that Tso insisted Nanking could send in. The court threatened the southern commissioner with punishment; Tseng was thus obliged to send five after all. Li himself reported, after this threat of punishment to his southern counterpart, that he was readying two ships to join the five from the Nanyang fleet.⁵²

Actually, Li had been ordered to send five ships as well; that he undertook to send only two is instructive. But he was to take back even these two, although in a manner so circuitous as to allow him to escape the imperial wrath. Li had finally agreed to contribute the British-built ships *Ch'ao Yung* and *Yang Wei*, under the German Siebelin; Li's two ships were to join five Nanyang ships, under Wu An-k'ang, at Shanghai; the resultant seven-ship flotilla was to be under the command of Yang Yüeh-pin (who was ordered by the court to "soothe" the German). Li's two ships arrived in Shanghai early in December 1884.[53]

But to Li Hung-chang the Korean problem had priority. Japan was already showing a disturbing influence in the peninsula. On December 10, Li wired the Tsungli Yamen that the Japanese were in league with the French, and asked to have his two ships returned for duty in Korea. Ma Chien-chung, a Foochow academy graduate who had been in Li's Tientsin naval academy as an administrator, was prepared, on Li's orders, to bring the two ships back to northern waters.[54] Since Li's argument was not without merit, the court decided that although the two British-built ships might not be returned, the China-built Nanyang ships *Teng Ch'ing* and *Yu Yüan* would be detached from the Formosa relief expedition and sent north to Li. Perhaps as a political *quid-pro-quo* for Li's acceptance of two inferior ships, the German "guest commander," supposedly counted as a "Li man," would be in charge of the Formosa expedition in which Li's ships would be prominent.[55]

But Li had not waited. He replied that Ting Ju-ch'ang had already put to sea with the *Ch'ao Yung* and *Yang Wei*, northbound; since they were on the high seas, Li had no way to return them to Shanghai. He buttressed himself by a wire to Peking on December 15, reporting Japanese ships in Korean waters, where China as yet could make no naval show.[56]

Li had acted on his own authority. Events saved him. An edict of December 15 took cognizance of a Japanese threat to Chinese interests in Korea. As for the Formosan expedition, it was after all to consist of the five Nanyang ships named above, under Wu An-k'ang (Siebelin having returned to Li with Li's ships), with Yang Yüeh-pin to take command from Foochow to Formosa.[57] But the ships never went so far south as Foochow. The French saw to that — although they were greatly aided by the tactical notions of the Chinese command. The following account is taken in part from the account of L. C. Arlington, Li Hung-chang's erstwhile drill instructor, who served in the harried Nanyang relief flotilla.[58]

After signing on with Li Hung-chang at Tientsin, Arlington

was informed late in 1884 by "S" (Siebelin) that Li wanted to transfer him to Nanyang fleet. Wanting action (and anticipating none in the Peiyang fleet), Arlington accepted with alacrity. "S" then selected other foreigners from Li's establishment. After arrival at Shanghai, these foreigners signed into the Nanyang flagship *K'ai Chi*. "S" returned to the north — to waylay the French, it was said. (Exeunt *Ch'ao Yung* and *Yang Wei*.)

Arlington (under a new contract, since his contract with Li meant nothing in the Nanyang fleet) observed that *K'ai Chi* was undermanned and the crew underpaid. But the officers had a good life. Admiral Wu had never been on a ship save as a passenger, and although once decorated for bravery, had been assigned to this post to redeem himself after his alleged peculation as commander of the Woosung forts. By way of contrast, "Ting Ju-ch'ang," the second-in-command of the flotilla, was a brave and competent naval man. Arlington was here assuredly referring to Ting *Hua-jung*; Ting Ju-ch'ang was Li's admiral and was then with Li's ships in Korea. The other officers impressed this observer as brave men, despite their distaste for the Manchu government; Arlington made no remark on their training.

Fuss and delay kept the ships at Shanghai. Drill took most of the time, conducted in English for small arms and in German for big arms. The foreigners were resented by the Chinese officers, who had only a rudimentary knowledge (said Arlington) of gunnery. Late in December 1884 the five ships left Shanghai, only to anchor at Woosung, where the foreigners were tested in gunnery. Thence the fleet took a secret southerly course, the foreigners being doubtful that Admiral Wu really wanted to find anything. The ships moved only by day, and were always in sight of the coast. Two weeks of drill and coaling at Chusan came next — with sleeping sentries, dice and cards below, and the ships illuminated "as if a pleasure party had command." Three unnamed captains dallied in Ningpo, leaving their ships under the "pilots."

Late in January 1885 the fleet again headed south. Its meanderings are indicative of the combination of untrained leaders and a decrepit strategy that linked ships with guns ashore. On January 25, the fleet anchored at Nan-k'ou; the next day it was at Yü-huan, 200 miles north of Foochow; thence it steamed to nearby Wenchow where it was planned to test the Formosa blockade by planting rumors of the existence of the relief expedition; Admiral Wu tried a real probe by sending in the merchant ship *Hua An*. Next the ships were reported safe in Shih-p'u and Lin-hai, on the Chekiang coast. Thereafter they wandered irresolutely about Chenhai's waters, with the French en route to intercept them. On February 10, they crossed to Tinghai; on February 11, they were back at Woosung; February 12 found them again at Tinghai; and on the 13th, they moved to the sheltered Shih-p'u haven again. On the last of the Chinese year of 1884, the *K'ai Chi*, *Nan Ch'en*, and *Nan Shui* went to Chenhai, but left shortly, damaging the (submarine?) telegraph wires and so keeping Tseng Kuo-ch'uan from knowing the whereabouts of the other two. Then the five rejoined at Shih-p'u.[59]

The leaders who worked out this itinerary were a motley group. We have already seen Arlington's comments on Admiral Wu. Arlington also recorded that the captain of the flagship, one "Ssu," had once been the pilot of the old *Confucius* of Taiping days in Shanghai; that the captains of the *Nan Ch'en* and *Nan Shui* were ex-China Merchants Company pursers who had bought their captaincies. The captain of the *Yu Yüan* was Chin Yung, a traditional water force man with some sea experience. Chiang Ch'ao-ying, captain of the *Teng Ch'ing*, was the only Foochow academy graduate, and Arlington probably referred to him when he said that one of the captains had had experience in a foreign navy.[60]

It is not surprising that Liu Ming-ch'uan appealed to Li Hung-chang for aid on February 16, 1885, and that Li was again ordered by the court to send his modern ships to the relief flotilla.[61] But by then disaster had overtaken the relief expedition. On February 13, Tseng Kuo-ch'uan reported that the five ships met the enemy off the Chekiang coast in wind and fog. In the battle, the Chinese ships had become separated, so that the slowest of them, *Teng Ch'ing* and *Yu Yüan*, put back into Shih-p'u, while the other three fled to Chenhai. The two stragglers were sunk in Shih-p'u, and the other three were blockaded in Chenhai harbor and could not help defend the Yangtze estuary.[62]

The details are instructive. It was rumored that the *Yu Yüan* and *Teng Ch'ing* had been deliberately scuttled in Shih-p'u to prevent bombardment of the populated area from the sea. There were also hints that torpedoes — even Japanese ones — had sunk them.

The court ordered an investigation.⁶³ Tseng Kuo-ch'uan used care in making the inquiry. Local persons of repute, even foreign newspapers, were consulted. It emerged that torpedoes had hit, and that the captains had then scuttled the Shih-p'u ships to keep fire from the magazines. The crews had fled. Yet the attack had been silent. How had the attack been made? Tseng felt that even if only small torpedo craft had been involved, the captains should have been alert enough to repel them.⁶⁴

Although he was two days off in his chronology, Arlington's recollections of his eyewitness experience at Shih-p'u are interesting. On February 11th (in fact, the 13th), at 3:00 p.m., fishermen reported to the five ships at Shih-p'u that a French fleet was approaching. General quarters was sounded (Arlington observed only general confusion). At ten that night, the enemy was reported just outside the enclosed harbor. Admiral Wu sent Arlington with a reconaissance party to a vantage point to verify the report. Some sparks in the dark, possibly from a French steam launch, excited the men in Arlington's party and they opened a wild fire, which brought on firing from the tense Chinese crews on the waiting warships. Arlington was amazed that he finally managed to return safely aboard. The flagship was in an uproar, with piping for general quarters, weighing of anchors, and similar frenetic activity. The next day, nine ships were seen outside. These opened a heavy fire, and (after one of the foreigners in the flagship had told the Chinese commanders to go to the devil, in disgust at their hesitation) the Chinese finally decided to emerge and give battle to the enemy.

Battle formation was centered on the flagship *K'ai Chi*, with *Nan Ch'en* and *Nan Shui* in the right echelon and *Yu Yüan* and *Teng Ch'ing* in the left. The crews were drunk but manful enough, Arlington recalled. The God of War was consulted. As the ships cleared Shih-p'u harbor, it was determined that the flagship and the right echelon would run for Chenhai, while the slow, China-built *Yu Yüan* and *Teng Ch'ing* were to put back into Shih-p'u.

This plan, wrote Arlington, was machiavellian. "Ting Ju-ch'ang" (Ting Hua-jung) was left in command of the Shih-p'u pair because Admiral Wu disliked him, and perhaps wished to see him killed, or at least to be made the scapegoat for the loss of the two slow ships that Wu knew would encumber him. Only the night before, Ting had been secretly transferred to the *Yu Yüan*, with Arlington coming along also a little later. (Since there were no foreign mentors aboard the *Yu Yüan*, discipline was lax, wrote Arlington.)

Ting Hua-jung, abandoned, received no help from officials ashore.[65] Captains Chin Yung and Chiang Ch'ao-ying, in direct command under Ting, selected good anchorages, but Arlington saw that Chin Yung had no guns loaded. Therefore Arlington personally loaded the Nordenfeldt guns on the *Yu Yüan's* bridge, and left a call with the deck officer for notification if any junks entered Shih-p'u. After midnight he was called, and saw many lights, those of fishermen. Again at 4:30 a.m. word was passed that the enemy was entering. Arlington counted sixty-five lights, and saw a few junks moving near the entrance. To scare these, he fired his Nordenfeldts high, when, "like a flash of lighting," something approached from behind a junk, and a torpedo struck. Later it developed that the enemy torpedo launch had come in under the lee of a "well-paid" fisherman. It was the end of the *Yu Yüan*. Arlington does not say when the *Teng Ch'ing* was hit, but notes that it was.

The ensuing scene "beggared description." Soldiers, sailors, ducks, geese, baggage, and similar flotsam from the deck were in the water in a mad scramble. In twenty minutes the battle was over. Chin Yung stayed in his *Yu Yüan* until the end (he could have scuttled her) in an act of bravery which offsets somewhat Arlington's conclusion that "the fault rested entirely with the Chinese." [66]

Admiral Courbet himself recorded that on the night of February 13–14, two thirty-foot launches with silent engines and black hulls, bearing twenty-nine-pound-charge spar torpedoes, entered the harbor. After a difficult search they found their victims (Arlington's firing of the bridge guns may have helped) and attacked at 3:30 a.m. Only one ship was hit; the other (*Teng Ch'ing*) was then apparently scuttled by her crew.[67]

The foreign descriptions may not be definitive, and Tseng Kuoch'uan's report (cited above) on the scuttling of the ships, along with the motives for it, may be correct. There remained the other three ships of the ill-starred Formosa relief expedition.

Admiral Wu, at Chenhai, was furious about the Shih-p'u news, and when Ting Hua-jung, Chin Yung, Chiang Ch'ao-ying, and Arlington reported to him, a "court martial" (Arlington's phrase) was held. As far as Arlington could see, Wu was the entire court, and Ting was silenced. After the "formal" proceedings were over, a long and loud wrangle went on in Wu's cabin between the two principals. Still, Ting was retained in the *K'ai Chi*, as was Arlington.[68] There was not much to do, with the French blockading ships pressing closely outside the harbor, and gambling and visits ashore the rule on the beleaguered ships. It was safer at Chenhai than at Shih-p'u.

Actually, there were five Chinese ships blockaded in Chenhai. The three Nanyang ships were joined by the *Ch'ao Wu* and *Yuan K'ai*, described by Arlington as two "Kwangtung ships having no connection with our squadron, nor did they want any."[69] Four, then seven, French ships watched. For that matter, Wu himself had had a difficult time getting in, for his three hotly pursued ships had been ordered off by the determined guardians of Ningpo, and he had to come in by force.[70] And he came in to stay, despite orders to proceed to the Yangtze, where another blockading French force would have kept him out.[71]

Li Hung-chang might have broken the Chenhai deadlock by sending down ships to blockade the French blockaders, but to an order to that effect he replied, logically enough, that if the French could keep the Chenhai fleet *in*, they could just as well keep his two ships *out*. The stalemate continued until April 15, 1885, when hostilities were suspended. The last French ship left Chenhai on June 28, 1885.[72]

Arlington's account of life in the blockaded ships is full of petty incidents: gawking gentry visitors, sentries asleep in boats sent out to watch the rock barrier, near mutiny, and the like. Of great interest was the attitude of the local population. The natives of the region during this trying time exhibited indifference to the plight of Chenhai's "defenders," which indifference betokened that lack of support for the fighting man which increased the social isolation of the new navy. There was no nationalism.[73] After the occasional gunnery exchanges between the Chinese and French ships, the peasants made a practice of digging up unexploded French shells from the river mud flats and offering them for sale, although sometimes the shells went off and killed these entrepreneurs. Since some naval officers also sold shells, it is possible that some enemy missiles were re-used in Chinese barrels, a most marvelous economy! Finally, Arlington reported that many of the Chinese shots were blanks.[74]

In accordance with the suggestions of Tso Tsung-t'ang, there were punishments meted out. Chang Ch'eng, who fled the stricken flagship *Yang Wu* in the Ma-wei battle, was beheaded. So too was Li Shih-chen, a subordinate officer on the *Yu Yüan*, who also decamped. Tso asked that Chin Yung and Chiang Ch'ao-ying be demoted but not exiled; nonetheless, they were exiled. Ting Hua-jung and Admiral Wu were exonerated. The court even ordered that Tso himself and Li Hung-chang be punished, but it is not surprising that these two influential officials escaped punishment.[75] In the absence of detailed records, such as would be left by a court martial trial, it can only be said that punishments prescribed seemed to be not entirely consistent, and that the weight of these penalties bore most heavily at the bottom of the chain of command.

From Arlington's account and other sources, it may be concluded that the level of training in the Nanyang fleet was not high. Presumably the Foochow fleet, with a higher percentage of trained captains, was a better trained and more disciplined force. There was only one instance of attempted insubordination in the Ma-wei battle: the gunners of the *Fu Hsing* pleaded with the Foochow-trained captain Ch'en Ying to quit the scene of battle, but he refused. Arlington reports only one mutinous situation at Chenhai, but that one could only be resolved by a foreigner brandishing a pistol, rather than by any effective exhortations of the appropriate native leader. The difference is crucial.[76]

China lost the war with France, but the explanation is not simply that France was overwhelmingly stronger. Although France had a margin of naval superiority in this first of China's modern naval wars, it was nothing like the superiority enjoyed by the British in the Opium War, or the allies in the Second China War of 1856–1860. China's problems in the war with France were not based on the material aspects of her navy as much as they were on the structure of leadership and the political organization of the empire. Her naval personnel was insufficiently trained, and had no grasp of a naval strategy appropriate to the new ships. The shift to modern naval materiel had been subject to numerous social, political, and financial frictions. In the institutional matrix of Confucian China, the navy of the "self-strengtheners" on the occasion of its first real test was still isolated.

VII

NAVAL DEVELOPMENTS AFTER 1885: THE EMERGENCE OF THE PEIYANG FLEET

China's defeat at the hands of the French did convince some of China's leaders that naval centralization was needed. Tso Tsung-t'ang asked for the creation of a single director of a national fleet, which was to consist of ten large squadrons rotating through eight coastal bases, with two squadrons always on roving missions, including trips to the West.[1] This recommendation was part of a lengthy memorial which was Tso's valedictory address to the throne; Tso died shortly after writing the memorial, and the idea of naval centralization had to find other sponsors.

Chang P'ei-lun, although under sentence for his wartime malfeasance, was one of these sponsors. He called for a *shui-shih yamen*, or navy board. Hsü Ching-ch'eng, minister to France, Germany, Italy, Holland, and Austria, submitted to the court a study of the naval forces of nineteen Western nations, and also supported centralization.[2] Spurred by defeat, the court ordered Li Hung-chang, Prince Ch'un, and the Tsungli Yamen to study these suggestions. On October 12, 1885, the *Peking Gazette* stated:

Let Prince Ch'un be appointed chief controller of naval affairs, and all measures of coast defense will be decided by him. Let Prince Ch'ing and the Grand Secretary and Viceroy of Chihli, Li Hung-chang, be appointed as his colleagues in this management, and the Lt.-General of the Chinese Red Banner Corps, Shan Ch'ing, and the Junior Vice-President of the Board of War, Tseng Chi-tse, be assistant managers. Li Hung-chang will be made solely responsible for the reorganization of naval affairs on the northern coast.[3]

Robert Hart was elated by this news. Perhaps British influence could permeate such a central board. He wired to the British Foreign Office:

I suggested Admiralty in 1861; result was Lay-Osborn flotilla, but its collapse killed progress; suggestion renewed in 1873, result was gunboat fleet; resumed suggestion 1883, and suggested Seventh Prince for Chief, and now decree constitutes Admiralty with that Prince for chief! French, Germans, and Americans tried to secure lead, but I kept Navy in English hands. Admiralty is immense step forward and China wants Lang. Splendid opening. If lost, opportunity cannot recur. Make him come! China really begins to move.[4]

Lang did return to China, as we shall see, but his influence was not extensive. The American minister Denby,, who foresaw large demands for foreign machinery from an agency headed by what Denby called a "very liberal" man, who had organized an arsenal near Peking in the past, still feared that German influence would dominate the new navy board.[5] Markets and influence were the stuff of progress to such observers.

The modern Chinese historian Li Chien-nung sees Li Hung-chang as the principal architect of the new Naval Board.[6] But with Prince Kung out of favor at court, Li's influence was not what it had been. Prince Ch'un, or I-huan, half brother of the cashiered Prince Kung, was the new man of the day. His past associations with the centrally organized Peking Field Force (the *lien-chün*, already mentioned) was a factor in his selection. He had also been a leader of the "war-at-any-price" school in Peking, and might have been named as naval chief to counterbalance the more cautious views of Li Hung-chang. The Empress Dowager had long used him in her contest with Prince Kung. With I-huan also rose I-k'uang, the new head of the Tsungli Yamen. Both men were pliable to the will of the Empress Dowager. Prince Ch'un was also the father of the Kuang-hsü Emperor, and that young man, who was in 1885 close to reaching his majority, might be kept off the throne for a while longer because of the impossible awkwardness of requiring a chief minister to make obeisance to his own son. In 1886 when the emperor did come of age, Prince Ch'un begged the empress to prolong her regency for three years, so that the son might be more fully educated.[7] The considerations leading to the appointment of Prince Ch'un to the new post of naval chief probably included political calculations which had little to do with his specific competence.

Prince Ch'un was enthusiastic about his new assignment; he even wrote poetry about the navy.[8] But he never made the Navy Board into a real central directorate of naval affairs. It gradually became the instrument of the Nei-wu Fu, or Imperial Household, whose officers made an entirely non-naval use of the annual four-million-tael budget nominally assigned to the Navy Board.[9] Li Hung-chang, who was a member of the board as well as northern commissioner, had suggested the diversion of the old Sea Defense Fund from the two regional commissioners to the new Navy Board, perhaps in the hope that in this way he could at last realize the primacy in naval expenditures he had sought so long.[10] But it was to be the Summer Palace that was built, or refurbished, rather than Li's Peiyang fleet. The only pavilion in the Summer Palace which had any connection with the sea was the Marble Boat, so-called because this two-storeyed structure, rising from the lake bottom, was built on a marble foundation formed in the shape of a junk's hull, complete with fanciful paddle boxes wherein were imaginary paddles to drive it into the realms of pleasure. To jaundiced foreigners, here was the "Chinese navy." Whatever Tseng Chi-tse hoped of the new board, it was said that his Manchu superiors harassed him into an early grave.[11]

At first, the Navy Board made gestures toward naval reform. In September 1885 a Board of Revenue order forbade provincial officers to purchase naval materiel without clearing with the Board of Revenue and the Navy Board. On November 28, 1886, P'ei Yin-sen, superintendent of the Foochow dockyard, dutifully asked for permission to buy guns from Germany.[12] The new board also conducted fleet inspections. Early in 1886, Tseng Kuo-ch'uan sent the remaining Nanyang ships to the north for joint maneuvers with the Peiyang fleet, and shortly thereafter Prince Ch'un, Li Hung-chang, and Shan Ch'ing, who were inspecting coastal fortifications, witnessed joint drills at Port Arthur and Weihaiwei.[13]

But this seeming centralization of naval affairs was not to last. Chang Chih-tung, then Canton governor-general, in 1887 ordered eight gunboats from the Foochow dockyard without going through the new channels, although he reported his action to the throne. The Board of Revenue denounced the action, but P'ei Yin-sen supported Chang, for without such provincial orders the dockyard would have to close. The order stood.[14]

The purchase of naval materiel from overseas, which was increasingly the principal mode of naval development, was far beyond the Navy Board's control. Hsüeh Fu-ch'eng, as ambassador to Britain, complained of arms smuggling into China, and proposed that the Tsungli Yamen should inform the foreign consuls that all arms shipments to China, unless authorized by the southern and northern commissioners, the Navy Board, or the several provincial authorities involved, should be illegal.[15] The naming of so many alternative authorizing officials indicates that at best purchasing still conformed to the old decentralized system.

Furthermore, by 1892 Prince Ch'un had died, and the Navy Board was under men even less experienced. Its absorption by the Nei-wu Fu was almost complete. The formal demise of the Navy Board did not come until after the Sino-Japanese War, but it made no contribution to China's preparation for that war. It was not inactive; Li's letters to it show its interest in railroads, mining, and commerce, but this sort of thing was at best peripheral to its intended function.[16]

To Li Hung-chang, since he was unable to use the Navy Board and was consequently forced back into his accustomed regional role, the new would-be centralization of funds became a threat. The pooled budget of the Navy Board drew in even his own share of the Sea Defense Fund, so that he had to seek permission to disburse what had been his own income. He extricated himself from this situation by arranging for an edict giving him primacy in training a fleet for northern waters.[17] But his purchases were curtailed, and save for a few new acquisitions the Peiyang fleet was obsolescent. He played the old regional game. In the middle of 1885 P'ei Yin-sen complained that Li was trying to pre-empt the one remaining Foochow ship, the *Heng Hai*. Li made concilatory gestures, but in 1886, after Li was assigned to the new Navy Board, P'ei again complained, in a matter concerning personnel. P'ei wanted to bring back to Foochow the once-slighted Wu Chung-hsiang, then in the service of Li Hung-chang. Even Tso Tsung-t'ang had wanted Wu back, but Li had refused to send him. Now that Wu was on leave in his native place, P'ei moved again.[18] Others also resented the northern commissioner. In 1891 Liu K'un-i grumbled that Li had had the best chance to build up a fleet; for over twenty years he had been the single incumbent in Chihli, while the southern commissionership changed hands so frequently that no continuous naval program was possible. Liu himself had held the Nanking post for three widely separated periods over the preceding fifteen years.[19]

It was true that Li Hung-chang had a formidable aggregation of concurrencies, including even a position in the capital, and was favored by the decision to start postwar naval reconstruction with his unscathed Peiyang fleet. But he was still essentially a regional official, and by himself could not bring about naval unity in the decade after the Sino-French War any more than he could in the decade preceding it.[20]

However, Li did reorganize his Peiyang flotilla — and, in seeking to make the Peiyang regulations of 1888 a model for other fleets, he was seeking for some extension of his control. On September 30, 1888, Prince Ch'un submitted to the throne Li's new naval regulations for his twenty-five-ship fleet. British and German precedents were acknowledged, but did not supersede all native experience.[21] Peiyang command was vested in Admiral Ting Ju-ch'ang, aided by the post captains Lin T'ai-tseng and Liu Pu-ch'an. Captains, while required to obey the admiral, in their turn had complete authority on their ships, even over students in training. Land officials, civil, or military, were denied any authority over Peiyang ships.[22] The fleet was divided into seven functional squadrons. The seagoing fighting ships were put into three "wings" of three ships each, with the battleships *Ting Yüan* and *Chen Yüan* respectively in the right and left wings. The other four wings (squadrons) had support tasks: a squadron of harbor craft was created, as were a torpedo squadron, a training unit, and a transport contingent. The rank of wing commanders was determined by the size and character of the command. This arrangement was a reflection of British influence, and shows strategic sophistication.[23]

German precedents dominated Peiyang naval staff organization. There was a single admiral, rather than three navy lords in the British style. Li pointed out that there had never been several admirals in a single Chinese organization. Lin T'ai-tseng and Liu Pu-ch'an each commanded one of the German battleships, with headquarters in Port Arthur. Ting's staff included commanders for Personnel, Engineering, and Victualing, and a lieutenant-commanding for Fleet Weapons. Detailed regulations covered the activities of each of these officers, sometimes even setting the number of their bodyguards.[24]

In the provisions for joint maneuvers, Li's contribution and perhaps ulterior motives may be seen. Each winter, the Peiyang fleet was supposed to steam to Nanyang waters, for a joint north-south cruise along the southern coasts. While south, Peiyang captains would deliver daily logs to the Navy Board, via Admiral Ting Ju-ch'ang and the northern commissioner. If such joint maneuvers were "inconvenient," the northern commissioner would so advise the southern naval commander (the regulations noted that there was no southern admiral) who would then so advise the southern commissioner.

Reciprocally, each spring all southern seagoing fighting ships (the regulations named them all) would be ordered by the Navy Board to visit northern waters. While there, the southerners would be under the orders of the northern commissioner, who would carry out inspections and distribute rewards and punishments. The northern commissioner would communicate with his Nanking counterpart as to salaries, coal consumed, and similar expenses of the Nanyang ships, which were to be paid by the southern commissioner. In the fall, the Nanyang ships would return home, with their logs going to the Navy Board by way of Nanking. Somewhat gratuitously, it was urged in the regulations that the southern commissioner should not avoid drilling his ships just because he was far away.[25]

While on northern maneuvers, all ships would cruise off Fengtien, Chihli, Shantung, Korea, and "the Russian and Japanese islands." Itineraries were subject to the approval of the northern commissioner. If a warship was to be dispatched by the Navy Board or northern commissioner to a treaty power, or sent on a commerce-protecting mission, all details would be forwarded to the Navy Board in a "communication" (the term signifying communication between equals) from the northern commissioner, who would record personal merits and demerits for all personnel. Protocol for diplomatic missions was carefully set forth. If any mission involved an imperial commissioner, the northern commissioner would report to the Navy Board and its parent Tsungli Yamen, and would bear the expenses of such missions in the national interest on his own accounts.[26]

Li Hung-chang clearly recognized, in his regulations, that a new era of diplomacy was at hand. But it may also be said that these 1888 regulations were Li's exploitation of his advantage as a "national" official in the Navy Board in order to enhance his influence as northern commissioner. In the first capacity, he could send out ships from any part of China, the while paying for such diplomatic missions and serving as the channel of information in his regional capacity, thus enhancing the status of the latter position. Even in mere drills he could dispense rewards and punishments to southerners as well as northerners. Undoubtedly this would enable him to draw loyalties to himself. Provisions in the 1888 regulations for Peiyang ships in Nanyang waters were brief and vague, stipulating mainly that all northern ships, wherever berthed, were answerable to Admirable Ting — wherever he might be in person. The regulations were not fully reciprocal. This lack of reciprocity, however, was not baldly exposed in a single consecutive section of the regulations; the detailed provisions which gave the advantage to Li Hung-chang were scattered through separate parts of the whole text.

Li's regulations were adopted. They were not entirely a paper aggrandizement of his position. In 1890, the Nanyang ship *Teng Ying Chou* was sent to Korea to bestow a third-rank concubine on the Korean king — a delicate piece of diplomacy. In the next year, the southern commissioner "imitated" Li's regulations in the Nanyang fleet, and took part in a grand maneuver in Li's northern waters, showing six vessels to Li's four, with even the Kwangtung fleet sending up three. The inspecting party included Li Hung-chang, Governor Chang Yao of Shantung, senior Kwangtung naval officer Yu Hsiung-fei, and the Nanyang commander Kuo Pao-chiang. Li Hung-chang, who was of course the senior official in the party, wrote the report, praising Prince Ch'un for the fine show. In 1894, another joint review took place in northern waters, with a similar make-up.[27]

These maneuvers did not represent real unification. There were still four fleets, with Li's the largest. China was perhaps fortunate in 1894 that it was this largest of China's fleets that was engaged by Japan, but this fact was more coincidence than evidence of a grand plan. In the year of crisis, no one, not even Li Hung-chang, could assemble a "national" fleet.

For that matter, disorganization was marked even within the Peiyang fleet itself. W. F. Tyler, an Englishman who served in Li's battleship in the war with Japan, said of Li's Peiyang naval establishment: "In all this machine — which included not only the fleet but all cognate to it, from the Viceroy to the arsenal director — the groups of wheels revolved to no general purpose but only to their own. The various groups engaged and disengaged when necessary, by some process of give-and-take which caused the least inconvenience. It was the antithesis of an ordered regimen from the stand-point of efficiency; but it was disorder curiously ordered, and — in peace-time — worked without a rattle, well-greased with peculation, and with nepotism." Evidently the 1888 regulations did not regularize everything in the Peiyang fleet. Of Li himself, Tyler wrote: "The corruption, peculation, and nepotism which infested his organizations had their fountainhead in Li himself, and to an extent that was exceptional even for a Chinese official. He was himself enmeshed in the national machine of organized inefficiency; to him also it was a normal condition — yet he was without doubt a fervent patriot; and there is an example of a Chinese puzzle."[28]

Material developments in this decade between the Sino-French and Sino-Japanese Wars were not promising. Li Hung-chang had to curtail his purchases; and the one serious naval building facility, the dockyard at Foochow, found no relief from its constrictions.

Tso Tsung-t'ang's valedictory memorial had touched on many naval problems, including the lack of technical standardization of the unspecialized Foochow line of ships. He also asked that three or four million taels be expended annually by the dockyard, which he wished to have enlarged. Tso soon died — and Hart, among others, regretted this death particularly, since he feared it would devitalize a naval reform movement which had been inspired by the defeat of China in the recent war with France.[29]

Whatever might have been achieved had Tso lived, the postwar Foochow dockyard superintendent, P'ei Yin-sen, encountered financial trouble. Construction money was still being diverted into maintenance. After the war, Ch'ang P'ei-lun had suggested that the maintenance accounts for the nine destroyed ships be continued, but applied to new construction. The Fukien Rehabilitation Bureau disallowed the plan. At any rate, P'ei complained of construction-fund arrears. By long-standing arrangements the yard was supposed to get 20,000 taels monthly from the Fukien forty percent, and another 30,000 monthly from the sixty percent.

In July 1886 P'ei reported that he had received only a portion of the sum due from the first fund for 1884; in the much-contested sixty percent, the deficit came to nearly two and one-half million taels — about seven years' worth![30]

There was some material progress at the dockyard. Hart wrote of a graving dock and a gun factory (although the latter was not being used to build guns). Work on the dock as late as 1891 was going on only "languidly," according to Hart. The dockyard was still isolated economically. Hart commented that "owing to the lack of enterprise among the natives and encouragement from the governing classes, no special development is perceptible in any of the existing local industries." [31]

In P'ei Yin-sen's view, the outstanding plants at the dockyard in 1885 were the engine and iron-casting shops. By late 1886, a torpedo plant was producing. Of course P'ei had concerned himself with shipbuilding. France, he said, had won the war because of her "two or three" armored ships. China should build such ships. The returned construction men Wei Han, Ch'en Ch'ao-ao, and Cheng Ch'ing-lien were capable of directing the work, and Tso Tsung-t'ang, Mu T'u-shan, and the Min-Che governor-general Yang Ch'ang-jui were agreed that the effort should be made.[32]

In the meantime, the composite *Heng Hai* was being completed, and another was under construction. P'ei wanted to build no more of the old hybrid vessels, since they had been no more than armed merchant ships; his new iron-hulled ships were to be entirely naval. Power would be increased to 1600 horsepower, and the ships made a little wider. Since British power plants were installed in the composites mentioned above, we may wonder how well the existing plant was actually serving P'ei's ambitions.[33] Iron ships were a sign of progress, to be sure, but Europe was then turning to steel warships of up to 15,000 tons. P'ei also wanted to build torpedo boats, and in September 1886 a torpedo boat ordered by Chang P'ei-lun arrived from Germany, and P'ei planned to use it as a prototype.[34]

Understandably P'ei was opposed to buying foreign-built warships. Wei Han had inspected Li Hung-chang's latest British and German ships, and argued that the Foochow dockyard could duplicate them at a lower price. Accordingly, P'ei late in 1886 asked for funds to build the indicated types for delivery to the

Peiyang fleet. After a space, P'ei reported the laying of the keel of the Foochow dockyard's first armored ship, in the construction of which not a single foreigner was to be involved.[35]

But P'ei's attempts to create a national policy favoring home-built ships were in vain. On March 2, 1887, Li Hung-chang reported his plans for the delivery of the ships which Wei Han had seen in Europe, and asked for (and got) a sum of 220,000 taels for the round trip of the needed crews — the sum being close to half the average prewar income of the Foochow dockyard.[36] Small wonder that P'ei fought for provincial orders for ships, as mentioned, whether or not such orders came through the new Navy Board channel.

P'ei continued building ships, but at a retarded rate. In 1887 the 200,000-tael composite *Kwang Chia* was launched for the Canton governor-general. This 222-footer was engined by a British firm. The *Huan T'ai* of that year (1887) was China's first self-built ironclad ship; this 2400-horsepower ship was for the southern commissioner.[37] Although the dockyard had to meet only half of the construction costs, P'ei, through September of 1889, wrote at least six pleas for help from Peking. His troubles depressed this "old scholar of sixty," and in 1889 an Englishman reported to friends: "I say, the Commissioner has just tried to commit suicide; he jumped off the slip on the sly, whilst pretending to inspect a steamer under repair; but they got him out in time."[38] In 1890, P'ei retired. But the financial problem continued, and Pien Pao-ti, P'ei's successor as dockyard superintendent, wrote about it twice in 1891.[39]

Characteristically, the Foochow dockyard did not show deficits during the decade between the Sino-French and Sino-Japanese wars. Its average annual expenditure was about half a million taels, or about twenty percent less than the average annual income for the years 1883–1893. In this decade, the yard spent 4,986,888 taels — which was just about what Tso in 1885 vainly sought to have made available to it for every year, and what Li Hung-chang would have liked to have for a single year of ship-buying.[40]

Li Hung-chang, on his opposite course, did not have clear sailing. He was disappointed in the new Navy Board, to which he made repeated but unavailing requests for income. He averaged an annual 1.2 million taels from 1882 to 1891, but this was not enough. His balances dropped, and his buying was curtailed. Lang urged buying ever more ships, but Li could do little. Furthermore, although his annual income was reasonably steady, there were telling readjustments in the sums contributing to it. His collections from provincial maritime customs came more and more from the northern coastal provinces only. In 1883, Li's receipts for his "poor province" — that is, a province (Chihli) which by fixed practice received subventions from other "rich" provinces — had come from the entire littoral, but by 1888, the Shanghai customs was the most southerly donor. This was a reflection of the rivalry endemic in China's fiscal system. When Chang Chih-tung ordered small craft at Foochow, he had to pay for them, and he guarded his funds, saving them for ships which he intended to use strictly in his own waters.

In a way, Li Hung-chang was his own most wily competitor. His land army, the Anhwei army, during this period enjoyed two or three times the income of his modern navy. Even this privileged land force saw a drop in income from about 4.2 million taels in 1873 to about 2.8 million taels in 1892.[41]

Li did what he might. In October 1884, before the end of the Sino-French War, he arranged to receive the German sister battleships, *Ting* and *Chen*, ordered long before.[42] In 1885, he ordered four more ships, two from England and two from Germany. Tseng Chi-tse and Hsü Ching-ch'eng had wondered about types; some manufacturers were leaving off armor in the interest of greater speed, and, among armored vessels, there were those with only a central citadel, and those with water-line belts. The court referred the questions to Li Hung-chang, who answered that China should experiment with various types. Later he suggested to Tseng that unarmored, shallow-draught ships, with torpedoes, and capable of seventeen or eighteen knots, would be best for fighting and patrol in Asian waters. As it came out, two ships were ordered from both England and Germany in November 1885. These ships (which Wei Han believed could be more cheaply built at the Foochow dockyard) were not pairs of national sisters. The British ships, *Chih Yüan* and *Ching Yüan*, were respectively 2300 and 2850 tons, and respectively unarmored and armored, with differences too in armament and speed. The two German ships, *Ching Yüan* and *Lai Yüan*, also unarmored and armored, showed similar displacements and characteristics. Captain Lang led a mission to take delivery of the four ships in 1887.[43]

Before the delivery of these ships, Li was talking about buying still others. In January 1886 he complained to the Navy Board that he had only five ships suitable for ocean missions. He mentioned the coming four, desiring next to buy three shallow-draught steel armored fast ships and five or six torpedo boats. He also urged setting up a big shipyard. Li also criticized Hart (who was still urging various ship types on China) as a rank amateur.[44]

But Li had come nearly to the end of his purchases of naval materiel. In 1887, after helping the court borrow some money for a "naval academy" in Peking (to be discussed later), he ordered six torpedo boats. He also bought a dredger for his Port Arthur naval facility.[45] But after this, he placed no more orders for naval vessels.

Li's rivals, of course, included the court itself. It was not that the central government sought its own countervailing naval power. The court's object was the satisfaction of the pleasure of the insatiable Empress Dowager, who was encouraged — if she needed encouragement — by the eunuch Li Lien-ying. The southern commissioner felt the pressure as well. And so this chapter returns to the subject of the refurbishing of the Summer Palace.

In his recent study of the Chinese navy, Pao Tsen-peng states that after funds from the southern and northern commissioners were assigned to the Navy Board, there was misappropriation of them for "internal uses." Tseng Kuo-ch'uan, the southern commissioner, before the assignment of his Sea Defense monies to the Navy Board, had had a defense income of about 400,000 taels a year — at that, only a fifth of the supposed two millions he was supposed to disburse. Li Hung-chang's navy, in Tseng's view, had been favored; but if even Li had insufficient funds, what of Nanking? Coastal defense money was going to "internal uses," and Tseng could not get "the smallest drop," although he "cried out" for it. The new Navy Board had made things worse.[46]

Furthermore, the Navy Board made requests for additional special contributions from the provincial officials. While Li Hung-chang was urging a special assessment in Chihli for his use in paying for the Port Arthur complex, the Navy Board ordered him to withdraw 300,000 taels from his navy funds in the Hong Kong and Shanghai Bank, which was to go for certain construction on the "san-hai," or Peking lakes. Li countered that he had four ships on order, had already delayed certain Kiaochow fortifications to release funds for Port Arthur, and had been asked to decommission some of his existing ships. Nonetheless, he was shortly ordered, via Prince Ch'un, to borrow up to 800,000 taels for the projected "works," which were in fact to be a rest-house for the Empress. Ruses were suggested to cover any possible embarrassment he might feel in approaching foreign bankers; e.g., that the money was to be used for a "naval academy." In December 1886 Li talked with foreign bankers, who were keenly competitive for his business. Here was the origin of the "K'un-ming Naval Academy" at the capital — where later it could at least be said that genuine steam launches towed barges filled with court ladies around the pleasure lakes.[47]

In 1888, Li (having reorganized his fleet) reported spending 1,768,100 taels for the maintenance of his nine modern vessels. In order to add certain needed ships, he wanted an additional three million taels.[48] But he asked in vain. In that year, the Western Park, or Lake Palace, near the Forbidden City, was repaired as a temporary spa for Tz'u-hsi while the Ch'ien-lung Emperor's old residence at Wan-shou Shan on K'un-ming Lake was made suitably resplendent for her. She was about to "retire." According to one report, "About the time she was ready to begin the work, the Navy Bureau asked for 10,000,000 for a modern navy, a project which seemed so useless to the Empress Dowager that the officials, who were completely under her influence, sent in petitions urging that a garden be provided for the approaching birthday celebrations of the Empress Dowager."[49] Her retirement came in 1889; the birthday — her sixtieth — was not to come until 1894. The garden plan was a grandiose one, and according to the censor Lin Shao-nien the provincial governor-generals arranged to establish a special naval defense fund, for deposit with the northern commissioner, for her use in realizing it. The special fund was achieved in 1889.[50]

More exactly, it was arranged by Prince Ch'un that Li Hung-chang should appear to be the prime mover for the "naval fund." Li wrote to Tseng Kuo-ch'uan about the fund, saying that it was really to be used for the pleasure of the Empress Dowager. Tseng passed along the information to the governor of Kiangsi in 1889, in a letter which he wrote with small enthusiasm. Tseng feared that such special funds would be exacted every year.[51]

While China's great officials were making their quiet arrangements, the censor Lin Shao-nien raised his voice. Surely, he said, revelation of the fraud would bring on popular revolt. A gift for the empress should come openly from the Board of Revenue; all funds deviously collected on any other pretext should be returned. According to the official record, an order for such a return of irregular funds was issued. But it is doubtful if there was complete restitution. Tseng Kuo-ch'uan listed monies collected in this area for the "naval fund": Kiangsi provided 100,000 taels; Kiangsu, Kiangning, and the Liang-huai had put up 700,000. The first sum had been returned, but not the larger second one, and he wanted an investigation of the use of the money, for these sums had been raised painfully, often being taken from local defense budgets. Tseng observed that even the China Merchants Company had put up 100,000 taels — which interested him because that company owed as much to Kiangsu, but had apparently diverted it to this more politic use.[52]

In addition, the Liang-Kwang governor-general put in one million taels, and Chihli and Szechwan 200,000 each. In sum, at least 2.2 million taels went into this 1889 "naval fund." There had been a similar levy in 1887, nominally over and above the supposed regular income of the Navy Board, the four-million-tael Sea Defense Fund which of course was never fully realized. Still, after allowing for Peiyang fleet expenses, the Navy Board probably disposed of some 8.5 million taels in the six years 1889–1894, apart from the special levies.[53] But it was not building a navy. Its real activity is suggested by a Navy Board petition on the eve of the Sino-Japanese War, asking that the continuing expenses of the completed Summer Palace be taken from likin collections; that is, from some source other than the Navy Board.[54]

It is difficult to assess the cost of the Summer Palace to the naval program, for one must deal with an unrealized "regular" Navy Board income as well as with special levies and palace savings which might have been used for a "crash" naval program if the coming crisis with Japan had been properly anticipated — as it was by Li Hung-chang. It has been said that ninety percent of the navy's money was diverted into palace-building by Li Lien-ying, and that even Li Hung-chang dared not speak of it.[55] One competent estimate is that "squeeze" — evidently from a "regular" Navy Board income — came to 400,000 taels each year.[56] According to another, some three million taels of navy money was taken from the fleets; over the six years, 1889–1894, this would come to (approximately) a half million taels in each year just mentioned.[57] Even if this was ninety percent of the regular income of the Navy Board it should be recalled that such a sum would have run the Foochow dockyard for a year, or paid for the wages and food of the entire Nanyang fleet.[58]

Other accounts speak of the total cost of the Summer Palace, with its gardens and useless Marble Boat. One study puts this total at 100,000,000 taels, and cites a "local tradition" that some 70,000,000 of these taels came from foreign loans. If so, then 30,000,000 taels must have been found at home.[59] Perhaps most of this huge sum came from the mooted palace savings, reputedly some 20,000,000 taels, gathered from the sale of offices. On the other hand, just before the Sino-Japanese War an American official reported that by 1894 the Empress Dowager had reluctantly decided to divert 60,000,000 taels which had been collected for her birthday fête to the meeting of the problem in Korea.[60]

Whatever the total cost of the Summer Palace complex, the navy lost a great deal of money that might have been used for buying and building ships. Pao Tsen-peng cites the careful Lo Erh-kang as saying that at least 10,000,000 of naval funds were so misused. Pao himself inclines to double the amount, including both "regular" and "special" funds.[61] Perhaps the matter may never be definitively settled. It may at least be said that a differently organized and well-led China might have put up a more potent naval opposition to Japan in 1894. China was not a poor country.

It is also clear that Li and the Navy Board were competitors for funds — and that Li's buying program was halted. In 1891 the Board of Revenue put a formal end to Li's buying program by asking that all purchases, north and south, be suspended for two years, to allow for an interval of saving. Ting Ju-ch'ang and others protested vigorously, but uselessly.[62] Late in December of 1891, Li asked for money, citing his formal dependence on funds from the Navy Board, which were now all the more vital to Li, in view of provincial defaults to his defense fund.[63] The request was in vain.

To eke out income for his obsolescent fleet, Li resorted to unorthodox expedients. In 1891 foreigners observed that "Chinese gun vessels and the colliers do an increasing passenger trade between Chefoo and the naval stations of Port Arthur and Weihaiwei." The next year brought further surprised foreign comment: "A large number of war vessels go backwards and forwards between this [Chefoo] and Port Arthur. They certainly make a regular business of carrying passengers, and in China, where native passengers travel, large quantities of merchandise are carried as luggage." Foreign observers never quite accustomed themselves to this practice. Another note of 1893 reads: "The employment of war vessels as passenger steamers strikes Europeans as very extraordinary. The war vessels for this purpose are principally the smaller gun vessels of the Northern Squadron, which are constantly going to and from . . . Passenger tickets for passengers on board men-of-war are to be bought at the Imperial Telegraph Office." [64] After the Sino-Japanese War, foreign observers stated that the boilers of some of the ships in the Yalu battle were worn out.[65] Hard use in the carrying trade, together with indifferent maintenance, may account for this deterioration.

About three months before the Sino-Japanese War, Li wanted to buy twenty-one assorted new Krupp quick-firers for his biggest ships. The Navy Board and the Board of Revenue denied to him the required 610,000 taels, so Li took 200,000 taels from his maintenance funds and in this way purchased twelve of the new pieces.[66]

During the Sino-Japanese war, when the petulant court tried to blame all of China's losses on Admiral Ting Ju-ch'ang, Li in his defense of his admiral cautiously returned the blame to the court:

Careful examination of the naval publications of the various countries shows that of the twenty-one fast ships available to the Japanese, there are nine which have been built since Kuang-hsü's fifteenth year [1889] . . . and the fastest makes twenty-three knots [this was the *Yoshino*], with the next, twenty. . . . When our ships were first built, Western marine engineering had not developed so far. . . In recent years the [Hu] Pu has decided to stop buying ships and weapons; since 1888 we have not added a single ship to our fleet.[67]

EMERGENCE OF THE PEIYANG FLEET

Li might have put a keener edge on his thrust had he added that just before the war the British had urged him to buy two fast ships, but Li had encountered the refusal of the Board of Revenue. The Japanese then bought the two ships, and to one of them they gave the name *Yoshino*.[68]

If Li's skill availed him nothing in the fight for funds, other purchasers were even more sorely limited. The only late purchases for the southern fleet were torpedo boats, not all of them satisfactory. In the war, Nanking disposed only of the old German-built *Nan Shui* and *Nan Ch'en* and the still older four "gamma" gunboats.[69] We can hardly call this a fleet.

Building did not stop completely. In 1889 the Foochow dockyard launched the 2850-ton steel *P'ing Yüan*, which, with its eight-inch armor belt, cost 524,000 taels. But while on the ways, the ship had been shortened (financial trouble again) and her lines were ruined, so that she made only about ten knots. In the same year, the dockyard launched the smaller composite *Kuang Keng*, which went to the Nanyang fleet. The slightly larger, 1000-ton steel *Kuang I* of 1890 went to Canton, as did her unarmored sister, the *Kuang Ping* of 1891. In 1893, the *Fu Ching*, of about 2000 tons, was launched for the Foochow squadron. Finally, in 1894 the dockyard completed the all-steel trainer *T'ung Chi*.[70] To build all-steel ships was progress, but it is safe to say that the progress would have been greater had there been a better coordination of the national military effort. No other great shipbuilding facilities were created.

There was considerable technical advance in arsenals and yards during this last interwar period, for example, the building of a small dockyard and arsenal at Canton, docks at Amoy, improvements at Nanking, and also the great industrial works of Chang Chih-tung at Hankow.[71]

The Kiangnan arsenal continued to command the respect of foreigners. In 1889 one Westerner found it to be "an immense arsenal," with an iron-ship yard, "with costly and ponderous machinery capable of building modern ironclads of large size," and a 400-foot dock.[72] Nonetheless, only one important ship was built during the inter-war decade, the 1500-ton ironclad *Pao Min*. This sixteen-knot ship of 1885 went to the Nanyang fleet. That the foreigners in Shanghai dubbed her "The Terror of the Western

Nations" is suggestive. Two small gunboats were also built, but in those days of hulking Western dreadnoughts, these hardly merit mention.[73] Unfortunately the Kiangnan dock, as well as the other five docks on the river at Shanghai, rested on the alluvium, which afforded "ample" support for cruisers and unarmored ships, but not for heavier vessels, the docking of which would involve a "considerable" risk.[74] It was not for shipbuilding, or even for ship repair, that Kiangnan was notable during this period.

The Kiangnan arsenal in 1889 was making Remingtons — dozens daily. Much of the work was done by hand, with costly machinery standing idle. No foreigners were involved. In 1891, the Shanghai customs commissioner Bredon visited the place after a twenty-year absence, and he — an admitted nonexpert — had only praise for "the facility with which native foremen handled the ponderous machinery. The cannon foundry, rifle factory, and shot and shell works impressed me as wonderfully in advance of anything I thought existed in China . . . the provincial officials have every reason to be proud." [75] In 1893, the cannon plant was making twelve-inch breech-loading guns, all of native manufacture save for the "tubes" (apparently the barrel-liners).[76]

After the Sino-Japanese War, the junketing Englishman Lord Beresford was impressed (in 1898) by the Kiangnan arsenal, but observed that in the midst of 9.2-inch "hydropneumatic" disappearing guns and quick-firers were steel barrels for "the useless gingals . . . incredible though it seems." [77]

The evidence suggests that the Kiangnan arsenal was hastily filled with "beautiful and delicate machinery" right after the Sino-French War, as a response to the defeat of China, but that the plant was overbuilt. It was probably operated at less than capacity. The governor of Taiwan observed in 1894 that the products of Kiangnan coming to him were sufficient only for peacetime maneuver; Beresford, on the other hand, wrote that the cartridge plant could turn out "millions" annually. One foreign comment is significant: "The Kiangnan Arsenal seems to have been a sort of stepping post to higher posts, for three of its Directors have been sent as Ministers to foreign countries, while those in lower positions have been drafted to many important positions in the home and foreign service." [78] The arsenal career had not yet been properly accepted, apparently.

In the north, Li Hung-chang had expanded his Tientsin facilities. He had added a shipyard at Taku, which had "an extensive engineering establishment" and a drydock 340 feet long. In 1888 a steel screw tugboat, the *Yu Hsün*, was launched there, and later two small armored steamers. The Taku yard was mainly devoted to the building of maintenance and service craft, such as dredgers and tugs.[79]

Li built his principal naval station at Port Arthur, or Lu-hsün. He had wanted a dockyard for some time; in 1885 he reported to the Navy Board that his steel ships had to be docked twice a year. His Taku yard could take his small ships, but the *Ch'ao Yung* and *Yang Wei*, with their draughts of fifteen feet, had to go to foreign docks at Shanghai, and the twenty-foot-deep battleships could be taken only in docks at Hong Kong or Yokohama.[80]

Li began the Port Arthur project in 1881. A German army engineer on his staff, Constantin von Hannecken, was given overall direction of the preparation and fortification of Port Arthur, which was initially no more than a "wind-bound" junk harbor. Von Hannecken was primarily in charge of fortification; a contract for dredging was given to a French engineer. In 1894, when the dredging was completed, the entrance sill was twenty-five feet deep, and this depth prevailed in the inner waters. An extensive shore establishment had been put up, at a total cost of 1,393,500 taels, which had come from various sources, including Chihli maritime defense levies and a surplus remaining from Li's last ship purchases. Evidently Li had not given his all to the Summer Palace "navy fund."

The plant ashore included a dockyard, machine shops, warehouses, a railroad, an electric lighting system, and breakwater. The 400-foot stone dock was pumped by steam power. There was also a ship-pool, formed by two stone jetties, one of which was 400 feet long and could take ships on three faces. Although it was too cold to paint ships from November to March, Li was proud that ships could have their undersides repaired while repairs were going on topside. There was also a small torpedo boat dock, and an iron supply T-warf. Torpedoes could be tested and regulated in what a foreigner described as a "small but efficient" torpedo depot.

The shops — including a boiler shop, machine shop, pump

shop, stonework shop, brass works, iron foundry, and a forge — contained "the most modern engines"; Li was persuaded that China had never had such a modern repair yard. Indeed, during the Sino-Japanese War, seven ships, some heavily damaged, put into Port Arthur for repairs.[81]

Li's facilities had a formidable appearance, but his system of supply left much to be desired. In his 1888 Peiyang navy regulations, Li included a section entitled *hou-lu* (the "rear road") which dealt with supply. The regulations stated that in the West the function of supply was given to a specialist; Chinese practice, on the other hand, was to make concurrent use of men otherwise engaged. However, the regulations continued, since supply was a vital function, such men must be able.[82]

Li's supply system included the Ship Supply Depot at Port Arthur; the Tientsin Coastal Defense Fund, under a taotai; the Port Arthur Ordnance Office, with another at Tientsin; the Weihaiwei Machine shop; the Tientsin Machinery Bureau, or arsenal; and the Inspector-General of Naval Affairs, whose duties included stockpiling. All of these offices were subordinate to the northern commissioner, and were supported by Peiyang funds. Annual reports on the supply organization were sent by the northern commissioner to the Navy Board, as well as certain details to the Board of Revenue.

Li did not rely on domestic supply entirely; he continued to make purchases of foreign arms. He was aware of developments in Western ordnance; e.g., the abandonment of muzzle-loading. He urged the adoption of a single type of ordnance for China's ships, himself favoring Krupp products.[83] But Li's pro-German bias did not make his supply of guns and ammunition uniform. Krupp representatives, using one of his nephews as an agent, sold Li some obsolete equipment; Sheng Hsuan-huai, another agent for Li, placed orders through Mandl, a German who was close to Detring and Von Hannecken;[84] Hsü Ching-ch'eng, China's minister to Germany, also placed orders.[85] In 1894, the *Columbia*, a 2000-ton American steamer, "long, low, and sharp," smuggled to Li's Tientsin agents a load of American arms of all descriptions, camouflaged as foodstuff; and despite the enthusiastic efforts of the smugglers (intercepted by the Japanese, they pitched the boarding officer overboard and ran for it), this cargo can hardly have reduced Li's difficulties with ammunition. Li's warships, coming from two countries, doubtless posed a problem for the logistician.[86]

There was trouble in Li's own supply organization. In August 1894 a shortage of ammunition was uncovered in the ships which had just been challenged by Japan in the sinking of the transport *Kowhsing*. Von Hannecken and Tyler, who were serving in Li's flagship, wired to Li that China's fate depended on the Tientsin arsenal, and asked him to urge it personally to full output. Li did not do so, but in a month some shells were shipped out, with a letter from Chang P'ei-lun, Li's son-in-law and the director of the arsenal, saying that certain large-caliber shells could not be made. Later some Chinese gunnery lieutenants tried to reopen the matter through Admiral Ting, but without result. Tyler and Von Hannecken did no more. They felt that their foreignness worked against them, whereas Chang P'ei-lun's personal link to Li worked for him. More objections from them would have "upset the whole machine, such as it was . . ." Indeed, in the great naval review of 1893 there were already ammunition shortages in Li's fleet of a year's standing, but no one then had been so discourteous as to suggest to Li Hung-chang that his fleet looked mightier than it really was.[87]

Tyler laid responsibility for these shortages at the door of the "notorious" Chang P'ei-lun. Philo McGiffen, an American who was also in Li's naval service, hinted at "corruption and treachery ashore." A Chinese historian writes that during the Sino-Japanese War some ammunition did not fit the guns, and also blamed the Tientsin establishment. It seems that some clerks in that establishment were spies for Japan; among other things, they gave information on the sailing of the transport *Kowhsing*, whose sinking by Japan really started the war. These clerks sabotaged supply lines during the crucial months.[88] Li's *hou-lu*, then, was not in operation what it was on paper.

If Li's supply was not standardized, neither were the systems of supply elsewhere in China, nor were the gun types used in the coastal fortifications. In these fortifications, Krupps, Nordenfeldts, and Armstrongs were in common use. There was no single system of supply. In 1898 Lord Beresford visited some forty forts on China's coasts and rivers, noting "every conceivable sort of gun," with most forts still using muzzle-loading pieces. Some had breech-loaders "of the very best description," often made in China to British or German specifications. But most forts used Chinese powder, which was apparently more apt to burst the gun than to hurl the shell. In one fort, Beresford wondered if this was not the case, and was laconically informed that the powder did indeed sometimes blow up the ordnance. He saw Krupps fitted with Armstrong breeches, the original part having been blown off, but allowed that "these guns had been beautifully converted at the Shanghai Arsenal." [89] Although he wrote after the war, Beresford's notes are useful still, since he suggested implicitly that the Sino-Japanese War was not a powerful stimulus to military progress.

The material immediately preceding suggests that the traditional concern with fixed shore fortifications was still much in evidence on the eve of the Sino-Japanese War. Li Hung-chang was an outstanding builder of such shore installations, which were best exemplified in his massive Gulf of Chihli installations.

The Port Arthur forts were very impressive. The East Port area, covering thirty-two acres of water, was well protected. On one side of the narrow entrance were the Hwang-chin bluffs, which in 1894 presented three eight-inch Krupps. Other hills commanded the yards area. Opposite the Kwang-chin hill, across the entrance, were the eight Tiger Tail Promontory forts, with thirty-nine modern guns. In the surrounding hills were more guns, the largest running over six inches in caliber. A contemporary American estimate was that the whole installation showed good utilization of opportunities, so as to create a defense of "the most formidable character." [90] In taking Port Arthur (from the rear) in November 1894, Japan got "the best dockyard in the Far East, provided with every requisite for the repairing of vessels . . . a splendid naval base of operations at the enemy's door . . . Port Arthur represented a value of sixty million yen, about six million pounds sterling." [91]

Across the gulf was Weihaiwei. Here was an excellent harbor with islands so placed across its entrance (Liu-kung, Kwang, and Jih islands) that ships could enter only by a western pass right under the Liu-kung and west-shore forts. On the islands and in the hills around the harbor were seventeen forts, mounting fifty-five guns, from four to ten inches, some of them quick-firers. Four of the island guns were of the latest disappearing type. The guns bore only to seaward. The water entrances were guarded by a quintuple bank of torpedoes, a quadruple series of sunken magnetic mines, and a massive boom made up of three strands of three-inch steel cable floated on heavy timber balks, well anchored to the bottom.[92]

Li's anchorage at Talienwan was also fortified, with eighteen large pieces. There were forts at Chin-shou, Chefoo, and Kiaochow Bay — although the last-named works had been suspended for lack of funds.[93]

Ballard, the British naval historian, observed that these forts, with Li's fleet, gave strategic advantages to China which might have been exploited so as to frustrate Japan as the Korean admiral Yi-sun had done four centuries before. In the 1890's as in the 1590's, defeat at sea for China need not mean a total defeat, as it must for the aggressive Japanese.[94] Li Hung-chang was well situated for one wishing to defend Korea, and from the siting of his forts, it is apparent that he was not basing his defense on the ultimate inner point, that is, on the old Taku Forts, but expressed in his disposition of defenses a more outgoing strategic idea than was traditional.

The southern coasts were also richly planted with forts, but they were hardly involved in the Sino-Japanese War. In 1891 the Hainan authorities pushed construction of a new fort at Shuiying for five Krupps, up to eight inches. On Formosa, Governor Liu Ming-ch'uan energetically erected "vast earthworks," with guns from "a well-known German firm." It was said by foreigners that his forts were based on "the prescribed pattern of centuries." An Englishman in 1892 was of the opinion that China, in her chain of coastal and river forts, was still invoking the spirit of the Great Wall.[95]

In other ways the traditional element appeared in China's prewar naval situation. The traditional Yangtze water force in 1893 was warned against living ashore and taking its ease. There had been cutbacks in the traditional coastal water forces, but they had not been replaced by modern fleets.[96] Harbor blocking was still done in the old way. The Ningpo authorities in 1894, in the midst of the crisis, drove piles and sank stone-filled junks, as did the officials in the Foochow approaches after an ominous "courtesy visit" of three Japanese ships on June 2, 1894. The Foochow authorities evidently intended to allow no more of the naval infiltration which the French practiced in the weeks preceding the destruction of the dockyard in 1884.[97]

But the closing of harbors was not done only with the ancient paraphernalia. Ningpo also prepared torpedoes. The Shanghai defenses were sown with mines (so poorly mapped, to be sure, that many innocent junkmen were blown to bits before the mines could be removed by the intrepid customs service after the war).[98] Perhaps the master harbor-blocker was Chang Chih-tung. As early as 1886 he called for the permanent sealing off of Canton, despite the angry objections of foreign consuls. He put down massive blocks of stone and screw piles, leaving only a narrow channel, and thus brought on with these peacetime efforts many foreign epithets, which may be summarized in the British comment that they were "absurd."[99]

Perhaps the most "modern" application of the old close-the-harbors-and-wait formula was made at Shanghai. There the major defense was international law. Although the Kiangnan arsenal continued to make and ship its products, Liu K'un-i attempted to have Shanghai classified by international accord as a civilian place, outside the military sphere. Trade-hungry foreign officials supported the governor-general in this. If trade could continue, let China have its wars — elsewhere. Liu was successful in arranging for the isolation of Shanghai, but he took the precaution, nonetheless, of dumping stones in the Woosung channel.[100]

The variety of coastal defense preparations signified the continuing political fragmentation of the empire, and the continuing vitality of the traditional strategic concepts. At times, however, a more modern strategic idea was manifested in the prewar years. Captain Lang, Li Hung-chang's naval trainer, took Li's ships on flag-showing trips to the South Seas in the interwar period. And, after the Japanese three-ship "courtesy visit" to Foochow in June 1894, the governor-general there did not content himself with dumping stones into the river. He also urged the Tsungli Yamen to send six Chinese warships to Japan on a similar "courteous" visit.[101]

Li Hung-chang best exemplified a modern appreciation of the

diplomatic utility of a well-armed fleet in full movement. In 1886 he sent the just-delivered *Chen Yüan* and *Ting Yüan* to Korea, where the British were in occupation of Port Hamilton; in 1891, he sent his six best warships to Japan on a visit which happened to coincide with the growing tension between the two countries over Korea.[102]

During these years, the West was also uncertain about naval strategy. Even in Britain, the navy suffered a decline in prestige, and emphasis was laid on land preparations. Britain's heavy coastal forts, "Palmerston's follies," were solid evidence of the popularity of the "brick and mortar school" of national defense. The "blue-water school," not surprisingly made up of Royal Navy men, began a slow self-assertion after the Anglo-French crisis of the mid 1880's. British naval authorities (along with Mahan in America) stressed the idea that an enemy with command of the sea need not invade England; he could starve her out. England held a sharp debate at the end of the century, with land-military men insisting that ironclads were liable to run into each other or be dispersed by storms, and calling for a powerful army to defend the shores of home.[103]

The "science" of naval strategy was being remade by the impacts of steam, steel, and shell. As late as 1905, boarding stations and sword-and-cutlass drills were standard in British men-of-war. Such exercises bespoke a lingering attachment to the tactical idea of the melée and the use of the ram, rather than a full awareness of the potency of big naval guns. It is well known that changes in weapons-systems are attended by ardent strategic debate.

Still, it was not merely true that China's leaders were having only those conceptual uncertainties of their foreign naval mentors. There was after all a "Chinese" element in China. There was no real national debate there; rather, there were individual defensive arrangements variously manifesting old and new ideas, and incorporating patchwork separate fleets still showing the sails of many war junks.[104] If there was any instance of a "national policy," it was in the decision to refurbish the Summer Palace.

VIII

NAVAL TRAINING, 1885–1894

In the decade between the Sino-French and Sino-Japanese wars, there was an increase in Chinese official interest in naval training. In the early 1890's, there were training academies at Foochow, Canton, Nanking, Tientsin, and Weihaiwei — and even at Peking, if the K'un-ming Academy may properly be called a naval training establishment.[1]

The Foochow dockyard naval academy clearly lost its primacy. In 1885, dockyard superintendent P'ei Yin-sen, in a significant move, sought to increase the amount of sea time required of cadets in training.[2] Right after the Sino-French War there came another conservative attack on the academy, to the effect that it was employing too many men and wasting money, partly in the form of excessively high salaries paid to returned student-engineers. P'ei denied that anyone was being overpaid, adding that Tso Tsungt'ang had stipulated the foreign pay scale for returned students.[3] On the other hand, Li Hung-chang still cooperated with the academy in joint overseas training missions, and in April 1886, after his urging of it, a third Foochow mission departed for Europe, numbering twenty-four Foochow academy graduates and nine from Li's Tientsin establishment. About half of the trainees were in navigation, and after appropriate training in England — occupying three years and including a world cruise — these men returned. Interestingly, most of the remainder, construction or engineering graduates, took advanced training in fields outside their original specialization, such as international law or bridge construction.[4]

This third mission so depleted the Foochow navigation school roster that only seven remained. Consequently P'ei discontinued the maintenance of his training ship, proposing to send his few cadets for a tour in Li Hung-chang's *Wei Yüan*, and putting his own trainer into a Foochow-Formosa transport run for the time being.[5] It was planned to send another mission to Europe in 1894, but the war with Japan intervened.[6]

The Foochow academy was sporadically in operation in the 1890's. During active periods, Foochow graduates assisted the foreign instructional staff. This situation silenced some earlier complaints about the lack of opportunity for official employment. But by 1896 the discouragement of the graduates on this score was serious enough to elicit comment from the Tsungli Yamen. In 1900, foreign opinion was that the Foochow schools "had been practically discontinued for some years." [7]

At Canton, there had been for some time a school for training in a miscellany of foreign skills. In 1880 Governor-General Chang Shu-sheng imported two Canton gentry brothers who had been teaching in the Foochow schools. When Chang Chih-tung succeeded Chang Shu-sheng in 1884, he found fifty students bonded to remain for a five-year Western curriculum, with a rigorous schedule. After the Sino-French War, Chang changed the school into what was primarily a naval academy, and brought in the much-sought Wu Chung-hsiang from Foochow, P'ei Yin-sen having in the meantime managed to get Wu back from Li Hung-chang. Wu took fifty students from the Foochow school to Canton — a real depletion of the Foochow roster. The Canton Shui-lu hsüeh-t'ang (navy and army school) had a curriculum patterned on that of the Foochow academy, although it called for six years of study, rather than five; that is, three years of theory and three at sea, which is reminiscent of P'ei Yin-sen's desire to increase the amount of sea time in the Foochow curriculum. In 1889, Chang Chih-tung observed that only thirty-eight of the seventy students who transferred from the original Canton technical school passed the qualifying examinations set for the Canton naval academy. The senior class of deck officers then numbered only fourteen persons. In 1889, thirty-seven Foochow navigation students transferred to the Canton academy, and were shortly joined by twenty more from Tientsin, some going into the land-military branch of the Canton academy.[8]

In 1889 Chang Chih-tung was transferred to Wuchang as governor-general of Hunan and Hupeh. After this departure of the school's mentor, it was observed at Canton that the "great works was to some extent checked." [9] In 1891 some twenty-five students were enrolled, under four Chinese and two English instructors. Contemporary observers suggest that the school concentrated on torpedo-boat training. The school was losing about 10,000 taels per year. But by 1893, Governor-General T'ang Chung-lin, who had once been associated with the Foochow dockyard, reportedly cut back the Canton academy roster to ninety students, and later to thirty.[10] Evidently after Chang's departure the school had a fitful career, and during the governorship of the reactionary Kang-i (1892–1894), the school was once entirely closed, and the Canton fleet idled.[11]

At Nanking in 1889 Tseng Kuo-ch'uan established a naval academy, at the urging of Kuei Sung-ch'ing, of the Kiangnan Defense Bureau. The Nanking academy was patterned on the Tientsin academy of Li Hung-chang. But Tseng died shortly after the 120-student school was opened, and Liu K'un-i, who followed Tseng as Liang-Kiang governor-general, had difficulties. Financial troubles forced a cutback. Further, Liu in 1891 experienced another vexation. By order of the Navy Board in Peking, his students were supposed to go to the Peiyang fleet for shipboard training. But Li Hung-chang refused to take any Nanking students, saying that he had no room. Liu thus dropped his forty students and four instructors, and closed his torpedo factory. He said that when there were more ships (a futile hope, then), he would reopen his academy.[12] In 1894 an English instructor at the Nanking academy, which had reopened, observed that the test papers of his cadets were as good as those of English naval cadets. The first class did not graduate, however, until after the war with Japan. After the turn of the century, it was said about the Nanking naval students that there was among them a "pretty general endeavor to evade the government service, and the grievances of which they complain are in keeping with what is known generally of official management in China." [13]

During the interim between the wars with France and Japan, Li Hung-chang reorganized his training activities. In 1888, he placed all of his naval activities under a Tsung-li Shui-shih Ying-wu-ch'u, or general office of naval affairs, responsible to the northern commissioner. His most important naval training center was still the Tientsin naval academy, although he had established in 1885 a school in Tientsin for the training of land military men, partly for maritime defense (the Wu-pei Hsüeh-t'ang). Port Arthur had a school for mine and torpedo men. At Liu Kung Tao, in Weihaiwei harbor, there was a naval school under Admiral Ting

Ju-ch'ang, the Hai-chün Hsüeh-t'ang, mainly for in-service refresher courses, although the school did enroll some new recruits.[14] One of the instructors at Weihaiwei was an American, Philo McGiffen, an Annapolis graduate who later served in the naval war with Japan. Naval training was also carried on in torpedo and mine installations at Taku, Shanhaikuan, Pei-t'ang, and Weihaiwei.[15]

Lang, now on his second China tour, supervised Li's naval training system until 1890. Lang had been reluctant to return, but Hart had prevailed over his grievances, which had accumulated during his first period of service with Li Hung-chang, including rude treatment from people like Chang P'ei-lun and the fact that his first commission had come only from Li, rather than from Peking. For his second entry into Li's service, Lang insisted that he be given an imperial commission, that the training system be entirely British, that he bring certain aides at stipulated salaries, and that he have sole charge of Li's fleet organization and naval yards. Shortly after his return in March 1886, he was made admiral by imperial decree, and then was commissioned by Li Hung-chang as Instructor to the Peiyang fleet — which of course already had an admiral, Ting Ju-ch'ang. Lang smarted over this anomaly, but Hart, still holding grand views, persuaded him to stay. Lang did so, and threw himself into his work with great vigor and considerable achievement.[16]

The Tientsin naval academy was directly under the Tientsin taotai. In 1888, the navigation branch, called the Executive Branch, was under Yen Tsung-kwang (Yen Fu), former student at Foochow and Greenwich. The Engineering Branch was directed by two English professors. One of these foreigners started a torpedo department, with complete facilities for instruction in this "sine qua non of modern naval warfare." [17]

The preamble to the section in Li Hung-chang's 1888 naval regulations on examinations stressed the importance of naval academies in the West, where a naval career was given much honor. The Peiyang fleet was fairly large, but "calculating that each student needs at least ten years of training, and that about fifty percent of them drop out along the way [for personal reasons, cowardice, etc.], we can see the need for widely establishing schools and encouraging students to do energetic work." [18]

Li's cadets had to be healthy (with good teeth and without

tuberculosis) and to be from fourteen to seventeen years of age on entry. They had to be able to read the *Three Character Classic* as another prerequisite. Each had to have a parental guarantee binding him to the school. Success in a preliminary examination would lead to a quarter's study of English, after which there would be another weeding out. The best students would be retained as naval officer cadets, ready to enter on formal naval training.[19]

Some students came from other schools in Li's training system, but most were Tientsin boys from scholarly homes. In 1888 the taotai appealed to the ambitious with a flyer reporting that thirty cadets who had graduated from Li's Tientsin academy between 1881 and 1888 were currently getting "substantial salaries" and "substantial promotions." In 1888, another nine students graduated. Li's naval academy was still a small one.[20]

The curriculum established in the 1888 regulations covered six years and nine months, of which twenty-seven months were to be spent afloat in training ships. The courses were like those at the Foochow academy, and there was also careful provision for regular examinations. Graduates were to be designated expectant *ch'ien-tsung* — approximately, sub-lieutenants. Here began the naval career as such.[21]

It took time for Li's training to develop. In 1893, Li advised the Navy Board that thirty-five men had just been given a final examination by Li himself, and that only two thirds of them had been passed; the rest were sent home.[22] Foreigners observed that too much time was spent on elementary mathematics, taught by men who were competent to present much more advanced material. Comments made during the war with Japan suggest that coastal mapping was not very far advanced.[23]

The examination system included in-service tests for captains and their aides, who were required to write essays annually on naval topics, for ranking and publication. Rewards or punishments were determined in part by the results of these tests. Li still had to face the fact that his trainees tended to prefer identification with the civil service to identification with the naval service. In 1888, when mathematics was admitted as an allowable subject in the civil service examinations, Li got permission to send some of his academy graduates to the Tsungli Yamen to be examined for the *chü-jen* degree. The ancient civil service must have been a powerful lure, particularly for Li's officer cadets. Li's system also included elaborate provisions for the training of enlisted men, but presumably these institutional tensions were not felt at this level as much as they were among China's future naval leaders, and so this account will emphasize the training of naval officers.[24]

Rewards and punishments were carefully provided for in Li's 1888 naval regulations. A system of reviews culminated in triennial reviews of the entire fleet by the president of the Navy Board (who was required to go to sea in person for these grand reviews). The reviews gave an occasion for the dispensing of rewards or punishments. Even dockyard workers, or persons making useful translations of Western works, were to be included in these periodic dispensations, as were Navy Board people and officials in the northern commissioner's shore establishments. Significantly, it was stipulated that all persons decorated in a triennial inspection were to be ineligible for decoration by provincial officials; this provision was apparently designed to ensure that the eyes of China's naval officers would be fixed expectantly on Peiyang or Peking naval authorities, rather than on civil provincial officials, many of them in the south, where many of Li's naval captains were trained. In wartime, the northern commissioner could make promotions without regard to the basic three-year-in-one-grade intervals which otherwise underlay the system of merits and advancement. Throughout the detailed regulations governing advancement, we may detect a concern with giving incentive to naval officers to become "professionals" in their chosen new field of endeavor.[25]

The preamble to the part of the 1888 regulations devoted to promotions dwelt on British precedent, and the text has a Western look. Officers were divided into three categories – "fighting officers," "engineer officers," and "petty officers" – and each category had its own line of promotion. The "fighting officers" were divided into groups. First came the "outer-seas" class, made up of officers assigned to deep-water fighting ships. Next came the "outer-seas ordinary-vessel" class, whose officers were in harbor defense, transport, or training assignments. Third was the "inner-waters" class, for officers on ships so classified, or in dockyards, schools, or machine shops ashore. Different salary rates were assigned to these three classes of deck or line officers, and service time accumulated in one class was not freely interchangeable with time accumulated in the others. Two years in "inner-waters" berths could count for only one unit of seniority in "outer-seas" ships, and at that only for a year in "outer-seas ordinary-vessels," rather than for a year in a high-seas fighting ship. In general, all berths were to be filled by candidates from the rank next below, with priority given to men from the fighting ships. For all promotions from the rank of senior lieutenant upward, a memorial from the northern commissioner to the throne was stipulated. For promotion to the rank of senior post captain, only three years in fighting ships in the grade next below would qualify a candidate.

There were some interesting special arrangements. One was for the officer who found no empty berth in the rank above his own, who could then be promoted to other provincial assignments, even if only as an expectant; that is, as an official with a certain rank waiting for an opening. The regulations observed that in the West a naval officer whose naval advance was thus temporarily blocked was given a salary increase, but China could not do this. On the other hand, in the opposite situation where no suitable candidate could be found for a promotion, then a "person of merit" might be taken in on probation to fill the berth, or the incumbent might be kept on for another tour, at full salary.[26]

Thus the traffic might move out or in. A naval officer might become unwilling to continue in his new career if a civil appointment of appropriate rank became a possibility; he might then leave the navy, to be later "borrowed" back again by the navy, at the right rank and pay, from a kind of naval reserve. Thus a man choosing the navy need not entirely forswear all hope of identification with the honored civil service. On the other hand, a provincial official could submit his qualifications to the northern commissioner, who might then recommend him for naval service to the admiral (it was not the admiral who advised the northern commissioner in such cases). Such "meritorious" persons, after a three-year probation at reduced pay, might be absorbed into the naval hierarchy. Perhaps not many civilian officials would try for this dubious honor, but the arrangement did open the door to certain men who could be useful to Li Hung-chang. Thus southern-trained captains, outside of Li's own Peiyang promotion system, might enter Li's service. The arrangement also opened the door to such a man as Admiral Ting Ju-ch'ang, whose induction as admiral without *naval* merit (he was an ex-Anhwei army man, but one of Li's "own") made it possible for Li to be independent of the southern schools in selecting an admiral for the Peiyang fleet.

That the intention was to interlink the more honorific civil service with the unsung naval service is further shown by a provision in the 1888 Peiyang regulations that naval officers ashore were to wear the dress uniform of their civilian opposite numbers.[27]

The regulations also included a section dealing with punishments. For serious peacetime offenses, officers might be demoted but kept in their posts for self-redemption (at half-pay); they might also be separated from the service. For less serious offenses they were fined. Offenses of enlisted men in peacetime were usually punished with a beating. Wartime punishments were more stringent. For the most serious omissions or commissions in battle, punishments were meted out by the admiral, guided by a section on wartime land military discipline in the 1726 edition of the dynastic statutes, from which twenty-six articles deemed most pertinent to naval situations had been taken. Of the twenty-six, eighteen called for the death penalty, and of these, ten dealt with battle situations. Most of them apply reasonably to any military body engaged with the enemy; thus, for desertion, telling of secrets, cowardice, and fomenting mutiny, death was indicated. Some of the clauses were anachronistic, for example, those enjoining that all bows, arrows, quivers, knives and such battle issue should be preserved by the recipient. That this ancient code was lifted verbatim from the past and wedged into a set of naval regulations carefully written for a modern fleet is perhaps because in such weighty matters, tradition speaks most clearly.[28]

But the code is also interesting for what it omits. The primary role of the throne in matters of discipline was assumed, and so not mentioned. Beyond that, there was no provision for appeal, or for the regular constitution of a body of naval officers to investigate charges and technical evidence, a body which, in a highly technical situation, might at least balance the moral variables involved in the failure of an officer to do his duty or complete his assigned task. Only one stipulation, that the captain involved and the admiral were to conduct inquiries into equipment damage, suggests anything like a court-martial system. Captains were given considerable discretion in some matters, and all punishments were to be reported quarterly by the admiral to the northern commissioner, the provincial treasury (in matters involving pay), and the governor-general's military staff. Records of demotion were sent by the northern commissioner to the Navy Board. Short of the throne, the northern commissioner was the ultimate court. To what extent this traditional system of judgment was a discouragement to highly-trained professional naval officers, aware of the possible inadequacy of judgment by a single nonexpert given to a Confucian moral bias and open to many suggestions by unnamed persons, can only be guessed.

Pay is a form of reward, and Li's 1888 regulations were detailed in this respect. Following Western precedent, pay was divided into two categories. Four tenths of each compensation was called personal pay; six tenths was called ship or command pay. This new system was designed to absorb all older emoluments, such as anti-squeeze pay. The two-part system was flexible. Temporary or acting officers got only half of the personal pay appropriate to their rank, but full ship pay. Men assigned to temporary shore billets were given half of their personal pay, but none of the command pay. Various combinations of this kind were made. A table of compensation was included. An admiral's personal pay was 3360 taels and his command pay 5040 taels, for a total of 8400 taels per annum. For a senior post captain, the figures were 1584 and 2376 respectively; the lowest-ranking officer drew respectively 96 and 144 taels per year. If the system was flexible, it also put a premium on the actual performance of naval duty, rather than on the mere inactive or empty holding of a given rank.

Economy was desired. In the regulations Li demonstrated how savings were needed. He totaled a wage-and-salary bill of 669,100 taels per annum for the 1888 fleet, excluding the fleet engineer officer and the all-fleet ordnance inspector, to which posts no substantive appointments had then been made. The admiral's pay had been reduced by 1200 annually, taken from his personal pay; surely other officers had been subjected to the same rate and kind of cut. Already in 1888 Li was keeping four of his six Armstrong gunboats in "mothballs," and officers from these ships were sent to the ironclads. It is likely that they did not gain by the transfer into "acting" capacities. Economy was the rule.[29]

On the other hand, an authoritative British observer of the Sino-Japanese War wrote that Chinese crews were at half-strength, yet pay for full complements was being drawn.[30]

Prewar comments on Li's navy are interesting. A Shanghai paper in 1886 recorded the numerous movements of the Peiyang fleet, with its "powerful ironclads [and] swift torpedo cruisers." Two of the ships had wintered in Korea, where their "gallant commanders, courteous officers, and well-behaved crews have always been great favorites." Since "Admiral Lang" had "taken charge," German instructors were "rapidly being retired" — or so reported the American Minister Denby, who also cited the 1886 news dispatch mentioned above. It was said that "if the people on board the Peiyang squadron were called upon to show their teeth to an enemy they would render a different account of themselves than the unfortunate crew did at Pagoda anchorage [the Ma-wei battle of August 1884] . . . There can hardly be a doubt now that the Peiyang squadron alone is quite capable of coping single-handed with any other fleet at present stationed in East Asiatic waters." [31]

Military foreigners also made favorable comments. G. A. Ballard, who was a vice-admiral in the Royal Navy when he wrote his book on the importance of the sea in the political history of Japan, later recorded that Li's fleet in the 1890's was in "serviceable condition," with "excellent discipline" and "sound" training, and stores and equipment "up to establishment" both ashore and afloat. Externally, the ships were "smart and clean," and internally, in "good working order." Constant cruising had kept the crews alert. "In all respects," he recalled, "the fleet represented a force to be reckoned with at its face value." [32]

Chinese conservatives still harped on the corrupting influences of foreign training.[33] Other foreign reporters made reports that suggest that there was room for improvement. In 1888 the British consul at Foochow, E. H. Parker, called on Admiral Ting's ships there, as they returned from a cruise to Singapore. Parker, in a consular sampan pulled by uniformed boatmen, asked to see the admiral (when at last he had found the flagship), but the officer of the deck was at a loss as to "which Admiral" was wanted; in any event, neither Lang nor Ting was then aboard. The officer then desired to make the correct gun-salute to Parker, despite Parker's objection that he was not in the right uniform; still, the Chinese officer consulted a manual and Parker slowly drew off in his gig (out of the line of possible fire!) to allow time. Nothing happened. The meticulous Lang saw to it that the salute was duly discharged the next afternoon.[34] Protocol is closely related to discipline.

The matter of "which Admiral" was no joke to "Admiral" Lang. In fact, the problem led to Lang's resignation. The exact date of the last trouble is obscure, although the resignation came in August 1890. On one of the southern cruises of the Peiyang fleet in the late 1880's, Ting left his flagship for a side trip to Hong Kong. In his absence, Lang flew his own admiral's pennant, but Liu Pu-ch'an, the captain of the flagship, who held that he was the senior officer present, had Lang's flag hauled down and his own sent aloft. Lang was affronted, citing his rank as admiral by imperial commission. Liu did not have so high a rank. But Li Hung-chang upheld Liu Pu-ch'an when the fracas was brought to his attention, and Lang angrily resigned.[35]

Lang had taken his commission seriously. Tyler said that Lang had an authority "in ambiguous Chinese form which might mean anything from second-in-command to adviser with rank of Admiral." Lang believed himself to be second-in-command, after Ting; Ting regarded him as an adviser with rank of admiral.[36] The Chinese view of foreign admirals — indeed, of admirals as such — was illustrated by Chang Chih-tung in 1895, when he tried to get Lang back to China for the third time, to train Chang's fleet. He wired to the Tsungli Yamen suggesting the title of admiral as a lure to Lang; it was a title highly regarded by Englishmen, Chang said, but not by Chinese.[37]

The flag incident just discussed reveals other tensions in the Peiyang fleet. Lin T'ai-tseng, a Fukienese captain in Li Hung-chang's service, had supported Hart's endeavors to have Lang recalled to China in 1886. But on his return, Lang had proved to be a strict disciplinarian, and so had become unpopular, particularly with the Foochow academy officers, whose training was supposedly already complete. Inevitably, some of the resentments of the southerners came to rest on Li Hung-chang himself, who after all had hired Lang, and was keeping him on. Liu Pu-ch'an was a member of the southern clique, and his flag-switch may have been a signal rigged to attract the attention of Li Hung-chang, a sign of discontent. Admiral Ting though was an Anhwei man, isolated from the southern modern-trained group of officers; his small prestige was evidently no deterrent to Liu's irritation in the affair of the flags.[38]

Lang's own summary of his experience with Li Hung-chang, although hardly free of rancor, is illuminating. Of his frustrations, he wrote (in the third person):

Some of his critics have suggested that he wanted to get everything into his own hands, and was apt to forget that while he could command a squadron, he had no experience of office work ashore and of civil administration. He irked at the obstacles thrown in his path by ignorant and envious men; he felt that among the Chinese no one except the Viceroy [Li Hung-chang] took any real interest in the Navy, while the Viceroy himself was jealous of anyone interfering with it; he found it at times a heart-breaking matter to obtain proper supplies, while everything that was sanctioned was done as if it were conferring a very great favor.[39]

It was a very un-British situation.

China's loss of Lang in 1890 was important. An immediate result was the exclusion of Chinese students from British naval schools. Further, there is evidence that training went into a decline after his departure. In July 1891, the Peiyang fleet visited Yokohama, hardly with casual intent. The Stettin-built sister battleships *Ting* and *Chen* excited no small attention in Japanese naval circles. Togo of the Japanese fleet went over the flagship *Ting Yüan* with keen curiosity. But, to the astonishment of Admiral Ting, the Japanese visitor uttered no praise of the ship. To Togo, then commander of the Yokohama naval base, the crew lacked discipline; the guns were not clean, and were furthermore festooned with laundry. Togo was not impressed with a navy that treated its weapons in such a fashion.[40] Lang would never have permitted such laxity.

Admiral Ting was no professional naval man, and he was, furthermore, the first to admit it. Tyler recounted an episode in which Ting rebuked a foreign "expert" who had just ruined an expensive torpedo as follows: "The loss of a torpedo does not matter much, for unfortunately I see little chance of using them; but what I do not like about this affair is your pretense to be an expert. Here I am Admiral of the Fleet. Do I pretend? Do I assume to know anything about a ship or navigation? You know I do not; so take an example from me and pretend no more."[41]

The problem of making the navy a truly professional service was not eased under such leadership. E. H. Parker was a close friend of Teng Shih-ch'ang, one of Li Hung-chang's Foochow-trained captains. Parker spoke highly of Teng. His ship, the *Yang Wei*, was always clean, and Teng did not squeeze on oil and paint. His many attributes did not include aping foreigners; i.e., sprawling in chairs, puffing on cigars, bursting into guffaws, or starting fancy conversations. Teng was hard-working, ambitious, and a patriot. Parker felt that Teng had to a high degree "the mathematical and the naval capacity." Yet it was hard for Teng to use his capacity, and Parker concluded: "I do not quite know the relations which subsisted between Admiral Ting and Captain Teng, but I do know that the gallant Admiral, although a brave man, was grossly incompetent; and I am satisfied that Captain Teng spent many bitter hours in reflecting on the hopelessness of his aspirations." [42]

One observer put the matter this way: both the Chinese and the Japanese navies were trained by the British, but only the Japanese listened.[43] The comment is a misstatement; it overlooks the differing institutional aspects of training Chinese and Japanese. Not even Li Hung-chang could make the navy into a respected profession or career in China. A foreigner put the matter in these words, speaking of China's new naval officers: "They were outsiders from the Chinese official point of view, but had to be tolerated because the exigencies of coast defense demanded the Navy." [44] The best-trained men in Li's fleet were further isolated by their southernness, and they were handicapped by poor leadership and an outmoded fleet. But even the most modern ships would not, in themselves, have constituted a modern navy as an institution which could have been accepted in China.

IX

DISASTER IN THE NORTH: NAVAL ASPECTS OF THE SINO-JAPANESE WAR, 1894–1895

Japanese interest in Korea long predated the Sino-Japanese War. We may trace that interest back to Hideyoshi, who invaded the peninsula at the end of the sixteenth century. Japanese once again became interested almost immediately after the Meiji Restoration of 1868, which induced many tensions within Japan. The expedition to Formosa in 1874 was in part engineered by the Japanese oligarchs as an alternative to a proposed expedition to Korea. Japan used force to induce Korea to sign the treaty of Kianghwa of 1876, in which Korea was described as an independent entity. Thus began the process by which Japan sought to substitute her own influence in the peninsula for that of China, to which Korea was a tributary.

In the early 1880's, while China was increasingly absorbed with French aggression in Annam, Japan took advantage of disturbances in Korea caused by pro-Japanese elements to send troops to Korea. We have seen that Li Hung-chang, in withholding his fleet from the relief of Formosa in 1884, argued that the Korean problem could not be ignored. The Tientsin Convention of 1885 between Li and Ito in effect made Korea a protectorate of both China and Japan. China's concession to Japan at this time reflected the facts that China was weak and her war with France had not yet been concluded. Li was not entirely incorrect when he said that Japan was working hand-in-glove with France. After 1885, Li relied on his agent in Korea, Yüan Shih-k'ai; Japan, on her part, continued to try to encourage pro-Japanese elements, and to create a situation in which both China and Japan, in accordance with the Tientsin Convention, would send troops to Korea. In 1894, a pro-Japanese Korean was assassinated in Shanghai; in the same year a rebellion broke out in Korea, led by reactionary pro-Chinese forces, the so-called Tonghaks. Japan actually abetted the Tonghaks in order to induce China to send troops to Korea, thus setting the stage for a showdown. Although Li Hung-chang was extremely reluctant to enter a conflict, these were the raw materials from which the conflict was built.[1]

The war ended in defeat for China — and the loss of Korea, Formosa, and a great indemnity as well. The defeat ended the influence of Li Hung-chang, and was a blow to the prestige of the dynasty that it could not sustain, since Japan, the "dwarfs," were the victors. Japan was encouraged to further aggression on the mainland, with results of epochal importance for the history of the twentieth century. China's defeat is one of the most important in history. Yet, if she had defeated Japan at sea, Japan's thrust would have been totally frustrated. This chapter will examine the naval aspects of the Sino-Japanese War of 1894–1895.

If we make a comparison between the fleets of China and Japan, we may conclude that China might well have won the war at sea. By 1894, the Japanese fleet totaled thirty-two warships and twenty-three torpedo boats, manned by 13,928 men. Some of her ships were obsolete, but of the better ones, ten had been built in British yards and two in French. The 4277-ton *Matsushima* was built in France in 1890, and the *Yoshino*, 4150 tons, was launched by Armstrong's in 1893. The *Yoshino* did twenty-three knots on her trials, and this ship (which Li Hung-chang might have purchased) was known as the fastest ship in the world.[2] The Japanese-built steel *Hashidate* was built at Yokosuka in 1891, and was similar to the latest French types in her 4277-ton class. There were other Japanese building yards at Sasebo, Kure, and Kobe.[3]

Japanese naval training had kept pace with her naval growth. Satsuma navy men had gone overseas since the 1860's, and Annapolis had graduated two Japanese annually since 1870. At home in Japan, training had long been directed by Admiral Archibald Douglas of the Royal Navy, with over fifty French and British aides.[4]

Perhaps the greatest contrast between the navies of China and Japan in the 1890's lay in the fact that Japan's fleet was unified, whereas China still had the familiar fourfold division into the Peiyang, Nanyang, Fukien, and Kwangtung fleets. In 1894, these four fleets had some sixty-five large ships, with about forty-three torpedo boats.⁵ The strongest fleet was the Peiyang fleet of Li Hung-chang. This single fleet about equaled that of Japan. The Kwangtung fleet was the weakest.

The principal provincial figure involved in the Sino-Japanese war, thus, was Li Hung-chang, who had long dominated China's diplomatic relations. The Navy Board played only a subordinate role. One edict during the war sent to Li was addressed to him as the general supervisor of the navy; he often received direct edicts which bypassed the Navy Board. But the court did not use him as the exclusive transmitter of its wartime orders; others of equal or lesser rank received direct instructions and submitted their own reports.⁶ The Grand Council, of the several agencies in the capital, was most involved in the evolution of policy.⁷

There was some coordination of China's fleets. On July 18, 1894, Governor Shao Yu-lien of Taiwan asked the Grand Council for two Nanyang ships, and got them. But Li Hung-chang would not help him.⁸ Li at the time wanted southern help himself. He did get some, although it was inadvertent and mainly from Kwangtung. The *Kwang Ping*, *Kwang Chia*, and *Kwang I* were on joint north-south naval maneuvers in the summer of 1894, and tarried long enough to be unable to avoid action. Furthermore, a Nanyang ship, the *Ts'ao Chiang*, came north on an unrelated mission at the crucial time, and was caught in the war. Although the 1000-ton *Kwang Ping*, a steel torpedo cruiser, had been built at the Foochow dockyard as recently as 1891, these reluctant helpers had little effect on the outcome.⁹

Still, Li's own fleet outnumbered even the British fleet in those waters, and the general opinion of Westerners favored him over Japan.¹⁰ The Japanese themselves were not confident. There had been much bitterness in the new Diet in the 1890's over foreign policy, and many Japanese were surprised at their victory over China.

By July 1894, both China and Japan had troops in Korea. Japan was unwilling to withdraw after the suppression of the Tonghaks, however, and demanded Chinese cooperation in the reorganization of the Korean government. China would not agree. Li Hung-chang did not want to send more troops, as this would risk war; on the other hand, if he did not send more men, he would have to rely on Western mediation in the dispute, and this was not certain either. Li ordered Admiral Ting to keep his men out of incidents ashore in Korea; on July 1 he even took his ships out of Korean waters.[11] This settled nothing.

Li reluctantly decided to send more troops to Korea. On July 16, 8000 Chinese troops were landed from a convoy of eleven rented steamers. Later he sent more troops, in three ships — one of them being the *Kao Sheng*, or *Kowhsing*, under naval protection. On the 23rd of July, Japan seized the Korean king, and put in as regent a man who on the 27th declared war on China.

By that time, however, China and Japan had had their first naval engagement. This took place on July 25, and was won by Japan. The details and sequel of this encounter, fought in the vicinity of Feng-tao, or Baker Island, off the mouth of the Han River, are instructive.

When the Japanese learned that Li was sending three more troopships to Korea (and we have been told that spies in Li Hung-chang's Tientsin establishment told them of it, as mentioned in an earlier chapter),[12] they sent a naval detachment, their so-called Flying Squadron, consisting of the *Akitsushima, Yoshino, Naniwa*, and *Takachiho*, to intercept the convoy. The Chinese ships covering the convoy were the *Chi Yüan, Wei Yüan, Kwang I*, and *Ts'ao Chiang*. The first three Chinese warships and two of the troopships arrived at Asan on July 23, and the troops were discharged on the 24th. The *Kowhsing*, protected by the small, Shanghai-built *Ts'ao Chiang* (built in 1869) was still en route.

On the evening of July 24, the convoy commander, Fang Pai-ch'ien of the *Chi Yüan*, sent the *Wei Yüan* back to China. He took the *Chi Yüan* and *Kwang I* to sea shortly thereafter, either to return to China or to ensure the arrival of the *Kowhsing*. Early on July 25 the *Chi Yüan* and *Kwang I* encountered the *Yoshino, Naniwa*, and *Akitsushima* near Feng-tao.[13]

China's two warships were no match for their Japanese opponents. The 600-ton *Kwang I* was not formidable, and although the *Chi Yüan* was a German-built unarmored cruiser of 2355 tons, with two eight-inch Krupps in her main battery, she was outclassed by each of the three Japanese ships which found her. Admiral Ting had earlier asked to have larger ships sent out, but Liu Pu-ch'an had made his telegram look like a demand for belligerent action, and so Li Hung-chang had kept the protective force as inoffensive as possible.[14]

The *Chi Yüan* was put to flight in the ensuing battle, and the *Kwang I* beached and burned. The *Chi Yüan* was seen from the *Kowhsing*, which was still inbound with troops aboard; according to the *Kowhsing* report, the *Chi Yüan* was fleeing for Port Arthur, showing a white flag and a Japanese one, with the swift *Yoshino* in hot pursuit.[15] The *Kowhsing* herself was shortly thereafter sunk (after a troop mutiny and abandonment of the ship), and her escort, the *Ts'ao Chiang*, was captured. The loss of about 1000 troops in the *Kowhsing* fiasco was equivalent to the loss of a major land battle, and General Yeh Chih-ch'ao, for whom the reinforcements were intended, had to withdraw from Asan. The *Chi Yüan* limped into Port Arthur for repairs. The episode led to a storm of controversy and doubt about the future.[16]

In response to the Feng-tao defeat, Admiral Ting and Li Hung-chang worked out a strategy, which was to defend China's coasts between Weihaiwei and the mouth of the Yalu River. Naval cruising was to be confined within a line drawn between these two points. This strategy meant abandoning the hard-pressed General Yeh in the Asan area, and leaving the coasts of Korea, west as well as east, open to Japanese troop landings. Ting and Li also talked of buying more ships, but they had nonetheless put a strategic limitation on the use of the Peiyang fleet which Yi-sun, the sixteenth-century Korean admiral who cut the sea communications of the invading Hideyoshi, would never have accepted for himself.[17]

Within these limits, Admiral Ting late in July and early in August sallied forth from Weihaiwei or Port Arthur at least three times. China declared war on Japan on August 1, 1894. Philo McGiffen, serving in the battleship *Chen Yüan*, expected fighting, and hoped Ting would find and "sink the dogs," although he understood that "at the last moment" there came a "direct cable from the Tsungli Yamen" forbidding Ting to go to Chemulpo. Thus the "line" was made known to McGiffen. He said the *Chen Yüan* was a cheerful ship, tidily cleared for action, expecting no quarter and proposing to give none.[18]

On August 2, the Grand Council ordered Ting to aid General Yeh (which suggests that it was Li Hung-chang who drew the Weihaiwei-Yalu River line, rather than Peking, or else, if McGiffen's account is correct, that there was much inconsistency in Peking). The next day Peking wanted to know if Ting was hiding somewhere. There had been complaints about the admiral; a replacement, it was said, might be necessary.[19] Li Hung-chang promptly replied, giving arguments for not going to the relief of General Yeh. A near approach to the Korean coast (Li took his argument from Admiral Ting) would expose China's ships to mine fields and other dangers, while staying in open water would give China's heavier ships a chance to defeat the faster-firing Japanese. The Peiyang fleet had only seven reliable ships, he said; these were the *Ting* and *Chen Yüan, Lai Yüan, Chih Yüan, Chi Yüan*, and the two homophonically designated *Ching Yüan*. Admiral Ting would "watch the door to the Peiyang" closely; as for Yeh, something would be done.[20]

But when Li heard through spies that enemy ships were en route to the Yalu to harass General Yeh, he did not recommend any action. When the emperor ordered all Chinese ships to go there, Li replied that he had already issued such an order.[21] The emperor reverted to rumors that Ting would avoid contact with the enemy, and warned Li that he, Li, was ultimately responsible.[22] Li retorted that there were unconfirmed reports of gunfire in the Asan area, suggesting a contact there. He parried thrusts at Ting and himself by insisting that China had too few ships, adding that since his men were Western-trained, it would be unwise to consider replacing their admiral in the midst of battle. If Ting must be replaced, Li himself must ask for that replacement.[23]

Ting had several detractors. Earlier he had argued with Tai Tsung-ch'ien, commander of the Weihaiwei forts which Ting wished to destroy before their inevitable fall into enemy hands, and Tai had slandered Ting, both to Li and in Peking.[24] Nor was Li himself invulnerable. August 7 brought a telegram to him from the court recalling that he had long been in charge of the navy, and had succeeded before in coping with Japanese threats in Korea, whereas now he offered only excuses. If the navy needed more ships, let Li be specific, and all officials were ordered to cooperate.[25]

On August 10, while this wrangle was going on, Japanese ships bombarded Weihaiwei, in Ting's absence. Twenty enemy vessels threw in about 100 rounds, and then departed. The defenders found some of their pieces jammed, but soon hit home with some

Kiangnan-built four-inch quick-firers which had just been installed, and one of the attackers had to be towed off. But the Japanese ships bombarded Port Arthur on the same day.[26]

Li's reaction to the Weihaiwei raid was galvanic. Admiral Ting was recalled from his patrol, ostensibly because of weather danger to the torpedo craft, and the defense perimeter was pulled even farther back toward the west, to a line between Weihaiwei and Talienwan, almost due north.[27] At about this time, too, Li heard that Japan was buying more gunboats from Britain. There were rumors that Li had taken a Japanese bribe to keep the Peiyang fleet back, away from the Korean sea lanes.[28] This was probably no more than rumor, but it does seem that Li was mainly concerned with cutting his losses and keeping his ships.

The court was also stunned by the August 10 raids, and on August 12 decreed that Ting should guard Weihaiwei and Taku. The Court wanted to know where Ting was.[29] Shortly thereafter Hart advised the Grand Council that the Japanese might land at Port Arthur. The next few days brought at least three impeachments of the hapless admiral.[30]

On August 22, Li reported that Ting was en route to Weihaiwei from Port Arthur. No one knew where the next blow would fall. The court ordered Ting to be most vigilant, under threat of dreadful punishment. But Ting had little chance to redeem himself; on August 25, the Grand Council sought to have him replaced, as a coward, and Li was told to submit a list of suitable replacements. The next day Li was commanded to cashier Ting, although keeping him at his post to greet his successor and to redeem his many errors.[31] The day after, Ting was charged with abandoning General Yeh and with cowardice, and was dismissed. Li was told to make no excuses this time.[32]

Li was still not discountenanced. On August 29 he wired the Grand Council, reviewing the sorry history of his naval buying program. He said his fleet was old; Ting, furthermore, was the only experienced man. Liu Pu-ch'an and Lin T'ai-tseng were the only possible alternates, but both lacked battle experience — and if some person were imported from another province, there would be trouble.[33] Actually, both Liu and Lin were also then under attack in Peking for being cowardly, which dubious circumstances may have aided Li in his defense of Ting.[34] The admiral finally got off with a warning and suspended judgment,[35] but we may wonder how these events affected his morale as he entered the climactic Yalu battle a few weeks later — or how this bickering further eroded the strategic notions of Li Hung-chang.

Meanwhile, there had been talk of buying more ships, and, perhaps more to the point, two Gruson 1.97-inch quick-firing guns had been mounted on the *Chi Yüan* and some twenty others distributed to the other ships.[36] But Japan had not eased her land campaign on the Korean peninsula, and the battle of Pyongyang in September brought a concentration of Japanese military shipping in the Korean Sea. Li decided to send a large convoy, with Ting's protection, to the Yalu River. On September 14, five steamers left Taku with 4000 men. The main Peiyang fleet rendezvoused with these ships at Talienwan.[37] Here was the start of a movement of ships which was to culminate in the great battle off the mouth of the Yalu River, on September 17, 1894.

In the Yalu battle, China and Japan each had twelve ships. A professional Western naval man concluded that China had the edge in armor and weight of single salvo, while Japan had the advantage in speed of ships and weight of metal thrown in any sustained exchange of salvos. That is, Japan had "overwhelming superiority" in quick-firing guns, so that in multiple salvos she could throw three times the weight of metal that China could, offsetting China's possession of more guns of from six to twelve inches caliber. The quick-firers distributed to Li's fleet were not mounted in time.[38]

However, theoretical maxima do not always win battles, and other variables, such as leadership, maneuver, and availability of shells, were important. As for the first, leadership in the Peiyang fleet was an uncertain element.

Admiral Ting was at the top of the naval hierarchy. No one who knew him doubted his personal bravery, but this old Anhwei army cavalry officer was out of his element in the navy. A postwar Chinese official observer, Governor Hu Yu-fen of Kwangsi, wrote that the navy was under the army. In the West, admirals were expertly trained, and were furthermore popular with their men.[39] Ting was neither expertly trained nor popular.

Not surprisingly, Ting sought advice wherever he might find

it, and his staff included foreigners. In 1894 Constantin von Hannecken was made inspector-general of the navy, and since he was sometimes called adviser to the admiral, and sometimes co-admiral, his was an important post.[40] He came from the German army, and had served Li in various ways since 1880, among others, as we have seen, in the building of Li's heavy fortifications. Von Hannecken was in charge of the army reinforcements aboard the doomed *Kowhsing*, and had shown high courage in the mutiny that preceded the sinking. After the Yalu battle, Von Hannecken asked to be transferred to Li's land forces, where he undoubtedly felt more at home. Tyler, who wondered about a "soldier-engineer" serving as "an Admiral," observed that Von Hannecken was made co-admiral "to save Admiral Ting from summary decapitation in case of a reverse." [41] In any event, Von Hannecken was an active shipboard adviser of Admiral Ting during the Yalu battle.

Tyler himself had an important position. In 1891, as a young British naval sublieutenant, he had first seen Chinese naval ships in Kowloon Bay. Later he signed into Li's forces, seeing China as a country with "a reasonable chance." In the Yalu battle he was co-commander of the flagship *Ting Yüan* with Li Ting-hsin; that is, a kind of co-executive officer to the captain of the vessel, Liu Pu-ch'an. Tyler regretted that he had no real authority, and could only give advice. Li Ting-hsin was polite to him, and let him use the "exec's" suite, but was preoccupied with his relations with Liu Pu-ch'an. So Tyler "pottered along," overhauling the signal system and similar things that occurred to him. After the Yalu battle, Tyler was to find himself "more or less effective," for he was later made "Senior Executive Officer" in the *Chen Yüan*, with Li Ting-hsin then helping Tyler. But, although he had "considerable authority," this British officer was never fully accepted. But (as co-commander) Tyler stood on the *Ting Yüan's* bridge with Ting and Von Hannecken when the shooting started off the mouth of the Yalu. We shall see that his suggestions were important.[42]

Tyler believed that Ting was completely open to suggestion. He wrote that Ting would have kept up the Yalu fight after the Japanese break-off if he had been so advised, for "Ting would have agreed to anything we asked." [43]

The ranks, Tyler recalled of the days before the Yalu battle, were cheerful. Brisk and smart seamen had lovingly decorated their guns. Less optimistic were the officers, "in cloth top-boots, baggy trousers, and semiforeign coats with the dragon stripes and colored buttons of their rank," for, said Tyler, there was among them "that thing so indescribable, the enervating presence of mandarinism." He believed that they at least "respected and admired" the admiral. On the other hand, Philo McGiffen, whose position in the *Chen Yüan* during the Yalu battle was much like Tyler's in the *Ting Yüan*, stated that the admiral had to contend with "disaffections existing in a certain clique of his officers." [44] For that matter, the Cantonese captain Teng Shih-ch'ang complained of Fukien influence in the Peiyang fleet.[45] Who, then, were Li's captains?

Of the twelve captains fighting for Li in the Yalu battle, nine were graduates of the Foochow naval academy, and of these nine, seven had been in the first graduating class. Some (for example, Teng Shih-ch'ang and Lin T'ai-tseng) had been with Li for over a decade, but had no battle experience. Teng and Lin might have gotten battle experience in the Taiwan relief expedition of 1884–1885, but Li saved them (and their ships) for another day.

As for the supposed disaffections, one American eyewitness recorded that the Fukien officers tended to be cowards, while others fought manfully.[46] This statement is wide of the truth. There is not much evidence of favoritism in the assignment of commands. Tientsin academy graduates were unlikely to have full captaincies in 1894; this explains the southern dominance. The southerners in command in 1894 had ships whose size roughly reflected the experience and seniority of their captains. The two battleship captains, Liu Pu-ch'an and Lin T'ai-tseng, had been pronounced ready for command by Giquel as of 1874, twenty years before the Yalu battle. It seems that the foreign-built ships were put under the most senior men. Teng Shih-ch'ang put his first ship on a rock in 1880; this black mark may explain why this classmate of Liu Pu-ch'an was not a captain of the largest of Li's foreign-built cruisers in 1894 — and it may also explain why this Cantonese complained of Fukien "influence." [47]

It is doubtful that by 1894 Li Hung-chang really feared the "southernness" of these men — although it is likely that he did not forget it, and so was reluctant to use one of them as a replacement for Admiral Ting, who was indubitably Li's "own." The Yalu battle was not a test of Li's Tientsin officer-training system, in any event. As for the influence of cliques among Li's officers, it is impossible to be definitive. Indeed, foreign influence is much more clearly traceable, through the battle advice of such as Tyler.

Philo McGiffen called himself "commander" of the *Chen Yüan*. This Annapolis man was honorably discharged from the American navy in 1882, as a "past midshipman." His academy career was largely distinguished by horseplay (rolling cannonballs down stairs, for example). During the Sino-French War, he applied to Li Hung-chang and got an imperial commission; he taught seamanship and gunnery at Tientsin and Weihaiwei. His attitude during the Yalu battle is at least suggested by a friend who visited him years later, to see a derelict and senile McGiffen, in his bloodied Yalu uniform, try to relive the day. The friend speculated on McGiffen's action off the Yalu as follows: "There was no patriotism behind it; no lofty motive; no desire to protect; no self-sacrifice; no flag. For China, he had only contempt. He praised her sailormen for bravery and endurance, but denounced her officials, Admiral Ting always excepted, as traitors, even drawing monthly salaries from the enemy." [48] Tyler said of McGiffen simply that "he was not quite all there." [49] We may say, at least, that Li's naval leadership in the Yalu battle was made up of an odd assortment.

Other foreigners were in lesser positions, and the names Purvis, Albrecht, Heckman, Nichols, and some others will be encountered below. There were also a few of the former China Educational Mission "boys" in subordinate officer positions. Flag-Lieutenant Woo, nicknamed "Stork" (a "great wag") was also known to Tyler. To Tyler, deck and engine personnel were excellent, as were the warrant officers.[50]

The Yalu battle has been exhaustively described and analyzed, for in winning this early modern naval battle, Japan forced herself on the attention of Western naval specialists.[51] We need consider only parts of it here, with a view to discussing some of the problems which have been raised in this study of China's attempt to acquire and use a modern navy.

Since it reflected the command situation, and had much to do with the outcome of the Yalu battle, the battle formation deserves attention. It is not clear that Ting expected the action; still, the ships had been cleared for action.[52] Boats, handrails, and the like were removed; even the heavy steel shields from the Krupp twelve-inchers were removed, for the Feng-tao action had shown these to be splinter traps. Bags of coal were piled around the guns; the decks were sanded and flooded to check fire (at least on the flagship), and men scattered about to pass power charges. So much McGiffen reported, but the danger of fire, which feeds as much on disorganization as on inflammable materials, had not been well met throughout the fleet, as we shall see.[53]

The fleet was at anchor in the Yalu estuary when word was passed at noon on September 17 that smoke had been sighted. Tyler, just sitting down to a roast-pigeon dinner, took time to finish, and then conferred with Ting and Von Hannecken. Steam was gotten up and the flag-lieutenant busied himself with his buntings. Tyler had time to check guns, magazines, and projectiles, and to observe the cheerfulness of the crew despite the "damning fact of the shortage of projectiles," which Tyler linked to his doubts about Captain Liu Pu-ch'an, who was "cowering" in the conning tower. Here was the main chance. The army had failed in Korea, and the navy, said Tyler, knew that "on it alone now lay the fate of China; on it, had we but known it, depended more; the epoch of a series of world events that led to the Great War." [54]

As for battle formation, the choice lay between line ahead or line abreast (that is, follow-the-leader or side-by-side), and there was room for disagreement. Lang had argued for line abreast, with two echeloned divisions. Line abreast would also favor ramming, which was still an esteemed tactic.[55] Further, the design of the battleships *Chen* and *Ting*, with their two pairs each of twelve-inch Krupp breech-loaders in staggered side-mount barbettes, which could fire simultaneous salvos only right off the beam, but were rather more widely useful when fired ahead or astern, argued for line abreast.[56] True, the increasing Western use of quick-firing ordnance (lighter weapons that were best arranged along a vessel's sides) had already made the *Chen-Ting* design obsolete, and made for a preference for line ahead; but China's ships were not so prepared.[57] On the other hand, there were difficulties about line abreast. Range changes rapidly when opposing fleets in line abreast approach each other head-on; furthermore, an enemy has a better chance of hitting one's ships if they are head-on to him, for in that way they present their length as a target; since range of fire is harder to adjust than its lateral training, this is advantageous. Line abreast also calls for wheeling maneuvers of impossible speed for ships on the outside of the turn; of course, a ninety-degree turn in line by each ship in line abreast will put all into line ahead, but such a maneuver calls for nice coordination.

Von Hannecken had already concluded that the existing Chinese flag codes were not adequate to Li's needs, for in the Peiyang fleet there were unequal speeds and turning radii.[58] But there had been no time to make a basic change, and so on the eve of the war with Japan there had been issued — through Admiral Ting, of course — a set of what foreigners called "fatal general instructions," or "commands of the crudest description." These were: in action, sister ships or other assigned pairs were to keep together; all ships, if possible, were to fight end-on; and, if possible, all ships were to follow the visible movements of the flagship.[59] Clearly, this directive preferred line abreast, but for teams, rather than a fleet.

Yet Tyler reported that last-minute deliberations before meeting the Japanese ships off the Yalu had settled on line ahead for sections; that is, a line of pairs, each pair to the rear and side of the one before it. But when the ships were raggedly getting under way, Tyler saw a signal made for *line abreast*. This, he said, was Liu Pu-ch'an's master stroke, for the change would bring his two battleships into a seemingly protected middle, and save Liu's skin.[60] Admiral Ting and Von Hannecken did not spot the change, so Tyler urgently told them of it. Still, since vast confusion would have resulted from an attempted re-formation into line ahead, Tyler recommended that Liu's change be kept. All of this confusion, plus speed differentials, bent the Chinese ships into a crescent, with ships approximately abreast, moving roughly southwest at about six knots.[61]

The Japanese came on in the opposite direction at about ten knots, in line ahead, which favored their quick-firing broadsides and facilitated the tight maneuver and circling which distinguished their attack.⁶² They began a flanking turn around Admiral Ting's right end, which gave China the chance to make a right quarter-turn in line, to "cross the Japanese T," which would allow the Chinese ships, in line ahead, to pass in a northwesterly direction across the head of the enemy column, with each Chinese ship throwing in succession raking broadsides down the whole Japanese line. "Immense yellow ensigns" were hoisted, but Captain Liu Pu-ch'an on the flagship did not recommend the quarter-turn maneuver, which would have exposed his own flanks, and Ting and Von Hannecken did not see the opportunity. So Tyler made the suggestion, and it was approved. The signal was made, but the other ships lingered to see what the flagship would do. Liu Pu-ch'an did nothing, whereon Tyler prompted him; Liu gave the order for right rudder, but immediately in a low voice countermanded himself. Before Tyler could report Liu's insubordination to Ting (so says Tyler), Liu gave the order to fire, although the range was still too open. This order came at 12:50 p.m. The great salvo from the battleship's four twelve-inch guns set up a terrible concussion, which demolished the temporary flying bridge on which Ting and Tyler were standing. Ting sustained severe leg injuries, and had to be removed to his cabin, despite his gallant objections. Tyler was thrown thirty feet, and temporarily blinded. The big chance was lost. Tyler unequivocally laid this loss to the cowardice of Liu Pu-ch'an.⁶³

Even if Tyler was correct, we cannot argue here that China in this battle was given an initial and costly handicap because the conflict between Confucian values and those of modern naval training was bound to produce cowardly leaders. Cowardice is universal, as is heroism, of which there was a great deal among China's navy men in the Yalu battle. We can however state that Liu's alleged cowardice was greatly magnified because the admiral (with some of his advisers) in that naval chain of command was incompetent, and could not offset Liu's cowardice with the expected authority of a professional admiral. Admiral Ting had been selected by Li Hung-chang for political reasons, and the leadership of the entire Peiyang fleet was accordingly weakened. We may also wonder how it was not known, after nearly a decade of presumed training on the *Ting* and *Chen*, that firing the big twelve-inchers dead ahead would blow away the flying bridge. Perhaps it was known.

THE SINO-JAPANESE WAR, 1894–1895

For another *twenty minutes* the Japanese held their fire. Admiral Ito kept on his flanking course, but, probably because he expected a Chinese turn-in-line, changed course enough to produce a parallel line ahead for both fleets. This relative formation did not appear. Then the Japanese Flying Division, under Tsuboi on the *Yoshino*, increased to fourteen knots and started around what remained of Ting's right end. In another ten minutes, the signal halyards on the Chinese flagship had been shot away, so that even the material devices of leadership were lost.[64] The resulting formation was reported by a foreign eyewitness, who observed the battle from high bluffs to the north:

By this time it was half-past two p.m., and the battle had been in progress nearly three hours [this seems excessive]. Not having seen the commencement of the affair, we were for some time unable to make head or tail of it. The ships were mixed up and scattered . . . the struggle was nearing the coast . . . many were well within two miles . . . This of course enabled us to distinguish the vessels better, and we began to make out evident signs that John Chinaman was getting the worst of it. The Japanese vessels, working in concert and keeping together, as we began to perceive, seemed to sail around and around the enemy pouring on them an incessant cannonade, and excelling them in rapidity of fire and maneuvering. Some of the Chinese vessels appeared to me to present an appearance of helplessness, and there was no indication of combination as amongst their opponents.[65]

The Japanese divided into Flying and Main divisions. The first was circling Ting's right end, where were the two old British cruisers *Ch'ao Yung* and *Yang Wei*. Both had their heavy guns fore-and-aft, connected by a passage through officers' country. This sanctum was distinguished by elegant varnished paneling, which had not been stripped away for battle. The Japanese attack turned these alleys into roaring drafts of flame, cutting off the guns. The captains fought creditably but hopelessly; respectively, they were the Foochow academy men Huang Chien-hsün and Lin Li-chung. Both drowned. The observers ashore said: "The Chao Yung, an absolute ruin, drifted helplessly ashore, half a league from where we stood . . . her upper works knocked to pieces; her decks, strewn with mutilated bodies, an indiscriminate mass of wreck and carnage . . . Subsequently the Yang Wei went ashore similarly battered to pieces and burning. She was much farther off . . ."[66]

According to McGiffen, this same first hour of the battle saw the running away of Captain Fang Pai-ch'ien in his *Chi Yüan*, and the similar desertion of the non-Foochow-academy captain Wu Ching-jung in the Canton ship *Kwang Chia*. These two ships escaped from the extreme left wing, passing behind the entire fleet in their flight. The *Kwang Chia* grounded in Talienwan and was later destroyed by the Japanese. The *Chi Yüan* made it to Port Arthur — some say she rammed the hard-pressed *Yang Wei* as she ran — seven hours in advance of the crippled remainder of the Peiyang fleet, and Captain Fang started another controversy over his personal bravery, which continued long after his summary execution.[67]

The Japanese Flying Division next observed two more Chinese ships, to the north, with some torpedo boats. The *P'ing Yüan* and *Kwang Ping* had started tardily, and some say they did not join in the battle at all, but fled when the *Yoshino* bore down on them.[68] Others say the two attacked the hard-pressed Japanese converted merchant-warship *Saikyo*, and even put some shells into the *Matsushima*. If so, it is strange that they failed to sink the slow and weak *Saikyo*, which was so far out of control that she nearly rammed the *Naniwa*. In any event, these two Chinese ships also departed, after whatever degree of contact.[69] By loss and defection, the Chinese fleet was cut in half, and more ships were yet to be lost.

The *Chih Yüan*, under the Foochow-academy-trained Captain Teng Shih-ch'ang, went next, although it was observed from the shore that Captain Teng handled his "fine Elswick cruiser" with "admirable coolness," trying to ram the *Yoshino* after his own ship was "badly hulled . . . and took a strong list to starboard." Apparently he intercepted a torpedo from the *Yoshino* which was intended for the *Ting Yüan*. With her steam pumps hard at work, and her guns served until she sank, but without support, the *Chih Yüan* went down at about 3:30 p.m. with all of her 250 hands, accompanied by "yelling sounds of triumph from the Japanese ships . . ."[70] Captain Teng refused a life ring offered him by his servant, and even fought off the attempts made by his pet dog to rescue him.[71]

The *Ching Yüan*, under Captain Lin I-sheng (apparently not a Foochow academy man), was sunk about an hour later, with all hands. But it took the *Takachiho*, *Akitsushima*, and *Yoshino* an hour to do the job. There were later questions about this sinking. Some said that proper fire damage control could have saved her: "The King Yuan was not sunk by the Japanese, but simply allowed to burn out. A shell from a hostile ship struck her woodwork, setting it on fire. It was only a small affair, and could have been easily extinguished with a few buckets of water. But no fire brigade had been organized on board, and everybody bolted as far away as he could until the fire spread over the whole ship." [72]

Evidently training — perhaps since Lang's departure — had been remiss. There was also an organizational deficiency on the flagship. The Japanese were most interested in the battleships *Ting* and *Chen*, but were stopped by their big guns and heavy armor. Ship-handling in the *Ting* was shared by the Foochow academy men Li Ting-hsin and Liu Pu-ch'an, who maneuvered well. Von Hannecken, Tyler, Nichols, and Albrecht also worked efficiently. The ship engaged the *Matsushima*, Ito's flagship, in a "dreadful" exchange, and one of the *Ting's* ten-inch shells burst on the enemy, setting fire to ammunition and killing or wounding eighty men outright. Ito had to withdraw and transfer his flag, but the *Ting Yüan* also had to retreat — under cover of the *Chen Yüan* — to cope with a bad fire. Some small gear had been set afire in the forward lazarette. It was said that "everything was so upset that nobody thought of fighting the ship. Albrecht, however, by personal example mostly, got the pumps at work, and stood there amidst the shot and shell directing the stream of water until he had well-nigh flooded the room." Otherwise, the ship might have been "lost or badly crippled." [73]

The two battleships worked closely together; indeed, once two Japanese ships, caught in between them, escaped because *Ting* and *Chen* had to cease fire to keep from hitting each other.[74] The *Chen Yüan*, under Foochow Captain Lin T'ai-tseng and the non-Foochow executive officer (?) Yang Yung-lin, fought well, and a foreign gunner in the ship, Heckman, claimed credit for the shot which so sorely hurt the *Matsushima*.[75] There was high courage also in the heavily damaged *Lai Yüan*. In all, only four ships stayed or survived the Yalu battle; four were sunk or destroyed; and four departed, of which one was totally lost.

Ito called off the action at sunset, although his fleet was still intact, if battered. Chinese torpedo boats had come up, and he feared an after-dark attack by them. He steered for Weihaiwei, to cut off Admiral Ting, but the surviving Chinese ships went the other way, to Port Arthur. The Chinese break-off signal was made by the Foochow academy man Captain Yeh Tsu-kuei, of the surviving *Ching Yüan*.[76] Foreigners were amazed at the battered veterans which put into Port Arthur: "The Lai Yuan had her superstructure damaged by fire and shell more than any ship in the fleet, and was an appalling sight. . . . the foreigners who have seen her deem it a marvel that she could ever have been brought into port, so completely wrecked is the deck gear. Essentially, however, the ship is sound in both hull, armament, and engines." [77] Both battleships showed numerous hits, about 350 between them, mostly high on their superstructures.[78]

One careful observer recorded that China fired 197 twelve-inch projectiles, half of them being solid shot rather than explosive shell, and scored ten hits, with six shots and four shells. From her smaller guns, China fired 482 shots and registered fifty-eight hits, twenty-two on the *Hiyei*. China also loosed five torpedoes, without hits. China scored about ten percent of her tries; the Japanese, with their quick-firers, scored about fifteen percent of theirs.[79]

The Chinese were hampered by "woeful" shortages of ammunition, particularly for the big guns. It was said that she entered the battle with but fifteen rounds of "common shell" for each of the eight twelve-inch guns, with the rest of the rounds only armor-piercing shot. McGiffen believed that the *Hiyei* escaped because only armor-piercing shot was used against her. All but three of the shot for the big guns had been used when the action ended. To McGiffen, it was a "mystery" that Ito failed to finish the job.[80]

With regard to explosive projectiles, it was often true that powder was not good, or that shells did not fit. A 10.2-inch shell from the *Chen Yüan* struck the *Matsushima*, killing four men at the port torpedo tube aft, striking the barbette, and coursing through storerooms and an oil tank. But it broke when it struck the barbette, and proved to be filled with cement. Two "enormous shells" passed clear through the *Saikyo*.[81] Foreign criticisms of Li Hung-chang's "hou-lu," or supply establishment, were evidently not mistaken.

THE SINO-JAPANESE WAR, 1894–1895

To be sure, the Japanese had faulty ammunition too. It is a wonder that the *Ch'ao Yung* and *Yang Wei* were not sunk outright. The Japanese were never able to penetrate more than five inches of the Chinese battleships' fourteen-inch armor belts. Some of their shots were duds, and a Japanese complained that some "copper shot" used on that day was useless. Leadership and training were not everything.[82]

As for other material factors, evidently speed and rapidity of fire were more important — assuming maintenance of formation — than weight of vessel and armor. One Westerner observed that heavy waterline belt armor was demonstrably useless if it made a ship unsinkable but still reducible to a floating hulk with useless guns.[83] Statements of this kind show that even Western naval experts were trying to take lessons from the Yalu battle. Still, China's Peiyang fleet was obsolete, compared even to Japan's, and her personnel, though not without training, was not sufficiently trained or well enough led to meet the test which Japan put to China. There was also lack of proper support from the fleet's shore establishments.

The Sino-Japanese War did not end with the Yalu battle. Shore engagements continued. The remains of the Peiyang fleet undergoing (unhurried) repairs at Port Arthur was still a fleet-in-being. Li still had seven serviceable ships, including two battleships, and these ships could still at least have done effective convoy service, or could have harassed Japanese sea communications. Li Hung-chang, smarting at having been deprived of his three-eyed peacock feather and Yellow Jacket (symbols of honor earlier bestowed by the court, and removed as punishment for the Yalu defeat), was goaded by imperial demands to see the ships repaired and sent to sea. There were many conjectures as to where the Japanese would strike next.[84] A Westerner commented on the slowness of repairs: "One thing was evident at Port Arthur above all else — that was, that the officers and sailors did not seem very anxious to get their ships refitted for sea. For more than a week after the fight the wreckage was allowed to lie about, and on board the Ting Yuan a decomposed body was discovered nearly a fortnight later. And the Ting Yuan is one of the crack ships of the Chinese navy!"[85]

The court tried the old expedients. A "new man" — it was old

Prince Kung — was called in, to take over a super-military-directorate.[86] Von Hannecken declined the proffered command of the Peiyang fleet, so that Admiral Ting remained, assisted by Tyler and Vice-Admiral McClure. McClure, the new expert, had had nautical experience, but since it was limited to tugboating in Tientsin waters, where he had a reputation as a tippler, one may wonder even more about the "new" high command.[87] In November 1894, a new capital agency, the Tu-pan chün-wu-ch'u, or board of military affairs, was created, supplanting even the Grand Council.[88] These changes were both late and useless.

Help was sought from the south. Liu K'un-i, the southern commissioner, was told to send ships, but replied that he could spare none of his five. Later, Liu was brought north on a special military assignment, being replaced at Nanking *ad interim* by Chang Chih-tung, who was also instructed to send ships north.[89] There were two Kwangtung ships in the final naval stand, which was made at Weihaiwei at the end of 1894 and early in 1895; these were the *Kwang Ping*, which survived the Yalu battle (possibly because she prudently departed from it), and the *Kuang Keng*. Others came in 1895, but since these ships were returned to their home fleets after the war, they must have come after the end of the Weihaiwei surrender, for all of the ships which were there passed into Japanese possession.[90] With only slight qualification, we may repeat that the Peiyang fleet was the only one involved in the Sino-Japanese War, from start to finish.

At the end of October, the Japanese made an unopposed landing at Hua-yuan-k'ou, on the northern part of the eastern shore of the Liaotung Peninsula. Li Hung-chang undoubtedly knew of these enemy preparations for an overland rear strike at Port Arthur. Early in November, Japan took an abandoned Talienwan, even finding plans of mine and torpedo defenses in the proud concrete batteries erected by Von Hannecken.[91] Meanwhile, there was official talk in China about buying more ships.[92]

The court could always vent its frustrations on Admiral Ting, and on November 3 he was singled out for punishment, while Li was ordered to get the ships out of Port Arthur to shell the Japanese overland approach to the base. Li replied that he had only six ships and two torpedo boats ready to oppose fourteen Japanese fast ships and seven torpedo boats. Repairs on the heavy

Peiyang ships had to be suspended, and Li had no transport to lift troops to Port Arthur. The court implacably replied that *McGiffen* should be given command, to bring in eight battalions of relieving troops. Li parried by quoting Von Hannecken's objections to the use of his warships for convoy, and promised to consult him and McClure. This reply doubtless crossed an order of November 10 ordering Li to get the ships out of Port Arthur; if Ting did not accomplish this evacuation (what *was* his status?) he must lose his head.[93]

Ting had already decided that Port Arthur was not defensible, partly because of the configuration of its forts, and partly because he could not get the cooperation of local authorities.[94] On the 11th of November, the Japanese fleet tried to draw him out to fight, but then laxly let him escape some days later. In letting Ting take his fleet to Weihaiwei, the Japanese only postponed the task of destroying that fleet. Some Western observers say that this was the only basic mistake made by Japan in the entire Port Arthur campaign.[95] In any event, Port Arthur, with Ting's fleet gone, fell on November 21, after stiff land fighting.

At about this time, Admiral Ting enjoyed some strong support. All his captains, including Liu Pu-ch'an — who may not have wanted the responsibility of taking over the admiral's job — endorsed his leadership, and were joined by officials ashore at Weihaiwei, even those who had earlier denounced him as a traitor. McClure added that Ting's removal would wreck morale.[96]

The fleet crossed the Gulf of Chihli without incident, but unfortunately the *Chen Yüan* hit some underwater obstruction as she entered Weihaiwei, with the terrible result that her captain, Lin T'ai-tseng, committed suicide.[97] By the end of November, the *Ting* and *Chen*, with the *Ching Yüan, Lai Yüan, P'ing Yüan, Chi Yüan, Wei Yüan, Kwang Ping, Kwang Keng,* the six Armstrong gunboats, and eleven torpedo boats were anchored in the Weihaiwei protected harbor.[98] Japan could not ignore the potential threat of this fleet.

But Li Hung-chang, under pressure of military defeat and political attack, had retreated into the traditional strategical formulation. The war was over; a new fleet would have to be built, and here was its nucleus. Let it be used, if it must, in conjunction with the massive forts at Weihaiwei. Tyler said succinctly: "We did not mean to fight . . . I heaved a sigh of relief when I heard that we were going to funk it in the harbor." [99] To be sure, some of the ships occasionally sallied as far as Tengchow to the west and Cheng-shan to the east, but the notion of fixed forts and fixed ships, waiting for the enemy, had taken over.[100]

Still the controversy over Admiral Ting continued. On December 16 came an order for his arrest, and that of General Yeh Chih-ch'ao as well. Ting was to be deprived of title but kept in office. Li Hung-chang asked for delay, but shortly began to consider possible replacements for the admiral. Liu Pu-ch'an would not do; a man should serve as senior post captain at least ten years before being elevated to admiral, said Li. The captain of the *P'ing Yüan*, Li Ho-lien (Foochow academy-trained), was mediocre; Yang Yung-lin of the *Chen Yüan* was able but had just been moved into the captain's berth after Lin's suicide, and could not be elevated again so soon. Hsü Chien-yen, the taotai sent by the court to inspect the damaged *Chen Yüan*, although he had had some contact with Ting, was a civilian and not suitable.[101] (Hsü was the son of Hsü Shou, Tseng Kuo-fan's steamer builder, and evidently knew ships, but it is almost incomprehensible, even in that context, that his name should appear in a consideration of replacements for an admiral.) Li tenaciously defended Ting, partly because he did have some understanding of modern naval needs, and partly, of course, in Li's own interest. Yet there came no formal forgiveness of Admiral Ting.

Ting's actions at Weihaiwei show a mixture of defiance and defeatism. He had long wished to destroy the forts there, and after his arrival persisted in the wish, meeting varying degrees of opposition and even sabotage of his efforts — the last not so much by patriots as by those who prudently preferred to turn them over intact to the invincible Japanese.[102] On the other hand, Ting personally took a ship (the *Ching Yüan*) into action against one of the forts after it had fallen to the enemy, and had the ship sunk under him so fast that the flag could not be lowered.[103]

Late in January 1895, a fifty-transport Japanese force landed east of Weihaiwei, with no trouble. Ting's ships were kept in by the Japanese, who from January 20 onward had kept a seaward watch of fortified Weihaiwei. On January 25, Ito felt confident enough to write to Ting urging a prudent and gentlemanly surrender. It is a measure of Ting's valor that he turned this letter over to Li Hung-chang, although to many it must have sounded very reasonable.[104] Liu K'un-i, special imperial commissioner for military affairs in the Shanhaikuan region, asked for an amnesty for Ting, a definite lifting of the charges against the admiral, but this proposal resulted in little more from the court than orders for the punishment of some of Ting's old enemies.[105]

Admiral Ting had one unenviable chance to save his fleet. February blew in on howling gales, so severe that the Japanese blockaders had to seek shelter. But Ting did not make a run.[106] He used the respite from Japanese naval shelling to destroy some of the forts not yet taken by Japanese shore forces, thus prolonging his resistance for a few days. By February 3, the Japanese were well established on the eastern and southern shores of the bay, and turned the captured guns on Ting's ships.

Ting's greatest problem was the mounting incidence of Japanese torpedo-boat attacks; the boats came in at night, after cutting the protecting boom. In February, these attacks became terribly efficient. On the night of February 4, the *Ting Yüan* was holed, and, her water-tight doors not being in order, she had to be beached and abandoned save as a fort.[107] The next night enemy torpedoes claimed the *Wei Yüan, Lai Yüan*, and a transport, the *Pao Hua*. These ships were still being lighted at night; there were claims that traitors homed-in the attack with Morse signals. It has also been reputably said that the captains of the *Wei* and *Lai*, Lin Ying-ch'i and Ch'iu Pao-jen (both Foochow academy men), were ashore in amorous dalliance at the moment of the attack.[108] Admiral Ting tried to delude his men with reports of help on the way from the governor of Shantung, Li Ping-heng, although he knew better.[109] The situation was out of his hands.

On February 7 the *Ching Yüan* was sunk while under Ting's temporary command, as seen above; her captain, Yeh Tsu-kuei (Foochow), was ashore on unspecified business. That same day the remaining Chinese torpedo boats tried to run the Japanese blockade. They were met with a storm of Japanese fire, and those that were not hung up on the boom were captured by the swift *Yoshino*. These torpedo captains were in a real dilemma; a few days before Ting had received a court order that none of his ships should fall into enemy hands, yet the disastrous run for freedom was swiftly followed by another court order for the beheading of the men who had taken this slim chance.[110] Perhaps the action of these torpedo captains was not so much a response to orders as it was a reflection of the total collapse of discipline.

Admiral Ting was faced with a mounting clamor for surrender, particularly from the soldiers on Liu-kung-tao. McClure also covertly recommended it. Ting resisted. He wanted his captains to sink their ships, but they demurred, for the practical reason that the enemy would take reprisals for such wanton destruction of good naval materiel which they would want for themselves after winning it in battle. Neither could Ting get agreement on a proposed break out of the harbor. On the 11th of February, when soldiers approached him with bared knives, he excused himself, retired to his cabin, and took an overdose of opium.[111]

Immediately after Ting's death, a surrender message was drawn up in taotai's office and delivered to Ito by Ch'en Pi-kwang, captain of the *Kwang Ping*, who traveled under a white flag on the Armstrong gunboat *Chen Pien* to deliver the message. This was on February 12, 1895. The Japanese victors graciously permitted the officers to leave, but all the remaining ships — save for the *Kwang Keng*, which was detailed to bear away in state the remains of Admiral Ting — were to be turned over to Japan. Thus the *Chen Yüan, Kwang Ping, Chi Yüan, P'ing Yüan*, and the six Armstrong gunboats passed to the enemy, and Li Hung-chang's Peiyang fleet was no more.[112] At the same time, Liu Pu-ch'an, Yang Yung-lin, Chang Wen-hsuan (commander of the Liu-kung-tao land forces), and Tai Tsung-ch'ien (a fortress commander) followed Admiral Ting in suicide.[113]

In retrospect, in all this grim and sad business, there was one nearly humorous ironic note. The *Kwang Keng* was left in Chinese hands for the solemn office mentioned above. The *Kwang Ping* was not so favored, and Ch'en Pi-kwang, her captain, who keenly felt that he must take his ship back to Canton, asked Ito for permission to retain her. He argued that she belonged to the Kwangtung squadron, which had really taken no part in the war. Ito failed to respond to this instructive logic.[114]

The foregoing selected comments on the Yalu and Weihaiwei

battles illustrate some of the political and institutional frictions which hampered China's effort to acquire and use a modern navy. Another interesting field for inquiry is that of rewards and punishments. The details that follow are taken from the sequels to the battles discussed above.

Directly after the Yalu battle of September 17, 1894, Li Hung-chang made recommendations for rewards. Surviving candidates included Liu Pu-ch'an, Lin T'ai-tseng, Yang Yung-lin, Li Ting-hsin, and of course Admiral Ting. Deceased heroes cited for posthumous honor were Teng Shih-ch'ang, Lin I-sheng, Huang Ch'iung-ch'en, and Lin Li-chung, of the four ships driven ashore or sunk. Li even included subordinates such as Shen Shou-ch'ang and K'o Chien-chang, killed in the *Chi Yüan* during the Feng-tao fight of July 25. For Fang Pai-ch'ien, who supposedly fled the Yalu battle, he asked for punishment, in the discretion of the throne. Four men who brought their ships back to Port Arthur after the Yalu disaster were passed over in silence: Yeh Tsu-Kuei of the *Ching Yüan*, Ch'iu Pao-jen of the *Lai Yüan*, Li Ho-lien of the *P'ing Yüan*, and Ch'en Pi-kwang of the *Kwang Ping*.[115] Not all of this is clear. For example, the *Lai Yüan* was that "appalling sight" reported in Port Arthur, and her captain certainly did not run from the battle. Even the court wondered if there had been at least one oversight for reward – Lin Kuo-hsiang of the *Kwang I*, lost off Feng-tao – and asked Li to investigate.[116]

The punishment code was specific enough. Tyler found that it was definitely in use. Floggings of enlisted men were often given with a bare sword, which could result in death.[117] Yet something seemed to be amiss with the way the code operated for China's naval officers. Perhaps it worked too well. Thus, after Teng Shih-ch'ang's suicide in the Yalu battle, Li, on representations from Admiral Ting, who pointed out that it took a long time to train a naval officer, drafted a code to discourage such expensive losses by suicide.[118] Yet a little later, in the Port Arthur panic, Li recommended capital punishment for cowardice – which surely was already required by the existing code, if it was consistently applied.[119]

Perhaps the trouble was that the code was not consistently applied. There was too great a chance that a man would not get justice. The final court, of course, was the emperor. Punitive codes usually provide for appeal to such an ultimate judge, but in this case, there were special problems. The emperor was often isolated from the facts. Wen T'ing-shih, a progressive member of the Hanlin Academy, observed that at the start of the war all important telegrams were edited by the court translation bureau before coming under the august eye. When Wen so advised the emperor, the emperor was angry enough, but Wen only succeeded in bringing on himself the hostility of Prince Ch'ing.[120] This situation made for uncertainty.

There was no court martial system. The ultimate criteria of responsibility or culpability, in the Confucian view, remained essentially moral. It need not be said that moral factors do indeed figure in human failures, but China's naval officers operated ships with intricate mechanisms in them, and in that new situation, room should have been made for technical considerations which could only be determined by exhaustive examination by expert judges; that is, by the naval peers of an accused officer. As it was, even the moral variables might be shifted and arranged by political confidantes close to the throne.

Liu Pu-ch'an's case is revealing. He had been close to Li for over a decade, although Li (as we saw in an earlier chapter) once had some doubts about his character. In Tyler's view, the man was a coward. Tyler's story has been accepted by Chang Yin-lin, an historian of these same events, although Chang was in some cases anxious to reverse established judgments; in particular, he tried to exonerate the executed Fang Pai-ch'ien.[121] Liu is not praised in any account this present writer has seen. Yet he was recommended for reward after the Yalu battle, despite what Tyler saw (and surely some others must have observed Liu's insubordination, even though Liu covered it by ordering that devastating first twelve-inch salvo), and only at the end, at Weihaiwei, did he take his own life. His suicide may have been the action of a guilty man, or the final gesture of the defeated hero. We cannot know which.

Fang Pai-ch'ien may well be an opposite case. Next to the admiral himself, there was no more controversial figure in the war, and the controversy did not end with his execution after the Yalu battle. The record goes back to the Feng-tao battle in July 1894, about which there were many questions concerning the hour of the engagement, the responsibility for opening fire, the participation of the *Kwang I*, and so on. Some say Fang expected to meet the Japanese ships; others deny this, arguing that he had to shoot away his own fantail awning to permit the use of his after-battery on the pursuing *Yoshino* — that is, he was not cleared for action.[122]

Fang's critics say he fled two battles. Off Feng-tao, the *Chi Yüan* lost her bow gun, twenty of her crew, and fled under a white and a Japanese flag; all the while Fang was hiding in his cabin, afraid to order his first and second officers to fire, even though they asked permission to do so. An angry sailor defied orders and fired at the pursuers, it is alleged.[123]

As for the Yalu battle, it is alleged that Fang's retreat was so headlong that he ran into the shallows, where he rammed the damaged *Yang Wei*. Thus: "Fang's navigation and pilotage were about equal to his courage; finding his soundings suddenly change he altered his course and fairly rammed his unhappy colleague; escaping himself, however, with a damaged bow."[124] The *Chi Yüan*, critics continue, then ran for Port Arthur, where Fang spread wild tales of the fight, claiming that his entire battery had been disabled. But line and engineer officers examined the ship (informally, it seems) and found his claims about his fused gun barrels to be untrue, although his after six-inch gun was lifted out of its seat. Other reports say that his guns had been damaged with a sledge hammer to enable him to make an "honorable" exit. Finally, Fang's critics looked to the foreign engineer who came ashore out of the *Chi Yüan* at Port Arthur and refused to serve further under such a captain.[125] Fang was executed.

But there are those who saw Fang as a slandered hero. The reports of his cowardice in the Feng-tao fight arose, it was said, from the jealousy of Lin Kuo-hsiang, who lost his *Kwang I* then. It was also said that Liu Pu-ch'an lied to Li Hung-chang about Fang. Another allegedly false witness was Mu Chin-shu, former first torpedo officer of the *Chi Yüan*, who was dismissed by Fang for failure to fire a torpedo during the Feng-tao battle.[126] It was said that Fang fought off Feng-tao as long as he could, through the death of his first officer, Shen Shou-ch'ang, who was standing so close to Fang that Fang was bloodied by the man's death. This early shot also killed a sub-lieutenant, wrecked the steering gear, voice tubes, engine telegraph, and other equipment. Another shot smashed the ammunition hoist for the 8.3-inch gun, and a third penetrated this barbette, killing seven officers and men and wounding fourteen more. The Japanese first raised the white flag; one of Fang's shots hit the enemy's bridge, killing the enemy admiral, whose body was seen turning over and over in the air. The Japanese ship was saved only when two other Japanese warships came up, and then, with her steering gear patched, the *Chi Yüan* had to flee what had become a hopelessly uneven match. It may be that the stern battery was then most involved. The vaunted *Yoshino* could not catch the slower *Chi Yüan* because the *Yoshino* had been put down by the head by Fang's shooting, The *Chi Yüan's* decks were a shambles, and fortunately for her some of the Japanese shots were duds.[127] It is interesting that Li Hung-chang did not recommend punishment for Fang until after the Yalu battle, which came about seven weeks after the disaster off Fengtao.

Fang's supporters said he showed no cowardice in the Yalu action, but fought his ship as long as the guns could be served. Indeed, that foreign officer who supposedly quit Fang in disgust — this was Hoffmann — did no such thing. He himself said:

It was the most tremendous fight I have ever dreamt about. Captain Fong fought the Tsi-yuen with courage and ability. We had seven or eight men killed on board, and continued firing away as fast as we could until between two and three o'clock in the afternoon, by which time we were terribly damaged and had to leave the scene of action. Our large gun aft, sixteen centimeter Krupp, was disabled, and the two forward guns had their gear destroyed so that they could not be used, and to all intents and purposes the ship was useless, so Captain Fong decided to get out of action . . . We arrived in Port Arthur five or six hours before the remainder of the fleet, which came in about eight o'clock. On the way in we had a collision with another vessel, which sank. From the injuries to the Tsi-yuen, which are all abaft the beam, I should say the other vessel rammed us. The water poured into the Tsi-yuen in a regular torrent, but we closed the water-tight doors and went on in safety. I do not think that the charges of cowardice which have been brought against Captain Fong can be supported for a moment; he fought his ship until it was no longer serviceable.[128]

Hoffman concluded that he left the ship because he considered it to be no longer seaworthy.

Fang's partisans could also adduce the evidence of the Japanese. When Ch'en Pi-kwang handed the Weihaiwei surrender to Ito, the Japanese asked why Fang had been beheaded. Ito felt that the man was a stout fighter, on the Feng-tao evidence. Chen replied: "This was because of His Majesty's order. Ting was very unwilling to do it." [129]

Surely the case of Fang Pai-ch'ien was a complicated one. It contained conflicting technical evidence of fused guns or sabotaged guns, damage either in the bows or "abaft the beam," and so on. Moral judgments were not sufficient. But there was no court-martial inquiry.

There were other inconsistencies in the pattern of action and subsequent judgment. Wu Ching-jung, captain of the *Kwang Chia*, who supposedly quit the Yalu battle when Fang did, was only cashiered.[130] And what of the men who were reportedly ashore with prostitutes when their ships were torpedoed in Weihaiwei harbor? Surely there could be no more flagrant dereliction; the *Ting Yüan* had been sunk the night before, and the absentees could hardly have pled that the situation was a peaceful one. There was also Yeh Tsu-kuei, who was ashore when his *Ching Yüan* was sunk on February 7 under the command of Admiral Ting. Whether his business was any more legitimate than that of the two captains just mentioned we do not know. There is no evidence of the supreme punishment for any of these men. Yeh Tsu-kuei, in fact, had a long subsequent naval career.[131] At least Yeh Tsu-kuei and Ch'iu Pao-jen (one of the delinquent pair above) were not recommended for advancement by Li Hung-chang after the Yalu battle, but this does not tell us much.

Another case was that of Tsai T'ing-kan, who had earned the sobriquet of "the fighting Chinee" in his younger days when he was a member of the China Educational Mission to the United States. He had a long naval career with Li, and was one of the torpedo-boat captains involved in the desperate break-out attempt of February 7, 1895. After ordering that all of these captains should be beheaded, the Empress Dowager later shifted the blame for the incident to the shoulders of Li Hung-chang, and Tsai, with the other survivors, was demoted and kept in limbo for years. In 1908, thanks to the intercession of Yüan Shih-k'ai, he was restored to rank, and was soon made admiral. Perhaps this was justice, for Tsai was not a coward; although wounded, he stayed with his torpedo boat until she sank under him. He was then captured. But justice cannot be entirely separated from consistency. The order for general decapitation was suspended, apparently because of a mood of the empress rather than from a detailed examination of the evidence.[132]

Although he was not a fighting man, Chang P'ei-lun also presents an interesting case. Among his several duties in Tientsin, he had been in charge of Li's arsenal, as we have seen. In the fall of 1894 he was dismissed. In subsequent letters — which were hardly entirely objective, but are still worthy of note — he charged that his fall was associated with rumors planted by Japanese agents, whose masters were angry with him because of his long-expressed belligerence toward them; with the gossip of Tientsin, which turned on his being Li's son-in-law, and so favored; and with the intrigues of the Fukien clique in the Peiyang fleet, which group feared that he knew too much of the Ma-wei battle (August 1884) disaster.[133] If justice was done in Chang's case, it seems that it came by a devious road.

We may conclude that the system of naval rewards and punishments in late nineteenth-century China operated with unpredictability and inequity. It is reasonable to assume that not all of the several suicides during this naval war can be attributed to ancient custom, or to the ethic of the defeated naval hero; some undoubtedly stemmed from a desperate uncertainty that justice would be done. The case of Lin T'ai-tseng seems most pertinent to this argument. He took his own life after his *Chen Yüan* struck something as she entered Weihaiwei for the last time. The damage was fairly serious, for the ship had to be beached. But there was apparently no certainty about what the obstruction was, or where the fault lay. Even the court, remote from mere technicalities, asked if the ship had not struck a torpedo — else why such a fuss? Li was told to make a full investigation, but the case broke down into recrimination. Why had a man of such small courage been given such an important command, it was asked. Could Lin's replacement, Yang Yung-lin (who was designated by the much-attacked admiral) be trusted? The court had heard that the captain of the *P'ing Yüan*, Li Ho-lien (who was *not* recommended by Li Hung-chang after the Yalu battle) was eligible for the berth. And so on.[134]

Some of the questions asked by the court in the aftermath of Lin T'ai-tseng's suicide were pertinent, but others illustrate the inexpert meddling in matters of naval personnel which was typical of the Confucian monarchy. Lin may have acted up to his highest idea of duty, but it is more likely that he feared that he would not have a proper day in court. In any event, he was not available to testify to anyone, let alone a naval court of inquiry, and so his death was doubly expensive. His successor Yang Yun-lin also committed suicide after the surrender.

The most famous suicide was that of Admiral Ting. Perhaps he was guided by ideas of propriety; on the other hand, he had long been under an attack that was animated by petulance as much as by rational consideration of the relationship between the moral and technical variables of modern naval warfare.

The punishment system in Li's fleet was not consonant with the needs of a modern navy. To have effected changes in the system would have required the interposing of a board of review between the emperor and his naval servitors, a board staffed by technical experts who could have attempted to determine whether, in these several situations, it had been a fatigue of metal or morale which was most answerable. No one dared to question the ineffable judgment of the Son of Heaven. In the matter of discipline, a modern navy was incompatible with age-old tradition in Confucian China.

X

CONCLUSIONS

The story of the modernization of China's fleets does not end abruptly with the Sino-Japanese War. We might very well pursue it. The rivalries, whether inside or outside of China, were just as keen. Chang Chih-tung, who was building the Nanyang fleet, tried to persuade Lang to come back — although when the Tsungli Yamen issued the invitation, it was on behalf of the Peiyang fleet after all.[1] Foreign shipbuilders were as eager as ever to take orders from China, however they might be placed. Tyler, who joined the maritime customs service after the war, was buttonholed by Italian shipbuilders in Genoa when he passed through on leave; it had been rumored that Tyler was going home "to buy another fleet for China," and the Italians wanted to have the "first shot" at him. Tyler denied the "wretched story," but was expensively entertained nonetheless.[2] At about the same time, German suppliers were encouraged by the news that Von Hannecken had been asked to buy ships and hire training officers.[3] In 1898, Lord Beresford listed eleven ships in the Peiyang fleet, including three 3400-ton German cruisers, and fifteen ships in the Nanyang fleet — which had six German-built cruisers of about that size (the Nanyang fleet also included four "old-fashioned" 400-ton British gunboats, which were probably the old Armstrong boats purchased twenty years before).[4]

What may be suggested is that, as far as naval modernization was concerned, the Sino-Japanese War taught no lessons. Lang, who did not come back to China, said of the postwar ship-buying program: "It is a sad pity to see China ordering ships at random without any thought of homogeneity. I spoke to Li Hung-chang on this subject, and he perceived the mistake they are making at Peking. Li begged me to draw up a scheme for the reorganization of the navy, which I am now engaged upon in my spare time. I am very much afraid the Chinese are drifting into making the same blunder over again."[5] And so the story goes on. As late as

1914, British naval observers were still commenting on the "wobbling manner" in which China's officials, whether under the dynasty or the republic, conducted naval affairs.[6] It is not true, however, that nothing changed. For example, in 1904 the Foochow dockyard was at last placed under a professional naval officer (Yeh Tsu-kuei).[7]

Yet further pursuit of the naval history of the dynasty after the Sino-Japanese War is largely academic. However it was constituted, the navy was not tested in any war after that with Japan, and without such a test, there can be little measurement of the effectiveness of a military institution. We must therefore summarize what we have seen of China's naval modernization during the period when it was crucially tested.

China did indeed respond to the Western naval impact. In many ways, the accomplishment, which included the building of modern ships and the training of men, was impressive. However, the response was tardy, and it must be characterized as inadequate. We might expect that China's new and untried fleets would be defeated in the nineteenth century by Western navies, but that it was defeated by the Japanese navy, which was modernized no sooner, makes the point.

The problem is, why was China's response inadequate? The most frequently used explanation is that the dynasty was in decline. Some Western scholars, however, are not convinced that the concept of "dynastic decline," based as it was on the Confucian preoccupation with the moral attributes of the ruling family, is a sufficiently inclusive analytic device. The Chinese economy may have been expanding during this particular "decline."[8] China did not lose all of her battles, even with a Western power, as late as the 1880's. We know that a navy was built, or bought. On examination, the decline of the Manchus shows an interesting ambivalence.

Indeed, it may be said that this particular dynastic decline — marked as it was by military deterioration, defeat from the sea, rebellion, and the weakening of court leadership — helped naval innovation as much as it hindered it. That the weakened dynasty, during the rebellion, had to place greater reliance on Chinese provincial officials, such as Tseng Kuo-fan, Li Hung-chang, and Tso Tsung-t'ang, meant an increase in the power and prestige of those officials. Each of them developed an interest in military or naval reform, and, whatever their idiosyncracies, each had greater freedom to build plants or buy ships than had Lin Tse-hsü or the Cantonese gentry who sporadically experimented during and immediately after the Opium War.

In another way dynastic decline aided naval innovation. The old water force, which so amused Westerners, was of course affected by the general decline of leadership. Even during the early Manchu period, the water force had not been a powerful instrument. In the nineteenth century, the water force was not a great vested interest, set on the defiance of change. Although the old water forces, which were during our period never completely disbanded, did to some extent compete with the new fleets for funds, it may still be said that naval modernization was not hampered by entrenched professional conservatism, of which there was so much in Britain in that century. Occasionally a Sung Chin might say that the old war junks were adequate, but the water force officers who have figured in this study appear either as officers in the new ships, or else as actors in a bumbling farce, wherever their fleets were still maintained. For them, naval modernization took place almost in a different world.

On the other hand, the decline of the dynasty also hindered the naval modernization effort. The relative weakening of the central power after the rebellion increased the opportunities for competition between China's leaders, and basic questions, such as whether China should buy or build her navy, were left unresolved, subject to the tugging and hauling of rivals whose interests were complicated and no means impersonal. In 1884, the American minister to Peking put the problem in this way: "What Li, or Tso may have done towards the strengthening of the country can only be regarded as spasmodic and futile efforts, and not the outcome of a firm, generous, comprehensive policy, emanating from the Throne, pervading the whole Empire, and in the end enabling China to be, what she should be, a strong, wise, and civilized nation." [9] For that matter, inadequate leadership affected decision-making and morale at every point in the story. The fact that the fate of the dynasty rested in the hands of the Empress Dowager is largely a coincidence, not readily explainable in institutional or economic terms. The Confucian theory of dynastic decline, which explained such phenomena in moral terms, is not entirely devoid of pertinence.

The decline of the dynasty hindered naval modernization also in that the suppression of the Taiping Rebellion engendered in the minds of the saviors of the dynasty the "restoration" mood. The concept of a restoration, as deeply embedded in Chinese historical convention as the idea of "dynastic decline" itself, motivated China's modernizers to attempt to use "western studies" (in this case, naval modernization) for utilitarian purposes, while keeping "Chinese studies" (the whole range of Confucian values and institutions) as the core of society.

Thus Confucian institutions were to be defended with modern means. The formula was essentially conservative, and involved a contradiction between the Confucian institutions and the modern naval means which were created to defend them. It is this contradiction, whatever the accidental and personal factors which cluttered the story of naval modernization, which has largely concerned this study. Although the T'ung-chih Restoration was short-lived, it may very well be true that in this particular period of dynastic decline, given the conscious attempt to reinforce Confucian institutions, those institutions were stronger — or at least more inflexible — than at a time of dynastic vigor and confidence.

Let us then turn to the institutional and ideological factors in China's failure to modernize her naval defenses soon enough to meet her succession of challenges. The provincial organization of the empire may be classified as an institutional arrangement. However much the relations between the central government and the provinces were strained by the emergence, after the Taiping Rebellion, of such men as Li Hung-chang, the established provincial compartmentalization of China's military forces remained. If Li kept his ships out of the Sino-French War, the southern officials kept theirs, for the most part, out of the war with Japan. There was no national fleet, even on paper; certainly there was none in the minds of the men who directed the fleets or sailed the ships. Loyalties were provincial or personal. The water force had never been unified. Perhaps slow sailing speeds contributed to the parceling-out of responsibilities in that traditional force; this was no problem for the modern fleets. Nevertheless, the modern fleets were organized by province, or — and this was not much more effective — in accordance with the patterns of personal influence of such men as Li Hung-chang or Chang Chih-tung.

The political organization of the empire under what has been called the "Confucian constitution" was also reflected in the financial problems which attended the modernizing effort. China was not too poor to afford a modern navy. But there was no budget, and the revenues were divided by quota in such a way as to encourage rivalry between the central government and the provinces, and among the provinces, as well as among the parts of each provincial administration. In a time of dynastic decline, the customary perquisites were enlarged, and peculation was rife. But to have established a naval budget, administered in Peking, would have required a profound rearrangement of the organization of the empire, which not even a dynasty in its first vigor would have attempted.

Beyond these organizational encumbrances, there lay certain ideological factors which hampered naval modernization. Nationalism is a Western invention. The Chinese of the nineteenth century — even the late nineteenth century — hardly knew the feeling of identification with the "state," or the "nation." China's wars were regional affairs, of no general concern. In 1895, a customs officer said, "the war with Japan affected the province of Chihli to a slight degree only, and as far as one could see, the people of Tientsin regard it as a matter of no moment to them." [10] The men who engaged in those grim battles in the Gulf of Chihli or at Weihaiwei were isolated from their society.

In more general terms, it may be true that reformers are always isolated, but they were even more so in this context. In 1869, in the immediate aftermath of the Taiping Rebellion, which provided a stimulus for some reformers, Robert Hart said, "Some forty officials in the Provinces, and perhaps ten at Peking have a glimmering notion of what it is that the foreigner means when he speaks in general terms of progress; but of these fifty, not one is prepared to enter boldly on a career of progress." [11]

It was not that China's officials lacked conviction, but that their convictions were informed by Confucian values. To them, the central institution was the civil service examination system. Not only was this the principal means of personal advancement for China's men of ability; it was the bulwark of a host of values and preferences which elevated the scholar, with his nontechnical, literary, and artistic pursuits, at the expense of the military man and the technical knowledge required in naval modernization. It was difficult to find men to run China's arms establishments, and to keep them at it; it was at least as hard to train naval officers and persuade them to stay in their new and unsung profession. Dropout was high. In Appendix D of this study are the names of many Foochow academy men who appear in this story only as students. There are not many sketches of naval careers attached to the list. In part, this scarcity of evidence of the making of naval careers may be only a reflection of the way records were kept; also, not all naval officers were distinguished, or decorated, or killed in battle. But we do have Li Hung-chang's 1888 Peiyang naval regulations, which encouraged his cadets to hope for identification with the civil service, and Li's own statements on the high rate of attrition among his students, to give force to the argument that to most men, in the China we have studied, the military or naval career was not well regarded.

The failure to evolve a naval strategy suited to the potentialities of steam-powered ships shows another kind of resistance to the modernization process. To be sure, some progress was registered. The Yalu battle was fought in open water. But it was not fought in the Straits of Tsushima, between Korea and Japan, and the fleet had been severely limited in its strategic mission before the battle. After it, there was no strategy at all. The ships retreated to a fortified harbor; the ships were used as fixed forts. China's feeble strategic thinking may have been a function of the compartmentalization of the coasts; flotillas do not undertake the tasks appropriate to a combined "national" fleet. It would be neat to say, too, that inadequate financing led to this feeble strategy, but it would be at least as correct to reverse the terms. To relate strategy to finances or organization, however, takes us back to institutional matters.

At the heart of traditional China's Confucian institutions stood the throne. The emperor epitomized the personal, moralistic preference of Confucian thinking. His judgments could not be questioned, nor could his function as the ultimate judge of failure (failure itself was seen as a moral problem) be in any way usurped by intermediary devices of investigation and adjudication. Naval courts-martial would have introduced alien technical considerations, thereby weakening the supposed omniscience in matters of responsibility which the Son of Heaven possessed. Here was another institutional deterrent to the creation of a thoroughly professional modern naval force, confident of judgment on its own terms.

The complexity of China's response has been emphasized by pointing to the twenty-year hiatus between the Opium War and the start of naval reform in the 1860's. It is interesting to recollect that, even after the start of the modernization, probably the only clear-cut response to an overt naval challenge — that is, the only situation in which a Westerner can readily see and appreciate cause and effect — was the establishment of the Navy Board in 1885, after the Sino-French War. But that year also saw Chang Chih-tung attempt to effect the permanent sealing off of Canton. Here is a stark contrast in responses.

Of course China's failure to modernize her navy sufficiently is but part of her larger failure to industrialize. China's arsenals were not only socially isolated; they were economically isolated as well. Here also the basic explanation must invoke the Confucian values and institutions of traditional China.

In sum, naval reform in nineteenth-century China was undertaken by a few Chinese officials, each with his own evaluation of the problem, and each tremendously preoccupied with other concerns which were peripheral or even hostile to his separate naval program. China's naval modernizers were involved in a contradiction, which paralyzed their efforts, despite the enormous energies and abilities invested in these efforts.

NOTES

APPENDICES

BIBLIOGRAPHY

GLOSSARY

ABBREVIATIONS USED IN THE NOTES

BPP	*British Parliamentary Papers*
CCTY	*Ch'uan-cheng tsou-yi hui-pien*
CF	*Chung-Fa chan-cheng*
CJ	*Chung-Jih chan-cheng*
CKHP	*Huang-ch'ao chang-ku hui-pien*
CR	*Chinese Repository*
CSK	*Ch'ing-shih kao*
CTLT	*Huang-ch'ao cheng-tien lei-tsuan*
FRUS	*Foreign Relations of the United States*
HFT	*Hai-fang tang*
IMC	China, Imperial Maritime Customs
IWSM	*Ch'ou-pan i-wu shih-mo*
KNCTCC	*Kiang-nan chih-tsao-chü chi*
LWCK	*Li Wen-chung-kung ch'uan chi*
PYHC	*Pei-yang hai-chün chang ch'eng*
TWHK	*Tso Wen-hsiang-kung ch'uan-chi*
USNIP	*United States Naval Institute Proceedings*
WCSL	*Ch'ing-chi wai-chiao shih-liao*

NOTES

I. THE TRADITIONAL CHINESE WATER FORCE AND ITS FAILURE IN THE OPIUM WAR

1. For an analysis of some of the problems involved in the "decline" of the Manchus, see John K. Fairbank, Alexander Eckstein, and L. S. Yang, "Economic Change in Early Modern China: An Analytic Framework," *Economic Development and Cultural Change*, 9.1:18 (October 1960).
2. Unsigned article, "Military Skill and Power of the Chinese," *Chinese Repository*, 5.4:177 (August 1836), for critical comment; G. A. Ballard, *The Influence of the Sea on the Political History of Japan* (New York, 1921), pp. 135–136, for favorable comment from a British vice-admiral.
3. The basic narrative of the Opium War is found in H. B. Morse and H. F. MacNair, *Far Eastern International Relations* (Shanghai, 1928), Chap. 7. An excellent eyewitness British account is that of W. D. Bernard and W. H. Hall, *Narrative of the Voyages and Services of the Nemesis from 1840 to 1843, and of the Combined Naval and Military Operations in China*, 2 vols. (London, 1844).
4. For a table of the six naval rates in the Royal Navy, see John Masefield, *Sea Life in Nelson's Time* (New York, 1925), p. 11.
5. For sketches, see Pao Tsen-peng, *Chung-kuo hai-chün shih* (History of the Chinese Navy; Taipei: Chinese Naval Publication Office, 1951), pp. 82–88.
6. For discussion of the Board of Works, see Hsieh Pao-chao, *The Government of China, 1644–1911* (Baltimore, 1925), pp. 269–270. On provincial yards, see *CSK:PC*, 6:1b–3.
7. T. F. Wade, "The Army of the Chinese Empire: Its Two Great Divisions, the Bannermen or National Guard, and the Green Standard or Provincial Troops: Their Organization, Locations, Pay, Conditions, and etc.," *CR*, 20:378 (1851).
8. Repair schedules are given in *CSK:PC*, 6:1a–b. Also see Wade, p. 378, for annual rigging repairs in Kwangtung.
9. Masefield, p. 3.
10. See *CSK:PC*, 6:1b–5, for orders ranging from 1732 to 1840.
11. See Charles E. Gibson, *The Story of the Ship* (New York, 1948), Chaps. 13–14, for review of Western naval development. Pao Tsen-peng, pp. 87–88, discusses Ming-Ch'ing efforts to control commercial vessel size. See *CSK:PC*, 6:3–4, for orders to imitate commercial styles, the latest in 1804.
12. For instances of merchants providing their own protection, in 1740 and 1793, see *CSK:PC*, 6:3a–b. The 1809 episode is in H. B. Morse, *The Chronicles of the East India Company Trading to China, 1635–1834* (New York, 1926), III, 116–118.
13. Bernard and Hall, I, 277–278.
14. Lo Jung-pang, "The Decline of the Early Ming Navy," *Oriens Extremus*, 5.2:159 (December 1958).
15. For Board of Works list, see Wade, p. 379.
16. "Military Skill," p. 177.
17. *Ibid.*, p. 173.
18. Bernard and Hall, I, 287–281.
19. For example, see the fight at Anson's Bay of January 1841; Bernard and Hall, Vol. 1, Chap. 14.

NOTES TO CHAPTER I

20. Hsieh Pao-chao, p. 256. Also see H. S. Brunnert and V. V. Hagelstrom, *Present Day Political Organization of China*, tr. A. Beltchenko and E. E. Moran, rev. ed. (Shanghai, 1912), pp. 138–139.

21. Brunnert and Hagelstrom, p. 337; Hsieh Pao-chao, p. 291.

22. See *Ibid.*, p. 298; and Brunnert and Hagelstrom, p. 336, for discussion of high Manchu-Chinese relations. Wade, pp. 319–320, notes Manchu water force units at Foochow, Chapu, Canton, and Kinchow (Manchuria).

23. See Hsieh Pao-chao, pp. 259–60, 292, 299, for discussion of intraprovincial official relations, right of direct memorial, etc.

24. See reports by Wu-er-kung-o in July 1840, *IWSM:TK*, 11:7–10b, 13.

25. Wade, p. 255. This source has been supplemented with a list of Manchu Banner commands in Brunnert and Hagelstrom, p. 337.

26. Wade, pp. 373–374.

27. Ralph L. Powell, *The Rise of Chinese Military Power, 1895–1912* (Princeton, 1955), p. 14.

28. For table of ranks, with Chinese terms, see below, Appendix B.

29. The basic guide in this section on personnel is Wade. For specific instances of the buying of pirates see for example Morse, *Chronicles*, III, 144–145.

30. Charles Gutzlaff, *Journal of Three Voyages Along the Coast of China, 1831, 1832, and 1833, with Notices of Siam, Corea, and the Loo-Choo Islands*, 3rd ed. (London, 1841), p. 148. On p. 121 Gutzlaff wrote of a fight between Fukienese sailors in the Tientsin region and his own junkmen. *CSK:PC*, 6:4, notes that in 1816 when the Tientsin water force was re-established, it drew sailors from Fukien and other southern provinces.

31. Gutzlaff, *Journal*, pp. 205–219, covering his observations in the Woosung-Shanghai area.

32. See Wade, pp. 400–401, for detailed discussion of punishment system.

33. *CSK:PC*, 6:4b, for edicts of 1806, 1830, and 1835.

34. *IWSM:TK*, 12:11b–14b.

35. Gutzlaff, *Journal*, pp. 84–87. He traveled from Siam to Tientsin in a 250-ton commercial junk, with a crew of fifty men.

36. Wade, pp. 376–377, gives coverage for the entire coast. For further detail (Shantung, Chihli, Liaoning) see *CSK:PC*, 6:1a–b, 13b–14. There is mention of penalties in *ibid.*, 6:10a–b. For Min-Che arrangements, see *ibid.*, 6:1. Wade, p. 319, notes exclusion of Manchu units.

37. *CSK:PC*, 6:2a–b, and Wade, p. 378.

38. *CR*, 4:12, 562 (April 1836).

39. Powell, p. 15.

40. Wade, p. 379; totals for ocean water force only. On p. 378 he discusses cruising arrangements for Kwangtung; the average number of cruise ships for each of the five districts was thirteen.

41. Lo Jung-pang, p. 148, note 2.

42. *CR*, 4:12, 562 (April 1836).

43. Sir John F. Davis, *China During the War and Since the Peace*, 2 vols. (London, 1852), I, 3–4.

44. For description of the mile-long Amoy fort, see *ibid.*, I, 21, 156. See Wade, pp. 373–374, on Foochow Tartar general.

45. See entry for I-li-pu in Arthur W. Hummel, ed., *Eminent Chinese of the Ch'ing Period, 1644–1911*, 2 vols. (Washington, D.C.: 1943, 1944); also edict of July 20, 1840, in *IWSM:TK*, 11:7–10b.

46. *Ibid.*, 11:7–10b; 12:15a–b, 23a–b; 13:23b–25b.

47. *Ibid.*, 14:3b–4, 8b-9.

48. Brunnert and Hagelstrom, p. 337. Wade, p. 375, points out that the Chekiang water force was mainly a coastal conservancy unit, and the general did not really answer to the admiral, but, due to his rank, took his lead from the Min-Che governor-general.

49. H. B. Morse, *International Relations of the Chinese Empire*, 3 vols. (Shanghai, 1910–1918), I, 266, gives blockade arrangements.
50. See entries for Shih Lang, Shih Shih-p'iao, and Li Ch'ang-keng in Hummel.
51. Cited in Lo Jung-pang, p. 157.
52. Grace Fox, *British Admirals and Chinese Pirates, 1832–1869* (London, 1940), pp. 27–29, lists warship visits. Morse, *Chronicles*, Vol. 3, Chap. 61, Appendix P, lists them also.
53. For the *Doris* incident see *ibid.*, III, 214–222.
54. Fox, pp. 49–50.
55. *CR* 5.4:166–167 (August 1836); Morse, *International Relations*, I, 135.
56. Gutzlaff, *Journal*, pp. 170–183, 185–201, for visits to Foochow and the Ningpo-Chenhai area.
57. See Lo Jung-pang, pp. 162–168, for discussion.
58. For full description of the Canton fortifications, see Bernard and Hall, I, 238–241, 329–331, and Chap. 18. For comments on guns, see *ibid.*, I, 333–341; II, 32–33. On admission that some guns were liable to blow up, see report by Ch'i-shan, *IWSM:TK*, 20:27–32b.
59. On sandbags, overturned boats, etc., see memorial by Ch'i Chün-tsao, Teng T'ing-chen, and others of May 16, 1840, in *IWSM:TK*, 10:19b–23.
60. On Amoy forts, see Davis, I, 155–157; and Bernard and Hall, II, 123, which latter account contains the material quoted in the text.
61. *Ibid.*, Vol. 2, Chap. 33, contains the Chapu account. The British lost thirteen men — the largest loss in any action during the war.
62. Bernard and Hall, II, 285.
63. *Ibid.*, I, 329–331, contains details of British attack on chains and forts in January 1841; see also Ch'i-shan's report, Jan. 27 and 30, 1841, in *IWSM:TK*, 20:24b, 27–32b.
64. Bernard and Hall, Vol. 1, Chap. 18, has much on such devices.
65. Teng T'ing-chen et al., *IWSM:TK*, 6:6b.
66. The *Cambridge* was found on Feb. 27, 1841. Bernard and Hall, I, 353, 359.
67. For an order of 1736, see *CSK:PC*, 6:2b–3.
68. *Ibid.*, 6:12b, order of 1767.
69. On merchants' subscriptions for chains, etc., see memorial by Teng T'ing-chen et al., March 1839, in *IWSM:TK*, 6:3–6b. For memorial by Lin et al., see *ibid.*, 10:36–37.
70. *CR*, 11:432 (1842), and Bernard and Hall, I, 319–324.

II. CHINA'S DELAYED RESPONSE TO THE WESTERN NAVAL CHALLENGE

1. Lü Shih-ch'iang, *Chung-kuo tsao-ch'i ti lun-ch'uan ching-ying* (The early development of steamers in China; Taipei: Institute of Modern History, Academia Sinica, 1962), p. 9.
2. *Ibid.*, p. 10: Pao Tsen-peng, pp. 121–122, and Gideon Chen, *Lin Tse-hsü, Pioneer Promoter of the Adoption of Western Means of Maritime Defense in China* (Peking, 1934), pp. 20–21.
3. Chen, *Lin*, pp. 34–35, 43.
4. Bernard and Hall, II, 222, 296–297.
5. Chen, *Lin*, pp. 35–39; Pao Tsen-Peng, pp. 130–131.
6. Chen, *Lin*, pp. 36–45.
7. Bernard and Hall, I, 278–281.
8. Chen, *Lin*, p. 40.
9. Bernard and Hall, II, 226–227, 353–354; Lü Shih-ch'iang, pp. 11–12.
10. Lü Shih-ch'iang, p. 12; Earl Swisher, *China's Management of the American Barbarians* (New Haven, 1953), p. 38.
11. Pao Tsen-peng, pp. 129–130.

NOTES TO CHAPTER II

12. Lü Shih-ch'iang, pp. 28–29, argues in some detail that China had the money and skills.

13. See for example recommendations for more troops, forts, etc., by Teng T'ing-chen, Chi Chün-tsao, Huang Chüeh-tzu, May 16, 1840, in *IWSM:TK*, 10:19b–23; Yü-ch'ien's listing of barbarian weaknesses, Sept. 12, 1840, *ibid.*, 14:10–12; Lin Tse-hsü and I-liang on war junks, fire rafts, etc., Sept. 18, 1840, *ibid.*, 14:41b–42b; recommendations on staking harbors, sinking junks, disguising fishermen, etc., by I-li-pu and Liu Yün-k'o, Jan. 26, 1841, *ibid.*, 20:15a–b, 18, 19b. The summary is based on documents read in *IWSM* for the Opium War, and also on summaries and translations of these documents as presented in Arthur Waley, *The Opium War Through Chinese Eyes* (London, 1958); P. C. Kuo, *A Critical Study of the First Anglo-Chinese War, with Documents* (Shanghai, 1935); and Teng Ssu-yü, *Chang Hsi and the Treaty of Nanking, 1842* (Chicago, 1944).

14. Lü Shih-ch'iang, pp. 33–35, summarizes these memorials.

15. The recommendation by Teng, et al., dated Aug. 13, 1840, appears as Document 23 in Kuo, p. 256. For Lin's October 1840 memorial, see *IWSM:TK*, 16:21.

16. Chen, *Lin*, p. 20, citing *Hai-Kuo t'u-chih*, for the recommendation did not enter official records.

17. *IWSM:TK*, 14:10–12.

18. For statement by Teng T'ing-chen, see Kuo, Doc. 23, p. 256; for Lin's contradiction, see Waley, p. 123, citing memorial of Aug. 16, 1840. The emperor was angered by the contradiction.

19. Lü Shih-ch'iang, p. 35.

20. Yü-ch'ien reported this; Kuo, Doc. 28, p. 260. John K. Fairbank, *Trade and Diplomacy on the China Coast, 1842–1854*, 2 vols. (Cambridge, Mass., 1954), Chap. 1, gives this and other examples.

21. Waley, pp. 85–86.

22. *IWSM:TK*, 29:3b–4.

23. See Ch'i-shan memorial of January 30, 1841, in *ibid.*, 20:27–32b.

24. Teng, *Chang Hsi*, pp. 75, 78.

25. See Lo Jung-pang, "China's Paddle Wheel Boats," *Tsing Hua Journal of Chinese Studies, New Series*, 2.1:189–215 (May 1960), for detailed discussion of wheel-boats from Sung times on.

26. Waley, p. 71.

27. *Ibid.*, p. 100.

28. For the emperor's anger on false report of 1841 attack, see Kuo, Doc. 44, p. 286; for acceptance of 1842 report, see Teng, *Chang Hsi*, n. 242, pp. 165–166. Swisher, pp. 29–30, says the Tao-kuang Emperor was quite well informed on the strength of his armed forces.

29. Morse and MacNair, p. 63, note.

30. Lü Shih-ch'iang, pp. 30–33, places much emphasis on the personality of the emperor in explaining the termination of naval experimentation after the Opium War.

31. For review of movement for conciliation, see John K. Fairbank, "Chinese Diplomacy and the Nanking Treaty of 1842," *Journal of Modern History*, 12.1:1–29 (March 1940).

32. Chen, *Lin*, Chap. 3, "The Attitude of the Court and the Provinces," quotations on p. 60.

33. Lü Shih-ch'iang, pp. 36–37. The 30-month estimate is based on postface to Ting's book, *Yen-p'ao t'u-shuo*, in which he states that he submitted information on his work to Teng T'ing-ch'en at Canton — apparently late 1839 or early 1840. Chen, *Lin*, p. 54, cites this postface.

34. Lü Shih-ch'iang, p. 37.

35. *Ibid.*

36. See entry for I-shan in Hummel; for memorial, see Lü Shih-ch'iang, pp. 18–19.

37. Pao Tsen-peng, pp. 132–134.
38. For Bernard's comments, see Bernard and Hall, I, 278–281. *CR* (February 1843), p. 108, notes the purchase of the vessels named. Names of the purchasers are given by Swisher, p. 38.
39. Lü Shih-ch'iang, pp. 19–20, citing the *Shih-lu* rather than the *IWSM*, from which he draws the other documentation.
40. Chen, *Lin*, pp. 58–59.
41. Lü Shih-ch'iang, pp. 37–38, lists Admiral Wu, I-liang, Ch'i-ying, Niu Chien, I-li-pu, and a few others.
42. Chen, *Lin*, pp. 59–60.
43. *Hai-kuo t'u-chih*, 1:1, 3b; he also speaks of enticing the enemy into the inner waterways.
44. *CR*, 13.11:603 (November 1844).
45. For fuller treatment, see two works by Gideon Chen, *Tseng Kuo-fan, Pioneer Promoter of the Steamship in China* (Peiping, 1935), pp. 9, 18–20; and *Tso Tsung-t'ang, Pioneer Promoter of the Modern Dockyard and the Woolen Mill in China* (Peiping, 1938), pp. 4–6.
46. On Wu's activities, see T. T. Meadows, *The Chinese and Their Rebellions* (London, 1856), pp. 195, 208–210, 284; *BPP*: "Papers Respecting the Civil War in China" (1853), pp. 3–4; Chen, *Tseng*, pp. 31–32. Morse, *International Relations*, I, 406, 421–422, mentions the *Confucius* along with two others, the *Clown* and the *Compton* at Shanghai. See G. Lanning and S. Couling, *The History of Shanghai* (Shanghai, Hong Kong, Singapore, and Yokohama, 1921), p. 384, for some details on the *Confucius*.
47. Chen, *Tseng*, pp. 32–33.
48. John King, "Progress in China," Pt. 2, *Blackwood's Edinburgh Magazine*, February 1863.
49. Swisher, p. 22.
50. See entry for P'eng Yü-lin in Hummel.
51. Two detailed accounts of the Western naval revolution may be found in Bernard Brodie, *Sea Power in the Machine Age* (Princeton, 1941); and J. P. Baxter, *The Introduction of the Ironclad Warship* (Cambridge, Mass., 1933).
52. For the background of the Second China War and coverage of the war, see Morse and MacNair, Chap. 10 and 11. A detailed account based on official British reports is D. Bonner-Smith and E. W. R. Lumby, *The Second China War, 1856–1860*, Publications of the Navy Board Society, Vol. 95 (Greenwich: Royal Naval College, 1954).
53. Seymour to Admiralty, June 10, 1857, in Bonner-Smith and Lumby, pp. 204–208.
54. Chen, *Tseng*, p. 10.
55. See Chap. 1, n. 13.
56. Seymour to Admiralty, Dec. 29, 1856, in Bonner-Smith and Lumby, p. 151; Bowring to Clarendon, Dec. 31, 1856, in *ibid.*, p. 154.
57. For description of forts, see Seymour to Elgin, May 14, 1858, in *ibid.*, p. 328. Other descriptions in *North China Herald* (extra of May 27, 1858), p. 174; (May 29), p. 186; and (June 19), p. 170.
58. For re-establishment of the Tientsin water force, see *CSK:PC*, 6:7; descriptions of forts in *North China Herald* (July 9, 1859); Hope to Admiralty, July 5, 1859, in Bonner-Smith and Lumby, pp. 393–400.
59. Morse, *International Relations*, I, 576–584, for details of the encounter.
60. For full account see *ibid.*, Vol. 1, Chap. 26; for further details, comments on guns, etc., see *North China Herald* (Aug. 18, 1860), p. 130; (Sept. 8, 1860), p. 43; (Sept. 22, 1860), p. 151.
61. For a careful study of the Tsungli Yamen (*tsung-li ke-kuo shih-wu ya-men*), see Meng Ssu-ming, "The Organization and Functions of the Tsungli Yamen," Ph.D. thesis (Harvard, 1949), Chaps. 5 and 6.

NOTES TO CHAPTER II

62. Li Chien-nung, *The Political History of China, 1840-1928*, tr. Ssu-yü Teng and Jeremy Ingalls (New York, 1956), pp. 70-75, discusses phases of the rebellion and treats 1860 as a turning point.

63. For a careful study of the Restoration, including introductory comments on the historical precedents of it, see Mary Wright, *The Last Stand of Chinese Conservatism* (Stanford, 1957).

64. On the Ever-Victorious Army and Ward, see Morse and MacNair, p. 338; on Admiral Hope's agreement, see Andrew Wilson, *The Ever-Victorious Army* (London, 1868), p. 388.

65. For Yüan's memorial, see *IWSM:HF*, 71:34b. For a memorial on the subject from Tseng Kuo-fan, and the emperor's reaction, see *ibid.*, 72:3-9b.

66. For samples of this British view, see Bruce to Russell, May 13, 1862, in *BPP: Further Papers Relative to the Rebellion in China*, 1863, p. 9; Bruce to Stavely, Oct. 24, 1862, enclosed in Bruce to Russell, Nov. 25, 1862, *ibid.*, p. 154; Bruce to Kuper, Nov. 22, 1862, *ibid.*, p. 146.

67. The section on the Lay-Osborn flotilla is based on John L. Rawlinson, "The Lay-Osborn Flotilla: Its Development and Significance," *Papers on China*, 4:58-93 (Harvard University, East Asian Research Center, 1950). A few of the specific references will be given in the following notes.

68. *IWSM:HF*, 72:3, Jan. 19, 1861.

69. *IWSM:TC*, 1:22b, Sept. 9, 1861.

70. Chen, *Tseng*, pp. 40-42; see also *North China Herald and Market Report*, Sept. 5, 1868, p. 427, and Jan. 29, 1880, p. 22, for interesting details on this ship and her builders.

71. For correspondence between Tseng and the court, see memorial by Tseng, Sept. 9, 1861 in *IWSM:TC*, 1:22b; memorial by Prince Kung and edict, Feb. 9, 1862, *ibid.*, 4:9-12b; memorial by Tseng and edict, Jan. 24, 1862, *ibid.*, 4:51b-52b; memorial by Prince Kung, Nov. 18, 1862, and edict of same date, *ibid.*, 10:16, 20; for memorial of Tseng and edict, Feb. 7, 1863, *ibid.*, 12:35b-37b; for letter of Tseng, Nov. 17, 1863, *ibid.*, 21:19.

72. Andrew Wilson, *Lieutenant-Colonel Gordon's Chinese Campaigns and the Taiping Rebellion* (Edinburgh and London, 1868), pp. 265-266.

73. Lü Shih-ch'iang, pp. 115-116.

74. Baxter, pp. 155-159, gives *Warrior* details.

75. For translation of Li's letter, see Teng Ssu-yü and John K. Fairbank, *China's Response to the West* (Cambridge, Mass., 1954), p. 69.

76. Demetrius C. Boulger, *The Life of Sir Halliday Macartney, K.C.M.G.* (New York and London, 1908), p. 79.

77. On Osborn's machinery, see Boulger, pp. 125-131.

78. On the Chinese in Li's plants, see Ch'uan Han-sheng, *Ch'ing-chi ti Kiang-nan chih-tsao-chu* (The Kiangnan arsenal in Ch'ing times; Formosa, 1951), pp. 146-147, and Stanley Spector, *Li Hung-chang and the Huai Army* (Seattle, 1964) pp. 155-157.

79. Chen, *Tso*, pp. 8-13. Quotation on pp. 12-13.

80. *Ibid.*, pp. 1-4.

81. See Fox, pp. 150-172, for full discussion of the piracy problem and proposals. On Tso's proposal, see Chen, *Tso*, p. 17. The memorial appears in *CCTY*, 1:1-8b, June 25, 1866.

82. For discussion of the "self-strengthening" idea, see Teng and Fairbank, Chap. 5.

83. Chen, *Tso*, pp. 80-81.

84. See n. 63, above.

85. On Feng Kuei-fen, see Teng and Fairbank, pp. 50-55.

SELF-STRENGTHENING MOVEMENT

III. THE MILITARY SELF-STRENGTHENING MOVEMENT, TO 1875

1. There were other arsenals, in Fukien, Kirin, and at Nanking. The Fukien arsenal was set up by Ying-kuei; *IWSM:TC*, 89:19. In 1881 Wu Ta-ch'eng built a plant at Kirin; see *IMC: Dec. Reps., 1882–1891*, Newchwang, p. 33. Apart from the few notes in this text, there is little on the Nanking arsenal; see Chen, *Tseng*, pp. 24–25.

2. On Yung Wing's activities, see Yung Wing, *My Life in China and America* (New York, 1909), Chaps. 14 and 15. There is some confusion as to the early leadership at the arsenal. Li Hung-chang *(IWSM:TC*, 35:2) said that Feng and Shen were in charge. *Kiang-nan chih-tsao-chü chi* (The record of the Kiangnan arsenal; Shanghai, 1905), 6:40–44, presents a classified list of all arsenal leaders from 1865 to 1905, and there the first leaders given for general managers were Ting and Ying.

3. For Li's report on the purchase of the yard, see *IWSM:TC*, 35:2. T. E. LaFargue, *China's First Hundred* (Pullman, Wash., 1942), pp. 68–69, adds some information, as do Pao Tsen-peng, p. 184, and Lanning and Couling, p. 384. Spector, p. 303, speaks of the expansion of the arsenal. For Tseng's 1867 memorial, see *IWSM: TC*, 61:27–31b.

4. Report by Tseng, *ibid.*, 61:27–31b; also Chen, *Tseng*, p. 47.

5. List of works in *KNCTCC*, 2:2–11b; the 1905 date of this work makes it difficult to tell which shops were working by 1875. Ch'uan Han-sheng gives the number of shops by 1875 as seventeen. One of the important activities was the translation bureau set up in 1867 by Hsü Shou and Hua Heng-fang; see Knight Biggerstaff, *The Earliest Modern Government Schools in China* (Ithaca, 1961), pp. 173–174.

6. See Appendix C for further detail on ships mentioned in this book. The ships named here all appear in a list of Kiangnan ships, in *KNCTCC*, 3:55. The 1872 quotation comes from *BPP*: "Commercial Reports," 1872, v. lxvi, Shanghai, p. 152.

7. See list of Kiangnan ships, *KNCTCC*, 3:55. The remarks on the *Hai An* are found in *BPP*: "Commercial Reports," 1872, v. lxvi, Shanghai, p. 152. Shen Pao-chen in 1874 used only the *Ts'e Hai*; *IWSM:TC*, 97:7–8. The last ship built at Kiangnan was the *Pao Min*, 1885.

8. Tseng memorial of 1868, *IWSM:TC*, 61:27–31b; 1872 British comment in *BPP*: "Commercial Reports," 1872, v. lxvi, Shanghai, p. 152.

9. See report by Tseng Kuo-fan to Tsungli Yamen, Mar. 17, 1872, in *HFT: Fu-chou, shang*, p. 325; Ho Ching to Tsungli Yamen, July 23, 1872, in *HFT*: "Kiangnan," pp. 95–110. For material on the Sun Chin attack, see coverage of the Foochow dockyard, below.

10. See *KNCTCC*, 2:2–11b, for list of plant additions. For comments by Li Hung-chang on the Kiangnan arsenal, see Li memorial of 1874 in *IWSM:TC*, 99:13–31b; also Ch'uan Han-sheng, pp. 151–153, citing Li Hung-chang.

11. See *BPP*: "Commercial Reports," 1869, v. lx, Tientsin, p. 142; *LWCK*: Memorials, 17:16–17b; *PYHC*, item 8, on the two branches; and *LWCK*: Memorials, 33:25ff., for memorial by Li mentioning distribution of the Tientsin product.

12. Boulger, pp. 191–194.

13. Memorial by Li in 1874 in *IWSM:TC*, 99:13–31b.

14. Tso's memorial in *CCTY*, 1:1–8b; for discussion and partial translation, see Chen, *Tso*, pp. 16–19. There were other shipyard schemes; see report by Chiang I-feng, governor of Kwangtung, in *IWSM:TC*, 43:17.

15. For letter from French minister to Tsungli Yamen, Sept. 22, 1866, see *HFT: Fu-chou, shang*, p. 13; for orders and delay granted Nov. 18, 1866, see *CCTY*, 1:10–12b, and *HFT: Fu-chou, shang*, p. 17; Ying-kuei's takeover noted in *ibid.*, p. 17. For discussion, see Chen, *Tso*, p. 23, and Pao Tsen-peng, p. 181.

16. For discussion and arrangements, see Chen, *Tso*, pp. 30–31; and Prosper Giquel, *The Foochow Arsenal and Its Results: From Commencement in 1867 to the End of the Foreign Directorate on 16 February, 1874*, tr. from French by H. Lang

NOTES TO CHAPTER III

(Shanghai, 1874), pp. 9–10, 13–14. Edict of Nov. 18, 1866, cited in n. 15, acknowledges Tso's popularity with the gentry.

17. See Giquel, p. 13; Shen to Tsungli Yamen, Sept. 27, 1867, in *HFT: Fu-chou, shang*, pp. 80–81; for wages of apprentices, see LaFargue, p. 6; for court assurances to Tso and arrangements for signature, see edicts in *CCTY*, 2:1–19b, and *HFT: Fu-chou, shang*, pp. 45–46.

18. On the DeMeritens affair, see Ying-kuei report of Mar. 27, 1867, in *HFT: Fu-chou, shang*, p. 64; Shen's fears about the loyalty of the two Frenchmen, Aug. 8, 1867, *ibid.*, p. 73; Tsungli Yamen reply, *ibid.*, p. 78; Shen's support of Giquel, Nov. 27, 1867, *ibid.*, p. 95; Tsungli Yamen communication to Tso, Ying-kuei, Shen, in this and Wu T'ang affair, *ibid.*, pp. 101–103; reply to Tsungli Yamen, Feb. 2, 1868, *ibid.*, p. 104; report by Ying Kuei, Dec. 3, 1869, *ibid.*, p. 201; Tsungli Yamen to Shen, Dec. 10, 1869, *ibid.*, p. 204.

19. For Shen report on Wu T'ang, see *CCTY*, 3:17–19, 20–22; also in *IWSM:TC*, 51:13b–17b. Tso's memorial of the 10th month, 1867 (Oct. 27–Nov. 25) is in *ibid.*, 51:18–19. Wu T'ang was not opposed to steamers or shipbuilding; he bought a steamer in 1869, and in 1867 had signed a memorial with Ying-kuei, Fukien Tartar general, and Li Fu-t'ai, the Fukien governor, asking for money for shipbuilding; *ibid.*, 50:9b–10. Apparently Wu T'ang wanted the Foochow yard to be under his own control.

20. On D'Aiguebelle's trip to Kansu, after resignation, see Shen to Tsungli Yamen, Mar. 29, 1870, in *HFT: Fu-chou, shang*, p. 226. The rivalry between the two Frenchmen is mentioned in Chen, *Tso*, p. 40, and in Giquel, p. 17. Hart's comments on D'Aiguebelle appear in Stanley F. Wright, *Hart and the Chinese Customs* (Belfast: published for Queen's University by W. Mullan, 1950), p. 493. Tso had to ask Shen three times to take the superintendent's job; see Tso memorial in *HFT: Fu-chou, shang*, p. 20. Shen feared that as a member of the Fukien gentry he would be unable to get along with Peking appointees; he mentioned that he had already been placarded as a nepotist, etc.; *CCTY*, 3:1–6; also *IWSM:TC*, 50:1b, July 18, 1867.

21. Giquel, p. 10; and report by Shen, in *CCTY*, 2:6; also Chen, *Tso*, pp. 25, 34.

22. Reports by Shen, *CCTY*, 3:13b; 4:1–7b.

23. Foreign comment in *North China Herald and Market Report* (Aug. 8, 1868), p. 376; on plants, see Giquel, pp. 11–12, 28–29.

24. Apart from Giquel's coverage of plant (see n. 23), Shen spoke of docks, etc., in a memorial of Feb. 4, 1868, in *CCTY*, 4:1–7b; he also speaks of foreign experts in memorial of April 21, 1868, *CCTY*, 4:10–12b, as does Chen, *Tso*, pp. 81–82.

25. For Shen report on the ship, see *CCTY*, 6:5–8; for Ch'ung-hou report on his inspection, see *IWSM:TC*, 69:7–9b.

26. For Shen's reports on these ships, see *CCTY*, 6:9–10b, 12; 7:9–11b.

27. See Giquel, pp. 17–21, for quoted material and discussion of the program; see also Biggerstaff, pp. 210–212. Giquel says the school started with twenty-six students; Biggerstaff gives the figure twelve.

28. Giquel, pp. 21–22.

29. *Ibid.*, pp. 22–23; and Biggerstaff, pp. 212–214.

30. For Shen's reports on these ships, see *CCTY*, 7:6a–b, 15; 8:3, 4; 9:17b–18.

31. For Shen's report of the arrangement, see *CCTY*, 9:10b–12b.

32. For Shen's report on the shift, see *CCTY*, 8:4b; for his request to keep the Ch'en Hang, see *CCTY*, 10:8a–b. For the Formosa crisis, see the end of this chapter.

33. See Giquel, pp. 33–34, for his report to Shen. Shen reported on March 14, 1874, that all but two foreigners had left, with pay terminated on February 16; *CCTY*, 9:16–17.

34. Stanley Wright, p. 493.

35. Prince Kung memorialized in 1872 (*IWSM:TC*, 89:39–40) saying many of the ships were side-wheelers — a retrogression from the screw-driven *Wan Nien Ch'ing*.

Chen, *Tso*, p. 86, cites a foreign opinion that the fleet was obsolete; Stanley Wright, p. 493, cites Giquel as saying the ships were not formidable.

36. *IWSM:TC*, 84:35–36b.

37. *TWHK:* Memorials, 41:30–35b; Chen, *Tso*, pp. 40–41.

38. Li's memorial, *IWSM:TC*, 86:27–34b. Shen's memorial is in *ibid.*, 86:16b–22b. A summarizing memorial by Prince Kung is in *ibid.*, 87:23–25b.

39. For Tso's opinions, see letters to Wu T'ung-yün and Hsia Hsiao-t'ao, dockyard officers, probably in March 1872, in *TWHK:* Letters, 12:11a–b, 22. For Li's criticisms of the Foochow dockyard (for example, that the Kiangnan yard had gone ahead of the Foochow yard in having acquired plans for steel-armored Monitor-type harbor defense vessels), see his memorial, *IWSM:TC*, 87: 23–25b; see also translations from a letter in Spector, *Li Hung-chang*, p. 239. For recommendations on demobilizing old fleets, see *ibid.*, p. 177.

40. See Tso's original memorial, in *CCTY*, 1:1–8b; also report by Ying-kuei, Dec. 11, 1866, *HFT: Fu-chou, shang*, p. 27; permission of throne, Jan. 14 and 19, 1867, *ibid.*, p. 51 (two items). For Ying-kuei's request to be relieved from contribution to Tso, see his report to the Grand Council, Dec. 11, 1866, *ibid.*, pp. 28–29.

41. Ying-kuei to Grand Council, July 17, 1869, in *HFT: Fu-chou, shang*, p. 166; Grand Council to Tsungli Yamen, Aug. 7, 1869, *ibid.*, p. 169; Hu-pu request for report on Foochow maintenance costs, Jan. 15, 1870, *ibid.*, p. 219; Wen Yu report, Dec. 6, 1871, urging distribution of five ships, *ibid.*, p. 309; Tsungli Yamen approval, Dec. 17, 1871, *ibid.*, p. 311; Chekiang objections, Mar. 27, 1872, *ibid.*, pp. 318, 327; Li Hung-chang reaction, Apr. 14, 1872, *ibid.*, p. 336; Shantung reply, Apr. 27, 1872, *ibid.*, p. 341; Fengtien reply, May 21, 1872, *ibid.*, p. 344. All of this is from *HFT: Fu-chou*, Pt. 8, on ship distribution 1870–1882.

42. Prince Kung's suggestion in his memorial, in *IWSM:TC*, 87:23–25b (July 6–Aug. 3, 1872). Comment by British consul in *BPP:* "Commercial Reports," 1870, Foochow, p. 80.

43. See Wen Yu to Grand Council and Tsungli Yamen, May 20, 1871, in *HFT: Fu-chou, shang*, p. 291; and Ying-kuei report to Tsungli Yamen, June 21, 1871, *ibid.*, p. 294. See also Li to Tsungli Yamen, June 26, 1872, *ibid.*, pp. 374–375.

44. Tso request in early 1873, in *IWSM:TC*, 89: 14b–17b; Shen, et al., report of Feb. 24, 1873, *CCTY*, 8:6–9b; Peking authorization, July 4, 1873, *CCTY*, 9–1b.

45. On increasing guns, see Shen report, *CCTY*, 16:20–30; Shen's summary, *IWSM:TC*, 92:15–17 (Dec. 20, 1873–Jan. 17, 1874); Prince Kung's recommendation, *ibid.*, 92:22–24.

46. Li to Tsungli Yamen, Feb. 8, 1874, in *HFT: Fu-chou, shang*, p. 486. Tso Tsung-t'ang supported the two-ships-a-year idea (*ibid.*, pp. 487–489, Feb. 15, 1874). See also Li to Tsungli Yamen, Apr. 5, 1874, *ibid.*, p. 502. Li Tsung-hsi to Tsungli Yamen, Mar. 11, 1874, *ibid.*, p. 496. Li got the *Hai Ching* and *Ta Ya* during the Formosa crisis; see Shen to Tsungli Yamen, June 13, 1874, *ibid.*, p. 523.

47. Account in *CCTY*, 11:1–20b; for the item on opium taxes, see Shen's report in *CCTY*, 10:17a–b.

48. See memorials by Prince Kung in 1864, in *IWSM:TC*, 30:1–3, 5b–6, 8a–b, 9b, for mention of these several problems; also diary entry of Tseng Kuo-fan, October 1865, dealing with marching, small-arms drill, etc., in Chen, *Tseng*, p. 22. On Wojen, see Teng and Fairbank, pp. 75–77.

49. Giquel, p. 29; and 1870 memorial by Tseng Kuo-fan, in *IWSM:TC*, 74:29b–31b.

50. Pao Tsen-peng, pp. 223–224, makes the point about the "best" students. Biggerstaff, pp. 214–215, discusses the organization of the school.

51. Taken from discussion in 1882 of Li Hung-chang's Tientsin naval academy in Young to Frelinghausen, Dec. 12, 1882, *FRUS* (1883), p. 169.

52. Wang Hsing-chung, "Fu-chou ch'uan-ch'ang chi yen-ko" (Development of the Foochow dockyard), in Pao Tsen-peng, *Chung-kuo chin-tai-shih lun-ts'ung* (Discussions on modern Chinese history; Taipei, 1956), pp. 116–117.

NOTES TO CHAPTER III

53. On Wu Ta-t'ing's work, see Shen report, Mar. 8, 1870, in *HFT: Fu-chou, shang*, p. 255; on Western subjects, see Giquel, pp. 33–34; on traditional subjects, see Shen memorial, Sept. 27, 1867, in *IWSM:TC*, 50:21–24.

54. Pao Tsen-peng, p. 223; also Henry N. Shore, *The Flight of the Lapwing* (London, 1881), pp. 56–57, for report of a discussion between the author, who was in the Royal Navy, and one of the instructors at the dockyard.

55. On the trip, see Ch'ih Chung-yu, "Hai-chün ta-shih chi" (A record of important naval events), in Tso Shun-sheng, *Chung-kuo chin-pai-nien-shih tz'u-liao hsü-pien* (Additional materials on the history of China in the last 100 years), 2 vols. (Shanghai: China Book Company, 1933), pp. 325–326 — although Ch'ih's list of eighteen cruising cadets bears no correspondence to his list of candidates starting in the school in 1867. For Giquel's report, see Giquel, pp. 29–32. Comments on absences and examination performances in Biggerstaff, pp. 211–212, footnote; p. 215, footnote.

56. Report by Wen Yu to Tsungli Yamen, Apr. 1, 1871, in *HFT: Fu-chou, shang*, pp. 279–284; Shen report to Yamen, July 2, 1870, *ibid.*, p. 237.

57. Report by Shen, *IWSM:TC*, 71:34b–41b; also by Wen Yü, Apr. 11, 1871, *HFT: Fu-chou, shang*, pp. 279–284.

58. Shen report, *IWSM:TC*, 91:33b–35b; for waiving of archery, see Shen to Tsungli Yamen, Mar. 12, 1873, *HFT: Fu-chou, shang*, p. 429.

59. Shen reports, in *IWSM:TC*, 91:33b–35b, and *CCTY*, 9:20a–b.

60. Giguel made his report in mid-1873 (Giquel, pp. 29–34); the four men were Lu Han, Chang Ch'eng, Li T'ien, and Li Chia-pen. He also said that Li Kuo-hsiang, Yeh Fu, Teng Shih-ch'ang, and Li Ho (nien) would be ready at the end of 1873, and that Liu Pu-ch'an, Lin T'ai-tseng, Chiang Ch'ao-ying, Yen Tsung-kwang, Ho Hsin-ch'uan, and Huang Chien-hsün would be ready early in 1874.

61. Giquel, pp. 29–34. For Shen's overseas training proposal of Dec. 26, 1873, with support by Prince Kung, see *IWSM:TC*, 92:15–17, 22–24. Tso's support is in his memorial to the Tsungli Yamen, Feb. 15, 1874, *HFT: Fu-chou, shang*, pp. 487–489. Details of the plan are in a letter from Shen to Li Hung-chang, forwarded to the Tsungli Yamen, Apr. 5, 1874, *ibid.*, pp. 505–507. Shen had been urging overseas training for about a year with no result; see Biggerstaff, p. 23.

62. For detailed treatment, see Meng Ssu-ming, Chaps. 5 and 6.

63. *BPP: Correspondence Respecting the Revision of the Treaty of Tientsin*, 1871, p. 125.

64. For details, see T. F. Tsiang, "Sino-Japanese Diplomatic Relations, 1870–1894," *Chinese Social and Political Science Review*, XVII, 1 (1933).

65. See Spector, *Li Hung-chang*, pp. 179–181, for discussion of the background of the granting in 1875 to Li Hung-chang of coastal defense responsibility for the northern region, and the granting in 1879 of a similar charge to Ting Jih-ch'ang for the southern coasts.

66. See alarmist report by Lo Ta-ch'un, the Fukien general, on a supposed armada of twenty-six Japanese steamers, in *IWSM:TC*, 95:14b–19. The foreign estimates appear in *North China Daily News* of July 5, 7, and 14, 1874, with some details on the Japanese fleet.

67. For Shen's interest in keeping track of Foochow ships, see *CCTY*, 8:4–5, Jan. 8, 1870; see *IWSM:TC*, 91:19a–b, for Shen's request that recipient provinces keep the dockyard informed of the whereabouts of the ships. On Shen's powers, see Tsiang, "Diplomatic Relations," p. 22.

68. Shen's report of purchase, in *IWSM:TC*, 97:7–8, Sept. 11–Oct. 8, 1874.

69. For Shen's reports in September and October 1874, see *CCTY*, 10:17a–b; *IWSM:TC*, 97:19–24; *HFT: Fu-chou, shang*, pp. 525–527.

70. Stanley Wright, p. 465.

LI HUNG-CHANG

IV. HUNG-CHANG AND NAVAL DEVELOPMENT, 1875–1885

1. Spector, *Li Hung-chang*, pp. 160–162, 169–172; also occasional references to pertinent biographies in Hummel.
2. Memorial of Chang Chao-tung, governor of Kwangtung, 11th month (Oct. 10–Nov. 8), 1874, in *IWSM:TC*, 98:23b–27, enclosing Ting's suggestion; also memorial of Wen Pin, *ibid.*, 98:31–34.
3. See Spector, *Li Hung-chang*, pp. 179–181, for Li's reaction.
4. Hsien Yü-ch'ing, "Ch'ing-chi hai-chün chih hui-su" (A retrospect on the Ch'ing navy), *Tung-fang tsa-chih* (Eastern miscellany), 38.11:29–33 (June 15, 1941), gives the 1875 date for the fund. For later comments on it, confirming that it was to come from the customs 40 per cent, see memorials by Wen Yu to Tsungli Yamen of Jan. 30, 1877, and by Shen Pao-chen of Mar. 9, 1877, in *HFT:Fu-chou, hsia*, pp. 724 and 785; also letter of Li Hung-chang to Ting Jih-ch'ang, May 24, 1877, *LWCK: P'eng-liao*, 19:3b–4.
5. Ch'ih Chung-yu, pp. 327–328.
6. *CSK:PC*, 6:8a–b, mentions that Li Ch'ao-pin was proposed for the commandant, but Li's correspondence mentions the blocking of Hart's appointment to such a post in this year, so Hart must have been mentioned as well. See Li's letter to Shen Pao-chen, Sept. 26, 1879, in *LWCK:P'eng-liao*, 21:9–10b; to Li Feng-pao, Oct. 18, 1879, *ibid.*, 21:11; to Tseng Chi-tse, Oct. 19, 1879, *ibid.*, 21:13b–14; and to Shen Pao-chen, Nov. 30, 1879, *ibid.*, 21:20b–21.
7. Li Chien-nung, pp. 113–114, 123–124.
8. Stanley Wright, p. 496, n. 72. Yao Hsi-kuang, "Tung-fang ping-shih chi-lüeh" (A record of Eastern military matters), in Tso Shun-sheng, p. 194, notes that Hsüeh Fu-ch'eng and Li Hung-chang opposed the Hart nomination, and Stanley Wright, p. 481, confirms this. The Shufeldt episode is covered in P. H. Clyde, *United States Policy Toward China* (Chapel Hill, N.C., 1940), item 23, "Shufeldt's Indictment of China."
9. Stanley Wright, p. 490; and *WCSL*, 32:7.
10. Spector, *Li Hung-chang*, pp. 185–187, from a letter of Li's of Mar. 11, 1884.
11. Teng and Fairbank, Doc. 34, pp. 124–125; and Li Chien-nung, p. 124.
12. Clyde, p. 162. As for Li's influence in the south, note that he had personal representatives at important southern points. For example, see the report on the fall of Keelung, sent on Nov. 2, 1884, direct to Li from his "Foochow Bureau," in *WCSL*, 48:1. See also *WCSL*, 44:24, for a telegram from Li to the Grand Council dated Aug. 18, 1884, wherein Li reported a letter from Liu Ming-ch'uan which he had received in digest from his Shanghai agent, whom he had engaged to obtain material for the relief of Formosa.
13. For Jui-lin's report in 1868, see *IWSM:TC*, 55:5–6b. Appendix D lists ten Jui-lin gunboats, but those identifications that are uncertain are marked with a "?." For Ting's statement, see *IWSM:TC*, 74:15b.
14. Report of early 1871, in *ibid.*, 79:46.
15. For examples of defense recommendations, see memorial by Wen Yu, Wang K'ai-t'ai et al., *ibid.*, 96:22b–25b; Jui-lin, *ibid.*, 97:10–12; and Ting Jih-ch'ang, *ibid.*, 98:23–27. Jui-lin said the old ships were not enough; Ting called for larger vessels. For Wen-hsiang's recommendations and attached edict, see *ibid.*, 98:40–41.
16. Spector, *Li Hung-chang*, pp. 172–178; for soldier-farmer idea, see Li's letter of Feb. 10, 1875, in *LWCK: P'eng-liao*, 17:6.
Later Li argued that funds for the western campaigns should *not* be reduced; see letter of Mar. 17, 1875, *ibid.*, 17:8–9.
17. Translation from report by S. W. Williams to Hamilton Fish, Sept. 17, 1874, *FRUS* (1875), I, 200. On Wen-hsiang, see Teng and Fairbank, p. 90.
18. *IWSM:TC*, 99:13–31b.
19. Stanley Wright, pp. 467–470.
20. Shore, p. 504.

NOTES TO CHAPTER IV

21. For letter to Ting, Feb. 22, 1875, see *LWCK: P'eng-liao*, 17:5; letter to Shen, May 19, 1875, *ibid.*, 17:10b–11; letter to Shen, May 27, 1875, *ibid.*, 17:15–16b; letter to Shen, Aug. 19, 1875, *ibid.*, 17:18a–b; letters to Shen, Dec. 16, 1875, *ibid.*, 17:28b, 29a–b; letter to Shen, Feb. 20, 1876, *ibid.*, 18:2b–3b.

22. See letters to Shen cited in n. 21 above; also letter to Wu Ts'an-ch'eng, Oct. 10, 1876, *ibid.*, 18:21–22.

23. See entry for Hsüeh in Hummel.

24. Seward to Fish, Oct. 30, 1876, *FRUS* (1877), pp. 80–82.

25. For letter to Shen, Oct. 14, 1876, see *LWCK: P'eng-liao*, 18:23b; letter to Wu, Oct. 30, 1876, *ibid.*, 18:25b–26b; letter to Wu, Nov. 30, 1876, *ibid.*, 18:29–30b; letter to Ting, May 14, 1877, *ibid.*, 19:3b–4.

26. Letter to Kuo Sung-t'ao, May 14, 1877, *ibid.*, 19:7a–b; Stanley Wright, p. 476. Possibly Giquel was inquiring for Shen, while Li Feng-pao was secretly doing the same thing for Li Hung-chang. There is no evidence that Giquel actually purchased two such ships for Shen.

27. See letter to Ho Ching, Aug. 19, 1877, *LWCK: P'eng-liao*, 19:15a–b; for letters to Wu of Sept. 21, Oct. 9, and Nov. 26, 1877, and Feb. 9, 1878, see *ibid.*, 19:16b–17b, 20a–b, 28b–29b; 20:3.

28. See letter to Wu Ts'an-ch'eng, Nov. 11, 1877, on types, *ibid.*, 19:26; for letters to Wu of Sept. 21, and Dec. 24, 1877, mentioning possibility and cost of a new dockyard, see *ibid.*, 19:16b–17b, 34b–35b; Kuo, Dec. 8, 1877, *ibid.*, 19:30; letter to Wu, Feb. 9, 1878, mentioning concern about gunboats, *ibid.*, 20:3.

29. See letter to Wu, Feb. 9, 1878, *ibid.*, 20:3; Wu to Tsungli Yamen, Feb. 10, 1878, *HFT: Fu-chou, hsia*, p. 753.

30. Pao Tsen-peng, pp. 209–210.

31. See letter to Ho Ching, Mar. 13, 1878, calling the fund a trick, *LWCK: P'eng-liao*, 20:7a–b; letter to Wu, Mar. 19, 1878, *ibid.*, 20:8b–9.

32. Of the 18 ships built at the Foochow dockyard, 6 had been distributed; of the 12 still maintained by the yard, Wu considered only 3 usable in 1878, and these were the merchantmen sent to Li, which he promised to return; see Wu to Grand Council, Apr. 8, 1878, *HFT: Fu-chou, hsia*, p. 762; and Li to Wu, May 11, 1878, *LWCK: P'eng-liao*, 20:12a–b.

33. Wu to Tsungli Yamen, Aug. 5, 1878, *HFT: Fu-chou, hsia*, p. 769.

34. Pao Tsen-peng, pp. 209–210; Ch'ih Chung-yu, p. 329.

35. Report of Shen, Mar. 9, 1879, *HFT: Fu-chou, hsia*, p. 785.

36. For letters to Li Feng-pao and Shen Pao-chen, July 27 and Aug. 11, 1879, see *LWCK: P'eng-liao*, 21:3b–4, 4b.

37. For letters to Shen, Li Feng-pao, and Tseng, Sept. 26, Oct. 18, and Oct. 19, 1879, see *ibid.*, 21:9–10b, 11, 20b–21.

38. For letters to Shen and Tseng, Nov. 30 and Dec. 7, 1879, see *ibid.*, 21:13b–14, 14b–15.

39. Wu to Tsungli Yamen, Aug. 17, 1879, *HFT: Fu-chou, hsia*, pp. 816–817.

40. Stanley Wright, p. 476. The ships were the *Ch'ao Yung* and *Yang Wei*.

41. Letter to Chou Fu-k'ai, Feb. 6, 1880, *LWCK: P'eng-liao*, 21:17a–b.

42. Letters to T'an Wen-ch'ing and Chou Fu-k'ai, Feb. 26, 1880, *ibid.*, 21:18, 18b–19; for Shantung purchases, see Stanley Wright, p. 475; and Ch'ih Chung-yu, p. 330. Wright also refers to the Kwangtung purchases.

43. Letter to Li Feng-pao, Mar. 30, 1880, *LWCK: P'eng-liao*, 21:19b–20b.

44. Letter to Ho Ching, Apr. 2, 1880, *ibid.*, 21:21.

45. Letter to Li Chao-t'ang, Apr. 28, 1880, *ibid.*, 22:6–7.

46. Letters to Li Feng-pao, Ho Ching, and Li Feng-pao, of May 25, June 10, and July 13, 1880, *ibid.*, 22:9a–b, 9b–10, 11–12. The Fukien provincial government raised 600,000 taels — better than a year's income for the dockyard; see letter from Li Hung-chang to Tsungli Yamen, Sept. 22, 1880, *HFT: Fu-chou, hsia*, p. 861.

47. For letters to Chang Yu-ch'iao and Li Feng-pao, Sept. 21, 1880, see *LWCK: P'eng-liao*, 21:15–16.

48. Letter to Liu Shen-san, Oct. 21, 1880, *ibid.*, 22:18b–19.

49. Li Chao-t'ang to Tsungli Yamen, Nov. 19, 1880, *HFT: Fu-chou, hsia*, p. 865; for letters to Li Feng-pao, Li Chao-t'ang, and Li Feng-pao, of Dec. 3, 1880, and Jan. 5, 1881, see *LWCK: P'eng-liao*, 22:20–21b, 21b–22, 24b–25. On Li's technical questions to the London legation, see Boulger, p. 445. The shift to German yards involved a political contest in China as well. Hart wanted to build up the Tsungli Yamen (to which he was responsible) in foreign affairs, but Li preferred to keep as much power as possible in his own hands, and so played the German Detring off against Hart; Stanley Wright, p. 534.

50. Li did not get three battleships. One of his German purchases was the *Chi Yüan*, a 236-foot steel unarmored cruiser of 2300 tons; the other two were the 7500-ton battleships *Ting Yüan* and *Chen Yüan*. None were delivered until after the Sino-French War. Li Feng-pao made sharp practice in placing bids for these ships; see Stanley Wright, pp. 476–477. See also letter to Li Chao-t'ang, Mar. 1, 1881, *LWCK: P'eng-liao*, 23:3–4.

51. For letters of May 22, June 29, and Oct. 9, 1881, to Li Chao-t'ang, Ting Pao-chen, and Li Feng-pao, see *ibid.*, 23:5b–6, 8, 16a–b.

52. Spector, *Li Hung-chang*, pp. 171, 181–183, discusses competition between the central government and Li, and Li's retention of his personal forces. Ma Chien-chung, one of Li's naval school directors, describes the corruption in Li's forces in Ma's "K'an Lü shun chi" (A record of an official investigation of Port Arthur), in *Hsiao-fang hu-chai yü-ti ts'ung-ch'ao* (Material on geography from the Hsiao-fang hu study), 71: 2; his visit was on Apr. 25, 1881.

53. Li Chao-t'ang to Tsungli Yamen, Nov. 26, 1881, *HFT: Fu-chou, hsia*, p. 894.

54. For letters to Li Feng-pao of Jan. 11, Mar. 8, and Oct. 20, 1882, see *LWCK: P'eng-liao*, 23:18a–b, 19b-20, 27b–28.

55. Li Chao-t'ang to Tsungli Yamen, May 25, 1882, *HFT: Fu-chou, hsia*, p. 910.

56. For growing trouble with Japan, see Tsiang, "Diplomatic Relations." For comments on Sea Defense money, see memorial by Li in 1882, *WCSL*, 29:22–24b. On cutback in Li's forces, see translation of a letter from Li in 1880, in Teng and Fairbank, p. 120.

57. For letters to Li Feng-pao and Li Chao-t'ang of Oct. 20 and Nov. 8, 1882, see *LWCK: P'eng-liao*, 23:27b–28, 29. See also Li Chao-t'ang report to Tsungli Yamen, Dec. 5, 1882, *HFT: Fu-chou, hsia*, p. 932.

58. For report of Tso Tsung-t'ang to Tsungli Yamen, Jan. 22, 1883, see *HFT: Fu-chou, hsia*, p. 934; report of Li Chao-t'ang to Tsungli Yamen, Feb. 1, 1883, *ibid.*, pp. 935–938; orders of Chang Meng-yüan, *ibid.*, p. 948.

59. Chang Meng-yüan to Tsungli Yamen, Sept. 6, 1883, *ibid.*, p. 982. For details on conservative attacks, see next chapter.

60. Tseng to Tsungli Yamen, May 20, 1871, *ibid., shang*, p. 242. A few examples of uncoordinated buying must suffice here: during the Sino-French War, Chang Chih-tung tried to borrow half a million pounds from a German firm (*WCSL*, 44:23b; 52:15). Guns bought by Tseng Kuo-ch'uan for Woosung and Kiangyin forts, eight in number, cost nearly twice what Jui-lin spent in the late 1860's for six gunboats (*WCSL*, 46:14a–b).

61. Clyde, item 23, "Shufeldt's Indictment of China, 1882;" and letter to Li Feng-pao, *LWCK: P'eng-liao*, 23:21b.

62. For order to Tseng Kuo-ch'uan, see *WCSL*, 38:5b–6; for his reply, *ibid.*, 38:22–23b; for Hsü's report, *ibid.*, 38:23b–24b.

63. Letter to Shen, May 19, 1875, *LWCK: P'eng-liao*, 17:10b–11. The foreign observer was Cyprian A. G. Bridge; see his "The Revival of the Warlike Power of China," *Fraser's Magazine* (June 1879), pp. 778–789.

64. Information on armament comes from reports by Wen Yu and Shen Pao-chen, in *CCTY*, 1:14b and 8:4; also from "Vladimir," *The China-Japan War* (New York, 1896), p. 77; also from Shore, Chap. 7. Chang P'ei-lun's report, in *WCSL*, 46:21–22b.

NOTES TO CHAPTER IV

65. On the duds, see edict in *WCSL*, 48:16; Tseng's comments are in *WCSL*, 49:12.
66. Boulger, pp. 248–251.
67. Report in *WCSL*, 45:25b–26.
68. On Shen and Tso's plants, see Spector, *Li Hung-chang*, pp. 165–166; on dismissal of Macartney, see Boulger, pp. 199–241.
69. *KNCTCC*, *chüan* 5, table of deliveries.
70. On Kuo Sung-t'ao, see letter to Shen Pao-chen, May 27, 1875, *LWCK: P'eng-liao*, 17:15b–16b; letters to Shen on Ting Jih-ch'ang in August and September 1875, *ibid.*, 17:14a–b, 18a–b, 25a–b; letter to Shen, Feb. 6, 1876, on Ting's having too much to do as concurrent superintendent and Fukien governor, *ibid.*, 18:1b–2; edict to Li to select either Wu Ts'an-ch'eng or Li Ch'ao-t'ang, Mar. 7, 1876, *HFT: Fu-chou, hsia*, p. 671; letter to Shen on Ting's resignation and recommending Li Chao-t'ang, early 1876, *LWCK: P'eng-liao*, 18:4b–5b; letter to Shen, Apr. 11, 1876, reversing self on Li Chao-t'ang and recommending Wu Ts'an-ch'eng, *ibid.*, 18:10b–11; desire of Wu to have T'ang T'ing-hsu and Wang Yung-ho, both ex-China Merchants Company, come to the dockyard, *HFT: Fu-chou, hsia*, p. 686; Li Hung-chang letter to Shen Pao-chen, Dec. 29, 1876, on Ting's resignation from Fukien governorship, *LWCK: P'eng-liao*, 19:36; letter of May 11, 1878 to Wu Ts'an-ch'eng, who was to succeed Ting as Fukien governor, expressing doubts as to Li Chao-t'ang taking over the dockyard post, *ibid.*, 20:12a–b; letters to Ho Ching and Shen Pao-chen, June 27 and July 21, 1878, *ibid.*, 20:14, 14b; letter to Li Feng-pao, regretting Wu Ts'an-ch'eng's intention to resign, July 27, 1879, *ibid.*, 21:3b–4; letter to Ho Ching, Sept. 12, 1879, expressing hope that Chang Meng-yüan would succeed Wu Ts'an-ch'eng, *ibid.*, 21:7b; memorial by Tso Tsung-t'ang expressing interest in successor but not naming one, Jan. 22, 1883, *HFT: Fu-chou, hsia*, p. 934. Chang Meng-yüan was appointed. Spector implies that Li began influencing the choice of superintendents in 1867, when the post "fell into the hands of Shen Pao-chen, a loyal follower of Tseng and close colleague of Li . . ." Spector, *Li Hung-Chang*, p. 173.
71. See letters to Wu Ts'an-ch'eng of May 11, 1878, to Ho Ching of June 27, 1878, and to Ho Ching, Sept. 26, 1879, cited in n. 70 above; also letter to Shen Pao-chen, Sept. 26, 1879, in *LWCK: P'eng-liao*, 21:9–10b.
72. See letter to Li Feng-pao, Mar. 30, 1880, *ibid.*, 21:19b–20b; edict ordering investigation, Dec. 17, 1880, *HFT: Fu-chou, hsia*, p. 866; Li Chao-t'ang to Tsungli Yamen, Feb. 5, 1881, *ibid.*, p. 871.
73. Letters to Li Chao-t'ang on Lü T'ing-chih, May 31 and July 15, 1881, *LWCK: P'eng-liao*, 23:7a–b, 10–11; Li Chao-t'ang to Tsungli Yamen on Lü (expectant Chihli taotai) to replace Wu Chung-hsiang, Sept. 23, 1881, *HFT: Fu-chou, hsia*, p. 892.
74. On Li's use of Foochow-built ships, see letter to Shen, Dec. 16, 1875, *LWCK: P'eng-liao*, 17:28b; to Wu, Mar. 19, 1878, *ibid.*, 20:8b–9; to Wu, May 11, 1878, *ibid.*, 20:12a–b; to Li Chao-t'ang, Nov. 8, 1882, *ibid.*, 23:29. For encouragement on product improvement, see letter to Wu, Oct. 10, 1876, *ibid.*, 18:22; to Wu, Oct. 30, 1876, *ibid.*, 18:25b–26b; to Wu, Nov. 30, 1876, *ibid.*, 18:29–30b; to Wu, Sept. 21, 1877, *ibid.*, 19:16b–17b; to Wu, Nov. 11, 1877, *ibid.*, 19:26; to Wu, Nov. 26, 1877, *ibid.*, 19:28b–29; to Wu, Dec. 24, 1877, *ibid.*, 19:34b–35b; to Wu, Feb. 9, 1878, *ibid.*, 20:3; to Kuo Sung-t'ao, Feb. 27, 1878, *ibid.*, 20:4b–6b; to Li Chao-t'ang, Aug. 26, 1880, *ibid.*, 22:13b–14; to Li Chao-t'ang, Dec. 3, 1880, *ibid.*, 22:21b–22; to Li Chao-t'ang, Mar. 1, 1881, *ibid.*, 23:3–4; to Li Chao-t'ang, Nov. 8, 1882, *ibid.*, 23:29. Li seems to have taken the most concentrated interest before his gunboats were delivered.
75. The sixty references run continuously through Li's letters, starting with the selected year 1875. On Kiangnan training, see *HFT*: "Kiangnan," *lun-ch'uan tsao-lien chü* (the program for training on the steamers).
76. Names appearing are those of Chang Ch'eng, Yen Tsung-kwang (Yen Fu), Ch'iu Pao-jen, Wu Shih-chung, Teng Shih-ch'ang, Li Ho (lien), Wu Meng-liang, Liu Pu-ch'an, Lin T'ai-tseng, Chang Chao-yün, Fang Pai-ch'ien, Lin Yung-sheng, Yeh Tsu-kuei, Huang Chien-hsün, Lin Ying-ch'i, and Yang Tse-che. On Li's doubts

on Liu and Ch'iu (both later had dubious histories in the Sino-Japanese War), see his letter to Wu Ts'an-ch'eng of May 3, 1877, *LWCK: P'eng-liao*, 19:3. In 1881 Li praised Liu Pu-ch'an, with others; Biggerstaff, p. 235.

77. Ibid.

78. See letter of Li Hung-chang to Li Chao-t'ang of Mar. 1, 1881, *LWCK: P'eng-liao*, 23:3–4; report of Li Ch'ao-t'ang of Feb. 1, 1883, *HFT: Fu-chou, hsia*, p. 935. Biggerstaff, p. 235, cites a report by Li Hung-chang giving Yang, Li, and Wu a secondary rating. Chang Meng-yüan report of Nov. 24, 1883, *HFT: Fu-chou, hsia*, p. 998.

79. Biggerstaff, p. 236; entry for Wu Ta-ch'eng in Hummel.

80. Even Kuo Sung-t'ao once questioned the usefulness of naval studies overseas; see Teng and Fairbank, p. 101, and letter to Kuo, July 11, 1877, *LWCK: P'eng-liao*, 19:11–13. Tseng Chi-tse went so far as to say that such training was useless; see letters to Tseng, July 27, Aug. 15, 1879, *ibid.*, 21:3b–4, 7a–b.

81. Li indirectly refused to send the desired aide to Wu; see letter to Shen Pao-chen, July 21, 1878, *ibid.*, 20:14b. On Li's attempts to hire one of the fired Foochow gentry (the man was kept on by Li Chao-t'ang as a personal secretary, despite Li's attempts), see Li Chao-t'ang to Tsungli Yamen, July 6, 1880, *HFT: Fu-chou, hsia*, pp. 856–858, and Li Hung-chang to Tsungli Yamen, Aug. 26, 1880, *LWCK: P'eng-liao*, 22:13b–14b. On the return of Li's captains, see letter to Shen, Nov. 30, 1879, *ibid.*, 21:13b–14. Liu Pu-ch'an and Lin T'ai-tseng were returned to Li.

82. Biggerstaff, pp. 229–232.

83. The students were Liu Pu-ch'an, Lin T'ai-tseng, Wei Han, Ch'en Ch'ao-ao, Ch'en Chi-tung, and possibly Chang Ch'eng. Ch'ih Chung-yu, p. 326, gives a list which does not include the last name, but Ting Jih-ch'ang in an 1876 memorial stated that Chang Ch'eng was abroad (*CCTY*, 13:19b). See also report by Shen of May 17, 1875, *HFT: Fu-chou, hsia*, p. 553. Ch'ih Chung-yu, p. 327, states that Wei Han and Ch'en Ch'ao-ao stayed in Europe.

84. See edict of Feb. 8, 1873, *HFT: Fu-chou, shang*, p. 417, on the Li-Lo shift, and memorial by Shen of April 9, 1875, *ibid., hsia*, p. 552, on Tsai Kuo-hsiang. On use of *Yang Wu*, see report in *CCTY*, 12:7. See also Shore, pp. 226–240.

85. On Wu, see Ting Jih-chang to Tsungli Yamen, Mar. 5, 1876, *HFT: Fu-chou, hsia*, p. 669. (By August of that year it was reported that cadets in training were better than regular sailors; *ibid.*, p. 695.) On criticism, see Shen to Tsungli Yamen, Mar. 5, 1876, *ibid.*, p. 663.

86. Biggerstaff, pp. 232–234.

87. Reports by Wu Ts'an-ch'eng to Tsungli Yamen, Nov. 11, 1876, and June 17, 1877, in *HFT: Fu-chou, hsia*, pp. 704, 733; on itinerary of Kiangnan arsenal trainer, *Hai An*, see memorial by Shen Pao-chen, Nov. 9, 1876, *HFT*: "Kiangnan," p. 141.

88. On objections of Kuo and Tseng, see n. 80 above. See also letter to Li Feng-pao, citing Ho Ching and Li Chao-t'ang on Tseng's motivation, Sept. 21, 1880, *LWCK: P'eng-liao*, 22:15–16.

89. Letter to Shen, Oct. 13, 1878, *ibid.*, 20:19.

90. See edict of Dec. 17, 1880, with charges, setting up the committee: *HFT: Fu-chou, hsia*, p. 866; reply of Ho Ching to Grand Council and Tsungli Yamen, Apr. 9, 1881, *ibid.*, p. 890.

91. Shore, pp. 60–61; for other of his notes on "drills" see pp. 79–80, 81, 139.

92. Biggerstaff, p. 236.

93. Chang's memorial in *CCTY*, 26:20–21; see also Biggerstaff, pp. 217, 226, 236–237.

94. On Li's ideas about place of professionals in the West, see Teng and Fairbank, pp. 70–72; for comments on the Japanese, see *IWSM:TC*, 55:25; on C.E.M., see *ibid.*, 82: 47–48. Many of the returned students did enter the naval service; see LaFargue, pp. 12–13, 29–31, and list, pp. 173–176.

95. On the examination system, see Biggerstaff's abstract of 1874 memorial by

NOTES TO CHAPTER IV

Li (pp. 26–27); on West Point request, see Avery to Fish, Nov. 23, 1874, *FRUS* (1875), I, 227.

96. On Hsü, see Pao Tsen-peng, p. 138; other notes from *CSK:PC*, 7:3b, and Ch'ih Chung-yu, p. 328.

97. On Wu's association with the China Merchants Company, see Wen Yu to Tsungli Yamen, June 16, 1876, *HFT: Fu-chou, hsia*, p. 686. On Wu's taking the arsenal post, see letter to Li Chao-t'ang, Aug. 26, 1880, *LWCK: P'eng-liao*, 22:13b–14b. On Yen Fu, see letter to Li Chao-t'ang, Apr. 28, 1880, *ibid.*, 22:6–7. Ch'ih Chung-yu, p. 329, records Wu's presence at Tientsin.

98. L. C. Arlington, *Through the Dragon's Eyes* (London, 1931), p. 13.

99. Pao Tsen-peng, pp. 231–232.

100. Proclamation translated and included in Young to Frelinghausen, Dec. 12, 1882, FRUS (1883), p. 169.

101. Letter of Aug. 15, 1882, *LWCK: P'eng-liao*, 23:23–24. Spector, p. 402, remarks that Li's school was designed to offset the Foochow element in "the Chinese navy."

102. Ch'ih Chung-yu, pp. 329–330. One of the foreign instructors was present.

103. For Shufeldt's comment, see Clyde, p. 163. The comment on the competition for students is in Ch'ih Chung-yu, p. 327.

104. Clyde, p. 163.

105. Stanley Wright, pp. 479–480.

106. Arlington, pp. 14–15. Arlington calls the German "Captain S." The name is given in James H. Wilson, *China: Travels and Investigations in the Middle Kingdom*, 3rd ed., rev. (New York, 1901), p. 73.

107. Biggerstaff, p. 52, gives figures on deck-officer graduates before the Sino-French War. LaFargue, p. 74, states that some of the captains at the Ma-wei battle were ex-C.E.M. "boys," but the names given, in Cantonese romanization only, can by no stretch of imagination correspond to Chinese captains' names given in the Chinese sources. The water force lieutenant with sea experience was Chin Yung (*WCSL*, 56:37).

108. Shore, pp. 56–57.

V. ACHIEVEMENTS AND PROBLEMS IN THE MILITARY BUILDING EFFORT, 1875–1884

1. For list of plant additions, see *KNCTCC*, 2:2–11b. On training, see Biggerstaff, pp. 46–47, 168–175. For 1877 comments, see Bridge, pp. 778–789.

2. Report on *Wei Yüan*, *CCTY*, 13:9–10.

3. Reports by Ting in *CCTY*, 12:16; 13:31–32b; 14:1b–2, 11b–12.

4. See Shore, Chap. 7, for details of his visit.

5. See 1879 report by Wu, in *CCTY*, 17:1–5b; also Wu to Tsungli Yamen, Aug. 16, 1879, *HFT: Fu-chou, hsia*, p. 800, and edict waiving repair-free period, *ibid.*, p. 833. To my knowledge, the *CCTY* as of 1879 records only three repair jobs: see Shen 1874 report, *CCTY*, 10:13a–b, and reports by Wu in 1878 in *CCTY*, 15:22, 34. 6, 1880, *HFT: Fu-chou, hsia*, p. 856; Li Hung-chang to Tsungli Yamen, Aug. 26, Yamen to Hart, May 14, 1880, *ibid.*, p. 850; Li to Tsungli Yamen, June 1, 1880, *ibid.*, p. 851; Wu Yuan-ping (Liang-Kiang governor-general) to Tsungli Yamen, June 3, 1880, *ibid.*, p. 852; Li Chao-t'ang to Tsungli Yamen, June 24, 1880, *ibid.*, p. 853, and July 6, 1880, *ibid.*, p. 856.

7. Li did not vigorously defend the yard, and suggested that perhaps Li Chao-t'ang was not without blame. See Li Chao-t'ang's report to Tsungli Yamen, July 6, 1880, *HFT: Fu-chou, hsia*, p. 856; Li Hung-chang to Tsungli Yamen, Aug. 26, 1880, *LWCK: P'eng-liao*, 22:13b–14b.

8. Edict of Dec. 17, 1880, with changes, setting up the committee of investigation including Ch'en Lan-pin and Li Hung-chang, in *HFT: Fu-chou, hsia*, p. 866; reply of Ho Ching to Grand Council and Tsungli Yamen, Apr. 9, 1881, *ibid.*, p. 890.

THE MILITARY BUILDING EFFORT

9. Report on *K'ai Chi, CCTY,* 22:27.

10. Chang to Tsungli Yamen, Sept. 6, 1883, *HFT: Fu-chou, hsia,* p. 982; Tso to Tsungli Yamen, Sept. 18, 1883, *ibid.,* pp. 984–985.

11. For Ho's reply to Tso's charges, see *CCTY,* 25:1–9b. Some ships were repaired at the Kiangnan arsenal; see *KNCTCC,* 3:56a–b, for an undated list with eleven entries.

12. On charges to 1875 sixty percent, see Wen Yu to Grand Council, Dec. 2, 1875, *HFT: Fu-chou, hsia,* p. 630. On spring 1875 requests, see *CCTY,* 12:1–3; and *HFT: Fu-chou, hsia,* p. 547. On Board ruling and subsequent developments, see Hu-pu to Tsungli Yamen, Apr. 7, 1875, *ibid.,* p. 550; Shen request of July 20, 1875, *CCTY,* 12:17–20; Wen Yu to Grand Council, Dec. 2, 1875, *HFT: Fu-chou, hsia,* p. 630.

13. Hu-pu to Tsungli Yamen, Aug. 22, 1875, *ibid.,* p. 581; edict of Oct. 16, 1875, *ibid.,* p. 616; report by Shen in Sept., 1875, *CCTY,* 12:27–28.

14. Ting reports, *CCTY,* 13:5–8; also *HFT: Fu-chou, hsia,* p. 655 (Jan. 18, 1876); edict of Dec. 30, 1875, *ibid.,* p. 642; action in the spring of 1876 mentioned by report of Wu Ts'an-ch'eng to Grand Council, Jan. 23, 1877, *ibid.,* pp. 714–715.

15. Wu's account, made August 1879, in *CCTY,* 17:19–36b. Chang statement in report of July 19, 1885, *CCTY,* 28:5–7b.

16. On arrears, see Wu account, *CCTY,* 17:19–36b; for request of Feb. 10, 1878, see his report to Tsungli Yamen, in *HFT: Fu-chou, hsia,* p. 749.

17. Wen Yu report Jan. 30, 1877, *ibid.,* p. 724; report of Mar. 24, 1877, *ibid.,* p. 726. Shen report, Mar. 9, 1879, *ibid.,* p. 785.

18. *CCTY,* 19:1–13b, June 29, 1881.

19. Report by Chang, *CCTY,* 22:22–25; his accounts, Aug. 7, 1883, *CCTY,* 21:13–27.

20. On Ho's shortages, see report of May 7, 1884, *CCTY,* 24:1b. On Tso's half-payment proposal, see Chen, *Tso,* p. 43; also reference to it by P'ei Yin-sen in report of Dec. 1, 1887, *CCTY,* 36:18–22. Tso and Liu K'un-i, as southern commissioners, each sent a subsidy of 40,000 taels; Kwangtung sent 70,000 in 1881–1882; see Ho Ching to Tsungli Yamen, June 27, 1880, *HFT: Fu-chou, hsia,* p. 856; Kwangtung customs to Tsungli Yamen, Mar. 28, 1881, *ibid.,* p. 883; Hu-pu to Tsungli Yamen, Apr. 25, 1882, *ibid.,* p. 909; and Li Chao-t'ang to Grand Council, May 27, 1882, *ibid.,* p. 914.

21. For offer to maintain a ship, see governor of Shantung to Tsungli Yamen, May 28, 1882, *ibid.,* pp. 915–920. The Chenhai item did not appear in Wu's accounts made Aug. 19, 1879, *CCTY,* 17:19–36b. On yard contribution to famine relief ship maintenance, see Wu to Grand Council, Apr. 8, 1878, *HFT: Fu-chou, hsia,* p. 762. The governor of Chekiang planned to return the *Fu Po* to the dockyard; see Ping-pu to Tsungli Yamen, June 14, 1882, *ibid.,* p. 922.

22. See report by Tso et al., in *CCTY,* 20:8–12b; also Tso to Tsungli Yamen, Jan. 22, 1883, *HFT: Fu-chou, hsia,* p. 934, on his change in plans, orders from Germany, etc.

23. Immanuel C. Y. Hsü, *China's Entrance into the Family of Nations* (Cambridge, Mass., 1960), p. 197.

24. Mary Wright, pp. 207–208.

25. Chen, *Tso,* pp. 77–78. Li Hung-chang had some idea of the need to create external economies, in the form of iron and coal mines, but he talked in terms of the "kuan-tu shang-pan" system, which was damaging to modernization; see Teng and Fairbank, p. 110.

26. Mary Wright, p. 248; and Biggerstaff, pp. 71–84.

27. The eight superintendents were Shen Pao-chen, 1867–1875; Ting Jih-ch'ang, 1875–1876; Wu Ts'an-ch'eng, 1876–1879; Li Chao-t'ang, 1879–1883; Chang Meng-yüan, 1883; Ho Ju-chang, 1883–1884; Chang P'ei-lun, 1884; P'ei Yin-sen followed Chang. Pao Tsen-peng, p. 182, gives six men for the period, leaving out Chang Meng-yüan and Ho Ju-chang, who served for very short periods; on the other

NOTES TO CHAPTER V

hand, he includes the names of Wu Chung-hsiang and Chou Mao-ch'i, as "substitutes" for Wu Ts'an Ch'eng and Chang P'ei-lun. Frequent use has been made of the Hummel biographies to supplement direct documentary evidence in tracing the careers of these men.

28. Pao Tsen-peng, p. 128, says "most" of the superintendents were concurrently Min-Che governors-general — an overstatement, but it substantiates the point of their being generally overworked or preoccupied.

29. For discussion of the *t'i-tiao* system, see Wang Hsin-chung, p. 117. Names of the first three appear in a report by Shen, *CCTY*, 3:17–19. For the data on the early working of the system presented here, see Shen to Tsungli Yamen, Feb. 25 and May 25, 1868, in *HFT: Fu-chou, shang*, pp. 117, 120–125, and June 2, 1869, *ibid.*, p. 158 (including complaints of Hsia Hsien-lun); on Wu Ta-t'ing, Tsungli Yamen to Shen, Dec. 10, 1869, *ibid.*, p. 204; Shen to Tsungli Yamen, Oct. 4, and Tsungli Yamen to Li-pu, Dec. 16, 1870, *ibid.*, pp. 253, 281. See also Li Tsung-hsi to Tsungli Yamen, Nov. 9, 1873, in *HFT:* "Kiangnan," p. 131.

30. Shen to Grand Council, Mar. 24, 1875, and Grand Council to Tsungli Yamen, July 15, 1875, *HFT: Fu-chou, shang*, pp. 547, 574.

31. For Wu's recommendation, see memorial to Tsungli Yamen, Apr. 23, 1879, *ibid.*, *hsia*, p. 793; for Li's doubts on Li Chao-t'ang, see letter to Wu, May 11, 1878, *LWCK: P'eng-liao*, pp. 12a–b.

32. Wu to Tsungli Yamen, Nov. 9, 1876, and Li-pu to Tsungli Yamen, Nov. 28, 1876 (2 items), *HFT: Fu-chou, hsia*, pp. 697–700, 706.

33. Biggerstaff, p. 206.

34. Memorials of Shen, July 15, 1875, and Wu, Aug. 17, 1879, *HFT: Fu-chou, hsia*, pp. 556, 805. On dropout, see Biggerstaff, p. 211.

35. The following argument is based on the classified list of Kiangnan arsenal officials in *KNCTCC*, 6:40–44, supplemented by references to available biographies in Hummel.

36. Swisher, p. 6, has a note on "expectants." Many were merchants who purchased their posts and would never have substantive official advancement, although entered on the register of the Board of Civil Office in Peking. How many of the "expectants" at Kiangnan were of this order, rather than being bona fide candidates, is not known.

37. Ch'uan Han-sheng, pp. 151–153.

38. Biggerstaff, pp. 91–92, lists outstanding graduates of the naval academies at Foochow, Tientsin, and Nanking, showing that many of them held civilian posts in the government in the Republican period.

VI. DISASTER IN THE SOUTH: THE CHINESE NAVY IN THE SINO-FRENCH WAR, 1884–1885

1. Li Chien-nung, p. 121.

2. Li Hung-chang, writing to Li Feng-pao on Jan. 11, 1882, said China had bought thirteen of the Armstrong gunboats; see *LWCK: P'eng-liao*, 23:18a–b. I have been able to find the names of only eleven of these "mosquito craft"; see Appendix C.

3. Pao Tsen-peng, p. 245, gives the Nanyang fleet seventeen ships, the Peiyang fourteen, and the Foochow fleet eleven, in 1884.

4. See Young to Frelinghuysen, Feb. 11, 1884, *FRUS* (1884), pp. 67–69, and Apr. 18, 1884, *ibid.*, p. 96. The Tsungli Yamen backed Chang Chih-tung's independence in this matter; Chang P'ei-lun stated that the Yamen would interfere only with "gravest hesitation." Later, when Chang P'ei-lun was in charge of Min River defenses, he would not block the river without an edict ordering it (*WCSL*, 44:1–3b, Aug. 11, 1884), Tso Tsung-t'ang acted on his own initiative in a similar situation later (*WCSL*, 53:8b, Feb. 18, 1885). Li Hung-chang's idea was that such blocks could be made in an emergency, although foreigners should be advised (by whom?), and he asked the Yamen for a circular to this effect (*WCSL*, 43:16b–17, July 2,

THE SINO-FRENCH WAR

1884). For further information on the river blockage at Canton, see IMC: *Dec. Reps., 1882–1891*, Canton, pp. 574–575.

5. For memorial from Min-Che governor-general and others, Aug. 12–Sept. 10, 1884, giving names of fortified places and other detailed data, see *IWSM:TC*, 96: 22b–25b.

6. See report by Chang P'ei-lun, Aug. 11, 1884, *WCSL*, 44:1–3b; also Capt. Chabaud-Arnault (French navy), "Combats in the Min River," tr. Lt. E. B. Barry, *USNIP*, 11.2:308 (1885). This latter item is based on Courbet's reports. See also H. W. Wilson, *Ironclads in Action*, 2 vols. (Boston, 1898), II, 2, and map on p. xix.

7. Li Hung-chang expressed concern on Aug. 30, 1884, *WCSL*, 45:25b; the court admission appears in an edict of Sept. 2, 1884, *WCSL*, 46:1b.

8. In July 1884 Tseng was made imperial commissioner to negotiate at Shanghai (*ch'üan-ch'uan ta-ch'en*), and telegrams to and from him included this plenipotential title; see *WCSL, passim*. Li did not get a similar title until early in 1885; *WCSL*, 54:28a–b, Mar. 22, 1885.

9. Sometimes Li Hung-chang was asked to pass a command of the court all along the coasts, as in June 1884 in the matter of prohibiting the aiding of the French by Chinese pilots, for which see *CF*, V, 419, and *WCSL*, 42:7; at other times court orders were dispatched to Tartar generals, governors, etc., without mention of routing by Li or Tseng Kuo-ch'uan, e.g., an edict calling for diligence, *WCSL*, 42: 4b–5. Some orders were sent to individuals, as for instance a telegram of late 1884 sent to Governor Liu Ping-chang of Chekiang, and separately to the governor of Shantung, and also to Li Hung-chang, urging vigilance; *WCSL*, 46:15a–b. The Shanghai taotai Shao Yu-lien provided direct intelligence to the Tsungli Yamen; e.g., *WCSL*, 45:11a–b; 46:5–6. For Chang Chih-tung reports, see *WCSL*, 52:34b; 53:30b.

10. For Li's wire, see *CF*, V, 408. As early as Apr. 25, 1884, the court was warned by Shao Yu-lien that France was bringing eight warships north; defense officials were accordingly warned by the court. See *Ch'ing Kuang-hsü-ch'ao Chung-fa chiao-she shih-liao* (Historical material on Sino-French relations in the Kuang-hsü period), cited in *CF*, V, 313.

11. Ho Ju-ch'ang reported the first ship in a wire received on July 19, 1884; *CCTY*, 25:10–11b; the date July 13 comes from the entry for Chang P'ei-lun in Hummel. On the "army people" and the blocking problem, see report by Chang P'ei-lun, Aug. 13, 1884, *WCSL*, 44:1–3b.

12. *CF*, V, 414; also *WCSL*, 41:27a–b.

13. Ch'ih Chung-yu, p. 365, discusses the legal situation created by these entries. The names of French ships given are my guesses, based on an attempt to relate names of known French vessels to the often obscure Chinese phonetic renditions.

14. On the deadline, see Li to Grand Council, July 19, 1884, *WCSL*, 42:6a–b. On the other ships, see report by Chang P'ei-lun, Aug. 14, 1884, *WCSL*, 44:9b–12.

15. Reports by Chang P'ei-lun, *WCSL*, 44:1–3b, 9b–12.

16. For wire by Chang P'ei-lun, see *WCSL*, 43:9; for Yamen's reply on blocking the river, Aug. 5, 1884, see *WCSL*, 43:11b. For Yamen's authorization for destruction of the dockyard, see *WCSL*, 44:4.

17. Mu's report, July 16, 1884, and edict, *WCSL*, 42:2b, 4b–5.

18. See Ho report, July 19, 1884, *CCTY*, 26:10–11b. Ho reported four French ships. Chang P'ei-lun, in a written report received on August 14, 1884, said that China had only three ships at that approximate time (*WCSL*, 44:9b–12). For other details, see *CCTY*, 26:12–14; and *WCSL*, 42:11, 19b–20.

19. Liu wire, *WCSL*, 42:19b–20; order to Li Hung-chang, July 25, 1884, *WCSL*, 42:20; Chang P'ei-lun report, July 26, 1884, *WCSL*, 42:21; Li's reply to order, *WCSL*, 42:21b; Chang P'ei-lun report, and court reply, July 29, 1884, *WCSL*, 42:30a–b; also *CF*, V, 447–448.

20. For written reports, see *WCSL*, 43:26–27; 44:1–3b, 9b–12, all received Aug. 13–14, 1884. For his wire, see *CF*, V, 430, July 27, 1884.

NOTES TO CHAPTER VI

21. Chang Chih-tung agreed that the dockyard was in a perilous situation; *WCSL*, 43:3b, Aug. 4, 1884. Both of the ships sent were described as Kwangtung ships by Chang Shu-sheng, acting northern commissioner, in *WCSL*, 45:28. For their maintenance, 1882–1884, see report by Li Ch'ao-t'ang, July 2, 1882, in *CCTY*. Both were sunk in the Ma-wei battle; *WCSL*, 45:19b–20.

22. *WCSL*, 43:10b–11. There is some evidence about the sequence of Chinese warship arrivals at the Ma-wei anchorage. In a memorial received Sept. 16, 1884, Chang P'ei-lun wrote that Ho Ju-ch'ang "brought back" the *Chen Wei* and *Fu Po*; Chang Chih-tung sent the *Fei Yün* and *Chi An*; the *Fu Hsing* and *I Hsin*, and "a warship and a merchant steamer" also came in. There is no note of dates, but — despite Li Hung-chang's fears — the French evidently let them come in. See Chang report in *WCSL*, 46:19–12.

23. *WCSL*, 43:26–27.

24. *WCSL*, 44:19a–b, 21, 24b, Aug. 14, 15, and 18, 1884.

25. *CF*, V, 502. See similar order to Tseng Kuo-ch'uan, same date, *CF*, V, 503.

26. Appeal for help by Foochow authorities, Aug. 19, 1884, *WCSL*, 44:29b; court inquiry about troops, *WCSL*, 44:30 (also Aug. 20, 1884; it may of course have been sent first); instructions to Chang P'ei-lun, *WCSL*, 45:1b; appointment of Tseng Kuoch'uan and order to Li, *WCSL*, 45:2b.

27. Ho report, *WCSL*, 45:4; new appeal for help and court acknowledgment, *WCSL*, 45:5a–b.

28. H. B. Morse, *The Trade and Administration of China* (Shanghai, 1913), pp. 41–42, argues that the telegraph tended to aid centralization of power.

29. Chabaud-Arnault, p. 296. See also *IMC: Dec. Reps., 1882–1891*, Foochow, p. 419. There is some difficulty making up an exact list of Chinese warships present. The figure eleven is given by Ch'ih and also by H. W. Wilson, *Ironclads*, II, 302. An item in *CF*, III, 131–132, gives nine ships and two transports (*Hai Ching*, 1450 tons, built at Foochow and listed by Li's China Merchants Company, and *T'ing Chen*, of which I have no previous record).

30. H. W. Wilson, *Ironclads*, II, Table X, p. 302, gives eight French ships present, and *IMC: Dec. Reps., 1882–1891*, Foochow, p. 419, gives nine. I have not been able to find more than eight names.

31. Chabaud-Arnault, p. 296, and H. W. Wilson, *Ironclads*, II, 4–12.

32. *IWSM:TC*, 50:2–4.

33. Ch'ih Chung-yu, p. 336, is critical of Chang Ch'eng.

34. See *CF*, III, 548–549, for passage from partial translation of Loir's *L'Escadre de L'Amiral Courbet*. From this passage comes Courbet's statement that Chinese hesitation was crucial; that his own battle was determined by the tide; that he counted on having the Chinese ships stern-to relative to his ships.

35. Ch'ih Chung-yu, p. 366.

36. Chang Tsu-keng, *Min-hsien hsiang-t'u chih* (Gazetteer of Foochow, 1903), p. 78b. The account is generally similar to Ch'ih's.

37. Aug. 24, 1884 (date of receipt); *WCSL*, 45:7b–8.

38. *CF*, V, 523–525.

39. For an account of the battle, see H. W. Wilson, *Ironclads*, II, 4–12.

40. Ch'ih Chung-yu, pp. 331–332.

41. *CF*, V, 132–133.

42. *WCSL*, 47:1–4, Sept. 19, 1884.

43. *CF*, V, 512, Aug. 23, 1884.

44. Ch'ih Chung-yu, pp. 365–366.

45. Cited in Chen, *Tso*, p. 44. The several accounts cited above have it that the *Yang Wu* was sunk; *Fu Hsing* exploded (doubtless she sank); *Chen Wei* was put out of action, afire; fire also claimed the *Fei Yün* and *Chi An* (sunk). The *Fu Sheng* was sunk; the *Chien Sheng* was sunk; the *Yung Pao* and *Ch'en Hang* were destroyed on the dockyard ways (although Ho Ju-chang later reported that these two collided in action; *WCSL*, 46:16–17b). The *I Hsin* and *Fu Po* fled the action.

THE SINO-FRENCH WAR

46. Chabaud-Arnault, p. 302.

47. The Foochow academy men were Chang Ch'eng (*Yang Wu*), Ch'en Ying (*Fu Hsing*), Yeh Ch'en *(Fu Sheng)*, and Lin Sen-lin *(Chien Sheng)*. The other captains were Hsü Shou-shen *(Chen Wei)*, Kao Teng-yün *(Fei Yün)*, Lü Wen-ying *(Fu Po)*, and Lin Tse-yu *(I Hsin)*. I have no record of the name of the captain of the *Chi An*.

48. *WCSL*, 46:12b.

49. *WCSL*, 46:12b, Sept. 7, 1884. Chang P'ei-lun was made concurrent dockyard superintendent.

50. An essay might be written on the reports of the battle and the use of such terms as "broken," "burned," "destroyed," for French ships. For some representative samples, see reports of Ho Ju-chang, *WCSL*, 46:16–17b; 47:1–4; and *CCTY*, 25:20; or of Chang P'ei-lun, *WCSL*, 45:8b–9; 46:19–21; *CCTY*, 28:12–14. For the declaration of war, see *CF*, V, 517–520.

51. *CSK:PC*. 7:5a–b.

52. For edict, see *WCSL*, 48:7b–8, Oct. 24, 1884; for Tso's report, see citation in the edict of Nov. 6, 1884, *WCSL*, 48:22, which also contains a threat of punishment to the southern commissioner. Li reported readying his *Ch'ao Yung* and *Yang Wei* on Nov. 9, 1884, *WCSL*, 48:24a–b.

53. Report of Tseng Kuo-ch'uan, *WCSL*, 48:27; report of Li Hung-chang, Nov. 16, 1884, in *WCSL*, 49:2b–4; arrival of Li's ships reported by Tseng Kuo-ch'uan on Dec. 6, 1884, *WCSL*, 49:22.

54. See communications between Li and the court, on Korean problem, need for ships, etc., in *WCSL*, 49:26b–27; 50:6, 9b, 10b–11, 12a–b, 12b–13, 17b.

55. *WCSL*, 50:6, Dec. 14, 1884.

56. *WCSL*, 50:9b, 10, Dec. 14 and 15, 1884.

57. For edict, see WCSL, 50:10b–12; on command of the relief flotilla, see *WCSL*, 50:12a–b, Dec. 17, 1884.

58. Arlington, Chaps. 3–8. Arlington wrote from memory many years after the events described, but his verifiable facts are in close harmony with the official record (although he is a day or two off in his chronology), and his unverifiable facts are plausible.

59. This itinerary has been pieced together from reports of Tseng Kuo-ch'uan, in *WCSL*, 52:20b, 21; 53:1; and from the account of Ch'ih Chung-yu.

60. Arlington, pp. 19–20; also *WCSL*, 56:37, for a report mentioning Chin Yung.

61. *WCSL*, 53:1b, 2.

62. Tseng Kuo-ch'uan report, Feb. 20, 1884, *WCSL*, 53:19b; also see a later report in *WCSL*, 54:25b–38. The governors of Fukien and Chekiang, and Chang Chih-tung, all reported separately on these developments; see *WCSL*, 54:17b–19b, Mar. 21, 1885; and *WCSL*, 56:14b–17b, Mar. 28, 1885.

63. Ch'ih Chung-yu, p. 370, takes the line that the ships were deliberately scuttled.

64. Report of Tseng Kuo-ch'uan, *WCSL*, 56:34b–37b, Apr. 25, 1885.

65. Ch'ih Chung-yu, p. 370, makes the point.

66. See Arlington, pp. 32–43, for the Shih-p'u sequence; the quotation is on p. 42.

67. H. W. Wilson, *Ironclads*, II, 13–15, citing Courbet. *IMC: Dec. Reps., 1882–1891*, Ningpo, pp. 346–347, says the French torpedo was launched from a small French vessel concealed between two fishing junks.

68. Arlington, pp. 49–50.

69. *Ibid.*, p. 48.

70. *Ibid.*, p. 50.

71. *WCSL*, 53:25, Mar. 2, 1885.

72. Report by Li, Mar. 8, 1885, *WCSL*, 54:3. Date of departure of last French ship in *IMC: Dec. Reps., 1882–1891*, Ningpo, p. 346.

73. An interesting early manifestation of nationalism among overseas Chinese was reported by Tseng Chi-tse, who wired the Tsungli Yamen that the British Foreign Office had reported to him that Chinese in Singapore had wrecked a French ship there (*WCSL*, 47:11, Sept. 28, 1884). On the mainland there had to be persistent

attempts to keep the populace from helping the French; e.g., see edict to Chang Chih-tung, *WCSL*, 45:10a–b, Aug. 24, 1884 — just after the Ma-wei disaster.

74. See Arlington, pp. 59–85, on the events at Chenhai; see *ibid.*, pp. 59–60, on the digging up of shells.

75. *WCSL*, 56:34b–37b, Mar. 25, 1885.

76. On the Ch'en Ying incident at Ma-wei, see *ibid.* On the quelling of the Chenhai mutiny, Arlington, pp. 60–62, reports that Admiral Wu ordered the foreigners to do it, the pistol-wielder being Arlington himself.

VII. NAVAL DEVELOPMENTS AFTER 1885: THE EMERGENCE OF THE PEIYANG FLEET

1. Tso's recommendations are translated in Denby to Bayard, Oct. 16, 1885, *FRUS* (1885), pp. 178–180. Tso's memorial was dated May 25, 1885. See also *CTLT*, 342:4–5b.

2. For Chang's suggestions, see *CTLT*, 342:5b–6b; for Hsü's, see entry on him in Hummel.

3. Cited material from Denby to Bayard, Oct. 14, 1885, *FRUS* (1885), pp. 173–174; see also *CTLT*, 342:7, for further details.

4. Hart to Pauncefote (Foreign Office), Oct. 17, 1885, cited in Stanley Wright, p. 480.

5. Denby to Bayard, Oct. 16, 1885, *FRUS* (1885), pp. 178–180.

6. Li Chien-nung, pp. 125–126.

7. Meng Ssu-ming, Chap. 6. Other sources discussing these political considerations are J.O.P. Bland and E. Backhouse, *China Under the Empress Dowager* (Philadelphia, 1911), pp. 154–160, and the entry for I-huan in Hummel. See also n. 13, below.

8. See entry for I-huan in Hummel.

9. Pao Tsen-peng, p. 209, records that the Navy Board received permission to control the Sea Defense Fund.

10. See *LWCK: Hai-chün han-kao*, for item dated Jan. 3, 1886.

11. Li Chien-nung, p. 126. Tseng tried to refuse the post.

12. P'ei memorial referring to the order, in *CCTY*, 34:10–12. The directive ended somewhat weakly, for it warned that if provincial purchases were made independently, the province involved must devise its own source of payment. P'ei, being an imperial commissioner and not a provincial official, had no means to raise money from provincial funds.

13. *WCSL*, 66:16a–b, and 16b–17. Evidently Li Hung-chang wanted Prince Ch'un to stay on as head of the Navy Board, for on July 16, 1886, he wrote to him urging him not to resign; the problem was that the Kuang-hsü Emperor might ascend the throne; see *LWCK: Hai-chün*, 1:30b–31.

14. For court approval of June 23, 1888, see *CCTY*, 36:1–4b, 18–22; 38:15–19.

15. *WCSL*, 85:9–11b, July 9, 1882.

16. See *LWCK: Hai-chün*, for over 115 letters, 1885–1894, to the Navy Board. For a sample on railroads, see also *WCSL*, 80:13b–14, May 5, 1889, which is an edict to the Navy Board to draw up a plan for railroad construction. Meng Ssu-ming, p. 124, says that railroad building and mining were "automatically" given to the Navy Board, since they were closely related to defense.

17. Spector, *Li Hung-chang*, pp. 186–190, 226–227.

18. Li's conciliatory gestures came at least in a letter to a friend, Wu Wei-yin, in which Li noted that the dockyard was short of funds, and all other provinces should order their ships there; *LWCK: P'eng-liao*, 24:25, Aug. 18, 1886. On Wu Chung-hsiang, see *CCTY*, 31:25–26, Jan. 14, 1886. Wu did go back to Foochow, for later he was transferred from there to Canton; see Chap. VIII, below.

19. *WCSL*, 84:25–27, July 28, 1891.

20. See Spector, *Li Hung-chang*, pp. 189–194, 259–261, for discussion of Li's position.

21. See *PYHC* for complete detail. See also letter of July 15, 1888, in *LWCK: Hai-chün*, 3:7b–8b, discussing precedents and China's inability to imitate Britain completely.
22. *PYHC, chüan* 2, "Chain of Command." The several sections of the regulations are separately paginated. Pao Tsen-peng, p. 139, gives the names of Ting, Lin, and Liu.
23. *PYHC, chüan* 1, "Officer System."
24. *PYHC, chüan* 1, "Ship System."
25. *PYHC, chüan* 2, "Inspections."
26. *PYHC, chüan* 2, esp. pp. 3b–4, on protocol.
27. Ch'ih Chung-yu, p. 336.
28. W. F. Tyler, *Pulling Strings in China* (London, 1929), pp. 41–42.
29. For Hart's comment on Tso's death, see *IMC: Dec. Reps., 1882–1891*, Foochow, pp. 426–427. For Tso's recommendations, see Denby to Bayard, Oct. 16, 1885, *FRUS* (1885), pp. 178–180.
30. Reports by P'ei Yin-sen of July 19, 1885, and Jan. 6, 1886, in *CCTY*, 28:5–7b; 3:9–14.
31. *IMC: Dec. Reps., 1882–1891*, Foochow, pp. 426–427.
32. For 1887 report by P'ei on development of plant, see *CCTY*, 25:1–7; on postwar plans for ships, see his report in *CCTY*, 27:7–10b.
33. Reports by P'ei, Dec. 1, 1885, *CCTY*, 30:5–9.
34. Report by P'ei, Nov. 28, 1886, *CCTY*, 34:6–7b. The torpedo boat, the *Fu Lung*, ultimately went to the Peiyang navy. It was a 144-foot craft which had steamed to China from Germany by itself.
35. Reports by P'ei, Nov. 3 and Dec. 11, 1886, *CCTY*, 34:1–5, 14–16.
36. Li to Navy Board, *LWCK: Hai-chün*, 2:22b.
37. Reports by P'ei, *CCTY*, 36:7b–8, 8b, 10–12; 37:1b–2.
38. For quote, see E. H. Parker, *John Chinaman and a Few Others* (New York and London, 1902), pp. 19–20. On Pei's complaints, see *CCTY*, 36:1b, July 5, 1887; 36:2, same date; 36:19, Nov. 31, 1887; 37:21, Apr. 16, 1888; 39:11b–12, Aug. 11, 1889; 39:18b, Sept. 4, 1889.
39. *CCTY*, 43:33, Jan. 4, 1891; and *CCTY*, 44:12–14, Nov. 26, 1891.
40. See *CCTY*, 40:10b–11, Feb. 3, 1881; 42:2b–4, Jan. 3, 1889; 44:19a–b, Feb. 8, 1891; and 45:17b–18, Feb. 5, 1893, for accounting-period totals on which calculation is based. *CSK:PC*, 7:10–12, gives total dockyard expenses: 19 million taels over a forty-year period.
41. For a discussion of Li Hung-chang's financial problem, see Spector, *Li Hung-chang*, Chap. 7: "Problems of Military Financing." For particulars, see *ibid.*, Table 11, p. 222; Table 14, p. 225; and Table 5, pp. 202–204.
42. See Li report. *WCSL*, 48:13.
43. For correspondence on the ships, see *WCSL*, 61:17a–b, edict of Oct. 23, 1885; 61:21a–b, Oct. 28, 1885; and 61:21b–22; also see Li to Tseng Chi-tse, *LWCK: P'eng-liao*, 24:21b–22b, Jan. 13, 1886; and *ibid.*, 24:23b, to same, June 13, 1886. The note of Lang's mission is in Ch'ih Chung-yu, p. 335. See Appendix C for the Chinese names of the two ships called *Ching Yüan*.
44. Li listed the *Ting Yüan* and *Chen Yüan*, *Chi Yüan*, *Ch'ao Yung*, and *Yang Wei* as deep-water ships; he also listed some Foochow dockyard-built ships assigned to local roles. He mentioned the dangers of allowing amateurs to dabble in naval matters (*LWCK: Hai-chün*, 1:1–3).
45. Ch'ih Chung-yu, p. 335. *CSK:PC*, 7:5b, records that one of the torpedo boats, the *Tso I*, was from England; the rest were German.
46. Pao Tsen-peng, pp. 209–210.
47. See 1886 letters to Navy Board, in *LWCK: Hai-chün*, 1:18b, Mar. 11; 1:19b, Apr. 27; 1:20b, June 25 and 30; 1:10b, Jan. 21 (on decommissioning); Prince Ch'un to Li, Dec. 13, *ibid.*, 2:23b; on Li's talks with bankers, letters of Dec. 13 and Jan. 3, 1887, *ibid.*, 2:24, 26. The information on the court ladies on the lakes comes

NOTES TO CHAPTER VII

from C. B. Malone, *History of the Peking Summer Palace* (Urbana, 1934), pp. 197–198.

48. For the total, see *PYHC*, chüan 2, "Summary of Expenses." For Li's wishes for ships, see *LWCK: Hai-chün*, 3:7b–8b, to Navy Board, July 15, 1888.
49. Malone, p. 198.
50. Pao Tsen-peng, p. 213, citing biography of Lin Shao-nien.
51. *Ibid.*, pp. 210–211.
52. *Ibid.*, pp. 211–213.
53. *Ibid.*, p. 213.
54. Malone, p. 198.
55. Bland and Backhouse, pp. 99–100. The Navy Board did not entirely cease payments to Li Hung-chang. In October 1894 Li received to 1.5 million taels from the Navy Board and the Board of Revenue each; *WCSL*, 98:7b–10b. In the period 1883–1891, Li's naval budget showed 8,340,000 taels; see Stanley Spector, "Li Hung-chang and the Huai-chün," Ph.D. thesis (University of Washington, 1953), p. 490.
56. *Ibid.*, p. 406.
57. Malone, p. 198.
58. On Nanyang expenses, see memorial by Liu K'un-i, July 29, 1891, *WCSL*, 84:25–27.
59. Malone, p. 198.
60. Sill to Gresham, June 28, 1894, Appendix I, "Chinese-Japanese War," *FRUS* (1894), p. 25.
61. Pao Tseng-peng, pp. 214–215.
62. Ch'ih Chung-yu, pp. 337–338.
63. *LWCK: Hai-chün*, 4:18b–20.
64. See reports on Chefoo trade for 1891, 1892, and 1893, in *BPP*: "Diplomatic and Consular Reports," 1892, v. lxxxi, 12; 1893, v. xcii, 13–14; and 1894, v. lxxxv, 10.
65. James Allan, *Under the Dragon Flag* (New York, 1898), p. 34. Allan, an American adventurer, talked with Purvis, a foreign engineer serving on the *Ch'ao Yung*, who particularly noted conditions in that ship.
66. Pao Tsen-peng, p. 214.
67. Ch'ih Chung-yu, pp. 376–377; and *WCSL*, 95:1–3b, Aug. 31, 1894.
68. Pao Tseng-peng, p. 214.
69. Report by Liu K'un-i, July 25, 1891, *WCSL*, 84:25–27. Li wrote the Navy Board that the Nanyang fleet had three seaworthy ships: *Nan Ch'en, Nan Shui*, and *K'ai Chi; LWCK: Hai-chün*, 2:3. Ch'ih Chung-yu, p. 342, mentions the four gunboats.
70. Ch'ih Chung-yu, p. 336.
71. On the Canton facilities, see *CSK:PC*, 7:17b; *IMC: Dec. Reps., 1882–1891*, Canton, p. 575; Denby to Blaine, Mar. 12, 1889, *FRUS* (1889), p. 108; Charles Beresford, *The Break-Up of China* (New York, 1899), pp. 301–302; and LaFargue, who writes (p. 9) that the Canton yard was modeled on that at Foochow. On the Amoy docks, see H. W. Wilson, *Ironclads*, II, 61; and "Bibliographical Notes," in *USNIP*, 14.1:278–279 (1888). On Nanking, see Beresford, pp. 298–299. For description of the Hankow works, see report of P. Scheldtweiler, Secretary to Provincial Board of Mines, dated Oct. 16, 1892, and approved by Chang Chih-tung, in *IMC: Dec. Reps., 1882–1891*, Hankow, pp. 187–190; and Beresford, p. 299. The present account will also bypass arsenals at Chengtu, Kirin, Taipei, and Tamsui, which did not figure in the hostilities of the period. *HFT*: "Kiangnan" contains extensive material on these facilities.
72. J. W. McClellan, *The Story of Shanghai* (Shanghai, 1889), pp. 64–66; and "Bibliographical Notes," *USNIP*, 14.1:278–279 (1888).
73. *CSK:PC*, 7:19; and McClellan, pp. 64–66.
74. See "Bibliographical Notes," *USNIP*, 14.1:278–279 (1888). For other docks in the Shanghai area, see also *IMC: Dec. Reps., 1882–1891*, Shanghai, p. 317. H. W. Wilson, *Ironclads*, II, 61, discusses docks in Japan, which makes comparisons available.

75. *IMC: Dec. Reps.*, *1882–1891*, Shanghai, p. 338. McClellan, pp. 64–66, mentions other impressions of foreigners.
76. Hilary A. Herbert, "Military Lessons of the Sino-Japanese War," *North American Review*, 160:685–698 (June 1895).
77. Beresford, pp. 294–298.
78. Governor of Taiwan, *WCSL*, 95:4–6b, Aug. 31, 1894; Western comment in McClellan, pp. 64–66.
79. *LWCK:Hai-chün*, 1:8b–9, Jan. 3, 1886; also *CSK:PC*, 7:17b. For improvements in Li's plant (powder mills) see H. Marion, abstract of a book on powder mills in China, in "Bibliographical Notes," *USNIP*, 14.3:615 (1888). In 1898 Beresford praised the Tientsin arsenal, but observed that its director was drastically underpaid in English terms; Beresford, pp. 292–294.
80. *LWCK: Hai-chün*, 1:1–3, Jan. 3, 1886. Ch'ih Chung-yu, p. 334, mentions a visit to Nagasaki of Li's ships, which involved a bloody fracas betwen Li's crews and Japanese police, so that Lang even urged a declaration of war, although Admiral Ting preferred a legal settlement. Another reason for keeping repairs at home!
81. Li report on Port Arthur in *WCSL*, 84:33b–36, Oct. 29, 1891. Allan, p. 40, remarked that the mines laid to protect the harbor by Li's Port Arthur experts were not always well adjusted; some showed above water.
82. *PYHC*, chüan 2, item 14, "Naval Supply Organization."
83. Letter of Jan. 3, 1886, *LWCK: Hai-chün*, 1:9.
84. Spector, "Li Hung-chang," pp. 407, 603.
85. See report on purchases, in *WCSL*, 95:12a–b, Sept. 14, 1894.
86. See Allan, *passim*, for the *Columbia's* voyage. Evidently Li did some standardizing of equipment, however, Both of his *Ching Yüan* vessels, English and German, purchased in 1885, had fixed torpedo tubes designated "Fish" (submerged) by T. A. Brassey in *The Naval Annual* (1894), Chinese listings.
87. Tyler, pp. 39–43.
88. See *ibid.*, p. 50, on Chang P'ei-lun; see also Philo McGiffen, "The Battle of the Yalu, Personal Recollections by the Commander of the Chinese Ironclad *Chen Yuen*," *Century Magazine* (August 1895), p. 593. Ch'ih Chung-yu, p. 380, mentions the treacherous clerks.
89. See Beresford, chap. 22, esp. p. 291, for reports on the forts visited.
90. For details see Inouye Jukichi, *The Japan-China War* (Shanghai, n.d.), Appendix 31. See also "Vladimir," p. 223.
91. "Valdimir," p. 231. The author was very pro-Japanese, and may have exaggerated Japan's triumph.
92. Richard Wallach, "The War in the East," *USNIP*, 21.3:723, 725 (1895), makes rather slighting references to Weihaiwei; see also Inouye, Appendices 26 and 27; and "Vladimir," p. 276, for many details.
93. On Talienwan, see Inouye, section "On the Regent's Sword," p. 8. On Chefoo, see "Report for the Year 1892 on the Trade of Chefoo," *BPP*: "Diplomatic and Consular Reports," v. xcii; *IMC: Dec. Reps.*, *1882–1891*, Chefoo, pp. 74–75, and *ibid.*, *1892–1901*, Chefoo, pp. 66–67. On Tsingtao (Kiaochow), see *CTLT*, 342: 9a–b; *IMC: Dec. Reps.*, *1882–1891*, Kiaochow, p. 74, and *ibid.*, *1892–1901*, Tsingtao, p. 89.
94. Ballard, p. 1.
95. On Shuiying, see "Report for the Year 1891 on the Trade of Kiungchow," *BPP*: "Diplomatic and Consular Reports," 1892, v. lxxxi. For Formosa, see *BPP*: "Commercial Reports," 1886, v. lxvi, Tamsuy and Keelung, p. 27. The 1892 English comment is from "Report for the Year 1892 on the Trade of Chefoo," *BPP*: "Diplomatic and Consular Reports," 1893, v. xcii.
96. *CSK:PC*, 6:9b, a note of 1889 for the Fukien water force; by 1893, repeated trimming had cut the force to 30 war junks; *ibid.*, 6:9.
97. *IMC: Dec. Reps.*, *1892–1901*, II, Ningpo, p. 37. On Foochow, see *WCSL*, 92:2a–b, July 3, 1894.

NOTES TO CHAPTER VII

98. Tyler, p. 113.
99. "Report for the Year 1887 on the Trade and Commerce of Canton," *BPP*: "Diplomatic and Consular Reports," 1888, Vol. 100, for consular reaction. For Chang's ideas on permanent blocks, see *WCSL*, 66:1–3b.
100. A full treatment of this matter would take a separate essay; Liu K'un-i was uncertain; the Japanese changed their minds; there were the arsenal problem, the interests of the British, and so on. Liu raised the matter in a telegram to the Tsungli Yamen late in July 1894, *WCSL*, 93:10b. See *WCSL*, 93:13a–b, 15b; 94:2b; 95:9, 4–6b, 100:12b–13, for correspondence going into December 1894. Denby summarized, to Gresham, Sept. 15, 1894, in Appendix I, *FRUS* (1894), pp. 58–59.
101. Governor-general T'ang Chun-lin, *WCSL*, 92:2a–b, July 3, 1894.
102. On these visits, see Ch'ih Chung-yu, pp. 334, 338.
103. A. J. Marder, The *Anatomy of British Sea Power* (New York, 1940), Chap. 5, summarizes Britain's strategic debates.
104. The Yangtze water force was supposedly reinvigorated with orders to its officers to cease living ashore, etc. Its admiral, Huang I-sheng, approached the Min-Che officials with a scheme of cooperation. There were two troop steamers in Chekiang and three in Fukien, and he planned joint maneuvers with them. *CSK:PC*, 6:9b.

VIII. NAVAL TRAINING, 1885–1894

1. Although the K'un-ming Academy did not outlast the Sino-Japanese War, it did have some serious intent. In 1887, after an inspection of coasts and rivers, Prince Ch'un asked for the founding of a school near the capital to train Manchus in naval skills. The school was built on K'un-ming Lake, near the I-ho Yuan, and opened at the end of 1887 or early in 1888. It imitated the format of the Tientsin naval academy. Sixty students were initially called, and forty remained. The first class graduated in 1892 and was sent to the Tientsin naval academy for further study. In 1893 this class was granted a vacation, after which some of its members returned to K'un-ming and were absorbed into the Banners. In 1892 a second class of forty-four (still all Manchus, apparently) was called, but after the war the Navy Board petitioned to have the K'un-ming Academy closed. Perhaps the dynasty wanted to infiltrate some of its own men into Li's fleet. Pao Tsen-peng, pp. 232–233.
2. Biggerstaff, p. 222.
3. *CCTY*, 31:1–5, Jan. 14, 1886.
4. Biggerstaff, pp. 237–239; and *CCTY*, 32:4–6, May 10, 1886.
5. *CCTY*, 33:3–5, July 17, 1886.
6. Biggerstaff, p. 239.
7. Biggerstaff, pp. 224, 226–227; also "Naval Colleges in China," *Engineer* (June 8, 1900), pp. 600–601.
8. Pao Tsen-peng, pp. 227–230; and Biggerstaff, pp. 54–55, 227.
9. "Report for the Year 1889 on the Trade of Canton," p. 10, *BPP*: "Diplomatic and Consular Reports," 1890–1891, Vol. 85.
10. *IMC: Dec. Reps., 1882–1891*, Canton, p. 576; "Report for the Year 1888 on the Trade of Canton," p. 9, *BPP*: "Diplomatic and Consular Reports," 1889, v. lxxvii; Pao Tsen-peng, p. 230.
11. Biggerstaff, p. 56.
12. Pao Tsen-peng, pp. 234–236; and Liu report in *WCSL*, 84:25–27, July 28, 1891.
13. "Naval Colleges," pp. 600–601.
14. Pao Tsen-peng, pp. 233–234, 243, discusses the Weihaiwei school. Some recruits came from Kwangtung, brought back by the Peiyang fleet after a cruise in southern waters. Possibly Li used the Weihaiwei school as an induction center for such recruits, to prepare them for the Tientsin naval academy.
15. For fuller discussion of Li's various schools, see *PYHC*, chüan 1, item 7, and chüan 2, items 5, 8, and 14; *CTLT*, 342:9b; Ch'ih Chung-yu, p. 336; Pao Tsen-peng,

pp. 233–234; and E. H. Parker, "Militaryism in China," *China Review* (Sept.–Oct. 1885), p. 109.

16. Stanley Wright, pp. 480–481. Lang was praised for his work by Li and Prince Ch'un, May 20, 1886, *WCSL*, 66:16a–b.

17. Denby to Bayard, May 11, 1888, *FRUS* (1888), I, 301–303; also *PYHC, chüan* 2, "Miscellaneous Expenses," for further information on the academy's organization.

18. *PYHC*, 2:1–6b, "Examinations."

19. *Ibid.*

20. Ch'ih Chung-yu, p. 342, says that in 1895 Wang Wen-shao, governor of Chihli, sent undergraduates from the Liu-kung-tao school to the Tientsin academy. For the flyer, see Denby to Bayard, May 11, 1888, *FRUS* (1888), I, 301–303, based on a proclamation in *Shih pao* (Apr. 30, 1888), by "Sin" [sic], expectant Chihli taotai and manager of the school.

21. *PYHC, chüan* 2, "Examinations."

22. *LWCK: Hai-chun*, 4:22a–b (Aug. 25, 1893). Pao Tsen-peng, p. 231, gives numbers, ranging from eighteen to thirty, of graduating students.

23. On the elementary nature of the curriculum, see Denby to Bayard, May 11, 1888, *FRUS* (1888), I, 301–303. The comments on map work were indirect. A Japanese naval officer remarked that American maps of the Yellow Sea and Korea were the best available; see "Bibliographical Notes," *USNIP*, 21.4:860 (1894). Biggerstaff, p. 239, states that two of the naval students who went to Europe in 1886 studied cartography.

24. *PYHC, chüan* 2, "Examinations," including sections on enlisted personnel. The item on the *chü-jen* degree is in Biggerstaff, p. 182.

25. See material on reviews, rewards, from *PYHC, chüan* 2, "Reviews," which also contains material on north-south joint maneuvers.

26. *PYHC, chüan* 1, "Promotions."

27. *Ibid.*, "Ceremonial Regulations."

28. *Ibid.*, "Punishments." For the twenty-six articles, see pp. 4–7b.

29. *Ibid.*, "Salaries."

30. W. Laird-Clowes, "The Naval War Between China and Japan," Brassey (1895), pp. 90–126; statement made in *ibid.*, p. 116.

31. Denby to Bayard, May 14, 1886, *FRUS* (1886), pp. 83–84.

32. Ballard, pp. 135–136.

33. See *LWCK: Hai-chün*, 1:29b–30, July 16, 1886. Another kind of corruption was associated with the overseas training program. In 1890 P'ei Yin-sen recommended rewards for a group of students who had been overseas, but it was found that the list included Foochow dockyard staff personnel who had never been abroad. Wang Sung-ch'en, acting assistant superintendent, had forged the additions. See *CCTY*, 43:6a–b.

34. Parker, *John Chinaman*, pp. 241–244.

35. Stanley Wright, pp. 481–482; and Parker, *John Chinaman*, pp. 251–252.

36. Tyler, p. 36.

37. *WCSL*, 106:13a–b, Feb. 16, 1896.

38. Ch'ih Chung-yu, p. 334, and Yao, p. 197. Another interesting opinion is that the man behind Lang's ouster was Fang (Pai-ch'ien), also a member of the strong southern contingent in the Peiyang fleet; H. W. Wilson, *Ironclads*, II, 67.

39. Stanley Wright, pp. 481–482.

40. Edwin A. Falk, *Togo and the Rise of Japanese Sea Power* (New York and Toronto, 1936), pp. 131–132.

41. Tyler, p. 89.

42. Parker, *John Chinaman*, p. 259.

43. Herbert, "Lessons," p. 696.

44. Alfred Cunningham, *The Chinese Soldier and Other Sketches* (London, n.d.), pp. 30–31.

NOTES TO CHAPTER IX

IX. DISASTER IN THE NORTH: NAVAL ASPECTS OF THE
SINO-JAPANESE WAR, 1894–1895

1. Summary based on coverage in Li Chien-nung, pp. 127–139.
2. Figures on Japanese strength from W. H. Beckler, "A Review of Japanese Naval Financial Policy," *USNIP*, 37.3:789 (September 1911). Other accounts do not always agree; e.g., "Vladimir," pp. 87 and 168, gives only twenty-seven principal ships.
3. Herbert, "Lessons," speaks of Japanese facilities. Japanese yards were organized by Louis Emile Bertin; see Alfred Vagts, *Defense and Diplomacy: The Soldier and the Conduct of Foreign Relations* (New York, 1956), p. 184.
4. E. B. Potter and J. R. Fredlund, eds., *The United States and World Sea Power* (New York, 1955), p. 420, makes the point about Annapolis; and Vagts, p. 184 covers training in Japan.
5. H. W. Wilson, *Ironclads*, II, 62. "Vladimir" and Inouye give slightly different figures.
6. For example, see edict to Liao Shou-feng, ordering him to ready troops, *WCSL*, 97:1, Oct. 10, 1894. Admiral Ting occasionally submitted a direct report; see one to the new Chün-wu ch'u, *WCSL*, 100:9a–b.
7. Occasionally the Tsungli Yamen sent orders for the strengthening of local defenses, as to the Min-Che governor-general, via Li Hung-chang, acknowledged July 3, 1894 (*WCSL*, 92:2a–b); see also acknowledgment of similar instruction by the governor of Taiwan, Aug. 31, 1894, in *WCSL*, 95:4–6b.
8. On receipt of Nanyang ships, see *WCSL*, 93:2b–3b, July 18, 1894, and *WCSL*, 93:17a–b, July 29, 1894. In the last item Shao Yu-lien asked for Peiyang help too. At the end of August he asked for it again (*WCSL*, 95:4–6b). That there were not many ships available in southern waters is shown by the fact that after the P'eng-hu fight of April 1895, Chinese troops were evacuated by junk, although some officials escaped on British ships; see item by Hung Ch'i-fu, "Taiwan chan-chi" (Record of the fighting in Formosa), *CJ*, VI, 333, 348.
9. See accounts of Yalu and Weihaiwei naval battles, below, for the records of these southern ships.
10. For notes on other fleets, see "Bibliographical Notes," *USNIP*, 21.1:206 (1895), citing a German article entitled "Foreign Squadrons at the Seat of War in China," dated Dec. 5, 1894. An American naval officer remarked that all the world thought that China had a fleet better than Japan's; see Ensign Frank Marble, USN, "The Battle of the Yalu," *USNIP*, 21.3:521. Not all foreign opinion was favorable. Hart said in July 1894: "China is getting fighting material into line and is horrified to find how poor it is . . ."; Stanley Wright, pp. 642–643.
11. Yao Hsi-kuang p. 194.
12. On the convoy, see Li report of July 16, *WCSL*, 92:12b–14b. That the Japanese were not expecting this particular encounter — that is, that their espionage was not very exact — is suggested by Togo Heikachiro in his discussion of the sinking of the *Kowhsing*, as cited in *CJ*, VI: 30–35, in which he makes no mention of expecting the encounter.
13. Accounts of the Feng-tao battle include those of Morse and MacNair, pp. 577–578; "Vladimir," pp. 95–97; H. W. Wilson, *Ironclads*, II, 67; and Chang Yin-lin, "Chia-wu Chung-kuo hai-chün chan-chi kao" (Chinese naval campaigns in the Sino-Japanese War), *Ch'ing-hua hsüeh-pao*, 10.1:63–64 (Jan. 1935).
14. Chang Yin-lin, p. 64, makes the point about the editing of the telegram; Ch'ih Chung-yu, p. 375, and Yao Hsi-kuang, p. 198, also mention a holdback of larger units.
15. Taken from the "Vladimir" account, pp. 95–97.
16. The *Chi Yüan's* repairs included the installation of two new Gruson 1.97-inch, four-pound quick-firing guns, just arrived from Europe; Laird-Clowes, p. 98.
17. Chang Yin-lin, p. 73, mentions the Weihaiwei-Yalu line. As for Japanese

THE SINO-JAPANESE WAR, 1894–1895

troop landings, see for example the landing on September 12 of 10,000 soldiers, 4000 coolies, and 350 horses. Thanks to these reinforcements, which came through Chemulpo on the west coast, Pyongyang fell on Sept. 15 ("Vladimir," p. 118). On the line, see also n. 27, below.

18. McGiffen's account applies to a patrol of August 2; H. W. Wilson, *Ironclads*, II, pp. 80–81.
19. *WCSL*, 94:3a–b; and Chang Yin-lin, p. 74.
20. *WCSL*, 94:6a–b.
21. *WCSL*, 94:8a–b, 8b, 10a–b, for items from Li, the court, and Li, the last dated Aug. 6, 1894.
22. Grand Council to Li, Aug. 5, *CJ* III, 22–23.
23. *WCSL*, 94:10b–11, Aug. 6, 1894.
24. Ch'ih Chung-yu, pp. 376, 382–383. It was also being said that Ting was in secret contact with the enemy.
25. *WCSL*, 94:11a–b.
26. Laird-Clowes, p. 99. Chang Yin-lin, pp. 74–75, says the raid was a feint to cover troop movements, and China was deceived. H. W. Wilson, *Ironclads*, II, 80–81, also mentions the raid. Li's reports of it may be found in *WCSL*, 94:13–14, 17–18.
27. The rough-weather excuse is mentioned in Laird-Clowes, p. 99. He cites McGiffen as saying that the recall was "in consequence of the representations of Li Hung-chang." In a memorial of Aug. 29, 1894, Li (in a defense of Ting) argued that the proper use of the fleet was to guard the threshold, as defined by Port Arthur and Weihaiwei, instead of making active attacks; *CJ*, III, 71–73. This is the only official Chinese reference to a "line" I have been able to find. McGiffen claimed the line was drawn by the Tsungli Yamen, right after the "so-called bombardment of Weihaiwei," and was a "most positive order" not to go outside of a line drawn from the Shantung light to the Yalu's mouth; see McGiffen, p. 586. H. W. Wilson, *Ironclads*, II, 80–81, mentions the Weihaiwei-Yalu line, relating it to orders from Li Hung-chang. A. T. Mahan, "Lessons from the Yalu Fight," *Century Magazine*, 1.50:629 (August 1895), mentions a line. So does Falk, p. 177. These accounts are probably based on McGiffen. The point is a basic one, but it would seem that the line was drawn by Li Hung-chang.
28. Li reports on supposed Japanese purchases in *WCSL*, 94:25b, Aug. 12, 1894. Pao Tsen-peng, p. 297, mentions the rumor that Li was bribed; so too does Falk, p. 177, but he discounted the idea, although admitting that circumstantial evidence gave it some strength.
29. *WCSL*, 94:13–14, Aug. 12 and 13, 1894.
30. *WCSL*, 94:14a–b, on Hart. The impeachers of Ting were widely scattered, that is, one was in the Board of Rites in Peking, another was a district official censor in Kwangsi. See *CJ*, III, 39, 56–58, for impeachments during period Aug. 16 to 25, 1894.
31. For Li's report, and subsequent orders, see *WCSL*, 94:17–18, 18b, 20, under dates of Aug. 22, 23, and 26. For Grand Council order of Aug. 25, see *CJ*, III, 58.
32. *CJ*, III, 67.
33. *WCSL*, 95:1–3b, Aug. 31, 1894. Li had taken the precaution of sending Ting to convoy ships to Ta-tung-k'ou; *WCSL*, 94:22a–b, Aug. 28, 1894.
34. A complaint of Aug. 31, 1894, charged that Lin and Liu were "stupid and cowardly," given to hiding in their cabins; Ting's limitations were blamed on these two, and the emperor was asked to dismiss them. This was refused. See Chang Yin-lin, p. 75.
35. *WCSL*, 95:3b, Aug. 31, 1894.
36. For discussion of buying ships, see *WCSL*, 94:20b, Aug. 27; *WSCL*, 95:7b, Sept. 2; *WCSL*, 96:13, Sept. 23, 1894. An Wei-chün, a censor in Fukien, argued against letting Li Hung-chang make the purchases. Li, he said, already had his quota; the Nanyang fleet should be built up. He attacked Li, Liu, and Lin, and said that in

235

NOTES TO CHAPTER IX

the Feng-tao battle (near Asan) the *Kwang I* made a good fight, which to him proved the truth that the commander rather than the ship was important. See *CJ*, III, 77–78, Aug. 31, 1894. On the Gruson guns, see Laird-Clowes, p. 109.

37. Inouye, Pt. 1, p. 1, discusses the Japanese buildup, and states that Japan did *not* anticipate a sea contact with Chinese forces in the course of effecting troop landings on the west coast of Korea. Perhaps the Japanese knew of Li Hung-chang's defense line between Weihaiwei and the mouth of the Yalu, or Talienwan.

38. Ballard, pp. 139 ff., makes a lengthy technical comparison. Comparisons are also in H. W. Wilson, *Ironclads*, II, pp. 112–113, and Table XX, p. 307; and Hilary A. Herbert, "The Fight of the Yalu River," *North American Review* (November 1894), pp. 513–528.

39. *CTLT*, 324:11a–b.

40. Ch'ih Chung-yu, p. 339, calls him *tsung-ch'a*, or inspector-general; Laird-Clowes, p. 101, calls him Inspector of Coasts and Adviser to the Admiral; Tyler, p. 39, calls him Co-Admiral.

41. Tyler, p. 60. Vagts, in a chapter on "Military Missions and Instructors," discusses the problems of Von Hannecken, who had the rank of a Chinese general.

42. Tyler, pp. 36, 40–41, 43–44, 50, 64.

43. *Ibid.*, p. 52.

44. *Ibid.*, p. 62, and McGiffen.

45. Yao Hsi-kuang, p. 201.

46. Chang Yin-lin, p. 78, citing McGiffen.

47. For details, see battle accounts to follow and Appendices C and D, "Ships" and "List of Chinese Names." Von Hannecken, himself of uncertain naval competence, remarked that Li's Yalu captains had had little experience; Laird-Clowes, p. 116.

48. Daniel Henderson, *Yankee Ships in China Seas* (New York, 1946), pp. 249–250, citing an account by Park Benjamin. McGiffen also "zealously insisted on his rank of Commander in the Chinese Navy, which, he claimed, he held by imperial rescript, although he received no pay . . ." Falk, p. 176, called McGiffen a captain.

49. Tyler, p. 44.

50. The foreigners were: in the *Ting Yüan*, Von Hannecken, Tyler, Nichols (gunnery lt.), and Albrecht (chief engineer); in the *Chen Yüan*, McGiffen and Heckmann (gunnery lt.); in the *Chih Yüan*, Purvis (engineer); and in the *Chi Yüan*, Hoffman (engineer). Nichols and Purvis were killed. See Laird-Clowes, p. 110. Pao Tsen-peng, p. 310, gives the Chinese names of these men. There was a different group in the last stand at Weihaiwei; see Inouye, Sec. 2, "Fall of Wei-hai-wei," p. 25, "Woo" was Wu Ying-fu; see LaFargue, pp. 78–82.

51. See Inouye, Sec. 1, "The Naval Battle of Haiyang"; "Vladimir"; Falk; Marble; Potter and Fredlund; and H. W. Wilson, *Ironclads*, II, for detailed accounts.

52. Falk, p. 183, implies the battle was not expected, thus accounting for China's irregular battle line; Marble, p. 506, said Ting would have avoided contact if he had anticipated it (but Lt. W. P. White, in his discussion of Marble's article, says, Ting went out to fight even though he could have remained unseen in his Yalu estuary anchorage; see Marble, p. 515).

53. Details on clearing for battle from McGiffen, with added details from H. W. Wilson, *Ironclads*, II, 79; Falk, p. 176; and Laird-Clowes, p. 116.

54. Tyler, pp. 50–51.

55. On line-ahead vs. line-abreast, see Laird-Clowes, p. 116; also H. W. Wilson, *Battleships in Action*, 2 vols. (Boston, 1926), I, 102.

56. See H. W. Wilson, *Ironclads*, II, 63–64, for discussion; see also his *Battleships*, II, 92, for diagram of the *Chen-Ting* mount system. Marble (discussion by Lt. White, p. 508) reverses the placement of the barbettes, saying the starboard barbette was the farthest forward, which would affect ability to make a simultaneous salvo over the starboard bow. Potter and Fredlund, p. 425 n., argue that only on the

THE SINO-JAPANESE WAR, 1894–1895

broadside could such ships develop their maximum fire. Evidently this was a controversial design.

57. H. W. Wilson, *Ironclads*, II, 63–64, makes the point. As for the Japanese ships: the principal Japanese unarmored cruisers included two built in France and one in Japan to French plans. These three carried 12.8-inch Carnet guns, one on each, with two ships carrying them in a forward mount, and the third, in an after mount. This design embodied "the serious defect of an excessive development of fire from one end of the ship" (Ballard, p. 139). Still, the Japanese based their battle formation on these guns, which could be best fired over the side — hence, line-ahead. H. W. Wilson, *Ironclads*, II, p. 116, says that no large battleship of modern design fought for either side off the Yalu. The British *Royal Sovereign* displaced 14,510 tons — far beyond the 7430 tons of the *Ting Yüan* class.

58. For Li's coverage of signaling in his 1888 regulations, see *PYHC*, *chüan* 2, "Signal flags."

59. Laird-Clowes, p. 116, calls the instructions fatal; Ballard, chap. 5, calls them crude (and says that they amounted only to a permission to flee danger, pair by pair). Marble, p. 518, feels that Von Hannecken inspired them; Laird-Clowes and Ballard say that they originated with Ting. H. W. Wilson, *Ironclads*, II, 85–86, also discusses the problem.

60. Tyler, p. 57. Pao Tsen-peng, p. 306, agrees. However, Mahan, "Lessons," was of the opinion that it was logical to keep the two heavy battleships in the middle of a line-abreast. This may suggest again how complicated and controversial were these tactical matters.

61. As in all of these matters, there was disagreement in detail, but here is the Chinese line as given in Falk, p. 167, which corresponds as well as any with reported developments in the battle: from right wing to left, *Yang Wei*, *Ch'ao Yung*, *Ching Yüan*, *Lai Yüan*, *Chen Yüan*, and *Ting Yüan*, *Ching Yüan*, *Chih Yüan*, *Kwang Chia*, and *Chi Yüan*. The *P'ing Yüan* and *Kwang Ping* came up later, probably behind the right wing.

62. Speed given in comment by Lt. White to Marble, Marble, p. 514. The Japanese did not always use line-ahead; Yao Hsi-kuang, p. 200, says that in the August 10 raid on Weihaiwei, they came up line-abreast. Laird-Clowes, p. 101, gives an example of the Chinese use of line-ahead.

63. Tyler, pp. 50–52. Chang Yin-lin, pp. 78–80, follows Tyler's account. Allan, adds this note on disobedience: "As an instance of this, it is alleged that instructions telegraphed from the conning-tower of the flagship were varied or suppressed by the officer at that telegraph, and that a subsequent comparison of notes with the engineer officer afforded proof of this." (Albrecht was the engineer.) H. W. Wilson, *Ironclads*, II, 104, also mentions the incident. Liu fired his first salvo at 6000 meters; Inouye, Sec. 1, p. 3. These points may serve to underline the need for a technical inquiry into these matters, to determine responsibility.

64. The Japanese opened fire at 3000 meters; Inouye, Sec. 1, p. 3. Falk, p. 185, says Ito was surprised that Ting did not execute the quarter-turn-in-line, so as to bring on a broadside duel. Falk here makes the point that British instructors to Ting's fleet had stressed line-abreast as a *prelude* to battle. The destruction of signal halyards is mentioned in Ch'ih Chung-yu, p. 378; Ch'ih adds (p. 379) that the other ships were disconcerted by this.

65. Allan, pp. 30–31.
66. *Ibid.*, p. 32.
67. Hsien Yü-ch'ing, p. 31, says that *Chi Yüan* rammed the *Yang Wei*; H. W. Wilson, *Ironclads*, II, 92, agrees. However, in the discussion of the punishment of Fang Pai-ch'ien, later in this chapter, other evidence is introduced. As for *Kwang Chia*, Inouye, Sec. 1, p. 42, cites a *North China Daily News* correspondent as saying that her captain "kept such a keen eye aft that at 11 p.m. he ran on a reef 20 miles off Talien Bay." Conjectural, but good copy.

68. "Vladimir," p. 170, and Inouye, Sec. 1, p. 4, say these two ships were the

NOTES TO CHAPTER IX

old Armstrong gunboats *Chen Nan* and *Chen Pien*. The authors used sources which are not clear. Falk, p. 189, assigns the names used in this account, which seem to harmonize with other facts.

69. H. W. Wilson, *Ironclads*, II, 91, mentions the attack on the *Saikyo*, and on p. 97 expresses surprise that she was not sunk.

70. Newspaper dispatch cited in Inouye, Sec. 1, p. 14. The quotations come from Allan, p. 33.

71. Chang Yin-lin, pp. 81–82; Ch'ih Chung-yu, p. 377; and *CTLT*, 342:11, mention Teng's heroism and give details on his drowning.

72. Inouye, Sec. 1, pp. 19–20, citing newspaper report.

73. *Ibid.*, pp. 19–21, citing news coverage. H. W. Wilson, *Ironclads*, II, 113, lists these fires: the *Lai Yüan* almost reduced to a hulk; the *Ching Yüan* afire before sunk; the *Ting Yüan* had three fires; the *Yang Wei*, *Ch'ao Yung*, and *Kwang Chia* were all afire (the *Kwang Chia* apparently did not flee unscathed).

74. H. W. Wilson, *Ironclads*, II, 91; Falk, p. 191, lays the escape of the *Hiyei* to faulty Chinese ammunition.

75. Tyler, p. 54. Chang Yin-lin, p. 54, supports Tyler in this, arguing that the *Ting Yüan* claim was probably a lie of Liu Pu-ch'an's.

76. Chang Yin-lin, p. 85; also Falk, p. 197. The other *Ching Yüan* was sunk during the Yalu battle.

77. Inouye, Sec. 1, p. 18, citing news report.

78. H. W. Wilson, in *Battleships*, Vol. 1, Chap. 6, and in *Ironclads*, II, 109–110, concludes that the Japanese scored most with their six- to eight-inch quick-firers. Their big French Carnet twelve-inch rifles were supposed to penetrate thirty inches of armor, but no armor damage on the battleships' fourteen-inch belts exceeded four inches.

79. Figures on shells fired, hits, etc., from H. W. Wilson, *Ironclads*, II, 91, 99, 114; H. W. Wilson, *Battleships*, I, 105; Laird-Clowes, p. 109; and McGiffen, p. 601. Inouye, Sec. 1, p. 17, cites a news dispatch on the over-use and run-down condition of Chinese torpedo boats, and their consequent slow speed in this action. Chinese ships had forty-four torpedo tubes in all, as against thirty-two for Japan. Tyler, p. 54, says shooting was based on observation of shell splashes; another observer says the sight-bars were set and left unchanged throughout; another, that a table of distances based on the masthead angle of the *Matsushima* was later found in the *Ting Yüan*. See comments in Marble, pp. 502, 509.

80. On Chinese ammunition, see H. W. Wilson, *Ironclads*, II, 104; McGiffen, p. 599; Tyler, pp. 39–41; and Laird-Clowes, p. 109. McGiffen comments on the break-off on p. 601.

81. H. W. Wilson, *Ironclads*, II, 94–96. Cunningham says some of the shells were filled with sand. Laird-Clowes (p. 116) remarks that China marked her ammunition with the "broad arrow" in the belief that this old British naval symbol would bring good luck. Hsien Yü-ch'ing, p. 32, cites a number of critical articles, and concludes that Chinese powder was not good, that the shells did not fit — and that no one cared, since profit had been the chief consideration in their manufacture.

82. Hsien Yü-ch'ing, p. 32, citing a Japanese account.

83. "Professional Notes," *USNIP*, 21.4:897–898 (1895), for review of published item entitled "The Offensive and Defensive Weapons in the Battle of the Yalu." There were many such pronunciamentos on the "lessons" of this pioneer modern naval battle.

84. Charles Denby, *China and Her People*, 2 vols. (Boston, 1906), II, 136–137, talked of Li's soreness over the loss of his decoration; as for speculation on Japan's next blow, see *WCSL*, 96:14; 24b; 97:2b–3.

85. Inouye, Sec. 1, pp. 19–21, citing news dispatch.

86. *WCSL*, 97:3, Sept. 29, 1894, a directive by the Empress Dowager.

87. Tyler, pp. 60–61. Ch'ih Chung-yu, pp. 339–340, wrote that many foreigners held McClure's appointment to be unwise.

88. The new board was under Prince Kung, assisted by I-k'uang, Jung-lu, and Ch'ang-lin (all Manchus); *WCSL*, 99:8, Nov. 2, 1894. Wen T'ing-shih said that Prince Kung was old and out of touch, with only a few supporters (*CJ*, V, 498).

89. *WCSL*, 97:4, Oct. 2, 1894; and *WCSL*, 99:17, Nov. 8, 1894.

90. Ch'ih Chung-yu, p. 342, indicates that the *K'ai Chi*, *Ching Ch'ing*, *Huan T'ai*, *Nan Ch'en*, and *Fu Ching* were ordered to come north in 1895.

91. Li reports on Japanese movements in *WCSL*, 97:12b, 15, October 1894. See "Vladimir," pp. 205–207, for Japanese plans and unhampered execution of them. The taking of Talienwan is covered in *ibid*., pp. 213–217.

92. See Chang Chih-tung reports, *WCSL*, 98:13, Oct. 25; also *WCSL*, 95:4–6b; 98:1, 7b–10.

93. For orders and correspondence relative to Ting, see *WCSL*, 99:9, 10b–11, 13b–14, 16a–b, 18, 20a–b; 100:2b — all between Nov. 3 and 10, 1894.

94. Yao Hsi-kuang says Ting tried to persuade Li to fight a decisive battle at Port Arthur, but was reprimanded by Li. As for troubles with local authorities, see Ch'ih Chung-yu, pp. 381–382.

95. Ballard, Chap. 6, pronounces this as Japan's only basic mistake. Falk, p. 161, remarks that neither side was a master of strategy; even Western navies had only rudimentary strategic ideas, and were inclined to dismiss war colleges as "effeminate."

96. Ch'ih Chung-yu, p. 340.

97. Tyler, pp. 68–69; Ch'ih Chung-yu, p. 382.

98. There is some question — as usual — as to how many ships were in the Weihaiwei harbor. Ballard, Chap. 6, gives thirty-six; Yao Hsi-kuang, pp. 203–204, gives fourteen; "Vladimir," p. 276, gives twenty-six. Some of the discrepancy may be a matter of including merchant ships. The names given here figure in the action accounts.

99. Tyler, pp. 68–69. He had not been consulted.

100. Yao Hsi-kuang, p. 203. Li was ordered to send his ships to Taku for inspection, but evidently he did not send them so far. Hsü Chien-yen, taotai at Taku, and son of Tseng Kuo-fan's steamer-builder Hsü Shou, was to have done the inspecting; *WCSL*, 100:7, Nov. 16, 1894.

101. See *CJ*, III, 261–262, 263–264; and *WCSL*, 102:16a–b, 18b–19, the last date being Dec. 24, 1894.

102. Tai Tsung-ch'ien was Ting's principal opponent, but it was reported by Chou Fu that Tai was really gloomy about the Weihaiwei situation; *CJ*, V, 212. Once Ting tried to have some of the forts blown up, but traitors blocked the attempt, so that the powder had to be touched off by the flash of a pistol — risky, to say the least. On the other hand, Ting had trouble getting fort commanders to stay in their forts until he ordered them out — apparently only Sah Ping-chen would stay. See Ch'ih Chung-yu, pp. 340–341, 382–384; Tyler, pp. 67, 71; Laird-Clowes, p. 122; Inouye, Sec. 2, "The Fall of Wei-hai-wei." Appendices 26, 27; "Vladimir," pp. 278–285; for many details, see Cunningham. For a report to Peking by Li on the loss of the Lung-miao-tsui fort, where much cowardice was shown, see *WCSL*, 104:11b–13, Jan. 31, 1895.

103. The ship was holed on the waterline by a nine-inch shell; Ch'ih Chung-yu, p. 384; Tyler, p. 85. On the absence of Captain Yeh Tsu-kuei, see Yao Hsi-kuang, p. 200.

104. On Ito's letter, see Ch'ih Chung-yu, p. 340.

105. On request for amnesty, see *WCSL*, 103: 18b–19, Jan. 22, 1895. Liu Ch'ao-pei, implicated in the Lung-miao-tsui fort's fall (see n. 102, above), was punished, and one of the men who aided Ting in trying to blow up the forts was elevated to a magistracy. Ting was placed in command of all land and sea forces in the Weihaiwei area, in an apparent move of desperation (*WCSL*, 104: 11b–13, 13a–b, Jan. 31, 1895).

NOTES TO CHAPTER IX

106. Ballard, Chap. 6, makes much of Ting's lost chance. See also "Vladimir," pp. 282–285.

107. Tyler persuaded Ting to abandon the *Ting Yüan* before she settled; see Tyler, pp. 73–74; also "Vladimir," pp. 288–291, and Inouye, Sec. 2, pp. 14–15. The Japanese lost two torpedo boats on this raid.

108. Inouye, Sec. 2, p. 14; Ch'ih Chung-yu, p. 341; "Vladimir," p. 293. For Li's report to the Chün-wu ch'u, see *WCSL*, 105:22b, Feb. 9, 1895. Traitorous signals were suggested in "Capture of Weihaiwei," *USNIP*, 21.1:209–211 (1895). Yao Hsi-kuang, p. 200, makes the charge against the two captains.

109. Li Ping-heng, governor of Shantung, wired to Peking for help on Feb. 3 and 5, 1895 (*WCSL*, 104:16b). Unfortunately, his appeals arrived during the New Year holiday, and it was a week before a reply came — by which time, Weihaiwei had fallen; Ch'ih Chung-yu, p. 384. The governor soon fled to Lai-chou; Yao Hsi-kuang, pp. 200–201. For other details of Ting's attempts to get aid (including having messages swum ashore), see Ch'ih Chung-yu, p. 384. Tyler, pp. 68–78, talks of the crumbling of morale at Weihaiwei.

110. Yao Hsi-kuang, p. 202; Inouye, Sec. 2, p. 18; Cunningham, p. 41; "Vladimir," p. 295. The three remaining Chinese ships fired heavily at the Japanese outside, and damaged the *Fuso*. On the order to avoid capture, see *WCSL*, 104:14a–b; for execution order, *WCSL*, 105:29b–30, Feb. 11, 1895. Apparently the New Year holiday was over (see n. 109, above).

111. My account of the surrender has been much compressed from those of Tyler, pp. 79–85; Yao Hsi-kuang, pp. 204–205; Ch'ih Chung-yu, pp. 341–342. Their accounts do not agree in every detail.

112. The Japanese flag was hoisted on the grounded *Chen Yüan*, which was later repaired for Japan at Port Arthur. The Japanese lost no ships, and only 27 killed and 38 wounded during the entire Weihaiwei action, according to Inouye, Sec. 2, p. 26.

113. For Li's report on these suicides, see *WCSL*, 106: 3b–4, Feb. 14, 1895. For other accounts, see Lin Shu item in *CJ*, VI, 328–330; and Chou Fu in *CJ*, V, 208–209. Tyler (pp. 80–81) said Liu Pu-ch'an took opium several times, each time regretting it and calling a doctor; finally Tyler persuaded this hard-working foreign doctor (amputating in the Liu-kung-tao hospital) to let Liu die.

114. "Vladimir," p. 300. Yuan Tao-feng, "Li Hung-chang and the Sino-Japanese War," *T'ien-hsia Monthly*, 3.1:9–17 (Aug. 1936), also cites this request, as evidence of internal division in China.

115. *WCSL*, 95:16b–17, Sept. 19, 1894; also Ch'ih Chung-yu, pp. 380–381. Pao Tsen-peng, p. 308, says the *Ching Yüan* and *Lai Yüan* both fled — the latter late in the battle — which may throw some light on the omissions. Li could not satisfy Von Hanneken in the matter of a reward, which may have had something to do with the latter's quitting the Peiyang fleet; Ch'ih Chung-yu, pp. 339–340.

116. *WCSL*, 95:16b–17, Sept. 19, 1894. As for the captain of the *Kwang I*, see report of the censor in n. 36, above.

117. Tyler, p. 66.

118. *CTLT*, 342:11.

119. *WCSL*, 99:15a–b, Nov. 7, 1894.

120. Item by Wen T'ing-shih, in *CJ*, V, 496.

121. See Chang Yin-lin, *passim*. On the insubordination incident, Li Hung-chang reported that Ting was wounded by a Japanese shot, and that Liu replaced him temporarily; *WCSL*, 95:21b, Sept. 20, 1894. Yao Hsi-kuang, p. 202, supports the idea that Ting was wounded by a bullet, not, thus, by the early salvo of Liu Pu-ch'an.

122. Hoffman, engineer on Fang's ship, and Lin Kuo-hsiang, captain of the *Kwang I*, said the engagement was not expected; see Chang Yin-lin, p. 64. "Vladimir," p. 95, says the opposite. H. W. Wilson, *Ironclads*, II, 68, says the Chinese ships were not stripped for action. On the matter of when the fight began, Chang

CONCLUSIONS

Yin-lin accepted the testimony of the chief engineer of the *Kowhsing*, who placed it at 6:30 a.m. "Vladimir," p. 95, says China fired first (he was strongly pro-Japanese); Chang Yin-lin, pp. 63, 69, says the opposite; Laird-Clowes, p. 97, agrees with Chang; Li Hung-chang claimed that Japan fired first, *WCSL*, 93:14b–15, July 27, 1894. Chang Yin-lin (pp. 65–66) says Lin Kuo-hsiang lied about his active part in the encounter; Falk, says the *Kwang I* tried to ram Tsuboi's flagship; H. W. Wilson, *Ironclads*, II, 71, says the *Kwang I* lost thirty-seven men before running out of ammunition and being forced to withdraw. Perhaps it is not surprising that the court wondered whether Lin Kuo-hsiang had been slighted in Li's recommendations for reward; see nn. 36 and 116, above.

123. Chang Yin-lin, p. 67, surveying what he calls "traditional accounts," which allow for the discharge (a miss) of one torpedo. "Vladimir," pp. 349–369, discusses the flag question; Templin, the *Kowhsing's* first officer, spoke of the flags, but Von Hannecken, who was also present on the *Kowhsing*, saw no such flags, or didn't feel it important enough to mention.

124. Inouye, Sec. 1, pp. 15–16, citing news report; Yao, "Military," p. 202, agrees. See also n. 67, above.

125. Tyler, p. 57; Inouye, Sec. 1, pp. 15–16.

126. Chang Yin-lin, pp. 65–67.

127. *Ibid.*, pp. 68–69. "Vladimir," p. 97, tends to be sympathetic to Fang; Laird-Clowes, p. 98, supports the idea that Fang's ship shot well; H. W. Wilson, *Ironclads*, II, 70, 95–96, notes heavy damage to the *Chi Yüan*; Falk, p. 163, offers general support; Ch'ih Chung-yu, p. 380, is generally favorable to Fang, giving details of Chinese personnel killed; Yao Hsi-kuang, pp. 199–200, takes a middle position, saying Fang fired four shells *after* putting up the white flag, and managed to put the *Yoshino* down by the head; he also said that Fang "boasted" of having killed a high Japanese officer. Pao relies heavily on Ch'ih, but adds that Fang incorrectly reported killing the Japanese admiral; Pao Tsen-peng, pp. 293–296.

128. Inouye, Sec. 1, p. 16, citing the Shanghai *China Gazette*, no date given. Also cited in H. W. Wilson, *Ironclads*, II, 99–101. Wilson also cites McGiffen as saying that Fang's guns, save for the stern-chaser, were all in good condition after the Yalu fight.

129. Chang Yin-lin, pp. 67–68; "Vladimir," p. 97. It would not appear from Togo's journal that Togo himself was much impressed with Fang in the Feng-tao fight. He mentions the white and Japanese flags, and his chasing of the *Chi Yüan*. He does not say that Fang gave no fight, but does report that he quit the chase because he got an order to that effect from his own flagship; evidently the sinking of the *Kowhsing* was held to be more important. Item by Togo in *CJ*, V, 32–33.

130. *WCSL*, 96:13a–b, Sept. 23, 1894.

131. For Yeh, see Appendix D, "List of Chinese Names."

132. See LaFargue, pp. 78–82, on Tsai.

133. Letters of Chang P'ei-lun, in *CJ*, V, 224–227; see also entry for Chang in Hummel.

134. On the inquiry, see *WCSL*, 100:9a–b, Nov. 20, 1894. Ch'ih Chung-yu, pp. 339–340, says the ship hit a rock, but that Ting said it was a torpedo. Yao Hsi-kuang, p. 203, says she ran ashore on Nov. 22 and was damaged from engineroom to stern, with a hole thirty by five (Chinese) feet, and that it took six foreign technicians from the Kiangnan arsenal eight days to repair her.

X. CONCLUSIONS

1. For Chang's interest in Lang, see *WCSL*, 106:13–13b, Feb. 16, 1895; 116:39, Aug. 18, 1895. Stanley Wright, p. 482, deals with the Tsungli Yamen's invitation to Lang, in February 1896.

2. Tyler, p. 104.

3. On Von Hannecken, see *WCSL*, 100:7, Nov. 16, 1894; for further discussion

NOTES TO CHAPTER X

on buying ships, possibly from Brazil and Chile, see *WCSL*, 104:19b; 105:27b–29; 106:2b, Feb. 3, 11, and 12, 1895.

4. Beresford, Chap. 21, deals with his postwar naval observations. The fleets were undermanned (although the crews seemed to be well trained). Beresford recommended that the entire fleet be put to police uses, and undelivered ships sold (thus, two 4800-ton Armstrong cruisers, built and paid for but undelivered because of a shortage of men and facilities in China). The Foochow dockyard he dismissed as very wasteful; the drydock for 3000-ton ships was unsafe. He saw "hundreds" of useless war junks.

5. Boulger, p. 452.

6. Item from *United Service Gazette* (Great Britain), cited in "Professional Notes," *USNIP*, 40.4:1128 (July-August 1914).

7. *CSK:PC*, 7:7–8b.

8. Fairbank, Eckstein, and Yang, p. 24. The statement on which my comment is based reads: "In our present state of knowledge, we cannot determine whether the Chinese economy as a whole was expanding or contracting during this period."

9. Young to Frelinghuysen, Jan. 31, 1884, cited in Clyde, pp. 177–180.

10. *IMC: Returns of Trade and Trade Reports*, Statistical Series 3 and 4, 1895, Part II, *Tientsin*, p. 1.

11. In answer to a question put by J. Ross Browne, when that American diplomat first arrived; cited in Clyde, pp. 97–98.

APPENDIX A

TABLE OF ORGANIZATION

The basic command units, in descending order, for both land and sea forces, Green Banner:

piao	標	brigade
hsieh	協	regiment
ying	營	battalion
shao	哨	encampment, outpost
hsün	汛	post

The "direct commands," which were designated kuan-hsia:

t'i-piao	提標	under the general or admiral
tu-piao	督標	under the governor-general
fu-piao	撫標	under the governor

In the water-force, officers and units were linked thus:

t'i-piao	提標	the direct command of the admiral
chen-piao	鎮標	under a senior post-captain
hsieh-piao	協標	under a junior post-captain
ying	營	under officers from commander down through junior lieutenant
hsün	汛	under officers up to sub-lieutenant

Sources: Morse, <u>Trade and Administration</u>, pp. 63-64; Brunnert and Hagelstrom, p. 337; Wade, pp. 364-365; <u>CSK:PC</u>, 6:2a-b.

APPENDIX B

TABLE OF OFFICER RANKS

Rank	Land Equivalent	Naval Equivalent	Official Grade
T'i-tu 提督	General-in-chief	Admiral-in-chief	1b Same
Tsung-ping 總兵	Brigade-general	Sr. post-capt.	2a Admiral-of-divisions
Fu-chiang 副將	Colonel	Jr. post-capt.	2b Commodore
Ts'an-chiang 參將	Lt. colonel	Commander	3a Captain
Yu-chi 游擊	Major	Lt. commanding	3b Same
Tu-sze 都司	First captain	Sr. lieutenant	4a Commander
Shou-pei 守備	Second captain	Jr. lieutenant	5a Naval lt.
Ch'ien-tsung 千總	Lieutenant	Sub-lieutenant	6a Lieutenant
Pa-tsung 把總	Sergeant	Warrant?* Ensign?*	7a Ensign
Wai-wei ch'ien-tsung 外委千總	Second sgt.	Chief petty officer*	8a Sergeant
Wai-wei pa-tsung 外委把總	Corporal	Petty officer*	9b Lance sergeant

Sources: For land equivalents, see Mayers, pp. 65-66. Mayers states that army and navy ranks were the same in the Green Banner forces. On pp. 150-151 he gives Chinese renderings of

European naval ranks, from which I have derived the Naval Equivalent column, in part. His appendix is dated 1897 and starts with commander-in-chief, admiral, vice-admiral, rear-admiral, and commodore, to which he assigns Chinese ranks that do not appear in the traditional accounts. All of these additions fall between t'i-tu and tsung-ping, at which level he starts to use familiar Chinese ranks. His list also leaves out the last three naval ranks, so I have made the naval equivalents here, and have asterisked my own suggestions. This list of ranks has been used throughout this present book.

The last column, giving official grade and another set of naval equivalents, comes from Wade, p. 364, but since this list seems to mix land and naval ranks it is offered only for comparison.

APPENDIX C

LIST OF SHIPS, 1860-1895

Data for this appendix have been assembled from numerous sources, including CCTY; CSK; WCSL; Ch'ih Chung-yu; "Vladimir"; Inouye; Wilson, Ironclads. Listed alphabetically are Chinese ships, bought or built (for chronological lists, bought or built, without specifications, see Pao Tsen-peng, pp. 191 and 199). Not all of the ships listed here are mentioned in the text. I have tried to list all ship names encountered, even when the reference has been unclear, except that for the most part I have included only names identifiable in Chinese characters. A supplement to this appendix lists separately Japanese ships in the Yalu naval battle of September 1894.

Ships that were purchased are marked with an asterisk. Following the ship's name, in parentheses, is date of construction or order, place of origin, and squadron or fleet of registry. Next comes the class of the vessel, material of construction, and a note on armor; displacement, length, and speed; and armament. Miscellaneous remarks, if any, follow. Data not available are indicated by "n. a."

Many of the data must be approximations, for the sources do not always supply specifications, nor do they agree in detail. Classifications are not always clear: for instance, the Chinese terms ping-ch'uan 兵船 and p'ao-ch'uan 炮船 both mean "gun boat, " and in itself "gun boat" is not a clear designation. Chinese sources usually say little about guns, which forces reliance on late Western sources. Data must often be questioned. For example, Jui-lin purchased six gunboats in 1867, but from various sources we can find the names of ten boats linked to this purchase. In some cases contradictory data must be introduced.

Abbreviations Used

Armst, Armstrong gun(s)
bl, breech-loading guns
cm, centimeter
Chft, Chinese foot (feet)
Foo, Foochow dockyard
Fr, France
ft, foot (feet)
Fuk, Fukien squadron
GB, Great Britain
gb, gun boat
Ger, Germany
Hotch, Hotchkiss guns
hp, horsepower
in, inch(es)

kgt, kilogram tons
Kr, Krupp guns
Kwang, Kwangtung fleet
lb, pound(s)
mg, machine gun
ml, muzzle-loading guns
Nan, Nanyang fleet
Pei, Peiyang fleet
qf, quick-firing guns
Shai, the Kiangnan arsenal
tb, torpedo boat
torp, torpedo
US, United States

*AN LAN 安瀾 (1867?, GB, Kwang). One of 6 purchased by Jui-lin, governor-general of Kwangtung. Pao Tsen-peng, p. 199, calls this the AN NAN, and Fox, p. 183, calls it the AULAN.

AN LAN 安瀾 (1872, Foo, Fuk?); gb, wood, n.a.; 1000 kgt, 200 Chft, n.a.; 5 guns. Chen, Tso, pp. 36-37, calls this a transport, with a 400-ton freight capacity. Cost 165,000 taels. Sank in a storm off Taiwan in 1874.

*CH'ANG SHENG 長勝 (1865, GB, Fuk?). Purchased by Tso Tsung-t'ang to stop running of food to Taiping rebels; also used to ship rice to Formosa.

CH'AO WU 超武 (1878, Foo?, Nan or Fuk); gb, wood, n.a.; 1250 tons, 217 Chft, 11.5 knots; one 19-cm and four 40-lb guns. Iron-framed, 750-hp new horizontal model engine, 180-man crew. Cost 200,000 taels. Used in 1880 by Yeh Fu in attack on Chekiang pirate Huang Chin-man. Ch'ih Chung-yu does not mention where it was built, but

(p. 330) places it in the Nanyang squadron; "Vladimir" places it in the Fukien squadron.

*CH'AO YUNG 超勇 (1880-1881, GB, Pei); Armstrong ram cruiser, steel, unarmored; 1350 tons, 210 ft, 15-16 knots; two 10-in Armst, four 12-cm qf, two 1-in guns, 7 mg, 3 fixed torp tubes. Twin-screw, 2677 hp, 130-man crew.

*CHEN AN (1877?, GB?, Pei); gb, steel, n.a.; 440 tons, n.a., 10 knots; one 22-ton Armst, two 12-lb guns. "Vladimir," p. 77, mentions this vessel without giving Chinese characters. Possibly one of the Armstrong gunboats bought by Li Hung-chang.

*CHEN CHUNG 鎮中 (1879, GB, Pei); gb, steel, n.a.; 440 tons, n.a., 10 knots; one 25-ton Armst, two 22-lb guns. Ordered by Li Hung-chang for Shantung; arrived 1881. Crew of 119; cost 150,000 taels. Surrendered at Weihaiwei, February 1895.

*CHEN HAI (1877?, GB?, Pei); gb, steel?, n.a.; 440 tons, n.a., 10 knots; two 16-cm and four 12-cm guns. Mentioned in "Vladimir," p. 77, without Chinese characters. Same as next?

CHEN HAI 鎮海 (1871, Foo, Pei); "GB. despatch vessel," wood, unarmored; 572.5 tons, 166 Chft, n.a.; 6 guns. Crew of 70; 80-hp engine. Cost 109,000 taels.

*CHEN HAI 鎮海 (1867, GB, Kwang). One of the 6 gunboats purchased by Jui-lin.

*CHEN HSI 鎮西 (1875, GB, Pei); gb, steel, unarmored; 440 tons, 127 ft, 10 knots; one 35-ton Armst, two 22-lb guns. One of the double-ended, twin-screw (like a ferry-boat, to go either way) "epsilon" Armstrong gunboats ordered by the southern commissioner for 150,000 taels. On arrival in 1879, taken into Peiyang squadron. Observed patrolling Gulf of Chihli in 1880. Surrendered at Weihaiwei, February 1895.

*CHEN NAN 鎮南, see CHEN HSI for specifications.

*CHEN PEI 鎮北, see CHEN HSI for specifications.

*CHEN PIEN 鎮邊, see CHEN CHUNG for specifications.

*CHEN T'AO 鎮濤 (1867, GB, Kwang). One of the 6 gunboats purchased by Jui-lin.

*CHEN TUNG 鎮東, see CHEN HSI for specifications. Used by Li Hung-chang as a trainer in 1880.

CHEN WEI 振威 (1872, Foo, Fuk); gb, wood, unarmored; 572.5 tons, n.a., 10 knots; 6 guns. Cost 110,000 taels; 70-man crew. Paddles smashed at Foochow dockyard battle, August 1884. Same class as CHEN HAI.

*CHEN WU 鎮吳. One of the Lay-Osborn flotilla ships.

*CHEN YÜAN 鎮遠 (1880-1885, Ger, Pei); battleship, steel, 14-in armor belt; 7430 tons, 308 ft, 14.5 knots; four 12-in and two 6-in Kr, two Fish torp launching carriages, 8 mg. This Stettin-type, twin-screw, 6200 hp vessel drew 20 ft of water. With her armor she probably did no more than 10 knots. Cost 6.2 million marks. Probably launched in 1882, but not delivered until Sino-French hostilities ceased in 1885. In 1886 went to Korea; in 1891 partook in joint north-south maneuvers and went on a "courtesy call" to Japan. Played central role in Yalu battle, September 1894. Hit an obstruction entering Weihaiwei at the end of 1894. Surrendered to the Japanese in February 1895.

CH'EN HANG 琛航 (1874, Foo, Fuk); gb-transport, wood, unarmored; 1391 tons, n.a., n.a.; 2-3 guns. One of the Foochow dockyard ships made as a commercial vessel. During the battle at the Foochow dockyard in August 1884 she was damaged on the ways, evidently during conversion to a warship. "Vladimir," p. 77, speaks of a CHEN-HONG in the Kwangtung squadron at the time of the war with Japan, which was possibly this ship, repaired.

*CH'ENG CH'ING 澄清 (1867, Ger, Nan); probably gb, n.a., n.a.; 1209 tons, n.a., 12 knots; 5 guns. One of the 6 ships bought by Jui-lin? "Vladimir," p. 77, gives above specifications and calls the ship a Nanyang ship in his Sino-Japanese war listing. If the identification (without characters) is correct, it shows how old some of the Chinese ships were.

*CH'ENG PO 澄波. One of the 6 ships bought by Jui-lin?

CHI AN 濟安 (1873, Foo, Fuk); transport, wood, unarmored; 1258 tons, n.a., about 12 knots; 5 guns. Cost 163,000 taels. Described by Chang Shu-sheng (WCSL, 45:28) as a Kwangtung ship sunk in the Foochow dockyard battle in August 1884. "Vladimir," p. 76, lists a TSI-AN, a 1258-ton, 600 hp, 10-knot vessel, with one 16-cm and four 12-cm guns, which he says was added to the Peiyang fleet before the Sino-Japanese war, "from other squadrons."

*CHI YÜAN 濟遠 (1880-1885, Ger, Pei); cruiser, steel, unarmored; 2355 tons, 236 ft, 15 knots; three 8-in and two 6-in guns, four Fish torp, 9 mg. Launched probably in 1883, this twin-screw, 2800-hp ship was sent to China in 1885. Sent to Korea in 1886;

on joint north-south maneuvers in 1891; in Feng-tao naval fight in July 1894. Called "modern light cruiser." Surrendered to Japanese at Weihaiwei February 1895.

*CHIEN SHENG 建勝 (1874, US, Fuk). One of 2 ships ordered by Shen Pao-chen, via Fukien Reconstruction Bureau, during Sino-Japanese trouble of 1874; arrived 1876; sunk at Foochow dockyard battle, August 1884. Cost of this and FU SHENG, 240,000 taels.

*CHIEN WEI 建威 (1869, Ger, Foo). A "Prussian sailing ship" purchased by the Foochow dockyard as a trainer; some report she was bought from France.

*CHIH YÜAN 致遠 (1887, GB, Pei); cruiser, steel, unarmored; 2300 tons, 250 ft, 18 knots; three 8 1/4 unarmored in and two 6-in guns, seventeen qf, four torp tubes. This twin-screw, 7500-hp, 845,000-tael ship, with a 202-man crew, was delivered in 1887 by Capt. William Lang; in 1888 sent with CHING YUAN to put down Taiwan revolt; in 1891 part of naval escort for Russian heir-apparent, went on "courtesy call" to Japan, and in joint north-south maneuvers. Li reported her rated 18 knots had declined to about 15 in the Yalu battle of September 1894, in which she was sunk.

CHIN OU 金甌 (1876, Shai, Nan). Armored gb, 105 ft.

*CHIN T'AI 金臺. One of the Lay-Osborn flotilla ships.

CHING CH'ING 靖清 (1884, Foo, Nan); "fast" gb, composite, n.a. On 1891 diplomatic mission (see also CHIH YUAN) and joint north-south maneuvers. Ordered north to aid Peiyang fleet in 1895; returned in spring of 1896, evidently without having helped. 1100 tons; cost 366,000 taels.

*CHING HAI 靖海. Smuggler's ship captured by Tso Tsung-t'ang in 1865. With foreign captain and Chinese officers, was used for patrol. Later transferred to Canton customs office.

CHING WEI 靖威. Probably the same as WEI CHING.

CHING YÜAN 靖遠 (1872, Foo, Nan); gb, wood, unarmored; 572.5 tons, n.a., 8 knots; two 16-cm Vavasseur and two 40-lb guns. Cost 110,000 taels. "Vladimir," p. 77, gives the ship 480 hp and lists it in the Fukien squadron in the Sino-Japanese war period.

*CHING YÜAN 經遠 (1886, Ger, Pei); cruiser, steel?, unarmored; 2300 tons, 250 ft, 18 knots; two 8-in and two 6-in guns, 17 qf, 6 mg, 1 fixed Fish torp tube, 1 launching carriage. This 7500-hp, 202-man, twin-screw ship, costing about 365,000 taels, was sunk in the Yalu naval battle with Japan, September 1894.

*CHING YÜAN 靖遠 (1887, GB, Pei); cruiser, steel, armored with 9.5-in belt; 2850 tons, 270 ft, 16.5 knots; two 8-in and two 6-in guns, 17 qf, 9 mg, 1 fixed submerged Fish torp tube, 2 launching carriages. Cost 845,000 taels. Delivered by Captain Lang in 1887. In 1888 sent to Taiwan to quell revolt; in 1891 went on a "courtesy call" to Japan and then to Shanghai, during Ko Lao Hui uprising. Survived Yalu battle with Japan in September 1894, but was sunk in Weihaiwei harbor, February 1895.

CHUN HO 鈞和. Commercial vessel converted to military use by Kiangnan arsenal in 1882.

*FEI LUNG 飛龍 (1867, GB, Kwang?). One of 6 gunboats purchased by Jui-lin.

*FEI T'ING 飛霆 (1875, GB, Nan); gb, iron, n.a.; 400 tons, n.a., 9 knots; one 38-ton Armst, two 12-lb guns, 2 mg. One of the Armstrong gunboats purchased by Li Hung-chang in 1875; delivered in 1877 and picked up crew at Foochow dockyard. Transferred to Nanyang fleet in 1880.

*FEI T'ING 飛霆 (1894, GB?, Pei?). Purchased during the Sino-Japanese War; arrived in 1895. Hsien Yu-ch'ing, p. 33, calls it a German ship; CSK:PC, 7:15, calls it an Armstrong ship.

*FEI YING 飛鷹 (1895, Ger, n.a.). Purchased during the Sino-Japanese War; 850 tons.

FEI YÜN 飛雲 (1872, Foo, Fuk?); gb, wood, unarmored; 1258 tons, 200 Chft, about 13 knots; 5 Prussian bl. Cost 163,000 taels. Chen, Tso, pp. 36-37, calls it a transport, suggesting lack of clear differentiation between fighting and cargo types. Chang Shu-sheng (WCSL, 45:28) lists it as a Kwangtung ship destroyed in the Foochow dockyard battle, August 1884.

*FU AN 福安 (1894, GB, Foo). Armstrong gunboat.

FU CHING 福靖 (1893, Foo, Fuk); tb?, steel, armored?; 2200 tons, 233 Chft, 17 knots; two 8-in Armst, eight 4.7-in qf, 4 mg. Sent to Peiyang fleet to aid it in war with Japan, 1895; returned 1896, evidently without having helped. Sunk in storm near Port Arthur 1898.

FU HSING 福星 (1869, Foo, Fuk); gb?, wood, unarmored; 515 tons, n.a., n.a.; 3 guns. Cost 106,000 taels; 80-hp engine and crew of 70. Destroyed in the Foochow dockyard battle, August 1884.

*FU LUNG 福龍 (1886, Ger, Pei); tb, steel, n.a.; 144 tons, n.a.,
22.5 knots. Steamed to China. Originally commissioned at
Foochow, then sent north as training ship. In the Yalu battle,
September 1894.

FU PO 伏波 (1870, Foo, Fuk); gb, wood, unarmored; 1258 tons,
218 Chft, n.a.; 5 guns. Cost 161,000 taels; 560-ton freight
capacity; 150-hp engine. Used as a trainer, under a foreign
captain. Fled from the Foochow dockyard battle, August 1884;
Ch'ih Chung-yu, p. 332, says she was scuttled to block the exit.
"Vladimir," p. 77, listing ships of the 1890's includes this, and
gives her one 16-cm Vavasseur, one 9-ton, four 40-lb, and six
46-lb guns.

*FU SHENG 福勝 (1874, US, Fuk). Gunboat ordered by Shen Pao-chen,
arrived 1876 (see also CHIEN SHENG); sunk in Foochow dockyard
battle, August 1884.

HAI AN 海安 (1871, Shai, Nan); gb, wood?, unarmored; 2800 tons,
300 Chft, 12 knots; two 21-cm, four 15-cm, and two 12-cm Kr
(these guns probably mounted later). Tseng Kuo-fan was very
proud of her, noting her depth of "more than forty feet" (Chen,
Tseng, p. 48). She had an engine of about 1800 hp. In some
accounts called AN HAI (e.g., Hsien Yü-ch'ing, p. 30).

HAI CHING 海鏡 (1873, Foo, Pei); transport, wood, unarmored; 1391
tons, n.a., 9 knots; 3 guns. One of the converted warships taken
over by China Merchants Steam Navigation Co. "Vladimir,"
p. 77, lists her for the 1890's in the Kwangtung squadron (the
romanization is uncertain), citing 1450 tons, 600 hp, one 16-cm
and two 12-cm guns, 9 knots, and a 180-man crew.

*HAI TUNG YÜN 海東雲 (1869, Fr, Min-Che?). Purchased from a
foreign firm in 1869 by Min-Che governor-general. Chang Ch'eng,
one of the Foochow naval academy's first graduates, was made
captain in 1873.

HAI YEN 海晏. Pao Tsen-peng, p. 191, lists it as built at the
Kiangnan arsenal at Shanghai in 1872. Reference to HAI AN, above?

HENG HAI 橫海 (1886, Foo, Nan); gb, composite, unarmored; n.a.,
217 Chft, n.a.; two 15-cm, five 12-cm guns, and guns on bridge.
Cost 200,000-taels. Was held by foreigners to be third-rate.
After a grounding in 1886, was repaired in one month (at double
time). Had a 750-hp horizontal compound engine.

HSIA LEI 下雷 (1888?, Taku dock, Pei). Steel, tb?.

*HU WEI 虎威 (1875, GB, Nan); gb, iron, n.a.; 319 tons, 118 ft, n.a.; one 26.5-ton gun. One of the Armstrong gunboats ordered by Li Hung-chang in 1875, through Hart, for 150,000 taels. Arrived 1876, took on officers from the Foochow dockyard naval academy. Sent to P'eng-hu in 1877; sent north in 1878; commissioned in the southern commissioner's fleet in 1880.

*HUA FU PAO 華福寶. Purchased in Shanghai in 1866 by Fukien province.

HUAN T'AI 寰泰 (1887, Foo, Nan); gb, composite, unarmored; 1477 tons, 260 Chft, 15? knots; two 15-cm and five 12-cm Kr, 4 mg. Double-planked with compound horizontal 2400-hp engine; cost 366,000 taels. Participated in 1891 joint north-south maneuvers; ordered to go to aid of Peiyang fleet in 1895, but returned in 1896, evidently without having seen action. Sunk in collision in 1903.

HUI CHI 惠吉 (1868, Shai, n.a.); gb?, wood?, n.a.; n.a., 185 Chft, n.a. 392-hp; 600-ton cargo capacity. Later appeared on a chart of ships and units receiving ammunition from the Kiangnan arsenal.

I HSIN 藝新 (1876, Foo, Fuk); gb, wood, unarmored; n.a., 188 Chft, n.a. Entirely designed by Chinese students at the Foochow dockyard, the ship had engines below the water line. She was too small for action at the Foochow dockyard battle of August 1884, and fled; perhaps scuttled in an attempt to block the exit from the anchorage.

*I T'UNG 一統. One of the Lay-Osborn ships.

K'AI CHI 開濟 (1883, Foo, Nan); gb, composite, unarmored; 2153 tons, n.a., 15 knots; two 21-cm and six 12-cm Kr, 4 Nordenfeldt guns. 2400-hp; cost 386,000 taels. One of the Nanyang ships on the Taiwan relief expedition of 1884-1885 (Arlington, p. 19, reports that she had only 250 hp). In 1886, in joint training exercises with Peiyang fleet; participated in 1891 joint north-south maneuvers. In 1895 ordered to aid Peiyang fleet but evidently did not, since she was returned in 1896. Blew up in accident at Nanking in 1902 and sank.

K'ANG CHI 康濟 (1879, Foo, Pei); gb, composite, unarmored; 1200 hp, 217 Chft, n.a. 750-hp compound vertical engine; participated in joint north-south maneuvers in 1891.

*K'O FU 可敷 (1861, US, n.a.). One of 2 American ships fitted with arms and hired in 1861 to protect Shanghai. Known as the Confucius.

KUANG CHEN 廣貞 (1886, Canton, Kwang?). A shallow-draft gunboat for local use.

KUANG CHI. Splken of by "Vladimir," p. 76, as being in the last action at Weihaiwei in early 1895. He gives her 1030 tons, 2400 hp, two 12-cm qf guns, 8 mg. No ship by this name was built in China. This is probably the KUANG PING.

KUANG CHIA 廣甲 (1887, Foo, Kwang); gb, composite, unarmored; 1300 tons, 222 Chft, 14? knots; two 15-cm and four 12-cm guns. 160-hp; cost 220,000 taels. Destroyed in the Yalu naval battle, September 1894.

KUANG HENG 廣亨, see KUANG CHEN for specifications.

KUANG I 廣一 (1890, Foo, n.a.). Torpedo boat mentioned by Ch'ih Chung-yu (p. 336).

KUANG I 廣乙 (1890, Foo, Kwang); gb, steel, n.a.; 1000 tons, 235 Chft, 17? knots; three 12-cm qf?. Cost 200,000 taels. Convoyed troops to Korea in mid-1894, and so became involved in the first naval battle with Japan, off Feng-tao, in which she was destroyed. Although "Vladimir," p. 76, gives her only 600 tons, his statement on her armament, used above, is fairly close to the description of her armament in CCTY, 39:16.

KUANG KENG 廣庚 (1889, Foo, Kwang); shallow-draft gb, composite, n.a.; 320 tons, 144 Chft, 12? knots; one 12-cm gun at bow, one 10.5-cm gun at stern, 2 Hotch on sides. Cost 60,000 taels.

KUANG LI 廣利, see KUANG CHEN for specifications.

KUANG PING 廣丙 (1891, Foo, Kwang); torp cruiser, steel, n.a.; 1000 tons, n.a., 15 knots; one 12-cm gun, 8 Hotch. The designation "torpedo cruiser" comes from Brassey's 1894 Annual, although that description gives the ship no torpedo tubes, nor does the description in CCTY, 44:5b. Cost 120,000 taels. Entered the naval action off the Yalu in September 1894, coming on the scene late.

*KUANG WAN 廣萬. A Lay-Osborn ship.

KUANG YUAN 廣元, see KUANG CHEN for specifications.

*LAI YÜAN 來遠 (1887, Ger, Pei); cruiser, steel, armored; 2830 tons, 270 ft, 16.5 knots; two 8.25-in and two 6-in guns, 7 mg, one fixed submerged Fish trop tube, 3 launching carriages. Cost about 865,000 taels. This "modern armored cruiser" or "barbette ship," with twin screws, 3-in deck plates, minutely subdivided hull, cork-packed armor, and 202-man crew, probably did no better than 13 knots in the Yalu battle of September 1894. Participated in the 1891 joint north-south maneuvers, and went to Japan in that year. Li recognized that her 8-in armor, flush with the water-line, was not of the best design. Severely damaged in the Yalu battle and surrendered to the Japanese at Weihaiwei in February 1895.

*LEI CHEN 雷震 (1884, Ger, n.a.). Torpedo boat.

*LEI CHUNG 雷中 (1882, Ger, Kwang?). Torpedo boat.

*LEI HU 雷虎, see LEI CHUNG for details.

*LEI KAN 雷坎, see LEI CHEN for details.

*LEI K'AN 雷乾, see LEI CHEN for details.

*LEI K'UN 雷坤, see LEI CHEN for details.

*LEI LI 雷離, see LEI CHEN for details.

*LEI LIANG 雷良, see LEI CHEN for details.

*LEI LUNG 雷龍, see LEI CHUNG for details.

*LEI SUN 雷巽, see LEI CHEN for details.

*LEI TUI 雷兌, see LEI CHEN for details.

LUNG CH'ING 龍清 (1884, Foo, n.a.). Pao Tsen-peng, p. 193, lists this as a fast gunboat.

*LUNG HSIANG 龍驤 (1876, GB, Nan); gb, iron?, unarmored; 319 tons, 118 ft, n.a.; one 26.5-ton Armst. One of the Armstrong gunboats ordered by Li Hung-chang and in the 1880's registered with the Nanyang fleet. See also HU WEI.

LUNG WEI 龍威 (1889, Foo, n.a.). China's first steel ship. Design altered during construction and name changed to P'ING YUAN, q.v.

MEI YÜN 湄雲 (1869, Foo, Pei); gb, wood, n.a.; 515 tons, n.a., n.a.; 3 guns. 80-hp; 70-man crew; cost 163,000 taels. "Vladimir," p. 76, lists a vessel that could be this one, giving her 400 hp, however, and 7 Vavasseur guns. He adds that the ship was transferred to the Peiyang fleet for the Sino-Japanese War. Ch'ih Chung-yu, p. 342, indicates that she was returned (to which squadron?) after the war.

*MIN CHIEH 敏捷. Sailing ship, 700 tons, purchased in 1888 for trainer. Hsien Yu-ch'ing, p. 31, lists it as a Peiyang ship in 1887. Captured November 21, 1894, apparently in the taking of Port Arthur by Japan.

*NAN CH'EN 南琛 (1883, Ger, Nan); crusier, steel, n.a.; 2200 tons, n.a., 15 knots; two 8-in Armst, eight 12-cm qf. In the 1884-1885 Taiwan relief fleet; in joint drill with Peiyang fleet in 1886, and again in 1891. See also NAN SHUI.

*NAN SHUI 南瑞. Same specifications as NAN CH'EN. One of the southern ships sent north in 1895 and returned in 1896, apparently without having seen action against Japan. Arlington, p. 19, says these two ships were steel corvettes, with six 15-cm Krupp guns, and machine guns. They were rated at 18 knots, but in fact could steam at only 12 or 13.

*PAI YÜEH 百粵. A Lay-Osborn ship.

PAO MIN 保民 (1885, Shai, Nan); gb, steel, n.a.; 1477 tons, 225 Chft, 16 knots; two 200-lb and six 70-lb guns. This 1900-hp ship participated in the 1891 joint north-south maneuvers.

P'AO CH'UAN SHIH HAO 砲船十號. This is not a name, but a reference to "gunboat No. 10" which participated in the Foochow dockyard fight; Ch'ih Chung-yu, p. 365.

P'ING AN 平安. Gunboat No. 8, listed with No. 10, above; both vessels under Chien Ping-nan.

P'ING YÜAN 平遠 (1889, Foo, Pei); cruiser, steel, armored; 2850 tons, 200 ft, 10.5 knots; one 10.2-in and two 6-in Kr, 8 qf?, 1 fixed submerged Fish torp tube, 1 launching carriage. Originally the LUNG WEI, this 524,000-tael ship was shortened in the course of building (ruining her lines) and renamed; a shortage of money lay behind the change. She had an 8-in armor belt, and the heavy Krupp gun was mounted in a 5-in steel barbette forward. Inouye, Sec. 1, p. 3, calls this a 2000-ton, 14-knot ship. Surrendered to Japan at Weihaiwei, February 1895.

P'U CHI 普濟. Mentioned by Li Hung-chang as one of the Peiyang fleet during the Sino-French War, but too small to send on the Taiwan relief expedition (WCSL, 49:2b-4). No other record of this name.

*SAN WEI 三衛. A Lay-Osborn ship.

SHOU LEI 守雷. (1888 or later, Taku yard, Pei?); small steamer, steel, armored, screw-driven.

*SUI CHING 綏靖 (1867, GB, Kwang?). One of the 6 gunboats purchased by Jui-lin.

TA YA 大雅 (1874, Foo, n.a.); gb, wood, unarmored; 1391 tons, n.a., n.a. This 150-hp ship was one of those converted to commercial use. Sank in a storm in 1874.

T'AI AN 泰安 (1877, Foo, Pei); gb, wood, n.a.; 1258 tons, 204 Chft, 10 knots; 10 guns. Cost 162,000 taels.

*TE SHENG 得勝. A Lay-Osborn ship.

*TENG CH'ING 登清 (1867, GB, Kwang?). One of the 6 gunboats purchased by Jui-lin.

TENG CH'ING 登慶 (1880, Foo, Nan); gb, composite, n.a. Cost 200,000 taels. Was sunk or scuttled in Shih-p'u harbor during an action with the French early in 1885.

*TENG P'O 登波 (1868, Fr, n.a.). Pao Tsen-peng, p. 199, gives us the 1868 date; Hsien Yu-ch'ing, p. 30, gives 1869. Neither source gives the purchaser.

TENG YING CHOU 登瀛洲 (1877, Foo, Nan); gb, wood, unarmored; 1258 tons, 204 Chft, 10 knots; one 16-cm and four 12-cm guns. Cost 162,000 taels. Used in the winter of 1882 to help quell troubles in Korea.

TIEN CHI 恬吉 (1868, Shai, n.a.). Boiler and hull of this 185-ft ship were made at the Kiangnan arsenal, and a purchased and repaired engine was used (Chen, Tseng, p. 47).

*TIEN P'O 恬波 (1867?, Fr, Kwang?). One of the 6 gunboats purchased by Jui-lin? CSK:PC, 7:14, gives cost as 40,000 taels.

*T'IEN P'ING 天平. Purchased from Lay? after the disbanding of the Lay-Osborn flotilla, and used for coastal patrol (Ch'ih Chung-yu, p. 324).

*TING T'AO 定濤 (1867?, n.a., Kwang?). One of the 6 gunboats purchased by Jui-lin?

*TING YÜAN 定遠, see CHEN YUAN for specifications and other details. Surrendered (beached) to Japan in Weihaiwei harbor, February 1895.

*TORPEDO CRAFT, I, ERH, SAN SSU 一, 二, 三, 四 (1882, Ger, Pei).

*TORPEDO CRAFT, CH'EN, SU, LIEH, CHANG 辰, 宿, 列, 張 (1895, Ger?, Nan).

TS'AO CHIANG 操江 (1869, Shai, Nan?); gb, wood, unarmored; 640 tons, 180 Chft, 9 knots; four 16-cm Vavasseur guns. Convoyed Kowshing in 1894; captured by the Japanese ships in the Feng-tao battle.

TS'E HAI 測海 (1869, Shai, Nan); gb, wood, unarmored; 600 tons, 175 ft, 12? knots; fifteen 12-cm guns. Engine of 430 hp.

*TS'E TIEN 策電 (1875, GB, Nan); gb, iron, n.a.; 319 tons, 118 ft, n.a.; one 38.5-ton Armst, two 12-lb guns, two mg. One of the 4 Armstrong gunboats ordered by Li Hung-chang and later transferred to the Nanyang fleet.

*TSO ERH 左二 (1887, Ger, Pei). See also YO I.

*TSO I 左一 (1887, GB, Pei); large, fast tb. Cost 80,000 taels, with German equipment. See also TSO ERH.

*T'U CHIH PO 土只坡. One of the American steamers hired in 1861 to protect Shanghai--old convoys, fitted with arms.

T'UNG CHI 通濟 (1894, Foo, n.a.). 1900 tons.

WAN NIEN CH'ING 萬年清 (1869, Foo, Fuk); transport, wood, unarmored; 1450 tons, 238 Chft, about 15 knots with the wind (see CCTY, 6:6-7b, which allows only 12 knots against the wind); 6 guns. This screw-driven ship had a 150-hp engine and a cargo hold, and required a crew of 100 men. Sunk in collision in 1887.

WANG KAO. Launch of 25 ft and perhaps 6 knots, built by Hsü Shou for Tseng Kuo-fan in 1865.

WEI CHING 威靖 (1870, Shai, Nan); gb, wood?, n.a.; 1000 tons, 205 Chft, 12 knots. 600-hp engine.

WEI YÜAN 威遠 (1877, Foo, Pei); gb, iron-framed with wooden skin (composite), unarmored; 1300 tons, 217 Chft, about 16 knots with the wind; 7 guns. The iron frames and 750-hp engine came from France and Britain; her total cost was 195,000 taels. In 1886 she was sent to Korea; in 1891 she participated in joint north-south maneuvers. Sunk at Weihaiwei by Japanese torpedoes, early 1895. China's first iron-framed ship.

*YANG WEI 揚威 (1881, GB, Pei); cruiser, composite, unarmored but ram-equipped; 1350 tons, 210 ft, 15? knots; two 10-in Armst, four 12-cm qf, 3 fixed torp tubes. 2600-hp; twin-screw. Was sent by Li in 1884 to join the Taiwan relief expedition, but was recalled before seeing any action. In 1886, sent to Korea; in 1891, in joint north-south maneuvers. Destroyed in the Yalu battle with Japan, September 1894.

YANG WU 揚武 (1872, Foo, Fuk); gb, wood, unarmored; 1393 tons, 190 Chft, about 15 knots with the wind; 13 m1 guns from GB. 250-hp ship, with engine below the water-line; collapsible stack, and accommodations for a 200-man crew. Cost 254,000 taels. It was noted that costs had increased as compared with those of the FEI YUN (CCTY, 8:4). In 1875, used as trainer to South Seas and Japan. Flagship of the Foochow dockyard fleet; sunk by French in August 1884.

*YO I, ERH, SAN 右一, 二, 三 (1887, Ger, Pei). Torpedo boats.

YU AN 馭安 (1873, Shai, n.a.); gb? of 2800 tons, 300 ft. Not mentioned in most accounts; see listing in KNCTCC, 3:55b.

YÜ HSUN 遇順 (1875, Taku dock, Pei?). Steel tug, screw-driven.

YU YÜAN 馭遠 (1875, Shai, Nan); gb, wood?, unarmored; 2800 tons, 300 Chft, 14 knots; two 21-cm and four 15-cm Kr, twenty 12-cm guns. Arlington, p. 19, notes that the "I-yuan" was the slowest in the fleet; with 200 hp and 22 old m1 guns, she was "hardly fit for fighting pirates, let alone the French." When built she was rated at 1800 hp. Sunk in Shih-p'u harbor by French torpedo boat attack in 1885.

YUAN K'AI 元凱 (1875, Foo, Fuk); gb, wood, unarmored; 1250 tons, n.a., 10 knots; one 16-cm and four 40-lb guns. Cost 162,000 taels.

YUNG PAO 永保 (1873, Foo, Fuk); gb, wood, unarmored; 1391 tons, 218 Chft, n.a.; 3 guns. Ch'ih Chung-yu, p. 367, says the ship was destroyed by the French in the Foochow dockyard battle of August 1884 (the ship was on the ways at the time), but "Vladimir," p. 77, lists a ship with a name like this, of 2500 tons, three 8-in Krupps, 2400 hp engines, etc. Possibly the YUNG PAO was rebuilt, but this seems unlikely, for, even ignoring the tonnage difference (no wider than those appearing in other sets of figures for some ships), the likelihood of an old wooden ship taking such a big engine seems small. Her original engine was rated at 150 hp.

SUPPLEMENT TO APPENDIX C

JAPANESE SHIPS IN THE YALU BATTLE, SEPTEMBER 1894**

AKAGI (1888, Onohama); gb, steel, unarmored; 615 tons, 164 ft, 12 knots; one 24-cm and one 12-cm Kr, 2 mg (Inouye, sec. 1, p. 29; ibid., p. 30, says the ship was built in Britain).

AKITSUSHIMA (1892, Yokusuka); cruiser, steel, unarmored; 3150 tons, 302 ft, 19 knots; one 32-cm gun, twelve 12-cm qf, 6 mg, 4 fixed Fish torp tubes, 1 launching carriage. This 8400-hp, twin-screw ship had a protected deck.

*CHIYODA (1890, GB); cruiser, steel, armored; 2450 tons, 308 ft, 19 knots; ten 12-cm qf, fourteen 47-cm qf, 3 mg, 3 launching carriages for Fish torp. This 5600-hp, twin-screw ship had a 4.5-in armor belt, 84 water-tight compartments, and a double bottom amidships. Her armor was of chrome steel.

*FUSO (1877, GB); corvette, iron, armored; 3718 tons, 220 ft, 13 knots; four 24-cm and two 17-cm Kr, 4 light guns, 5 mg. This 3500-hp, twin-screw ship had a cruising radius of 3500 miles at 10 knots. She was bark-rigged, and obsolete.

HASHIDATE (1891, Yokosuka); coast defense ship, steel?, unarmored; 4277 tons, 295 ft, 17.5 knots; one 32-ton Canet gun, eleven 12-cm qf, six 3-lb guns, 6 mg, 4 fixed Fish torp tubes. This 5400-hp, twin-screw ship was a "sister-ship to cruisers of late design delivered in 1891 from yards at La Seyne, France" (Potter and Fredlund, p. 420). The big gun was in an open-topped steel barbette of 12-in plate; her main deck was an end-to-end 2-in steel turtleback.

*HIYEI (1877, GB); cruiser, composite, armored for one-quarter of length; 2200 tons, 231 ft, 13 knots; three 17-cm and six 15-cm Kr. When built this 2490-hp, single-screw ship had tubes for experimental torpedoes, but she was obsolete in 1894.

*ITSUKUSHIMA (1889, Fr), see HASHIDATE for all specifications.

*MATSUSHIMA (1890, Fr), see HASHIDATE for most specifications. Heavily armed with twelve 4.7-in qf on broadsides, in addition to Canet gun, etc.

**For Chinese names of these ships, see Ch'ih Chung-yu, p. 337.

*NANIWA (1885, GB); cruiser, steel, unarmored; 3650 tons, 300 ft, 18.7 knots; two 26-cm Armst, six 15-cm Kr, 2 qf, 10 mg, 4 fixed Fish torp tubes, 1 launching carriage. Twin-screw; 7325 hp.

SAIKYO. Armed merchant ship, not up to naval capacity of rest of Japanese fleet in the Yalu battle.

*TAKACHIHO, see NANIWA for specifications.

*YOSHINO (1893, GB); cruiser, steel, unarmored; 4150 tons, 350 ft, 23 knots; four 6-in and eight 4.7-in qf, twenty-three 3-lb qf, 5 fixed Fish torp tubes, 1 launching carriage. This 15,000-hp, twin-screw Armstrong cruiser, with 2-in armored deck and "minutely subdivided hull," was originally offered to Li Hung-chang, but he had no funds to buy her. She was held to be the fastest ship in the world when built.

APPENDIX D

CHINESE PERSONAL NAMES

This is a list of all Chinese personal names encountered in the modern naval context covered in this study, whether or not they are mentioned in the text. The annotations are not complete, although in some cases enough data have been found to provide a fair sketch of an officer's career.

Names are romanized according to the Wades-Giles system. In some cases romanizations based on Cantonese pronunciations are introduced (e.g., from Giquel and LaFargue), without Chinese characters. Wherever possible these names have been linked to others given in Wades-Giles style. Often the sources give slightly different versions of a name; these are linked together if possible.

CEM stands for China Educational Mission (1871-1880); "Greenwich" for the Royal Naval College there; "Cherbourg" for the Ecole de Construction Navale; and "Toulon" for the French navy yard there. Some details on overseas curriculum have been taken from Biggerstaff, The Earliest Modern Government Schools in China. An asterisk indicates that the individual was primarily associated with the modern naval or arms effort.

AN WEI-CHÜN 安維峻

*CH'AI CHO-CH'ÜN 柴桌犀 ; Foochow student, made Chien Wei training trip in 1871.

CHAN SHIH-CHIH 詹事志

CHANG CHAO-TUNG 張兆棟

CHANG CH'AO-FA 張朝發

*CHANG CHE-JUNG 張哲瀅 ; assistant chief officer on the Lai Yüan in 1894; fought well.

*CHANG CH'ENG 張成; Kwangtung man; one of the first students to go to the Foochow school, 1867; pronounced by Giquel to be ready for command in 1873 (as Tchang-sheng); 1873, captain of Hai Tung Yün; 1873-1874, of Ching Yüan; 1876, overseas; also captain of Lung Hsing for Li Hung-chang; 1877, captain of Wei Yüan; 1879, of K'ang Chi and Yang Wu, rank of yu-chi. In charge of tactics at Ma-wei battle in August 1884; escaped from sinking ship; beheaded.

*CHANG CH'I-CHIANG 張啟江; apprentice who went to France with Giquel in 1876 and 1878. (Ch'ih Chung-yu, p. 327, gives a Chang Ch'i-cheng ; the name Ch'i-chiang is from CCTY, 15:25.)

CHANG CH'I-KWANG 張其光; a tsung-ping of the water-force, served as officer in Foochow modern ships, 1870.

CHANG CHIH-TUNG 張之洞

*CHANG CHIN-SHENG 張金生; 1873, student in the Foochow construction school, placed in charge of the pattern shop (Giquel gives the name Tchang-king-cheng); in 1878, studying construction in France; specialized in mining and metallurgy.

*CHANG CHIN-SHENG 張金盛; recommended for posthumous honors after the Yalu battle of September 1894. Same as above?

CHANG CHING-HSIU 張敬修; commissioned by the emperor in 1853 to bring Cantonese shipwrights and foreign cannon to Hupeh.

CHANG CH'ING-PIAO 張清標; former Chapu fu-chiang at Foochow dockyard in 1878.

CHANG HSI 張喜

CHANG LIANG-CHI 張亮基

CHANG MENG-YÜAN 張夢元

CHANG P'EI-LUN 張佩綸

*CHANG PIN-YÜAN 張斌元; third engineer on the Lai Yüan in the Yalu battle.

*CHANG PING-FU 張炳福

*CHANG PING-KUEI 張秉圭; Foochow student sent to Britain 1886; studied naval law and English.

CHANG SHIH-HENG 張士珩

CHANG SHU-SHENG 張樹聲

*CHANG SHUN-KAO 張順高; captain of Tsao Chiang in 1872.

CHANG SZU-HSÜN 張斯㧰 ; 1876, with rank of expectant magistrate, sent from the Foochow yard to Peking for interview at Tsungli Yamen, as reward for service at yard, on recommendation of Shen Pao-chen; brother of Chang Szu-kuei.

CHANG SZU-KUEI 張斯桂 ; in 1857, in charge of the first gunboat owned by the Shanghai guild. Well versed in the use of foreign machines; an associate of Li Shan-lan.

CHANG WEN-HSÜAN 張文宣

CHANG YAO 張曜

CHANG YIN-HUAN 張蔭桓

*CHANG YUNG-CH'ING (Chang-yung-tsing); an engineer in the Foochow yard mentioned by Giquel in 1873.

CH'ANG CH'ING 長慶

*CHEN CH'ENG (Tchen-tcheng); recommended as an engine-shop supervisor by Giquel in 1873, to be aided by Leang-ping-nien.

*CH'EN CH'ANG-LING 陳長齡 ; Foochow construction student, sent in 1886 for six-year course at Cherbourg.

*CH'EN CHAO-AO 陳兆翱 ; entered the Foochow construction school in 1867 to study French, physics, etc.; in 1876 sent abroad and studied in Britain, France, and Germany, concentrating on engines; 1878, at Cherbourg; 1880, returned to Foochow to work in engine construction; later in 1880 sent to Germany to observe building of Ting Yüan; in 1881 appointed by Li Ch'ao-t'ang to work on P'eng Yü-lin's order for ten small gunboats; by 1885, head of engine shops at Foochow; shortly thereafter recommended by P'ei Yin-shen.

*CH'EN CHAO-I 陳兆藝 ; in 1882, sent to Britain to study navigation, one of ten; in cooperation with Northern Commissioner.

*CH'EN CHEN-P'EI 陳鎮培 ; one of a group sent to Britain in 1896 by the Tsungli Yamen to observe the building of ships just ordered.

*CH'EN CHI-T'UNG 陳季同 ; Foochow student sent to Britain and France in 1876; in 1878, reportedly studying law in France. Chinese secretary to Giquel.

*CH'EN CHIN-JUNG 陳錦榮 ; made 1871 training trip in the Foochow trainer Chien Wei; third-in-command of the Ching Yüan in Yalu battle 1894; killed.

*CH'EN CHIN-K'UEI 陳金揆; in 1888, went with Liu Kuang-hsiung to Formosa with two ships to quell riots; second-in-command of the Chih Yüan in Yalu battle 1894; drowned; recommended by Li Hung-chang for posthumous honors.

*CH'EN CHING-SHANG (Tchen-king-shang); an engineer at Foochow, mentioned by Giquel in 1873.

*CH'EN CH'UN-HSÜAN 岑春煊; 1904; opened torpedo establishment at Huang-p'u, Kwangtung.

*CH'EN EN-T'AO 陳恩燾; in third group of students sent abroad by the Foochow yard, in cooperation with the Northern Commissioner; a Tientsin naval academy man; served in a British trainer, but also studied drafting in France; also studied hydrography; in 1895, sent to Germany to take delivery of a ship; in 1896, the Tsungli Yamen sent him to Britain and Germany to observe the building of more ordered ships.

*CH'EN HO-CH'ING 陳和慶; mentioned as apprentice in Foochow in 1873 by Giquel (Tchen-heu-king); in 1880, sent by the Northern Commissioner to Germany, and again in 1885, to observe the building of ships for the Peiyang fleet.

*CH'EN HO-T'AN 陳鶴潭; one of a group sent by Foochow in 1886 for study in Europe.

*CH'EN K'O-HUI 陳可會; Foochow apprentice; 1876, sent to France with Giquel, remaining at least two years, studying construction.

*CH'EN KUANG-P'ING 陳廣平; in 1885, sent by Kiangnan arsenal in a student mission to Europe.

CH EN LAN-PIN 陳蘭彬

*CH'EN LIN-CHANG 陳林璋; Foochow construction student who went with Giquel to France in 1876; in 1878, at Cherbourg; in 1913, put in charge of reorganized Foochow construction school.

CH'EN PAO-CH'EN 陳寶琛

*CH'EN PI-KUANG 陳璧光; captain of the Kwang Ping at the Yalu battle, 1894; rank of tu-sze.

*CH'EN PING-KUO (Tchen-ping-kuo); in 1873, recommended by Giquel as an aide in the Foochow dockyard.

*CH'EN PO-CHANG 陳伯璋; member of Foochow dockyard-Peiyang joint student mission to Europe, 1881.

*CH'EN SHAO-FANG 陳紹芳; in 1879, captain of Ch'ang Sheng; recommended by Wu Ts'an-ch'eng to be promoted to ninth civil rank.

*CH'EN SHIH-AN 陳世安

*CH'EN SSU-CHAO 陳思照; gunnery instructor on the Ching Yüan in 1894 Yalu battle; killed.

*CH'EN SUNG-YING (Tchen-song-ying); cited by Giquel in 1873 as an aide in the Foochow building yard.

*CH'EN TS'AI-TUAN 陳才銳; admitted to drafting school at Foochow in 1871; 1879, recommended by Wu Ts'an-ch'eng to be promoted to ninth civil rank; 1881, sent to Germany to learn torpedo-building; returned Foochow 1884; torpedo supervisor at Foochow; 1885, official rank of 9b.

*CH'EN TU-HENG 陳杜衡; sent by Northern Commissioner to Europe in 1886, to Britain; naval gunnery.

*CH'EN YEN-NIEN (PO-HAN) 陳燕年(伯涵); praised by Wu Ts'an-ch'eng as outstanding Foochow student; sent to Europe in 1886 by Northern Commissioner.

*CH'EN YING 陳英; Foochow student, made Yang Wu training cruise in 1875; captain of Fu Hsing in Ma-wei battle, 1884.

*CH'EN YING-CH'I 陳英屺; same as CH'EN YING (both names from Ch'ih Chung-yu, pp. 326 and 366 respectively).

*CH'EN YÜ-SUNG 陳毓淞; Foochow student, took Chien Wei training cruise in 1871; captain of Chien Sheng in 1877.

*CHENG CH'ING-LIEN 鄭清濂; admitted to construction school at Foochow dockyard in 1867; cited (as Tchen-tsing-lien) by Giquel as being in charge of fitting and setting up shops, with aides, in 1873; in 1877, to Britain and Germany to study construction and gun-making; 1878, at Cherbourg; in 1880, sent by Li Hung-chang to observe building of Ting Yüan; in 1880's, started building stone dock at Foochow yard (finished 1896); cited by P'ei Yin-shen after the Sino-French War; as head of ship construction at Foochow, designed Heng Hai, Ching Ch'ing; supervised building of armored hulls; in 1885, cited as holding tu-sze rank, with peacock feather.

CHENG FU-KUANG 鄭復光; colleague of Kung Ch'en-lin; known as a "scientist" and so recommended to officials during the Opium War.

*CHENG JU-CH'ENG 鄭汝成; in 1886, sent by Northern Commissioner to Britain to study naval gunnery; mentioned in ship-building connection, 1907; sent to naval school in Britain in 1911.

*CHENG KUNG-KUEI (TCHENG-KONG-KOUEI); one of two directors of the pattern shop at Foochow, mentioned by Giquel in 1873.

*CHENG P'U-CH'UAN 鄭溥泉; Foochow student, made 1871 training cruise in Chien Wei; captain of Wan Nien Ch'ing in 1877.

*CHENG SHOU-CHEN 鄭守箴; Foochow construction graduate sent in 1886 for six-year course in France in naval mathematics and science.

*CHENG SHOU-CH'IN 鄭守箴; sent by Foochow dockyard to France to study naval construction, 1896.

CHENG TSAO-JU 鄭藻如

*CHENG WEN-YING 鄭文英; 1886, Foochow naval cadet sent to Britain to study ordnance.

*CHENG YÜ 鄭漁; in 1873, captain of Ching Yuan; in 1874, of Chi An; in 1876, of Teng Ying Chou.

CH'ENG JIH-PIAO 成日標; in charge of Tseng Kuo-fan's first shipyard at Hengchow, Hunan, 1853.

CH'ENG MING-PIAO 成名標; in 1860, used by Tseng Kuo-fan to buy foreign guns. Same as CH'ENG JIH-PIAO?

*CH'ENG PI-KUANG 程璧光; 1896, sent by Tsungli Yamen to Britain to oversee orders for cruisers; 1907, in charge of Foochow dockyard; 1909, commander of cruisers; 1910, took two ships to meet American vessels; 1911, to Britain for coronation.

CH'I CHÜN-TSAO 祁寯藻

CH'I-KUNG 祁墳

CH'I-SHAN 琦善

CH'I-YING 耆英

*CHIA NING-HSI 賈凝禧; Foochow student sent in 1886 to Europe; served on British trainer; world cruise; specialized in hydrography.

CHIA PU-WEI 賈步緯; compiled and published a naval almanac calculated for the longitude of Shanghai rather than Peking or Greenwich; also mathematical tables.

*CHIANG CH'AO-YING 蔣超英; Foochow student, training cruise in Chien Wei, 1871; mentioned by Giquel as being ready for command in 1874; overseas in 1877; served on British armored ship; captain of Teng Ch'ing, 1881-1885; was in Shih-p'u disaster in 1885. When made captain in 1881, had rank of expectant shou-pei.

CHIANG CHUNG-YÜAN 江忠源; as acting governor of Hupeh, created river flotilla with Kuo Sung-t'ao in early 1850's.

CHIANG HSI-FAN 蔣錫璠; a chü-jen, mentioned in buying materials for Foochow yard, 1869.

CHIANG I-FENG 蔣益灃

*CHIANG MOU-CHIH 江懋祉; Foochow student, training cruise in Yang Wu, 1875; 1878, trained on British ship; captain of Chien Sheng at Ma-wei battle, 1884.

*CHIEN PING-NAN 翦炳南; in charge of two small boats, Ma-wei battle, 1884.

*CH'IH CHAO-PIN 池兆瑸; third officer of the Chen Yüan in the Yalu battle, 1894; killed; recommended by Li Hung-chang for posthumous honors.

*CH'IH CHEN-CH'ÜAN 池貞銓; 1876, Foochow construction student sent to France with Giquel; in 1878, studying mining, metallurgy; 1880, returned, started iron mine; worked in metallurgical shops at Foochow yard. 1885, rank of shou-pei.

*CHIN JUNG 金榮; captain of the Yu Yüan in 1885 Shih-p'u disaster; traditional water-force background.

*CHIN KIN-KWAI; ex-CEM student, cited as naval officer (Lafargue, p. 176).

CHIN YING-LIN 金應麟

*CH'IU CHIH-FAN 邱志範; Foochow student, 1886 to Britain; gunnery, navigation.

*CH'IU KUO-AN 裘國安; possibly the Kiou-koon-ngan mentioned as apprentice by Giquel in 1873 at Foochow yard; to France in 1876 with Giquel; 1878, reported at molding works at Marseilles; 1885, sent by Northern Commissioner to Germany to observe building of ordered ships.

*CH'IU PAO-JEN 邱寶仁; Foochow student, made training cruise in Chien Wei in 1871; 1876, captain for Li of Hu Wei, although in 1877 Li thought him unqualified for assignment to a larger vessel; in 1887, to Britain, to take delivery of ships, as navigator; captain of Lai Yüan in 1890's, with rank of fu-chiang; ashore when his ship torpedoed in Weihaiwei.

*CHO KUAN-LÜEH 卓關略; Foochow student, navigation school, 1867.

*CHOU FENG-CHEN 周鳳震; captain of Wei Yüan, 1877, having been transferred from Wan Nien Ch'ing, with shou-pei rank; succeeded in Wei Yüan berth after four months by Lü Han.

CHOU FU 周馥

CHOU FU-KAI 周福陵

*CHOU HSIEN-CH'EN 周獻琛; sent by Foochow yard to Europe in 1886; served in British training ship. Studied hydrography.

*CHOU K'AI-HSI 周開錫; t'i-tiao at Foochow dockyard.

*CHOU KUAN-PEN (CHO-KWAN-PUN); mentioned by Giquel as an engineer, in 1873.

*CHOU MOU-CH'I 周懋琦; took students from Foochow, Tientsin, and Kiangnan arsenal to Europe in 1886; made supervisor of students overseas.

CHOU T'AO-FU 周弢甫; asked by Tseng Kuo-fan to inspect first purchased steamer, 1862.

CHOU WEN-HSIANG 周文祥; designated to be one of the Chinese captains for the Lay-Osborn ships.

CHU HSIAO-HSIEN 朱筱仙; in 1862, brought purchased steamer to Anhui for Tseng Kuo-fan.

CHU I-HSIN 朱一新

CHU T'ING-PIAO 祝廷彪

CH'UNG-HOU 崇厚

*FANG PAI-CH'IEN 方伯謙; made Chien Wei training trip in 1871; 1876, to France as navigation student; 1878, studying navigation, translation, at Greenwich; first noted by Li Hung-chang in 1881, and put in command of one of Li's Armstrong gunboats; captain of Chi Yüan in 1894; involved in Feng-tao and Yalu engagements; beheaded after Yalu battle.

FENG CHU-YÜ 馮竹漁; builder of iron-hulled launch at Nanking, 1871.

FENG CHÜN-KUANG 馮焌光

*FENG JUI-CHIN (FUNG-JUI-KIN); cited in 1873 by Giquel as an engineer at Foochow yard.

FENG KUEI-FEN 馮桂芬

FU TE-K'O 傅德柯; in charge of the 100 "swimming braves" at the Ma-wei battle, 1884.

*HAN TIEN-CHIA 韓殿甲

*HO CHAO-KUANG (HO-CHAO-KWANG); mentioned in 1873 by Giquel as engineer at Foochow.

HO CHING 何璟

HO-CH'UN 和春

*HO HSIN-CH'UAN 何心川 ; Foochow student, made 1871 training cruise in Chien Wei; 1877, navigation student, sent to Britain; 1878, studying navigation, translation, etc., at Greenwich; captain of K'ai Chi in 1883; fired by Tso Tsung-t'ang in 1884 for grounding his ship twice.

HO JU-CHANG 何如璋

HO LI-KUEI 何禮貴

*HO P'IN-CHANG 何品璋 ; first officer on Chen Yuan in 1894 Yalu battle; 1907, sent by Northern Commissioner with two ships on cruise in South Seas.

*HO TING-LIANG; ex-CEM student; mentioned by LaFargue as naval officer.

*HSIA HSIAO-T'AO 夏小濤 ; an officer in the Foochow dockyard, to whom Tso Tsung-t'ang wrote in connection with the 1872 Sung Ch'in attack.

*HSIA HSIEN-LUN 夏獻綸 ; a t'i-tiao at the Foochow yard.

HSIANG JUNG 何榮

*HSIEH JUN-TE 謝潤德 ; first officer of Fei Yün, killed at Ma-wei battle, 1884.

*HSIEH PAO-CHANG 謝葆璋 ; 1884 graduate of Tientsin naval academy; in 1894 Yalu battle as gunnery officer on Lai Yüan; 1903, put in charge of Chefoo naval school.

*HSIN CH'ENG-FA 忻成發 ; in 1886, ran Heng Hai ashore in a fog; demoted.

*HSÜ CHAO-CHI 許兆箕 ; praised in 1876 by Wu Ts'an-ch'eng as an "old student" at Foochow yard.

*HSÜ CHEN-P'ENG 許振鵬 ; gunnery officer on Ting Yüan in Yalu battle, 1894; recommended for promotion.

*HSÜ CHI-CH'UAN 許濟川 ; Foochow student; training trip in Yang Wu in 1875.

*HSÜ CHIEN-SHEN 許鈐身 ; in 1877, as expectant taotai of Chihli, placed in charge of gentry staff at Foochow yard by Tsungli Yamen, over objections of Wu Ts'an-ch'eng and Shen Pao-chen; in 1878, training director for Li Hung-chang; sent south to pick up the newly-arrived Armstrong gunboats.

*HSÜ CHIEN-YEN 徐建寅 ; son of Hsü Shou.

HSÜ CHING-CH'ENG 許景澄

*HSÜ CHING-YEN 徐景顏 ; Tientsin academy graduate; killed in Yalu battle, 1894.

*HSÜ CH'UN-CH'UAN 許淳川 ; captain of Fu Hsing in 1879.

HSÜ CHUNG-HU 徐仲虎

*HSÜ HSI-YEN 徐希顏 ; recommended by Li for posthumous honors after Yalu battle. Same as Hsü Ching-yen?

HSÜ HSIANG-KUANG 許祥光

HSÜ KUANG-CHIN 徐廣縉

HSÜ SHOU 徐壽

*HSÜ SHOU-JEN 許壽仁 ; Foochow construction student sent in 1886 to France for six-year course; studied international law.

*HSÜ SHOU-SHAN 許壽山 ; Foochow student, training trip in Chien Wei in 1871; captain of I Hsin, 1877, and of Chen Wei in Ma-wei battle, 1884; killed.

HSÜ T'ING-HSU 徐廷旭

HSÜ WEN-YÜAN 徐文淵 ; expectant secretary, Fukien financial commissioner's office; had studied Western books and experimented with guns; recommended to Shen Pao-chen by Tso Tsung-t'ang.

HSÜEH FU-CH'ENG 薛福成

*HU KUANG-YUNG 胡光墉 ; Foochow yard t'i-tiao, late 1860's.

HU LIN-I 胡林翼

HU YÜ-FEN 胡燏芬

*HUA HENG-FANG 華衡芳 ; one of Tseng Kuo-fan's steamer experimenters at Anking, 1862; to Kiangnan arsenal, 1872.

*HUANG CH'ENG-HSÜN 黃承勛 ; cadet on Chi Yuan in Feng-tao action, 1894; arm shot off.

*HUANG CHIEN-HSÜN 黃建勛 ; Foochow student, training cruise in Chien Wei in 1871; 1878, cadet in British ship, cruising possibly to the United States; in 1881, Li Hung-chang asked to have him in his torpedo establishment; captain of Ch'ao Yung in Yalu battle, 1894; drowned and recommended for posthumous honors. Rank of tu-sze. (Ch'ih Chung-yu, p. 377.) See also HUANG CHIUNG-CH'EN.

*HUANG CHIUNG-CH'EN 黃炯臣 ; captain of Ch'ao Yung, 1894 Yalu action; same as HUANG CHIEN-HSÜN above. This version of the name from Yao Hsi-kuang, p. 200.

HUANG CHÜEH-TZU 黃爵滋

HUANG EN-CHAO 黃恩詔

*HUANG HSÜN; mentioned by Giquel in 1873 as member of first class at Foochow yard; in that year, made assistant professor in engineer's school. Same as HUANG CHIEN-HSÜN?

HUANG I-SHENG 黃翼升; commander of the Yangtze water-force in 1870; in 1893, admiral in same.

*HUANG LIEN 黃漣; third officer on the Fu Hsing in the Ma-wei battle, 1884; fought with distinction after his captain's death, until ship blew up.

HUANG LIEN-K'AI 黃聯開; tsung-ping of water-force, recommended to be an officer in early Foochow ships.

HUANG MEI-SHENG 黃梅生; Kiangnan captain of T'ien Chi.

*HUANG MING-CH'IU 黃鳴球; navigation student, sent by Foochow to Britain in 1886.

*HUANG SHANG-CHI (I-CHI) 黃裳吉 (一治); sent by Northern Commissioner in 1886 for overseas study.

*HUANG TAI 黃帶; mentioned in 1873 by Giquel as foreman of setting-up shop at Foochow yard, after having successfully passed a detailed examination in engines; 1880, sent as apprentice to Germany.

*HUANG TE-CH'UN 黃德椿; Foochow student sent in 1896 to France to study naval construction.

*HUANG T'ING 黃庭; recommended by Wu Ts'an-ch'ang in 1879 to be ninth-rank civil officer; in 1881, sent by Foochow yard overseas to learn construction of fortifications in France.

HUANG WEI-HSÜAN 黃維煊; first recommended for employment at Foochow yard in 1866; as Fukien t'ung-chih, present on the test run of the Wan Nien Ch'ing to the north in 1869; died in 1875, as expectant chih-fu.

I-CHING 奕經
I-HSIN 奕訢
I-HUAN 奕譞
I-K'UANG 奕劻
I-LI-PU 伊里布

I-LIANG 怡良

I-SHAN 奕山

*JEN CHAO 任照; one of five apprentices sent by Foochow yard to France in 1878; studied drafting and armor-making.

JUI-LIN 瑞麟

JUNG-LU 榮祿

*K'ANG CH'ANG-CH'ING 康長慶; captain of Ching Hai in 1879, rank of shou-pei.

*KAO CH'ENG-HSI 高承錫; recommended for promotion by Li Hung-chang after the 1894 Yalu action.

*KAO ER-CH'IEN 高而謙; Foochow construction student sent in 1886 to France; studied international law.

*KAO T'ENG-YÜN 高騰雲; captain of Fei Yün in the Ma-wei battle of 1884; killed.

*K'O CHIEN-CHANG 柯建章; third officer on Chi Yuan in the 1894 Feng-tao fight; killed; shou-pei rank at death; recommended for posthumous honors by Li Hung-chang.

*K'O HUNG-NIEN 柯鴻年; Foochow construction student sent in 1886 to France; studied international law.

*KOU-CHEN-TEH; cited by Giquel in 1873 as ready to help direct the Foochow building yard.

*KU CHIH-CH'ENG 古之誠; drafting student, praised by Wu Tsan-ch'eng in 1876.

KUAN T'IEN-P'EI 關天培

*K'UANG TS'UNG 鄺聰; praised by Wu Ts'an-ch'eng as "old student" at Foochow yard.

KUEI-LIANG 桂良

KUEI SUNG-CH'ING 桂嵩慶

KUNG CHEN-LIN 龔振麟

KUNG CHIH-T'ANG 龔之棠; son of Kung Chen-lin.

*KUO CHING-LI (KWO-CHING-LI); engineer mentioned by Giquel at Foochow, 1873.

*KUO JUI-KUEI 郭瑞珪; Foochow apprentice; studying in Marseilles, 1878. Possibly the Ko-jouei-kouei mentioned by Giquel in 1873.

*KUO PAO-CH'ANG 郭寶昌; in charge of six Nanyang ships in 1891 joint north-south maneuvers.

KUO SUNG-T'AO 郭嵩燾

KUO TE-SHAN 郭德山; tu-sze brevetted to yu-chi, to have been one of the Lay-Osborn captains.

*KUO YAO-CHUNG 郭耀忠; recommended for posthumous honors by Li Hung-chang after the 1894 Yalu action.

*KWANG KWOK-KONG; ex-CEM student, mentioned by La Fargue as naval officer.

*KWONG WING-CHUNG; ex-CEM student, of whom it was noted that he was killed at the Ma-wei battle of 1884 (LaFargue, p. 73).

*KWONG PIN-KONG; ex-CEM student; mentioned by LaFargue as naval officer.

LAI CH'ANG 賴長

*LAN CHIEN-SHU 藍建樞; Foochow student, took training cruise in Yang Wu in 1875.

*LI-AH-PUN; mentioned by Giquel as engineering student at Foochow, 1873.

*LI-AH-WEN; same as LI-AH-PUN.

LI CH'ANG-KENG 李長庚

LI CHAO-T'ANG 黎兆棠

LI CH'AO-PIN 李朝斌

LI CH'ENG-MO 李成謀

*LI CHIA-PEN 黎家本; Kwangtung man, entered Foochow school in 1867; mentioned by Giquel in 1873 as ready for command.

*LI FANG-JUNG 李芳榮; Foochow student recommended in 1879 by Wu Ts'an-ch'eng to be ninth-rank civil officer; sent abroad in 1882.

LI FENG-PAO 李鳳苞; before his diplomatic assignment in the 1880's, had been official at Kiangnan and Foochow yards.

*LI-FOO; mentioned by Giquel as engineering student at Foochow yard, 1873.

LI FU-T'AI 李福泰

*LI HO-LIEN 李和練; entered Foochow academy 1867; declared ready for command in 1873, by Giquel; desired by Li Hung-chang in 1877 as gunboat captain; captain of P'ing Yüan in Yalu battle, 1894. Kwangtung man.

LI HO-NIEN 李鶴年

LI HSING-JUI 李興銳

LI HSING-YÜAN 李星沅

LI HSIU-CH'ENG 李秀成

LI HUNG-CHANG 李鴻章

*LI-KIA-LO; mentioned by Giquel as engineering student at Foochow yard, 1873.

*LI LIEN-FEN 李連芬 ; first officer on Ching Yuan in 1894 Yalu action; killed.

LI LIEN-YING 李蓮英

*LI PI-LIANG 黎弼良 ; in 1896, sent by Tsungli Yamen to Britain to supervise the building of two ordered vessels.

LI PING-HENG 李秉衡

LI SHAN-LAN 李善蘭

LI SHAO-FANG 李紹昉

*LI SHIH-CHEN 李時珍; officer on the Yu Yüan in the 1885 Shih-p'u disaster; decamped; Tso Tsung-t'ang recommended capital punishment for him.

*LI SHOU-T'IEN 李壽田 ; construction student at Foochow; after study overseas, made engines for K'ai Chi, Heng Hai, Ching Ch'ing; 1881, ordered to work on P'eng Yü-lin order for gunboats; 1885, brevetted to tu-sze rank; in 1887, one of those in charge of construction at the Foochow yard.

*LI TA-CH'ANG; mentioned by Giquel as in the first class in the English-language school at the Foochow yard; served as translator for Giquel.

*LI TA-SHOU 李大受 ; Foochow construction student sent to France in 1886 to study bridging, river control, and railroad building.

*LI T'IEN 李田 ; in 1873, pronounced ready for command by Giquel; 1879, captain of Chen Wei with shou-pei rank; 1902, captain of K'ai Chi when she exploded at Nanking, for which he was demoted and sent to the frontier.

*LI TING-HSIN 李鼎新; Foochow navigation student, sent abroad in 1882; executive officer on Ting Yüan in Yalu action, 1894; recommended by Li Hung-chang for promotion; later admiral.

LI TSUNG-HSI 李宗羲

LIANG CHANG-CHÜ 梁章鉅

*LIANG MING-CH'IEN 梁鳴謙; recommended to be t'i-tiao at Foochow yard, 1875.

*LIANG PING-NIEN 梁炳年; recommended by Giquel in 1873 as Leang-ping-nien to aid Tchen-tcheng (Ch'en Ch'eng) as superintendent of engine-building; sent in 1876 to Toulon, where he died.

*LIANG TSU-HSÜN 梁祖勳; first officer of the Chen Wei in the Ma-wei battle of 1884; killed.

*LIANG TZE-FANG 梁梓芳; entered English-language school at Foochow in 1867; in 1877, captain of Fei Yün and Chen Wei. Kwangtung man.

*LIN CHAN-HSIUNG 林占熊; praised by Wu Ts'an-ch'eng in 1876 as "old student" at Foochow yard.

*LIN CHEN-CHANG (LIN-TCHENG-TCHANG); cited by Giquel in 1873 as an aide in running the setting-up and fitting shops at Foochow yard.

*LIN CHEN-FENG 林振峯; Foochow construction student sent in 1886 to France to study naval mathematics.

*LIN CH'ENG-MU 林承謨; Foochow student, training trip in Chien Wei, 1871.

*LIN CHIH-JUNG 林志榮; sent to Europe by Kiangnan arsenal in 1885.

*LIN CH'ING-SHENG 林慶昇; 1867, entered Foochow school as construction student; 1876, sent to Europe, specializing in mining and metallurgy; returned 1880, and was involved in setting up an iron mine at Foochow; also went to Formosa to supervise coal mining, and returned to work in the iron works at the Foochow yard. In 1885, a member of a party drawing the Yunnan border.

*LIN FAN 林藩; Foochow construction student, sent in 1886 to France. Studied international law.

*LIN FU-CHEN 林福貞; Foochow student sent in 1896 to France to study construction.

*LIN HO-LIN (LIN-HO-LIN); mentioned by Giquel as engineering student at Foochow yard, 1873.

*LIN HSIANG-KUANG 林祥光; sent as artisan to Germany in 1880.

*LIN I-SHENG 林翼升 ; captain of Ching Yüan in 1894 Yalu action, rank of fu-chiang; killed.

*LIN I-YU 林怡游; Foochow construction student, sent to France in 1876; studied at Toulon.

*LIN JIH-CHANG 林日章 ; Foochow construction student, to France 1876, studied mining and engine construction. Aided in establishing Kaiping coal mines for Li Hung-chang; also the Mu-yuan mine at Foochow, 1885, employed in engine shop at Foochow yard, with rank of assistant district magistrate (8a).

*LIN KAO-HUI 林高輝; captain of Ch'en Hang, 1877, with rank of ch'ien-tsung.

*LIN KUO-HSI 林國禧; returned to China in 1899 from Germany, where he with others had been observing the building of ordered ships.

*LIN KUO-HSIANG 林國祥; Foochow student, navigation, 1867; 1874, captain of Shen Hang; 1877, of Fu Po; captain of Kwang I in 1894 Feng-tao action, in which he lost his ship; captured by the Japanese and released when he signed a bond saying he would fight no more; after Yalu battle, appointed captain of Chi Yuan (after the beheading of Fang Pai-ch'ien). In 1896, sent by Tsungli Yamen to Britain to observe work on ordered ships. Kwangtung man. Same as LIN KUO-HSI?

*LIN LI-CHUNG 林履中 ; Foochow student, training cruise in Yang Wu, 1875; captain of Yang Wei in 1894 Yalu battle; drowned; recommended by Li Hung-chang for posthumous honors. Rank of tu-sze at death.

*LIN MING-HSÜN 林鳴塤 ; in 1873, Giquel recommended a Lin-ming-sun to help in directing the Foochow yard; 1885, sent by Northern Commissioner to observe the building of two ships ordered in Britain; in 1896, sent by Tsungli Yamen to Germany to observe ships being built there.

*LIN PAO-I 林葆懌; one of a group of Foochow navigation graduates, ca. 1885; he and six others sent to Northern Commissioner in 1886, and were berthed in the Wei Yüan.

*LIN SEN-LIN 林森林 ; Foochow student, took training cruise in Yang Wu, 1875; captain of Chien Sheng at Ma-wei battle, 1884; killed.

LIN SHAO-NIEN 林紹年

LIN SHOU-T'U 林壽圖 ; in 1874, when Shen Pao-chen was ordered to Formosa, he asked that this Shensi financial commissioner not go north, but come to the Foochow yard as full-time "inspector."

*LIN T'AI-TSENG 林泰曾 ; Foochow student, made training cruise in Chien Wei, 1871; mentioned by Giquel as ready for command in 1874; 1878, serving on British training ship; 1879, captain of Fei T'ing; 1880, to Britain in mission to take delivery of ships for Li Hung-chang; 1884, took Ch'ao Yung on southern training cruise; captain of Chen Yüan in Yalu battle, 1894; suicide after running his ship on some obstruction when bringing her into Weihaiwei late in 1894. Fukien man. Rank of tsung-ping at death.

LIN TSE-HSÜ 林則徐

*LIN TSE-YU 林則友 ; captain of I Hsin, Ma-wei battle, 1884.

*LIN TSO-HSIN; in 1873, Giquel recommended that Lin-tsou-sin be placed in charge of the chronometer works at the Foochow yard.

*LIN TZU-HAN 林滋煤 ; drafting student at Foo.; praised in 1876.

*LIN WEN-HO 林文和 ; officer on Fei Yün, 1873; captain of Yung Pao, 1874.

*LIN YING-CH'I 林穎啟 ; Foochow navigation student; 1878, served on British trainer; requested by Li Hung-chang in 1881 for service in Peiyang torpedo force; captain of Wei Yüan in Weihaiwei in 1895, and ashore when his ship was torpedoed in the harbor in February 1895.

*LIN YING-T'AI 林穎泰 ; Foochow student; training trip in Yang Wu in 1875. Same as LIN YING-CH'I?

*LIN YUNG-SHENG 林永升 ; Foochow student, training trip in Chien Wei in 1871; 1878, studying navigation and natural science at Greenwich. In 1881, assigned to gunboat purchased by Li Hung-chang for Shantung; probably accompanied Lang to Britain in 1887 to take delivery of ships; captain of Ching Yüan in Yalu battle, 1894; killed; recommended for posthumous honors by Li Hung-chang.

LIU CH'ANG-YU 劉長佑

LIU CH'AO-P'EI 劉超佩

*LIU HAN-FANG 劉含芳 ; commander of Li Hung-chang's torpedo boats in 1886 review at Port Arthur.

LIU JUI-FEN 劉瑞芬

*LIU KUAN-HSIUNG 劉冠雄 ; 1886, student sent to Britain; 1888, took Chih Yüan and Ching Yüan to quell revolt in Taiwan; second-in-command on Ching Yüan in Yalu battle, 1894; 1895, sent to Germany to take delivery of a ship; 1904, cashiered for grounding his ship; 1911, investigated Foochow dockyard; later admiral and navy minister.

*LIU K'UN 劉鵾 ; signalman on Chi Yüan, killed in Feng-tao battle, 1894.

LIU K'UN-I 劉坤一

LIU MING-CH'UAN 劉銘傳

*LIU MOU-HSÜN 劉懋勳 ; recommended by Giquel in 1873 as Foochow student worth sending to Europe; 1878, studying in Marseilles.

LIU PING-CHANG 劉秉璋

*LIU PING-YUNG 劉秉鏞 ; graduate of Tientsin naval academy, 1890.

*LIU PU-CH'AN 劉步蟾 ; Foochow student; training cruise in Chien Wei, 1871; cited as ready for command by Giquel, 1874; to Britain for advanced study, including serving in a British naval ship; 1879, captain of Chen Pei; 1880, sent by Li Hung-chang to Germany to observe building of Ting Yüan; captain of Ting Yüan in 1894 Yalu action; recommended for promotion by Li Hung-chang after that action; suicide after Weihaiwei surrender, February 1895. Rank at death, tsung-ping.

LIU TZU-JEN 劉仔仁 ; Chihli chih-chou, wanted at Foochow yard in 1876. Fukien man.

LIU YÜN-K'O 劉韻珂

*LO CH'ANG-CHIH 羅昌智 ; captain of Chen Wei, 1873.

*LO CHEN-LU 羅臻祿 ; 1873, cited (as Lo-tchen-lo) by Giquel as an aide in the Foochow carpentry shop; studied mining in France, 1878.

*LO CHUNG-MING 羅忠銘 ; Foochow navigation student, to Europe, 1886.

*LO CHUNG-YAO 羅忠堯 ; Foochow navigation student, to Europe, 1886.

*LO FENG-LU 羅豐祿 ; translator to Giquel on trip to France, 1876. Had completed navigation course. Noted in 1878 as studying meterology, chemistry, and physics in London.

*LO HSI-LU 羅熙祿 ; "old student" at Foochow praised by Wu Ts'an-ch'eng in 1876; in 1879, recommended by Wu as expectant magistrate.

LO PING-CHANG 駱秉章

LO TA-CH'UN 羅大春

*LOO-I; mentioned by Giquel in 1873 as an engineering student at Foochow yard.

*LU HSÜEH-MENG 盧學孟 ; 1896, Foochow student sent to France to study naval construction.

*LU LIN-CH'ING 陸麟清; in 1880, sent to Germany bh Li Hung-chang to supervise building of Ting Yüan.

*LU LUN-HUA 陸綸華 ; 1873, captain of Chen Hai, with rank of pa-tsung. Ningpo man.

*LU SHOU-MENG 盧守孟 ; Foochow construction student sent to Cherbourg in 1886; 1896, sent by Tsungli Yamen to Europe to observe building of newly-ordered ships.

LUNG WEN 隆文

*LÜ HAN 呂瀚 ; 1867, navigation student at Foochow yard; cited as ready for command by Giquel, in 1873; captain of Ch'ang Sheng, 1873; in 1877, captain of Fei Yün and Wei Yüan; in 1884, captain of Fu Sheng. In the Ma-wei battle, 1884, in charge of the two American-built gunboats purchased by Shen Pao-chen in 1874; committed suicide after one of these was sunk. Kwangtung or Hongkong man.

*LÜ T'IAO-YUNG 呂調鏞 ; noted as returning in 1899 from Germany where he and others had observed the building of ordered ships.

*LÜ WEN-CHING 呂文經 ; captain of An Lan, 1873; in 1876, captain of Chi An, with rank of expectant tu-sze. Li Hung-chang was very critical of him as an officer of the Foochow yard in 1882 (Li felt firing was too good); in 1899, noted as returning from observing construction of ordered ships in Germany.

*LÜ WEN-YING 呂文英 ; captain of Fu Po, Ma-wei battle, 1884. Same as LÜ WEN-CHING?

*MA CHIEN-CHUNG 馬建忠 ; in Giquel's party to Europe, 1876; in 1878, studied law and negotiation in France; 1879, head of Tientsin naval training.

MA HSIN-I 馬新貽

*MA YING-PO 馬應波 ; engineer of the Fei Yün in the Ma-wei battle, 1884; killed.

MU-CH'ANG-A 穆彰阿

*MU CHIN-SHU 穆晉書

MU T'U-SHAN 穆圖善

NIEH CH'I-KUEI 聶緝槼
NIU CHIEN 牛鑑

*OU-TEN-CHAG; cited by Giquel in 1873 as aiding in the direction of the Foochow building yard.

OU-YANG FANG 歐陽芳; yu-chi, brevetted to ts'an-chiang, to be one of the Lay-Osborn captains. OU-TEN-CHAG may be a misprinted romanization of OU-YANG FANG.

P'AN CHENG-WEI 潘正煒
*P'AN HSI-CHI 潘錫基; engineer on the Fei Yün in the Ma-wei battle, 1884; killed.
P'AN PING-NIEN 潘炳年
P'AN SHIH-CH'ENG 潘仕成
P'AN SHIH-JUNG 潘仕榮

PEI CHIN-CH'UAN 貝錦泉; praised by Shen Pao-chen in 1866 as an ex-water-force captain, then in command of Hua Fu Pao; asked by Tso Tsung-t'ang to help build a navy in Fukien; as yu-chi in 1870 worked with Li Ch'eng-mo to recruit men in Ningpo area for navigation training at Foochow school; captain of Yang Wu, 1873; of Yüan K'ai, 1875; left about 1877 to be a tsung-ping in the Hai-t'an Island water-force unit. Ningpo man.

*PEI SAN-CH'UAN 貝珊泉; captain of Fu Po, 1873; of Yüan K'ai, 1885 (he had been in command of this ship since 1877). In 1877, rank of tu-sse. Brother of PEI CHIN-CH'UAN?

PEI YIN-SEN 裴陰森
P'ENG CH'U-HAN 彭楚漢
P'ENG YÜ-LIN 彭玉麟
PIEN CH'ANG-SHENG 卞長勝
PIEN PAO-CH'UAN 卞寶泉

PIEN PAO-TI 卞寶第; same as PIEN PAO-CH'UAN? Both listed as directors of the Foochow yard after the Sino-French War, in Pao Tsen-peng, p. 182.

*PUN-CHEW-SIN; cited by Giquel as engineer at Foochow yard, 1873.

*SAH CHEN-PING 薩鎮冰; Foochow student, made Yang Wu training cruise, 1875; in 1878, studying navigation, translation and natural science at Greenwich; 1899, made assistant to Yeh Tsu-kuei, with rank of ts'an-chiang; 1905, replaced Yeh Tsu-kuei; 1909, toured Europe with Tsai-hsün, taking students to Britain; 1910, made navy minister.

SENG-KO-LIN-CH'IN 僧格林沁

SHAN-CH'ING 善慶

SHAO YÜ-LIEN 邵友濂

*SHEN CHAO-CHANG; ex-CEM student; listed by LaFargue as naval officer, commander of the Tsai Yüan.

SHEN PAO-CHEN 沈葆禎

SHEN PAO-CHING 沈葆靖

SHEN PING-CH'ENG 沈秉成

*SHEN SHOU-CH'ANG 沈壽昌; officer on Chi Yuan, killed in Feng-tao action, 1894; recommended for posthumous honors by Li Hung-chang.

*SHEN SHOU-K'UN 沈壽堃; 1886, sent by Northern Commissioner to Britain, where he studied navigation and gunnery; 1894, gunnery officer in the Ting Yüan, and recommended for promotion by Li Hung-chang; 1905, assistant to Sa Chen-ping; 1909, commander of the Yangtze squadron.

*SHEN SHU-LING 沈叔齡; recommended for promotion by Li Hung-chang after the Yalu battle, 1894.

*SHEN SHUN-FA 沈順發; 1873, captain of Wan Nien Ch'ing.

*SHEN YU-HENG 沈有恒; Foochow student, training cruise in Chien Wei, 1871. Captain of I Hsin before becoming, in 1877, captain of Chen Wei.

SHENG CH'IU-CH'ING 盛求清; fu-chiang, brevetted as tsung-ping, to be one of the Lay-Osborn captains.

*SHIH CHIEN-CHUNG 史建中; Foochow student, made training cruise in Yang Wu in 1875.

*SHIH EN-FU 施恩孚; 1896, sent by Foochow yard to France, construction student.

SHIH LANG 施琅

SHIH SHIH-P'IAO 施世驃

*SHIH SHOU-CHEN 史壽箴 ; lookout on Ting Yüan when she was dismasted in Yalu battle, 1894; recommended for posthumous honors by Li Hung-chang.

*SIT YAU-FU; ex-CEM student; killed in Ma-wei battle, 1884.

*SUN CHING-JEN 孫景仁 ; after Yalu battle, 1894, recommended for posthumous reward by Li Hung-chang.

SUN SHAO-CHIN 孫紹鈞; captain of Wei Ching, 1872.

SUNG CHIN 宋晉

*SUNG MON-WAI; ex-CEM student, listed by LaFargue as naval officer.

*TAI PO-K'ANG 戴伯康 ; Foochow navigation student; training cruise on Yang Wu, 1875.

TAI TSUNG-CH'IEN 戴宗騫

T'AN CHUNG-LIN 譚鍾麐

*T'AN HSÜEH-HENG 譚學衡; 1896, sent to Britain to observe building of ships; 1910, assistant to Tsai-hsün in new navy department.

T'ANG CHIUNG 唐炯

*T'ANG T'ING-SHU 唐廷樞 ; China Merchants' Steamship Navigation Co. man, expectant taotai, with knowledge of Western languages; sought by Foochow yard in 1876.

*T'ANG WEN-CHING 湯文經 ; 1879, replaced Wu Shih-chung on Wu's death; T'ang then had rank of shou-pei. He then transferred to the Fei T'ing in the Peiyang fleet. Killed in Yalu action, 1894, and recommended by Li Hung-chang for posthumous honors.

*T'ANG YU 唐祐; "old student" at Foochow yard, priased by Wu Ts'an-ch'eng in 1876.

TENG HSIU-CHIH 鄧秀枝 ; yu-chi brevetted to ts'an-chiang to be one of the Lay-Osborn captains.

*TENG SHIH-CH'ANG 鄧世昌 ; Kwangtung man; entered Foochow navigation school, 1867; cited by Giquel as ready for command in 1873; 1877, sought by Li Hung-chang to be gunboat captain; 1880, grounded his ship in cruise in Chihli waters; sent by Li with Yang Wei on Formosa relief expedition, late 1884; 1887, went (as navigator) with Lang to Britain to take delivery of ships; captain of Chih Yüan in Yalu 1894 battle, with rank of fu-chiang; killed; recommended for posthumous honors by Li Hung-chang.

TENG T'ING-CHEN 鄧廷楨

*TENG TS'UNG-PAO 鄧驄保; captain of the Chao Wu when she was blockaded by the French in Chenhai harbor in 1885; rank of tu-sze.

*TING HUA-JUNG 丁華容

TING KUNG-CH'EN 丁拱辰

TING JIH-CH'ANG 丁日昌

*TING JU-CH'ANG 丁汝昌

TING MING-SHENG 丁鳴威; military officer, rank of ch'ien-tsung, helped build ships at Shanghai; praised in 1869.

TING PAO-CHEN 丁寶楨

TING PING-CHUNG 丁秉忠; military officer, rank of ch'ien-tsung, at the Kiangnan yard; praised in 1869. Same as TING MING-SHENG?

*TING P'ING-LAN 丁平瀾; sent by Foochow yard in 1896 to France to study ship construction.

TING SHOU-CH'ANG 丁壽昌

TING SHOU-TS'UN 丁守存

*TING SZE-CHUNG; ex-CEM student, listed by La Fargue as naval officer.

TING TAO-CHIEH 丁道杰; 1863, gunnery demonstrator for Tseng Kuo-fan at Anking arsenal.

*TS'AI HAO-YÜAN 蔡灝元; sent to Germany to observe shipbuilding; returned 1899.

*TS'AI HSIN-SHU 蔡馨書; after Yalu battle, 1894, recommended by Li Hung-chang for posthumous honors.

TS'AI HUI-TS'ANG 蔡滙滄

TS'AI JUI-AN 蔡瑞庵; recommended by Shen Pao-chen to Li Hung-chang as possible leader of Peiyang fleet.

TS'AI KUO-HSI 蔡國喜; Lay-Osborn commander.

*TS'AI KUO-HSIANG 蔡國祥; put in charge of training at Foochow yard, on the trainer Yang Wu, 1874. Same as TS'AI KUO-HSI.

*TS'AI T'ING-KAN 蔡廷幹

TSAO KA-HSIANG; ex-CEM student, listed by LaFargue as naval officer.

*TS'AO CHIA-HSIANG 曹嘉祥; gunnery officer on the Chen Yüan; recommended for promotion by Li Hung-chang after the Yalu battle, 1894. Probably the Tsao Ka-hsiang listed by LaFargue as ex-CEM navy man.

*TSENG CHAO-LIN 曾兆麟; graduate of the Tientsin naval academy, 1887.

TSENG CHI-TSE 曾紀澤

TSENG CH'I 增祺; Foochow Tartar general; one of the post-Sino-Japanese-War superintendents at the Foochow yard.

TSENG KUO-CH'UAN 曾國荃

TSENG KUO-FAN 曾國藩

*TSENG TSUNG-KUNG 曾宗鞏; graduate of the Tientsin naval academy, 1892.

*TSENG TSUNG-YING 曾宗瀛; in 1879, recommended by Wu Ts'an-ch'eng at Foochow yard for promotion to ninth official rank; in 1885, sent by Northern Commissioner to observe the building of ships ordered; 1896, sent by Tsungli Yamen to Germany for similar observation.

TSO TSUNG-T'ANG 左宗棠

*T'U TSUNG-NIEN 屠宗年; 1873, captain of Mei Yün.

*TUNG TSAI-T'ANG 佟在棠; in 1881, torpedo and mine expert at Foochow dockyard; 1883, left the yard.

WANG CHEN-CH'ANG 王鎮昌

*WANG CH'IAO-NIEN 汪喬年; a tu-sze, in charge of the building of the I Hsin; praised by Wu Ts'an-ch'eng in 1876. Had been translator at Kiangnan yard.

*WANG CH'ING-JUI 王慶瑞; Foochow apprentice; in 1879, recommended by Wu Ts'an-ch'eng for promotion to ninth civil rank; in 1886, sent with student mission to Europe.

*WANG FU-CH'ANG 王福昌; Foochow apprentice, recommended by Wu Ts'an-ch'eng in 1879 for promotion to ninth civil rank; 1882, sent to France, to study gunpowder.

*WANG HSI-SHAN 王錫山; on Chi Yuan in Feng-tao action, 1894; killed; recommended by Li Hung-chang for posthumous honors.

*WANG HSÜEH-LIEN 王學廉; in 1879, recommended for promotion to expectant magistrate by Wu Ts'an-ch'eng; in 1886, sent by Northern Commissioner to Britain, to study naval gunnery, navigation.

*WANG HUI-LAN 王迴瀾; in 1879, recommended by Wu Ts'an-ch'eng for promotion to ninth civil grade; sent overseas in 1882, studied fortification in France.

WANG JUNG-HO 王榮和; China Merchants' Steamship Navigation Co. man, having made translations of Western works on ships and guns, wanted at Foochow yard, 1876; rank of fu-chiang.

WANG K'AI-T'AI 王凱泰

*WANG KUEI-FANG 王桂芳; in 1878, Foochow apprentice in France, studying drafting and armor-making.

*WANG LAN-FEN 王蘭芬; cited by Li Hung-chang after the Yalu battle, 1894, for posthumous honors.

*WANG PAO-CH'EN 王葆辰; tsung chien-kung at Foochow yard in 1877; under attack in 1880-1881, with Wu Chung-hsiang.

*WANG SHOU-CH'ANG 王壽昌; Foochow construction student sent to France, 1886; studied international law.

*WANG SUNG-CH'EN 王崧辰; assistant superintendent at Foochow yard; forged recommendations for rewards in 1890.

WANG TING 王鼎

*WANG TSUNG-CH'IH 王宗墀; cited after Yalu battle, 1894, for posthumous honors, by Li Hung-chang.

*WANG T'UNG-CH'EN 王桐陳; Foochow construction student, sent to Britain in 1886 to study ship engines; in 1895, sent by Foochow yard to Europe; 1913, in charge of reorganization of the dockyard.

WANG WEN-SHAO 王文韶

*WEI CHEN-SHENG 韋振聲; 1875, Foochow student taking training cruise on Yang Wu; 1879, captain of Chien Sheng.

*WEI CHIAO-NIEN (OUAY-KIAO-NIEN); cited by Giquel in 1873 as ready to take charge of Foochow foundry, with Ch'en Chao-ao.

*WEI HAN 魏瀚; Foochow student, cited by Giquel (as Ouie-han) in 1873 as chief director of construction of hulls and equipment; in 1878, studied at Cherbourg; 1880, sent to Germany, to observe building of Ting Yüan; 1881, detailed to work on P'eng Yü-lin's order for gunboats; 1883, full faculty status at Foochow academy; 1885, recommended for reward by P'ei Yin-sen; 1887, noted as being in charge of construction at Foochow yard.

*WEI HSIEN 魏瀻; recommended by Wu Ts'an-ch'eng in 1879 for promotion to ninth civil rank; 1882, sent to Europe; returned Foochow 1885 after studying shipbuilding in France; held 9b official rank.

WEN-HSIANG 文祥

WEN PIN 文彬

WEN T'ING-SHIH 文廷式

WEN YÜ 文煜

*WENG SHOU-CHENG 翁守正; gunnery officer on Fu Sheng; killed in Ma-Wei battle, 1884.

*WONG CHU-LIN; ex-CEM student, listed by LaFargue as naval officer.

*WONG KUEI-LIANG; ex-CEM student, listed by LaFargue as naval officer.

*WOO KEE-TSAO; ex-CEM student, listed by LaFargue as naval officer.

*WU AN-K'ANG 吳安康

WU CHIEN-CHANG 吳健章

WU CHIEN-HSÜN 吳建勛

*WU CHING-JUNG 吳敬榮; 1894, captain of Kwang Chia, tu-sze rank; left Yalu battle and lost ship aground; 1907, in charge of four ships to root out arms smuggling at Macao; 1908, captured a Japanese ship in such activity.

WU CH'UAN-MEI 吳全美

*WU CHUNG-HSIANG 吳仲翔

WU-ERH-KUNG-O 烏爾恭阿

WU HSI-CHANG 吳錫章; a pa-tsung in 1870 recommended for an officer's post in one of the Foochow ships.

*WU HSUEH-CH'IANG 吳學鏘; apprentice at Foochow yard; in 1878, studying drafting and armor-making in France.

WU HUNG-YÜAN 吳鴻源; in 1865, in nominal command of the Ch'ang Sheng (a foreigner was in real command); formerly water-force tsung-ping at Wenchow.

*WU KUANG-CHIEN 伍光鑑; sent to Britain in 1886 by Northern Commissioner, to study naval sciences.

WU MENG-LIANG 吳夢良; sought by Li Hung-chang in 1877 as a captain; no mention by Giquel or others as being a Foochow man.

WU PING-CHIEN 伍秉鑑

*WU SHIH-CHUNG 吳世忠 ; at Foochow as yu-chi in 1869, with Yeh Wen-lan; 1873, captain of Fei Yün and Chi An; 1877, captain of Yang Wu. Water-force man.

WU TA-CH'ENG 吳大澂

*WU TA-T'ING 吳大廷 ; t'i-tiao at Foochow in 1870's.

WU T'ANG 吳棠

*WU TE-CHANG 吳德章 ; 1867, student in French school at Foochow yard; 1878, studying at Toulon; specialized in naval construction; 1885, recommended by P'ei Yin-sen; designed K'ai Chi, Heng Hai, Ching Ch'ing; in charge of armor works. In 1885, rank of shou-pei; in 1897, supervised taking Foochow students to Europe.

WU TSAN-CH'ENG 吳贊誠

WU TUNG-YÜN 吳彤雲 ; in 1871, commanded three ships built at Shanghai arsenal in demonstration maneuvers for Tseng Kuo-fan.

*WU YING-FU (WOO YING-FOO); ex-CEM student; later admiral. Flag-lieutenant on flagship, Yalu action, 1894. Attended the Foochow academy two years before going into Peiyang fleet. 1901-1908, in charge of Kiangnan arsenal; 1908, admiral of cruiser squadron; during the Republic, he was admiral, and minister of communications. Resigned in 1916.

*WU YING-K'O 吳應科 ; recommended by Li Hung-chang for promotion after the Yalu battle, 1894.

WU YUAN-PING 吳元炳

*YANG AN-TIEN 楊安典 ; 1891, commander of the Canton squadron.

YANG CH'ANG-JUI 楊昌濬

*YANG CHI-CH'ENG 楊濟成 ; 1895, sent by Kiangnan arsenal to Europe.

*YANG CHIEN-LO 楊建洛 ; third officer on the Chi Yüan; killed in Yalu battle, 1894; recommended by Li Hung-chang for posthumous honors.

*YANG CH'IN-KUEI (TANG-TSIN-KWEI); cited by Giquel in 1873 as engineering student at Foochow academy.

YANG FANG 楊芳

*YANG FANG-I (YANG-FONG-YI); cited by Giquel in 1873 for aiding in the direction of the Foochow building yard.

*YANG LIEN-CH'EN 楊廉臣; Foochow construction student admitted 1867; 1878, studying at Toulon; 1880, returned to Foochow yard; built engines for Heng Hai, Ching Ch'ing; rank of shou-pei, brevetted to tu-sze; cited for reward by P'ei Yin-sen in 1885.

YANG P'EI 楊霈

*YANG SEW-NAN; ex-CEM student; listed by LaFargue as naval officer killed at Ma-wei battle, 1884.

YANG T'ING-HUI 楊廷翬; water-force yu-chi kept on at Foochow yard in 1868 to be an officer.

*YANG YUNG-LIN 楊用霖; second-in-command on Chen Yüan in Yalu battle, 1894; fought well, recommended for promotion; succeeded Lin T'ai-tseng as captain when Lin committed suicide; jump in rank probably from yu-chi to tsung-ping. Ex-CEM? See YUNG LIANG.

*YANG YUNG-NIEN 楊永年 ; 1873, captain of Fu Hsing; promoted to ch'ien-tsung for help given to two English ships; 1878, ran his own ship aground; 1879, captain of Shen Hang, rank of tu-sze.

YANG YÜEH-PIN 楊岳斌

*YEH CH'EN 葉琛; Foochow student, Yang Wu training cruise 1875; 1879, recommended by Wu Ts'an-ch'eng for expectant magistracy; captain of Fu Sheng in Ma-wei battle, 1884; killed.

YEH CHIH-CH'AO 葉志超

*YEH FU 葉富 ; Foochow student, entered English school 1867; cited by Giquel as ready for command in 1873; 1880, took Ch'ao Wu on antipiratical mission; 1874, captain of Hai Tung Yün.

YEH MING-CH'EN 葉名琛

*YEH PO-YÜN 葉伯鋆 ; Foochow student; training cruise on Chien Wei, 1871.

*YEH TIEN-SHUO 葉殿鑠 ; Foochow apprentice, to France in 1878, studied drafting and armor-making.

YEH T'ING-CH'UN 葉廷春

*YEH TSU-KUEI 葉祖珪 ; Foochow student, 1871 Chien Wei training cruise; 1878, Greenwich; 1887, to Britain with Lang, as navigator, having been in Li's service since 1881; captain of Ching Yuan at Yalu battle, 1894, but not recommended for promotion by Li Hung-chang after that battle; ashore when his ship was sunk in Weihaiwei harbor; at the time, rank of fu-chiang; 1899, "restored" from disgrace;

1904, all dock installations placed under him. Pao Tsen-peng, p. 138, says that he was admiral of the Kwangtung fleet in 1904, and was also made <u>tsung-li nan-pei-yang hai-chün</u>, or commander of a joint north-south fleet. Died in 1905.

*YEH WEN-LAN 葉文瀾

YEN FU, see YEN TSUNG-KWANG.

*YEN LIANG-HSÜN 嚴良勳; student at T'ung-wen kuan at Shanghai; won official rank; studied at Peking T'ung-wen kuan; brought to Foochow in 1876 by Wu Ts'an-ch'eng; 1878, inspector of Foochow academy.

YEN PO-T'AO 顏伯燾

*YEN TSUNG-KWANG 嚴宗光; Foochow student; training trip in Chien Wei, 1871; cited by Giquel as ready for command in 1874; studied at Greenwich, 1878; 1880, director of training at Tientsin naval academy.

YI CH'ANG-HUA 易長華

YIN JU-CHANG 殷如璋

YING HAN 英翰

YING-KUEI 英桂

YING PAO SHIH 應寶時

*YOUNG SHANG-HIM; ex-CEM student, listed by LaFargue as naval officer.

*YU HSIUNG-FEI 余雄飛; leader of Kwangtung contingent in 1891 joint north-south naval maneuvers; rank of <u>fu-chiang</u>, vice-admiral of Kwangtung fleet.

*YU HSÜEH-K'AI 游學楷; in 1873, Giquel cited a Yio-sio-che for an aide to Wei Han; probably the same; in 1886, sent to France, studied international law.

*YU HSÜEH-SHIH 游學詩; Foochow construction student; praised by Wu Ts'an-ch'eng in 1876; recommended for expectant magistracy in 1879; 1883, sent to Taiwan to coal-mine work.

YU PU-YÜN 余步雲

YUAN CHIA-SAN 袁甲三

YUAN CHÜN 袁俊; <u>ts'an-chiang</u>, to be one of the Lay-Osborn captains.

*YUNG LIANG; cited by LaFargue as a survivor of the Ma-wei battle of 1884, who later became captain of Admiral Ting's flagship. YANG YUNG-LIN?

YUNG WING (YUNG HUNG) 容閎

YÜ-CH'IEN 裕謙

YÜ K'UAN 裕寬

BIBLIOGRAPHY

Allan, James. Under the Dragon Flag. New York, 1898.

Arlington, L. C. Through the Dragon's Eyes. London, 1931.

Ballard, G. A. The Influence of the Sea on the Political History of Japan. New York, 1921.

Barnaby, Nathanial. Naval Development in the Century (Nineteenth Century Series). London and Edinburgh, 1904.

Baxter, James Phinney. The Introduction of the Ironclad Warship. Cambridge, Mass., 1933.

Beckler, W. H. "A Review of Japanese Naval Financial Policy," United States Naval Institute Proceedings, 37.3:801-822 (September 1911).

Beresford, Charles. The Break-Up of China. New York, 1899.

Bernard, W. D. and W. H. Hall. Narrative of the Voyages and Services of the Nemesis from 1840 to 1843, and of the Combined Naval and Military Operations in China. 2 vols.; London, 1844.

Biggerstaff, Knight. The Earliest Modern Government Schools in China. Ithaca, 1961.

Bland, J. O. P. and E. Backhouse. China Under the Empress Dowager. Philadelphia, 1911.

Bonner-Smith, D. and E. W. R. Lumby. The Second China War, 1856-1860 (Publications of the Navy Board Society, Vol. 95). Greenwich: Royal Naval College, 1954.

Boulger, Demetrius C. The Life of Sir Halliday Macartney, K. C. M. G. New York and London, 1908.

BPP: British Parliamentary Papers
> Correspondence Respecting the Fitting Out, Dispatching to China, and Ultimate Withdrawal, of the Anglo-Chinese Fleet Under the Command of Sherard Osborn; and the Dismissal of Mr. Lay from the Chief Inspectorate of the Customs. 1864, Vol. 63.
>
> Papers Respecting the Civil War in China, 1852-1853. Vol. 69.
>
> Correspondence Affecting Affairs in China, 1859-1860. Vol. 69.
>
> Correspondence Respecting the Revision of the Treaty of Tientsin. 1871, Vol. 70.
>
> Further Papers Relative to the Rebellion in China. 1863, Vol. 73.
>
> "Accounts and Papers," including "Diplomatic and Consular Reports on Trade and Finance in China" and "Commercial Reports of Her Majesty's Consuls in China." Bound in with Parliamentary Papers, but with its own volume numbers for each year.

Brassey, T. A., ed. The Naval Annual. Portsmouth, England, 1886-1896.

Bredon, Juliet. Sir Robert Hart. New York, 1909.

Bridge, Cyprian A. G. "The Revival of the Warlike Power of China," Fraser's Magazine (June 1879), pp. 778-789.

British Parliamentary Papers, see BPP.

Brodie, Bernard. Sea Power in the Machine Age. Princeton, 1941.

Brunnert, H. S. and V. V. Hagelstrom. Present Day Political Organization of China, tr. A. Beltchenko and E. E. Moran. Rev. ed.; Shanghai, 1912.

Cameron, Meribeth E. "The Public Career of Chang Chih-tung, 1837-1909," Pacific Historical Review, 7.3:187-210 (September 1938).

"Capture of Weihaiwei," United States Naval Institute Proceedings, 16.1:209-211 (1895).

Carlson, Ellsworth C. "The Kailan Mines, 1878-1912," Papers on China, 3:24-77. Harvard University, East Asian Research Center, 1949.

CCTY: Ch'uan-cheng tsou-yi hui-pien 船政奏議彙編 (Memorials on the Foochow dockyard), comp. in part by Tso Tsung-t'ang. 54 chüan in 22 ts'e; last entry in 1902.

CF: Chung-Fa chan-cheng 中法戰爭 (The Sino-French war), ed. Shao Hsün-cheng 邵循正 et al. 7 vols.; Shanghai, 1955.

Chabaud-Arnault, Capt. "Combats on the Min River," tr. Lt. E. B. Barry, U.S.N., United States Naval Institute Proceedings, 11.2:295-320 (1885).

Chang P'ei-lun 張佩綸. "Han-kao" 函稿 (Letters); from Chien-yü chi 澗于集 (Works of Chang Pei-lun); in Chung-Jih chan-cheng, V, 224-232.

Chang Yin-lin 張蔭麟. "Chia-wu Chung-kuo hai-chün chan-chi k'ao" 甲午中國海軍戰蹟考 (Chinese naval campaigns in the Sino-Japanese war); Ch'ing-hua hsüeh-pao, 10.1:61-95 (January 1935).

Chen, Gideon. Lin Tse-hsu, Pioneer Promoter of the Adoption of Western Means of Maritime Defense in China. Peking, 1934.

------Tseng Kuo-fan, Pioneer Promoter of the Steamship in China. Peiping, 1935.

------Tso Tsung-t'ang, Pioneer Promoter of the Modern Dockyard and the Woolen Mill in China. Peiping, 1938.

Ch'en Hsin-te 陳信德, tr. "Tung-hsiang-p'ing-pa chi-ch'en Kao-sheng-hao jih-chi" 東鄉平八擊沉高陞號日記 (Togo's journal on the sinking of the Kowhsing); in Chung-Jih chan-cheng, VI, 30-32.

Cheng Tsu-keng 鄭祖庚. Min-hsien hsiang-t'u chih 閩縣鄉土志 (Gazetteer of Foochow). 1903.

Ch'ih Chung-yu 池仲祐. "Hai-chün ta-shih chi" 海軍大事記 (A record of important naval events); in Tso Shun-sheng,

Chung-kuo chin-pai-nien-shih tz'u-liao hsü-pien, pp. 323-385.

China, Imperial Maritime Customs, see IMC.

Chinese Repository, see CR.

Ch'ing-chi wai-chiao shih-liao, see WCSL.

Ch'ing-hua hsüeh-pao 清華學報 (The Tsing Hua journal). Tsing Hua University, Peking, 1924-, semiannually.

Ch'ing Kuang-hsü-ch'ao Chung-Fa chiao-she shih-liao 清光緒朝中法交涉史料 (Historical materials on Sino-French relations in the Kuang-hsü reign). Peiping: Palace Museum; reprinted in Chung-Fa chan-cheng, Vol. 5.

Ch'ing Kuang-hsü-ch'ao Chung-Jih chiao-she shih-liao 清光緒朝中日交涉史料 (Historical materials on Sino-Japanese relations in the Kuang-hsü reign). Peiping: Palace Museum; reprinted in Chung-Jih chan-cheng, Vols. 3 and 4.

Ch'ing-shih kao, see CSK.

Chou Fu 周馥. Chou-ch'üeh-shen-kung ch'uan-chi 周愨慎公全集 (Complete works of Chou Fu; excerpted in Chung-Jih chan-cheng, V, 208-214.

Ch'ou-pan i-wu shih-mo, see IWSM.

Ch'uan-cheng tsou-yi hui-pien, see CCTY.

Ch'uan Han-sheng 全漢昇. Ch'ing-chi ti Kiang-nan chih-tsao-chü 清季的江南製造局 (The Kiangnan arsenal in Ch'ing times). Formosa, 1951.

Chung-Fa chan-cheng, see CF.

Chung-Fa Yüeh-nan chiao-she shih-liao 中法越南交涉史料 (Historical materials on Sino-French relations over Annam). Peiping: Palace Museum; reprinted in Chung-Fa chan-cheng, V, 87-499.

Chung-Jih chan-cheng, see CJ.

CJ: Chung-Jih chan-cheng 中日戰爭 (The Sino-Japanese war), ed. Shao Hsün-cheng et al. 7 vols.; Shanghai, 1956.

CKHP: Huang-ch'ao chang-ku hui-pien 皇朝掌故彙編 (Collected historical records of the imperial dynasty), comp. Chang Shou-yung 張壽鏞 et al. Movable type ed., 1902; 100 chüan in 60 ts'e.

Clyde, P.H. United States Policy Toward China. Chapel Hill, N.C., 1940.

Cordier, H. Histoire des Relations de la Chine avec les Puissances Occidentales, 1860-1900. 4 vols.; Paris, 1901-1902.

CR: Chinese Repository. Macao and Canton, May 1832 to December 1851; monthly.

CSK: Ch'ing-shih kao 清史稿 (Draft history of the Ch'ing dynasty), comp. Chao Erh-hsün 趙爾巽 et al. Movable type ed., 1937; 536 chüan in 131 ts'e. See in particular Ping-chih 兵志: chüan 6, Shui-shih 水師 (Water force); chüan 7, Hai-chün 海軍 (Navy); chüan 9, Hai-fang 海防 (Coastal defense).

CTLT: Huang-ch'ao cheng-tien lei-tsuan 皇朝政典類纂 (A classified compendium of the administrative statutes of the imperial dynasty), comp. Hsi Yü-fu 席裕福 et al. Movable type ed., 1903; 500 chüan in 119 ts'e.

Cunningham, Alfred. The Chinese Soldier and Other Sketches. London, n.d.

Davis, Sir John F. China During the War and Since the Peace. 2 vols.; London, 1852.

Dawson, F.J. Jr. "Law and the Merchant in Traditional China," Papers on China, 2:55-92. Harvard University, East Asian Research Center, 1950.

Denby, Charles. China and Her People. 2 vols.; Boston, 1906.

Fairbank, John K. "Manchu Appeasement Policy, 1843," Journal of the American Oriental Society, 59.4:469-484 (December 1939).

------"Chinese Diplomacy and the Nanking Treaty of 1842," Journal of Modern History, 12.1:1-29 (March 1940).

------Trade and Diplomacy on the China Coast, 1842-1854. 2 vols.; Cambridge, Mass., 1954.

Fairbank, John K., Alexander Eckstein and L.S. Yang. "Economic Change in Early Modern China: An Analytic Framework," Economic Development and Cultural Change, 9.1:1-26 (October 1960).

Falk, Edwin A. Togo and the Rise of Japanese Sea Power. New York and Toronto, 1936.

Foreign Relations of the United States, see **FRUS**.

Fox, Grace. British Admirals and Chinese Pirates, 1832-1869. London, 1940.

FRUS: Foreign Relations of the United States. U.S. Department of State.

Gibson, Charles E. The Story of the Ship. New York, 1948.

Gilfillan, S.C. Inventing the Ship. Chicago, 1935.

Giquel, Prosper. The Foochow Arsenal and Its Results: From Commencement in 1867 to the End of the Foreign Directorate on 16 February ,1874, tr. from French by H. Lang. Shanghai, 1874.

Gutzlaff, Charles. Journal of Three Voyages Along the Coast of China, 1831, 1832, and 1833, with Notices of Siam, Corea, and the Loo-Choo Islands. 3rd ed.; London, 1841.

------The Life of Taou Kwang, Late Emperor of China. London, 1852.

Hai-fang tang, see HFT.

Hail, William. Tseng Kuo-fan and the Taiping Rebellion. New Haven, 1927.

Hannay, David. The Navy and Sea Power. London, 1913.

Henderson, Daniel M. Yankee Ships in China Seas. New York, 1946.

Herbert, Hilary A. "The Fight of the Yalu River," North American Review, 159:513-528 (November 1894).

------"Military Lessons of the Sino-Japanese War," North American Review, 160:685-698 (June 1895).

HFT: Hai-fang tang 海防檔 (Files on maritime defense), ed. Kuo T'ing-i 郭廷以 et al. Taipei: Institute of Modern History, Academia Sinica, 1957 (cloth ed). Section II, Fu-chou ch'uan-ch'ang 福州船廠 (Foochow dockyard), in 2 vols., shang 上, pp. 5-532, and hsia 下, pp. 533-1136. Section III, Nei chi-ch'i chü 內機器局 (Internal machine shops), in 1 vol., first item on "Kiang-nan chih-tsao-chü fu kiang-nan lun-ch'uan ts'ao-lien chü" 江南製造局附江南輪船操練局 (The Kiangnan arsenal and steamship training).

Hsieh Pao-chao. The Government of China, 1644-1911. Baltimore, 1925.

Hsien Yü-ch'ing 洗玉清. "Ch'ing-chi hai-chün chih hui-su" 清季海軍之回溯 (A retrospect on the Ch'ing navy); Tung-fang tsa-chih, 38.11:29-33 (June 15, 1941).

Hsü, Immanuel C.Y. China's Entrance into the Family of Nations: The Diplomatic Phase, 1858-1880. Cambridge, Mass., 1960.

Huang-ch'ao chang-ku hui-pien, see CKHP.

Huang-ch'ao cheng-tien lei-tsuan, see CTLT.

Hummel, Arthur W., ed. Eminent Chinese of the Ch'ing Period, 1644-1911. 2 vols.; Washington, D.C., 1943, 1944.

Hunter, W.C. The Fan Kwae at Canton Before Treaty Days, 1825-1844. Shanghai, 1911.

IMC: China, Imperial Maritime Customs, Returns of Trade and Trade Reports, Statistical Series 3 and 4, 1859-. Shanghai: Inspector General of Customs.

------Decennial Reports on the Trade, Navigation, Industries, etc., of the Ports Open to Foreign Commerce in China and Korea and on the Condition and Development of the Treaty Port Provinces, Statistical Series 6, first issue, 1882-1891; second issue, 1892-1901, in 2 vols. Shanghai: Inspector General of Customs, 1893 and 1906.

Inouye Jukichi. The Japan-China War. Shanghai, n.d.

IWSM: Ch'ou-pan i-wu shih-mo 籌辦夷務始末 (The complete account of our management of barbarian affairs). Photolithograph of the original compilation; Peiping, 1930. Later Tao-kuang period, 1836-1850, 80 chüan; Hsien-feng period, 1851-1861, 80 chüan; T'ung-chih period, 1862-1874, 100 chüan.

Kiang-nan chih-tsao-chü chi, see KNCTCC.

Kiernan, E.V.G. British Diplomacy in China, 1880-1885. Cambridge, England, 1939.

King, John. "Progress in China," Pt. 2, Blackwood's Edinburgh Magazine (February 1863).

Kirkaldy, A.W. British Shipping: Its History, Organization, and Importance. London and New York, 1914.

KNCTCC: Kiang-nan chih-tsao-chü chi 江南製造局記 (The record of the Kiangnan arsenal), comp. Wei Yun-kung 魏允恭. 10 chüan; Shanghai, 1905.

Kuo, P.C. A Critical Study of the First Anglo-Chinese War, with Documents. Shanghai, 1935.

LaFargue, T.E. China's First Hundred. Pullman, Washington, 1942.

Laird-Clowes, W. "The Naval War Between China and Japan," in
T.H. Brassey, ed., The Naval Annual (1895), pp. 90-126.

Lanning, G. and S. Couling. The History of Shanghai. Shanghai,
Hongkong, Singapore, and Yokohama, 1921.

Lephay, J. La Bataille Navale du Yalu. Paris, 1895.

Li Chien-nung. The Political History of China, 1840-1928, tr.
Ssu-yü Teng and Jeremy Ingalls. New York, 1956.

Li Wen-chung-kung ch'üan-chi, see LWCK.

Lin-le (Augustus F. Lindley). Ti-Ping Tien Kwok. London, 1866.

Little, Mrs. Archibald. Li Hung-chang. London, 1903.

Lo Jung-pang, "The Decline of the Early Ming Navy," Oriens Extremus,
5.2:147-168 (December 1958).

------"China's Paddle Wheel Boats," Tsing Hua Journal of Chinese
Studies, new ser., 2.1:189-215 (May 1960).

Lo-ya-erh 羅亞爾. "Chung-Fa hai-chan" 中法海戰 (The Sino-
French naval war); in Chung-Fa chan-cheng, III, 539-591.
Tr. from Maurice Loir, L'Escadre de l'Amiral Courbet (1886).

London Daily News.

London Times, The.

Lovette, Leland P. Naval Customs, Traditions, and Usage. 3rd
ed.; Annapolis: United States Naval Institute, 1939.

Lü Shih-ch'iang 呂實強. Chung-kuo tsao-ch'i ti lun-ch'uan ching-
ying 中國早期的輪船經營 (The early development
of steamers in China). Taipei: Institute of Modern History,
Academia Sinica, 1962.

LWCK: Li Wen-chung-kung han-kao 李文忠公函稿 (The letters
of Li Hung-chang), ed. Wu Ju-lun 吳汝綸 Shanghai?, 1902.
See in particular P'eng-liao han-kao 朋僚函稿 (Letters to

friends), 24 chüan, and Hai-chün han-kao 海軍函稿 (Letters to the Navy Board), 4 chüan.

Ma Chien-chung 馬建忠. "K'an Lü shun-chi" 勘旅順記 (A record of an official investigation of Port Arthur); in Hsiao-fang hu-chai yü-ti ts'ung-ch'ao 小方壺齋輿地叢鈔 (Material on geography from the Hsiao-fang hu study). 71 chüan; 1897.

McClellan, J.W. The Story of Shanghai. Shanghai, 1889.

McGiffen, Philo N. "The Battle of the Yalu: Personal Recollections by the Commander of the Chinese Ironclad Chen-Yuen," Century Magazine (August 1895), pp. 585-604.

Mahan, A.T. The Influence of Sea Power upon History, 1660-1783. 5th ed.; Boston, 1894.

------ "Lessons from the Yalu Fight," Century Magazine, 1.50:629-632 (August 1895).

Malone, C.B. History of the Peking Summer Palace. Urbana, 1934.

Marble, Frank. "The Battle of the Yalu," United States Naval Institute Proceedings, 21.3:479-499, followed by comments by others, pp. 499-521.

Marder, A.J. The Anatomy of British Sea Power. New York, 1940.

Masefield, John. Sea Life in Nelson's Time. New York, 1925.

Mayers, W.F. The Chinese Government. 3rd ed., rev. by G.H.H. Playfair; Shanghai, 1897.

Meadows, T.T. The Chinese and Their Rebellions. London, 1856.

Meng Ssu-ming. "The Organization and Functions of the Tsungli Yamen." Ph.D. thesis; Harvard University, 1949.

Michael, Franz. "Military Organization and Power Structure of China During the T'ai-p'ing Rebellion," Pacific Historical Review (November 1949).

"Military Skill and Power of the Chinese," Chinese Repository, 5.4:165-178 (August 1836).

Morse, H. B. International Relations of the Chinese Empire. 3 vols.; Shanghai, 1910-1918.

------The Trade and Administration of China. Shanghai, 1913.

------The Chronicles of the East India Company Trading to China, 1635-1834. 4 vols., New York, 1926; and Vol. 5 (1742-1774), New York, 1929.

Morse, H. B. and H. F. MacNair. Far Eastern International Relations. Shanghai, 1928.

"Naval Colleges in China," Engineer (June 8, 1900).

"Navy of China," Spectator (Jan. 21, 1882).

Pao Tsen-peng 包遵彭. Chung-kuo hai-chün shih 中國海軍史 (History of the Chinese Navy). Taipei: Chinese Naval Publication Office, 1951.

Parker, E. H. "Militaryism in China," China Review (September-October 1885), p. 109.

------John Chinaman and a Few Others. New York and London, 1902.

Paullin, Charles O. "The American Navy in the Orient in Recent Years," United States Naval Institute Proceedings, 37.4:1137-76 (December 1911).

Pei-yang hai-chün chang-ch'eng, see PYHC.

Pelcovits, N. A. Old China Hands and the Foreign Office. London, 1948.

Playfair, G. M. H. The Cities and Towns of China. Shanghai, 1910.

Potter, E. B. and J. R. Fredlund, eds. The United States and World Sea Power. New York, 1955.

Powell, Ralph L. The Rise of Chinese Military Power, 1895-1912. Princeton, 1955.

Pratt, Sir John T. China and Britain. London, n.d.

PYHC: Pei-yang hai-chün chang-ch'eng 北洋海軍章程 (Regulations of the Peiyang navy). 2 chüan in 1 ts'e; Tientsin, 1888; foreword by I-huan 弈譞 dated Sept. 30, 1888.

Rawlinson, John L. "The Lay-Osborn Flotilla: Its Development and Significance," Papers on China, 4:58-93. Harvard University, East Asian Research Center, 1950.

"Rebellion, Diplomacy, and Progress in China," Fraser's Magazine (February 1865).

Shore, Henry N. The Flight of the Lapwing. London, 1881.

Smith, H. Warrington. Mast and Sail in Europe and Asia. London and New York, 1906.

Spector, Stanley. "Li Hung-chang and the Huai-chün." Ph.D. thesis; University of Washington, 1953.

------Li Hung-chang and the Huai Army. Seattle, 1964.

Spense, G. J. A Forgotten Flotilla. Printed by the Kentish Times, n.d.

Sprout, Harold and Margaret. The Rise of American Naval Power. Rev. ed.; Princeton, 1942.

Swisher, Earl. China's Management of the American Barbarians. New Haven, 1953.

Teng Ssu-yü. Chang Hsi and the Treaty of Nanking, 1842. Chicago, 1944.

Teng Ssu-yü and John K. Fairbank. China's Response to the West. Cambridge, Mass., 1954.

Tsiang, T. F. "China After the Victory of Taku, 1859," American Historical Review, 35.1:79-84 (October 1929).

------"Sino-Japanese Diplomatic Relations, 1870-1894," Chinese Social and Political Science Review, 17.1:1-106 (1933).

Tso Shun-sheng 左舜生. Chung-kuo chin-pai-nien-shih tz'u-liao hsü-pien 中國近百年史資料續編 (Additional materials on the history of China in the last 100 years). 2 vols.; Shanghai: China Book Company, 1933.

Tso Wen-hsiang-kung ch'uan-chi, see TWHK.

Tung-fang tsa-chih 東方雜志 (The eastern miscellany). Shanghai, 1904-; monthly.

TWHK: Tso Wen-hsiang-kung ch'uan-chi 左文襄公全集 (Complete works of Tso Tsung-t'ang). 100 chüan in 96 ts'e; Changsha, 1889.

Tyler, W. F. Pulling Strings in China. London, 1929.

United States Naval Institute Proceedings, see USNIP.

USNIP: United States Naval Institute Proceedings. Annapolis: U.S. Naval Institute, 1874-; monthly.

Vagts, Alfred. Defense and Diplomacy, the Soldier and the Conduct of Foreign Relations. New York, 1956.

"Vladimir" (Zenone Volpicelli). The China-Japan War. New York, 1896.

Wade, T. F. "The Army of the Chinese Empire: Its Two Great Divisions, the Bannermen or National Guard, and the Green Standard or Provincial Troops: Their Organization, Locations, Pay, Conditions, and etc.," Chinese Repository, 20.5:250-280 (1851); ibid., 20.6: 300-340; ibid., 20.7:363-422.

Waley, Arthur. The Opium War Through Chinese Eyes. London, 1958.

Wallach, Capt. Richard. "The War in the East," United States Naval Institute Proceedings, 21.3:691-740 (1895).

Wang Hsin-chung 王信忠. "Fu-chou ch'uan-ch'ang-chih yen-ko " 福州船廠之沿革 (Development of the Foochow dockyard); in Pao Tsen-peng, Chung-kuo chin-tai-shih lun-ts'ung 中國近代史論叢 (Discussions on modern Chinese history). Taipei, 1956.

WCSL: Ch'ing-chi wai-chiao shih-liao 清季外交史料 (Historical materials on foreign relations in the latter part of the Ch'ing dynasty), comp. Wang T'ao-fu 王㪼夫 (Wang Yen-wei 王彥威), ed. and pub. Wang Liang 王亮 (Wang Hsi-yin 王希隱). 112 ts'e; Peiping, 1932.

Wei Yüan 魏源. Hai-kuo t'u-chih 海國圖志 (An illustrated gazetteer of the maritime countries). First block-print ed., 1844; 50 chüan.

Wen T'ing-shih 文廷式. "Wen-ch'en ou-chi" 聞塵偶記 (Diary); in Chung-Jih chan-cheng, V, 495-499.

Wilson, Andrew. The Ever-Victorious Army. London, 1868.

------Lieutenant-Colonel Gordon's Chinese Campaigns and the Taiping Rebellion. Edinburgh and London, 1868.

Wilson, H.W. Ironclads in Action. 2 vols.; Boston, 1898.

------Battleships in Action. 2 vols.; Boston, 1926.

Wilson, James H. China: Travels and Investigations in the Middle Kingdom. 3rd ed.; New York, 1901.

Wright, Mary C. The Last Stand of Chinese Conservatism. Stanford, 1957.

Wright, Stanley F. Hart and the Chinese Customs. Belfast, 1950.

Yao Hsi-kuang 姚錫光. "Tung-fang ping-shih chi-lüeh" 東方兵事紀略 (A record of Eastern military matters); in Tso Shun-sheng, Chung-kuo chin-pai-nien-shih tz'u-liao hsü-pien, pp. 133-243.

Yuan Tao-feng. "Li Hung-chang and the Sino-Japanese War," T'ien-hsia Monthly, 3.1:9-17 (August 1936).

Yung Wing. My Life in China and America. New York, 1909.

GLOSSARY OF TERMS AND TITLES

chih-fu 知府
ch'üan-ch'üan ta-ch'en 全權大臣
Chün-chi ch'u 軍機處

Hai-chün hsüeh-t'ang 海軍學堂
hai-fang 海防
hou-lu 後路
Hsien-feng (Emperor) 咸豐
Huai-chün 淮軍

I-ho-yüan 頤和園

K'ang-hsi (Emperor) 康熙
Kuang-hsü (Emperor) 光緒
K'un-ming Lake Naval Academy
昆明湖水師學堂

lien-chün 練軍
likin 釐金
lun-t'i 論題

Nanyang ta-ch'en 南洋大臣
Nei-wu fu 內務府

Peiyang ta-ch'en 北洋大臣
san-hai 三海
Sheng-yü kuang-hsün 聖諭廣訓
Shui-shih yamen 水師衙門
Shui-shih ying-wu ch'u
水師營務處

Tao-kuang (Emperor) 道光
taotai 道台
t'i-t'iao 提調
tsung-chien-kung 總監工
Tsung-li ko-kuo shih-wu yamen
總理各國事務衙門
tsung-pan 總辦
Tu-pan chün-wu ch'u
督辦軍務處
T'ung-chih (Emperor) 同治
t'ung-ling 統領
T'ung-wen kuan 同文館

Wan-shou shan 萬壽山
Wu-pei hsüeh-t'ang 武備學堂

INDEX

Academies, see Training
Admirals: position in water force, 8, 10, 11, 12; position in modern navy, 164, 174–175, 180
Admiralty, 65, 76, 94
Akitsushima, 170, 182
Albrecht, 177, 183
Alcock, Rutherford, 60
Amherst, 14
Ammunition: and Foochow dockyard, 52; bad quality of, 81; Kiangnan supply of, 82, 96, 146; in Peiyang fleet, 148–149; in Yalu battle, 184–185, 238n81. See also Guns
An Lan, 48, 59
An Wei-chün, 235n36
Anhwei army, 64, 78, 82, 139, 174
Annam, 167
Annapolis, 168
Apprentices, School of, see Foochow dockyard training programs
Arlington, L. C., 91, 121–127
Armored ships: in Western navies, 69, 139; Li Hung-chang's interest in, 72, 73, 74, 76, 78, 140; built in China, 96, 137, 138, 147; French, at Ma-wei battle, 116; in Sino-Japanese War, 174, 183
Armstrong gunboats: Li Hung-chang's interest in, 69–71, 72, 74, 78, 86, 90, 91, 93, 110, 224n2; in Nanyang fleet, 145; in Sino-Japanese War, 187, 190, 198
Armstrong guns, 32, 44, 96, 111, 149, 150
Arrow (lorcha), 30
Arsenals: Anking, 35, 38; Canton, 145; Fukien, 213n1; Hanyang, 108; Kiangnan (Shanghai), see Kiangnan arsenal; Kirin, 86, 213n1; Nanking, 38, 81–82, 145, 213n1; Soochow, 38, 41; Sungkiang, 38; Tientsin (Machinery Bureau), 41, 43–44, 63, 71, 81, 82, 84, 149; Tsinan, 108
Aspic, 116, 117

Baclé, 109
Baker Island, see Sino-Japanese War, Feng-tao battle

Ballard, G. A., 151, 163
Banner forces: command system, 8; Green Banner water force, organization, 6–7, personnel, 8–10, patrols, 10, financial problem of, 17–18; Manchu Banner water force, separate from Green Banner units, 6, 7, 208n22. See also Water force
Beresford, Lord Charles, 146, 149–150, 198
Bernard, W. D., 17, 20, 127
Biggerstaff, Knight, 104, 106
Black Flag troops, 109
Blakely ordnance, 80
Board of Civil Office, 84, 106
Board of Revenue, 53, 68, 131, 142, 144, 145
Board of Rites, 235n30
Board of War, 6, 7
Board of Works, 4
Bogue (Bocca Tigris), 14–16
Book of Filial Piety, 57
Breech-loading guns, 146, 149
Bridge, Sir Cyprian, 96
Bruce, Sir Frederick, 34, 35, 36
Bulwarks, 5
Burlingame, Anson, 35
Buying versus building problem: controversy over, 45–46, 62, 98; and Li Hung-chang, 67–79, 136; attempt to regulate, 131; and Foochow dockyard, 137–138; after Sino-Japanese war, 198; and Wu T'ang, 214n19

Cambridge, 17, 19
Captains, Western-trained: and Foochow dockyard fleet, 58–59, 87–88; and Li Hung-chang, 72, 85, 133, 159; in Sino-French War, 94, 119, 127, 227n47; in Sino-Japanese War, 176–177, 188, 191
Career, naval, isolation of, see Naval officers
Cargo-capacity of warships, see Warships
Carnet naval guns, 237n57, 238n78
Carroll, James, 57, 58, 59

INDEX

Censors, 24, 142
Centralization of power, see Political System
Chains, as harbor defense, 8, 16, 31
Chang Chao-tung, 217n2
Chang Chao-yün, 220n76
Chang Ch'eng, 58, 59, 88, 112, 117, 119, 127, 220n76, 221n83
Chang Chih-tung: opposition to Li Hung-chang, 76; in Sino-French War, 110–111, 112, 113; ship purchases after 1885, 131, 139; Hankow works, 145; defensive ideas, 152, 204; training activities, 155, 164, 198; in Sino-Japanese War, 186; personal influence, 202
Chang Ch'ing, 20, 25, 26
Chang Meng-yüan, 79, 83, 84, 86, 99, 102, 105
Chang P'ei-lun: naval centralization proposals of, 66, 129; belligerence of, 78; and Sino-French War, 81, 111, 112–115, 117–120; and Foochow dockyard, 83, 90, 101, 105; and Sino-Japanese War, 149, 196; Lang's complaint about, 157
Chang Shu-sheng, 155
Chang Sze kuang, 58
Chang Wen-hsuan, 190
Chang Yao, 135
Chang Yin-lin, 192
Ch'ang-lin, 239n88
Ch'ang Sheng, 59
Ch'ao Wu, 113, 126
Ch'ao Yung, 92, 110, 121, 122, 147, 181, 185, 218n40, 229n44
Chassepot gun, 44
Checks and balances, Manchu system of, 7–8, 23
Chen, Gideon, 104
Chen Hai, 48, 71
Chen Nan, 237n68
Chen Pien, 190, 237n68
Chen Tsao-ju, 107
Chen Wei, 50, 116, 117
Chen Yüan: Li Hung-chang's plans for, 94, 139, 153, 229n44; in reorganization of Peiyang fleet, 133; visit to Japan, 165; in action in Yalu battle, 171, 172, 175, 176, 178, 180, 183, 184; in action at Weihaiwei, 187, 188, 190, 196
Ch'en Ch'ao-ao, 85, 87, 137, 221n83
Ch'en Chi-tung, 221n83
Ch'en Hang, 51, 71, 78, 116
Ch'en Lan-pin, 84, 89, 107
Ch'en Pi-kwang, 190, 191, 195

Ch'en Ying, 127
Cheng Ch'ing-lien, 85, 137
Cheng Fu-kuang, 21
Cheng Ho, 5, 14, 15
Cheng Yü, 59, 88
Ch'eng Pu-ch'uan, 88
Chenhai harbor blockade, 123, 126–127
Cherbourg navy yard, Ecole de Construction, 88
Chi An, 50, 59, 77, 114, 116, 117
Chi Yüan: in Feng-tao battle, 171, 191, 193; in Yalu battle, 172, 174, 182, 193, 194; at Weihaiwei, 187, 190; Li Hung-chang's evaluation of, 229n44
Ch'i Chün-tsao, 22
Ch'i-kung, 3, 27
Ch'i-shan, 2, 3, 22, 23, 25, 209n58
Ch'i-ying, 3, 25, 27
Chiang Ch'ao-ying, 88, 123, 125, 126, 127, 216n60
Chiang I-feng, 213n14
Chien Sheng, 88, 113, 116
Chien Wei, 58
Chih Yüan, 139, 172
Chin Yung, 123, 125, 126, 127
China Educational Mission, 59, 107; and Li Hung-chang, 89, 90, 91, 94; C.E.M. "boys" in the Sino-Japanese War, 177, 195
China Merchants Steam Navigation Company, 51, 55, 67, 70, 72, 91, 123, 142
China's fighting ships, compared with Western ships, see Ships and fleets
Chinese Repository, 28
Ching Ch'ing, 98, 230n90
Ching Yüan (British-built) 139, 172, 184, 187, 188, 189, 191, 195
Ching Yüan (Chinese-built), 50, 54, 59
Ching Yüan (German-built), 139, 172, 182
Ch'iu Pao-jen, 85, 189, 191, 195, 220n76
Chou Feng-chien, 88
Chou Fu-k'ai, 218nn41, 42
Chou K'ai-hsi, 105, 106
Chronometers, made in China, 48
Chu T'ing-piao, 7
Ch'uan-cheng tso-yi, 83
Chuenpi battle, see Opium War
Chuenpi Convention, 2–3, 12
Ch'ung-hou, 43, 48
Chün-chi ch'u, see Grand Council
Civil service examination system, 2, 202. See also Institutional structure
Civil War (United States), 35
Cliques, naval officers', 164–165, 176, 196

308

INDEX

Clown, 211n46
Coastal defense: in Opium War, 8, 11–13, 15–18; in Second China War, 30–32; Li Hung-chang's early ideas on, 67; 1874 Formosa crisis, 68; mixture of old and new in, 80, 110–111, 113, 118, 149–150, 151–152. *See also* Forts; Strategy
Columbia, 148
Commercial use of warships, *see* Warships
Commissioner of Trade for Northern (or Southern) Ports, *see* Northern (or Southern) Commissioner
Competition: rivalries of Li Hungchang, 53, 63–64, 70, 71, 72, 74, 75, 78; intraprovincial, 53, 75, 99–100, 136–137; interprovincial, 53, 59, 67, 70, 139, 176, 190, 200–201, 222n101; between Peking and provinces, 33, 36–37, 54, 56, 70, 73, 100–102, 140–145, 202; regional, 93, 140, 164–165, 176–177; international, affecting China's naval modernization, 65, 78, 93, 130, 163, 198. *See also* Sea Defense Fund
Composite ships, 43. *See also* Iron
Compton, 211n46
Confucian values: and naval innovation in 19th century, 1, 2, 56, 202–203; Cheng Ho mission, 15; and naval innovation in Opium War period, 19, 21, 24; and T'ung-chih Restoration, 39–40; and naval training, 44, 57, 92; and arsenal work, 104, 108; and economic isolation of Foochow dockyard, 137; and discipline and punishments, 162, 180, 192, 197; and dynastic decline, 199. *See also* Conservative opposition; Institutional structure
Confucius, 29, 33, 123
Conservative opposition: to Foochow dockyard, 45–46, 52–54, 79, 84, 86, 89, 98; to all modernization, 56; to overseas training, 87–89, 154, 163. *See also* Confucian values; Naval officers
Construction, naval, training in, *see* Foochow dockyard training programs
Conversion of warships, *see* Warships
Cormorant, 31, 32
Coup d'état of 1861, 32–33
Courbet, Admiral Amédé A. P., 112, 113, 117, 118, 119, 120, 125
Courts-martial, need for, *see* Discipline
Coxinga, 13
Crews, water force, 9; for Lay-Osborn ships, 35, 36. *See also* Training, crews in action
Curriculum, naval, *see* Training; Foochow dockyard training programs
Cushing, Caleb, 28

D'Aiguebelle, Paul, 45, 46, 47, 56
De Meritens, Baron, 44, 46, 47
Decentralization of power, *see* Political system
Denby, Charles, 130, 163
Design, School of, and Office of, *see* Foochow dockyard training programs
D'Estaing, 112, 116
Detring, Gustav, 65, 76, 93, 148
Diet (Japanese), 169
Direct Commands, 11
Direct memorials, 6, 7, 10, 25
Discipline: water force, 9, 11–12, 25, 26; role of emperor in, 67, 197, 203–204; in Sino-French War, 114–115, 119–120, 126, 127; in 1888 Peiyang regulations, 161–162; in Sino-Japanese War, 172–174, 186–188, 191; need for court-martial system, 192–195, 197, 203–204
Distribution of Foochow-built ships, 61–62. *See also* Foochow dockyard, financial problems
Dockyards: Amoy, 145; Anking, 35, 36; Canton, 145; Foochow (Ma-wei), *see* Foochow dockyard; Taku, 86, 147; in Japan, 168
Doris, 14
Douglas, Admiral Archibald, 168
Duguay Trouin, 112, 116
Dynastic decline and naval modernization, 1–2, 199–201

East India Company, 14
Economic isolation of Foochow dockyard, 104
Elliot, Charles, 2, 3
Empress Dowager, 63, 66, 113, 130, 140, 141, 143, 195, 196, 200
Epsilon, *see* Armstrong gunboats
Espionage for Japan, 149, 170
Ever-Victorious Army, 33, 38, 65

Falsification of battle reports, 24–25, 120
Famine, 72, 103
Fang Pai-ch'ien, 170, 182, 191, 192–193, 220n76
Fatshan Creek battle, *see* Second China War
Fei Yün, 50, 54, 59, 114, 116, 147
Feng Chün-kuang, 40, 41, 107

309

INDEX

Feng-tao battle, *see* Sino-Japanese War

Financial problems hindering naval modernization, 134, 141, 151, 156, 162–163, 202; misuse of naval funds for rebuilding the Summer Palace, 32, 68, 73, 131, 140–145, 147. *See also* Foochow dockyard, financial problems

Fire rafts, 16, 24–25, 31, 80

"Fire-wheel boats," 26. *See also* Steam propulsion

Fires, in Yalu battle, 181, 183, 238n73

Fleets, modern, in China: attempts to create a single fleet, 60–62, 64–67, 129–130; in 1880's and Sino-French War, 79, 110, 113–116, 120–121, 126, 224n3; joint maneuvers, 131, 133–134, 149, 169; in the Sino-Japanese War, 135, 168–169, 180, 186, 201, 239n90. *See also* Foochow fleet; Kwangtung fleet; Nanyang fleet; Peiyang fleet

Flying Squadron (Japanese), 170, 181

Foochow dockyard: establishment of, 39, 41; early political troubles, 44–48; ships built to 1875, 48, 50–52; financial problems to 1875, 52–56, 61; conservative attack on, 86; building, 1875–1884, 96–99; financial problems, 1875–1884, 99–104, 131, 218nn32,46; after Sino-French War, 136–138, 143, 145, 169, 242n4; relations with Li Hung-chang, 70, 71, 72, 73, 81, 83–90; superintendents of, 83–84, 104–106, 199, 223n27

Foochow dockyard training programs: naval academy, 47, 56–60, 90, 154–155; naval construction schools (School of Naval Construction, School and Office of Design, School of Apprentices), 47, 48–50, 51, 85–86; advanced overseas training, 49–50, 59–60, 70, 85–90, 154. *See also* Training, officers in action

Foochow fleet, 61, 64, 74, 82, 145; captains and command of, 58, 85, 87–88, 227n47; discipline in Sino-French War, 127; size in 1884, 224n3

Foreign ships sold to China, *see* Appendix C

Foreigners: directing producing facilities, 44, 47, 79, 96, 97, 214n33; serving in navy during Sino-French War, 58, 94, 121–122, 125, 127; serving in navy during Sino-Japanese War, 175, 177, 236n50. *See also* Lang; Giquel

Formosa, relief of in 1884, *see* Sino-French War

Forts: in Opium War, 14–16; in Second China War, 31, 32, 44, 45, 80; in Sino-French War, 110, 111; in Sino-Japanese War, 150–151

France: and Second China War, 31–32; policy during Taiping Rebellion, 34; naval competition with Great Britain, 37; trouble with China in Annam, 109–110, 167; and advanced overseas training, 59, 87, 88; supplier of military goods to China, 45, 47, 67, 76; supplier of military goods to Japan, 168, 237n57, 238n78. *See also* Sino-French War

Fu Ching, 145, 239n90

Fu Hsing, 48, 113, 116, 127

Fu Po, 48, 80, 116

Fu Sheng, 113, 116

Functional ambivalence of China's warships, *see* Warships

Fuso, 240n110

Gamma, *see* Armstrong gunboats

Gatling guns, 82

Germany: Germans in Li Hung-chang's service, 65, 70; visited by Foochow graduates, 88, 163; and 1888 Peiyang reorganization, 133; ships sought by or sold to China, 78–79, 110, 120, 137, 139, 170, 198, 229n45; supplies from, and Li Hung-chang, 44, 71, 76–77, 78, 80, 115, 131, 148. *See also* Detring; Von Hannecken

Gingals, 7, 146

Giquel, Prosper: under contract to direct Foochow dockyard, 45, 46, 47, 51; and training at Foochow dockyard, 56, 58, 59, 176; role of in purchasing ships, 70, 71, 73, 218n26; and overseas training, 86, 88; post-contract work of at Foochow dockyard, and criticisms of, 97, 98, 99

God of War, 124

Goddess of Mercy, 23

Gordon, Charles ("Chinese"), 38, 65

Governors-general, military powers of, 7–8, 11, 12, 33

Graft, 68, 70

Grain boats, 6

Grand Council (Chün-chi ch'u), 6, 33, 60, 109, 113, 169, 171, 173, 186

Grand Secretariat, 52, 60

Grant, U. S., 93

Great Britain: 18th-century warships in China's waters, 13; naval policy toward China before Opium War, 13–14;

310

INDEX

in Opium War, 2, 7, 11–13, 15–17, 20, 21, 23, 24–25; and piracy, 30, 34; and Second China War, 30–32; policy in Taiping Rebellion, 33–35; naval competition with France, and technical advances, 30, 37, 69; and training of Chinese naval personnel, 59, 87, 88, 166; and 1888 Peiyang reorganization, 133, 159; ships sought and bought by China, 67, 69–70, 73–76, 78, 80, 110, 121, 139, 168, 181, 182, 229n45, 242n4; guns sold to China, 44; and sale of ship engines to China, 97, 110, 121, 137, 138, 139. *See also* Lang; Hart

Great Wall, 151
Greenwich, Royal Naval College, 88
Gruson quick-firing guns, 174
Gunports, 5, 20
Gunpowder, 6, 43, 127, 184
Guns: in Opium War, 6, 15, 20, 21, 22, 27; foreign, Chinese interest in during Taiping Rebellion, 29; in Second China War, 31–32; advances in Western, 32, 69, 70, 74–75; Li Hung-chang's interest in, 37, 38, 44, 76, 79, 148, 150–151; built in China, 42, 43, 44, 96, 137; on Foochow-built ships, 42, 48; in Sino-French War, 80–81, 116–117; smuggled into China, 131–132; in Sino-Japanese War, 174, 178, 180, 184–185, 193
Gutzlaff, Charles, 11, 14

Hai An, 42
Hai Ching, 51
Hai-chun hsüeh-t'ang, 157
Hai-fang fund, *see* Sea Defense Fund
Hai-fang Yamen, 65
Hai-kuo t'u-chih, 28
Hai Tung Yün, 59
Han T'ien-chia, 38, 41, 107
Hanlin Academy, 192
Hart, Sir Robert, 47, 51, 137, 173; and Lay-Osborn fleet, 34–35; and buying ships for China, 46, 62, 67–68, 69, 70–77, 90, 98, 140; and attempts to reorganize China's fleets, 65, 93–94, 111, 129–130, 136, 157; on progress in China, 202
Hashidate, 168
Heckman, 177, 183
Heng Hai, 132, 137
Hideyoshi, 167, 171
High command: in Sino-French War, 118, 119, 120, 122; in Peiyang organization, 163–165; in Sino-Japanese War, 174–176. *See also* Captains
Hiyei, 184
Ho Ching, 43, 52, 72, 83, 84, 88, 89, 98, 111, 114, 118
Ho Hsin-ch'uan, 216n60
Ho Ju-ch'ang, 99, 103, 112, 113, 115, 117, 118, 119
Ho Kuei-ch'ing, 29
Ho Li-kuei, 26
Hoffman, 194
Hong merchants, 18
Hongkong and Shanghai Bank, 140–141
Hope, Admiral James, 34
Hou-lu, 149, 184
Hsia Hsiao-t'ao, 215n39
Hsia Hsien-lun, 54, 83, 105
Hsiang Jung, 29
Hsien-feng Emperor, 32
Hsü Chien-yen, 108, 188, 239n100
Hsü Ching-ch'eng, 129, 139, 148
Hsü Hsiang-kuang, 25, 26
Hsü Shou, 36, 108, 188, 213n5
Hsü T'ing-hsu, 80
Hsüeh Fu-ch'eng, 71, 131, 217n8
Hu Kuang-yung, 46, 105
Hu Yu-fen, 174
Hua An, 123
Hua Heng-fang, 213n5
Huan T'ai, 138, 239n90
Huang Chien-hsün, 181, 216n60, 220n76
Huang Ch'iung-ch'en, 191
Huang Chüeh-tzu, 22, 210n13
Huang En-ch'ao, 107
Huang Lien-k'ai, 58
Huang Wei-hsuan, 58
Hui Chi, 42
Hunan militia, 33

I Hsin, 71, 97, 116
I-hsin, *see* Prince Kung
I-huan, *see* Prince Ch'un
I-k'uang, *see* Prince Ch'ing
I-li-pu, 11, 12, 22
I-liang, 18
I-shan, 3, 22, 23, 26, 27
Ideological problems in naval modernization, 202. *See also* Confucian values; Conservative opposition; Institutional structure
Imperial Household (Nei-wu Fu), 131, 132
Imperial Maritime Customs: and Lay-Osborn fleet, 29, 34; revenues for Kiangnan arsenal, 41; revenues for Foochow dockyard, 44, 53, 99–102, 136–

137; revenues sought by Li Hung-chang, 63, 65, 68, 69, 70, 72, 75, 139; revenues for arms purchases, 67–68; aides to Li Hung-chang, 91; criticism of Foochow dockyard ship, 98
Indirect commands, 8
Inspector-General of Naval Affairs, 148
Institutional structure: and naval innovation, 2, 201–202, 203–204; and training, 90, 91, 94–95, 156, 157, 158–159, 166; and dockyard careers, 104–108, 146, 199; and loss of naval wars, 127–128, 143; and financial problem, 103–104; and strategy, 153. *See also* Confucian values; Conservative opposition
Intelligence-gathering, 23
International law, and China's defense problems, 111–112, 113, 120, 152
International rivalry, and China's naval modernization, *see* Competition
Interprovincial rivalry, *see* Competition
Iron, in Chinese ship-building, 42, 43, 47, 48, 52, 70, 71, 97, 99, 137
Isolation of naval officers, *see* Naval officers
Ito, Admiral Yukyo, 181, 183, 184, 188, 190, 195

Japan: and Liu-chiu-Formosa crisis of 1870's, 42, 51, 55, 60–62, 64, 65, 68, 73, 74; and Korea, 78, 114, 121, 167–168; naval strength of, compared to China, 61, 168; references to by Li Hung-chang, 52, 90
Joint maneuvers, *see* Fleets, modern
Jui-lin, 61, 67, 217n15
Jung-lu, 239n88

K'ai Chi, 79, 86, 98, 99, 103, 114, 120, 122, 123, 124, 126
Kang-i, 156
K'ang Chi, 73, 97, 98, 102
K'ang-hsi Emperor, 8
Kao Sheng, see Kowhsing
Kestrel, 31
Kianghwa, treaty of, 167
Kiangnan arsenal: operations to 1875, 38, 41–43; concentration on ordnance, 42–43, 70, 96; and Li Hung-chang, 52, 53, 64, 69, 81–83; training at, 85; leadership at, 89, 106–108; and Tso Tsung-t'ang, 103; after Sino-French War, 145–146; in 1898, 150; in Sino-Japanese War, 152, 173
Kiangsi, 37

Kirin shipyard, 98
K'o Chien-chang, 191
Korea: treaty with United States, 65; and Sino-Japanese War, 78, 167–170
Kowhsing, 149, 170–171, 175
Krupp guns: Li Hung-chang's interest in, 43, 44, 76, 80, 144, 148; imitated at Kiangnan arsenal, 96; on Chinese ships, 98, 170, 178; in Chinese forts, 111, 149, 150, 151
Kuan T'ien-p'ei, 2, 11, 18
Kuan-tu shang-pan, 223n25
Kuang Chia, 138, 169, 182, 195
Kuang-hsü Emperor, 65, 130, 144
Kuang I, 145, 169, 170, 171, 191, 193, 235n36
Kuang Keng, 145, 186, 187, 190
Kuang Ping, 145, 169, 182, 186, 190, 191
Kuei Sung-ch'ing, 156
K'un-ming naval academy, 141
Kung Ch'en-lin, 19–20, 21, 25, 29
Kuo Pao-chiang, 135
Kuo Sung-t'ao, 66, 72, 83, 88, 105
Kwangtung fleet, 80, 135, 145, 168

La Fargue, Thomas, 107
Lai Yüan, 139, 172, 183, 184, 187, 189, 191
Lake Palace, 141
Lang, William: first hired, 93, 94; returns, 130, 157; training activities of, 140, 152, 178; anomalous position of, 163–165; decline of training after his resignation, 183; attempts to recall him, 198
Lapwing, 87, 89, 188
Last Stand of Chinese Conservatism, The, 40
Lay, Horatio Nelson, 29, 34, 35–37, 60
Lay-Osborn Fleet, 34–37
Lee, 31, 32
Lee magazine rifle, 96
Li Ch'ang-keng, 13
Li Ch'ao-pin, 217n6
Li Ch'ao-t'ang: relations with Li Hung-chang, 75, 77, 78, 79, 83, 85–86, 106; and *K'ang Chi* affair, 98; dockyard accounts of 1880, 102; qualifications for dockyard superintendent, 105
Li Ch'eng-mo, 54, 58, 61, 87, 120
Li Chia-pen, 216n60
Li Chien-nung, 110, 115, 130
Li Feng-pao: as ship-buying agent for Li Hung-chang, 71, 72, 75, 78, 80, 83, 84, 85, 88, 94; peculations of, 104, 219n50

INDEX

Li Fu-t'ai, 214n19
Li Ho-lien, 188, 191, 196, 216n60
Li Hsing-jui, 103, 107
Li Hung-chang: rise to power and experience with Western arms during Taiping Rebellion, 33, 36, 37-39, 199, 201; and Kiangnan arsenal, 41, 43, 53, 81-82; and Tientsin arsenal, 43-44, 82, 148-149; and Foochow dockyard, 51, 54, 55, 77, 79, 83-90, 91, 92, 98, 105, 106, 132, 154; and Sung Chin, 52-53; and Nanking arsenal, 82, 156; and purchase of ships and arms, 67-79, 138, 141, 143-145, 148-149; and Liu-chiu-Formosa crisis, 61-62; and attempts to reorganize fleets, 64-67, 129-135; and Sino-French War, to Ma-wei battle, 109, 111, 112, 113-114, 115, 118; and expedition for relief of Taiwan in Sino-French War, 120, 122, 123, 126, 127; and naval training and personnel system, 90-94, 156-163, 165, 166, 203; and 1888 reorganization of Peiyang fleet, 134-135, 159, 200; and Gulf of Chihli installations, 110, 147-148, 150-151; and Sino-Japanese War, to battle of Yalu, 167-168, 169-174, 175-177; and aftermath of Yalu battle, 185-189, 191-192, 194, 195, 196; strategic ideas of, 69, 76, 78, 151, 173, 187-188; rivalry with Tso Tsung-t'ang, 64, 68, 99; corruption and patriotism of, 136; personal influence of, 63-64, 100, 202, 217n12
Li Kuo-hsiang, 216n60
Li Lien-ying, 140, 143
Li Ping-heng, 189
Li Shao-fang, 7
Li Shih-chen, 127
Li Shou-t'ien, 86
Li T'ien, 216n60
Li Ting-hsin, 175, 183, 191
Li Tsung-hsi, 55, 61, 68, 70
Liang Men-ch'ien, 106
Liao Shou-feng, 234n6
Lien-chün, 45, 53, 63, 64, 82, 130
Lin I-sheng, 182, 191
Lin Kuo-hsiang, 191, 193, 240n22
Lin Li-chung, 181, 191
Lin Shao-nien, 141, 142
Lin T'ai-tseng: ready for command, 88, 216n60; service with Li Hung-chang, 92, 133, 164; in Yalu action, Sino-Japanese War, 173, 176, 183; suicide of, 187-188, 196; posthumous reward, 191

Lin Tse-hsü: and the Opium War, 2, 3, 15, 17, 18, 24; interest in naval change, 19-20, 22, 23, 25, 39, 45, 200
Lin Wen-ho, 59
Lin Ying-ch'i, 189, 220n76
Lin Yung-sheng, 220n76
Lintin, 27
Liu Ch'ao-pei, 239n105
Liu-chiu Islands, *see* Japan
Liu Jui-fen, 107
Liu K'un-i, 132, 152, 156, 186, 189
Liu Ming-ch'uan, 80, 111, 123, 151
Liu Ping-chang, 111, 113
Liu Pu-ch'an: training of, 88, 216n60; in 1888 Peiyang reorganization, 133, 164-165; in Sino-Japanese War before Yalu battle, 170, 173, 175, 176; in Yalu action, 178, 179, 180, 183, 191; and problem of replacing Admiral Ting, 187-188; suicide of, 190; character of, 85, 192-193, 238n75
Liu Yung-fu, 109
Liu Yün-k'o, 11, 20, 210n13
Lo Erh-kang, 143
Lo Ta-ch'un, 87, 216n66
Lu Han, 58, 88
Lu Wen-ch'ing, 59
Lü T'ung-chih, 84
Lynx, 116, 117

Ma Chien-chung, 121
Ma-wei battle, *see* Sino-French War
Ma-wei dockyard, *see* Foochow dockyard
Macartney, Halliday, 38, 44, 81, 82, 104
Mahan, Alfred, 15, 153
Maintenance of China-built ships, *see* Foochow dockyard, financial problems
Manchu Banner water force, *see* Banner forces
Mandl, 148
Mannix, William, 71
Maps and charts, 57-58, 158, 233n23
Marble Boat; *see* Financial Problems, misuse of funds
Marco Polo, 4
Margary affair, 71
Martini-Henry guns, 44
Matsushima, 168, 182, 183
McClure, Vice Admiral, 186, 187, 190
McGiffen, Philo, 149, 157, 171, 176, 177, 178, 181, 184, 187
Mei Yün, 48
Meiji Restoration, 167
Merchant ships built at Foochow dockyard, 51

INDEX

Mines (defensive weapon): in Second China War, 31–32; Li Hung-chang's interest in, 44, 76, 86, 91, 151, 157; at Kiangnan arsenal, 96; in Sino-Japanese War, 152, 172
Ming dynasty, 5, 11
Mohammedan revolt, 45
Morale of naval officers, *see* Naval officers; Discipline
Morse, Hosea B., 13
Morse, H. B., and H. F. MacNair, 109
Mu Chin-shu, 193
Mu T'u-shan, 111–114, 118–119, 137
Mutinous situations, 127
Muzzle-loading ordnance, 149

Nan Ch'en, 110, 120, 123, 124, 145, 230n 69, 239n90
Nan Shui, 110, 120, 123, 124, 145, 230n 69
Naniwa, 170, 182
Nanking, Treaty of, 1, 30
Nanking naval academy, *see* Training
Nanyang fleet, 143, 198; captains and training in, 123, 127; and Sino-French War, 66, 120–122; and Sino-Japanese War, 168, 169
Napier, Lord, 14
Nationalism, 202, 227n73
Naval academies, *see* Training
Naval architects, *see* Foochow dockyard training programs
Naval career, public denigration of, *see* Naval Officers
Naval construction training, *see* Foochow dockyard training programs
Naval ministry, 65. *See also* Admiralty; Navy Board
Naval officers, isolation of, 154–155, 166, 203; attempts by Li Hung-chang to circumvent, 158, 159, 160–161, 162. *See also* Confucian values; High command
Naval reviews, *see* Fleets, modern
Navy Board: establishment and functions of, 130–132, 138, 147, 156, 158, 169, 204; and Li Hung-chang, 134, 148, 159, 162; and misuse of funds for rebuilding Summer Palace, 140–145
Needle gun, 44
Nei-wu Fu, 131, 132
Nemesis, 6, 17, 21
Nichols, 177, 183
Nieh Ch'i-kuei, 107, 108
Niu Chien, 21, 23
Nordenfeldt guns, 125, 149

North-South joint naval maneuvers, *see* Fleets, modern
North Star, 12
Northern Commissioner: and 1874 Liuchiu-Formosa crisis, 60–62; and arms-producing centers in China, 81–82; powers of, 63–64, 86; attempts to increase powers of, 64–66, 132, 134, 135, 162; limitations on power of, 112, 132–133. *See also* Li Hung-chang

Office of Naval Affairs, 90
Opium tax, 53, 56
Opium War: action in, 1, 2, 3, 15–17; naval innovation during and immediately after, 19–28, 200, 204; and Second China War, 32. *See also* War junks
Ordnance, naval, *see* Guns
Organization of fleets, *see* Fleets, modern
Osborn, Sherard, 34–38
Overseas training, *see* Foochow dockyard training programs

Pagoda Anchorage battle, *see* Sino-French War
Palmerston's follies, 153
P'an Ch'eng-wei, 27
P'an Shih-ch'eng, 20, 25, 26, 27, 29
P'an Shih-yung, 21, 25, 26
Pao-chia, 114
Pao Hua, 189
Pao Min, 145, 213n7
Pao Tsen-peng, 143
Parker, E. H., 163–164, 166
Pay, in 1888 regulations, 162
Peculation, 68, 77, 79, 104. *See also* Financial problems, misuse of funds
Pei Chin-ch'uan, 38
P'ei Yin-sen, 131, 132, 136, 137–138, 154, 155
Peiyang fleet: and Robert Shufeldt, 65, 93; command of, 81, 85, 176–177, 186; and Sino-French War, 110, 114; in period 1884–1894, and reorganization of, 131, 133–136, 144, 148–149, 156, 157–163, 164, 198; obsolescence of, 140, 144, 172, 185; in Sino-Japanese War, 168, 169, 171, 174, 179, 180, 186, 187, 190, 198, 203; ships in line of battle in Yalu battle, and at Weihaiwei, 237n 61, 239n98
Peking Field Force, *see* Lien-chün

INDEX

Peking, rivalry with provinces, *see* Competition
P'eng Yü-lin, 29, 64, 103
P'i-shan p'ao, 81
Pien Pao-ti, 138
P'ing Yüan, 145, 182, 187, 188, 190, 191, 196
Piracy: and water force, 4, 5, 9, 13, 28; and growing official interest in steamers, 29, 34, 38–39, 54; international concern over, 45
Plover, 31, 32
Political system: and naval innovation, 23–25, 130; problem of decentralization of power, 6, 10, 11–12, 34–35, 60, 66, 224n4
Port Arthur, battle of, *see* Sino-Japanese War
Port Arthur naval base, 77, 147–148
Pottinger, Sir Henry, 3
Prince Ch'ing, 111, 129, 130, 192, 239n88
Prince Ch'un: before 1885, 65, 67, 111; and Navy Board, 129–132, 133, 135, 141
Prince Kung: and Lay-Osborn fleet, 34–35, 37; and international control of piracy, 39; and Sun Chin attack, 52, 54–55; and overseas training, 59; and naval centralization proposals, 66; influence of, 32, 60, 67, 68, 109, 111, 130, 186, 239n88
Provincial loyalties, 92–93
Provincial rivalries, *see* Competition
Punishments, *see* Discipline
Purvis, 177

Quality of Chinese ships and fleets, *see* Ships and fleets

Railroad engine, model of at Canton, 20
Ram cruisers, 74, 78
Ramiro, 27
Regulations, Peiyang Fleet, 1888, 133–135, 159
Remington rifles, 43, 44, 80, 96, 146
Repair of Foochow dockyard ships, 97, 99, 101, 222n5
Repairs to Chinese ships, after Yalu battle, 185
Restoration, T'ung-chih, 201
Reviews, naval, *see* Fleets, modern
Rewards: and punishments, in 1888 Peiyang regulations, 159; after Yalu battle, 191
Rockets, 44
Russell and Company, 29
Russia, 34, 75, 76, 77, 93, 110

"S", *see* Siebelin
Sah Ping-chen, 239n102
Saikyo, 182, 184
San-hai, 141
Scheldtweiler, P., 230n71
Schools, naval, *see* Training
Screw propulsion, 42, 48
Sea Defense Fund: and Li Hung-chang, 64, 70, 71, 73, 75, 78, 100; and Foochow dockyard, 101; and Navy Board, 131, 132, 140, 142. *See also* Competition
Second China War, 30–32
Segonzac, M., 97
Self-strengthening movement, 39, 44, 55, 74, 94–95, 99, 128
Seymour, Admiral, 31
Shan Ch'ing, 129, 131
Shanghai arsenal, *see* Kiangnan arsenal
Shao Yu-lien, 107, 169, 234n8
Shen Pao-chen: as superintendent of Foochow dockyard, 45–48, 51, 55–56, 105, 106, 117; and training work at Foochow dockyard, 50, 56, 57, 58–59; and 1874 Liu-chiu crisis, 51, 55, 61, 62, 116; and Sung Chin attack, 52, 54; and efforts to unify fleets, 64–65; and Li Hung-chang, 67, 70, 72, 74, 75, 80, 82, 83, 84, 86; and financial problems at Foochow dockyard, 99, 100, 101, 102
Shen Pao-ching, 41, 44, 107
Shen Shou-ch'ang, 191, 193
Sheng Hsuan-huai, 148
Sheng-yü kuang-hsün, 57
Shih Lang, 13
Shih Shih-p'iao, 13
Ship Supply Depot, Port Arthur, 148
Ships and fleets, Chinese, quality of: Western opinion of, 1–2, 47, 61, 79, 80, 163, 177, 189, 234n10; Chinese views of, 54–55, 71, 77, 79, 84–85, 99; compared with British, 3–4, 6, 52; compared with French, 116–117; compared with Japanese, 170, 174, 185
Shipyards, *see* Dockyards
Shore, Henry, 80, 87, 89, 95, 97
Shufeldt, Robert, 65, 79, 93
Shui-lu hsüeh-t'ang, 155
Shui-shih, *see* Water force
Shui-shih yamen, 129
Siebelin ("S"), 94, 121, 122
Sino-French War: background, 109–110; command structure in, 111–112; guns and ammunition in, 80, 82; captains at Ma-wei battle, 85, 94, 227n47; build-up of opposing fleets before Ma-wei

INDEX

battle, 112–116; Chinese ships compared with French, 116–117; Ma-wei battle, 116–119, 163, 196; ships sunk or destroyed at Ma-wei battle, 226n45; punishments after Ma-wei battle, 127; make-up of Taiwan blockade relief force, 120–123, 167, 176, 201; naval disaster at Shih-p'u, 123–126; Chenhai blockade, 123, 126–127; creation of Navy Board after war, 129; view of P'ei Yin-sen on French victory, 137

Sino-Japanese War, 150, 198, 201; background, 167–170; Feng-tao (Baker Island) battle, 170–171, 191, 192–194, 195; leadership in Yalu battle, 85, 174–177; Yalu battle ships, 144, 170, 174; crews in Yalu action, 163, 178; ammunition in Yalu battle, 184–185; action in Yalu battle, 179–185, 191, 193, 194, 203; Western assessment of Yalu battle, 185; Weihaiwei naval action, 187–190, 240n112; rewards and punishments, 191–192

Slow-down practices at Foochow dockyard, 98

Smuggling of arms into China, 131

Snider guns, 44, 80

Southern Commissioner, powers of, 60–62, 64–65, 112, 132, 134–135. *See also* Nanyang fleet

Standardization of naval and military materiel, need for, 5, 67, 79–81, 148–149, 152, 198

Staunch, 69

Steam propulsion in China: early experiments and interest in, 20, 21, 22, 25, 29, 31, 36, 37, 38–39; steam engines built in China, 42, 48, 97; steam engines purchased abroad, 41, 47, 51. *See also* Great Britain, sale of ship engines

Steel, in ships in China, 70, 74, 137, 145, 147

Stockpiling, 148

Strategy: early, 13–16; evolving tradition of, 81, 103, 122–123, 128, 151–152, 203; Li Hung-chang's notions of, 67, 69, 74, 76, 133, 151, 152–153; in Sino-Japanese War, 171–174, 187–188. *See also* Tactics

Subsidies for shipbuilding, 17, 53, 139; to Foochow dockyard, 55, 77, 83, 100, 103, 223n20

Suicides, 187–188, 190–192, 196–197

Summer Palace, *see* Financial Problems, misuse of funds

Sung Chin, 43, 52–54

Superintendent of Repair, 4

Supply, in Peiyang fleet, 148–149

Ta Ya, 51

Table of organization, Green Banner forces, 8

Tactics, 16–17, 78, 121; in Sino-Japanese War, 178–180

Tai Tsung-ch'ien, 172, 190

T'ai an, 97

Taiping Rebellion, relation of to military and naval modernization, 28, 33, 39, 56, 67, 102, 201, 202

Taiwan relief expedition, *see* Sino-French War

Takachiho, 170, 182

T'ang Chung-lin, 156

T'ang T'ing-hsu, 220n70

T'ang Wen-ch'ing, 218n42

Tao-kuang Emperor, 3, 25

Tartar Generals, powers of, 7, 8, 11

Telegraph and centralization, 115–116

Teng Chih-ch'ang, 92

Teng Ch'ing, 97, 103, 120, 121, 123, 124, 125

Teng Shih-ch'ang, 166, 176, 182, 191, 216n60, 220n76

Teng T'ing-chen, 11, 12, 22

Teng Ying Chou, 97, 135

Thistle, 31

Three Character Classic, 158

Thunderer, 52

T'i-tiao, 105–106

Tide, role of at Ma-wei battle, 114, 117–118

T'ien Chi, 41, 42, 48

Tientsin arsenal, *see* Arsenals

Tientsin Convention of 1885, 167

Tientsin Machinery Bureau, *see* Arsenals

Tientsin Massacre, 67

Tientsin treaties, 31, 32, 45, 47, 61

Ting Hua-jung, 122, 124, 126, 127

Ting Jih-ch'ang: arsenal experience of, 38, 41, 64; and Li Hung-chang, 67, 72, 75, 83; as Foochow dockyard superintendent, 97, 100, 105, 107; and misuse of funds for Summer Palace, 143

Ting Ju-ch'ang: position under Li Hung-chang, 90, 92, 133–135, 156–157; in Sino-French War, 122; in Sino-Japanese War, 144, 170–174, 175, 177, 178–181, 184, 186–190, 191, 195; anomalous position as admiral, 163–166; suicide, 190, 197

Ting Kung-ch'en, 20, 25, 26, 27

316

INDEX

Ting Shou-ts'un, 21
Ting Yüan, 133, 139, 153, 165, 172; in Yalu battle, 175–176, 178, 180, 182, 183; at Port Arthur, 185; at Weihaiwei, 187, 189, 195
Togo Heihachiro, 165, 234n12
Tonghaks, 168
Torpedoes and torpedo craft: bought by China, 44, 75, 76, 80, 139, 140, 145; built in China, 44, 71, 137, 147, 156; instruction and training in, 88, 157, 166; in Sino-French War, 116, 117, 119, 124–125; defensive preparations, 133, 151, 152; in Sino-Japanese War, 168, 169, 186, 187, 189–190, 193, 195–196; torpedo tubes in Chinese and Japanese ships, 231n86, 238n79
Toulon Navy Yard, 88
Tracy, Captain, 58
Trade, suspension of, 14
Training: in water force, 9–10; academy at Canton, 154–156; program at Foochow dockyard, *see* Foochow dockyard training programs; Kiangnan arsenal, 85, 96; K'un-ming academy at Peking, 154, 232n1; academy at Nanking, 154, 156; school at Peitang, 157; schools at Port Arthur, 156; schools at Shanhaikuan and Taku, 157; academy at Tientsin, 86, 90–94, 154, 156–158, 232n14, 233n20; schools at Weihaiwei, 154, 156, 157, 232n14; of crews in Sino-French War, 122, 124–125, 126, 127; of crews in Sino-Japanese War, 176, 178, 183; of officers in Sino-French War, 85, 94, 119, 123, 227n47; of officers in Sino-Japanese War, 85, 176, 181, 183, 184, 188, 189, 192–194; of modern naval personnel, comments on, 163–166; spread of Foochow academy regulations, 91, 156, 158, 232n1
Tribute system, 14, 15, 32, 109
Triomphante, 112, 116, 117, 118, 119
Tsai T'ing-kan, 195–196
Ts'ai Hui-ts'ang, 107
Ts'ai Kuo-hsiang, 36, 87
Tsao Chiang, 42, 169, 170, 171
Ts'e Hai, 42
Tseng Chi-tse: and Li Hung-chang, 74, 76, 77, 81, 88, 92; and Navy Board, 129, 131, 139; on overseas training, 221n80
Tseng Kuo-ch'uan, 37, 80, 131, 156; and Sino-French War, 111–115, 120, 123, 125; and misuse of funds for Summer Palace, 140–142

Tseng Kuo-fan: early interest in Western military materiel, 29, 33, 34–35, 36–37, 64, 188, 199; and the Kiangnan arsenal, 38, 39, 41–43; and buying versus building problem, 67, 79
Tso Tsung-t'ang, 66, 84; rise to power and early interest in Western military materiel, 29, 33, 38–39, 199; and Foochow dockyard, 44–47, 48, 52, 99, 137; and financial problem at Foochow dockyard, 53, 55, 56, 100, 101, 103, 138; and Foochow dockyard training program, 56–57, 59, 154; and functional ambivalence of China-built ships, 54, 136; and purchase of ships, 59, 67, 78–79; as rival of Li Hung-chang, 64, 66, 68, 76, 77, 81, 82, 83, 86, 132; and Sino-French War, 119, 120, 127; recommends naval centralization, 129; unable to effect profound change, 200
Tsung-chien-kung, 108
Tsung-li shui-shih ying-wu ch'u, 156
Tsung-pan, 107–108
Tsungli Yamen, 99, 100, 105, 152, 155, 158, 164, 171, 198, 234n7; start of, 33; not a powerful central agency, 60–62; and fleet organization, 66–68; and purchase of materiel, 69, 72, 74, 132; and Sino-French War, 111–112, 113, 121; and Navy Board, 129–130, 134
Tu-pan chün-wu ch'u, 186
T'ung-an vessel type, 27
T'ung Chi, 145
T'ung-chih Emperor, 32
T'ung-chih Restoration, 33, 39, 104
T'ung-wen kuan, 56
Tyler, William F.: comments on Li Hung-chang, 135–136; comments on Chang P'ei-lun, 149; comments on Admiral Ting, 165–166; comments on Liu Pu-ch'an, 180, 192; in Sino-Japanese War, 175–180, 183, 187, 240n107
Tzu-hsi, *see* Empress Dowager

United States weapons in China, 148

Vavasseur guns, 80, 116
Villars, 112, 116
Vipere, 117, 119
Volta, 112, 117
Von Hannecken, Constantin, 147, 175, 178, 179, 180, 183, 186, 187, 198

Wade, Thomas F., 10
Wade-Hart proposals, 45

INDEX

Waley, Arthur, 24
Wan Nien Ch'ing, 48, 52, 77, 88, 113n35
Wan-shou Shan, 141
Wang K'ai-t'ai, 52, 217n15
Wang Kao, 36
Wang Sung-ch'en, 233n33
Wang Yung-ho, 220n70
Wanghsia, Treaty of, 30
War junks: in Opium War, 3–6, 10–11; in Second China War, 31; in 1872, 52, 153; in Sino-French War, 116
Ward, Frederick T., 33
Warrior, 37
Warships, China's functionally ambivalent: design of, 42, 46, 48, 54; commercial use of, 87, 99, 144, 154; conversion of at Foochow dockyard, 54–55, 73, 77; attempts to make more martial, 54, 136, 137
Water force: in Second China War, 31; and Li Hung-chang, 68, 77; men serving in modern ships, 58–59, 87, 88, 94, 101–103, 123, 200; old units retained, 64, 82; in 1870's, 82, 89, 100; in 1890's, 151
"Water-thunder," 20, 27
Wei Ching, 42
Wei Han, 85, 87, 118, 137, 138, 139
Wei Yüan, 28, 77, 88, 97, 154, 170, 179, 187
Weihaiwei Machine Shop, 148
Weihaiwei forts, *see* Forts
Weihaiwei naval action, *see* Sino-Japanese War
Wen-hsiang, 60, 68
Wen Ping, 64
Wen T'ing-shih, 192
Wen Yu, 52, 54, 100, 102
West Point, 90
Western drill, 45
Western Park, 141
Wheel boats, 19, 21, 24
Whitworth guns, 44, 80
Wo-jen, 56
"Woo," *see* Wu Yung-fu
Woolich guns, 44
Wright, Mary, 104
Wu An-k'ang, Admiral, 121, 122, 124, 126, 127
Wu Chien-chang, 29
Wu Chien-hsün, Admiral, 21, 25, 26, 28
Wu Ching-yung, 182, 195
Wu Chung-hsiang, 83, 91, 106, 108, 132, 155
Wu-er-kung-o, 11, 12
Wu Hsi-ch'ang, 58

Wu-pei hsüeh-t'ang, 156
Wu Ping-chien, 27
Wu Shih-chung, 58, 59, 87, 220n76
Wu Ta-ch'eng, 86
Wu Ta-t'ing, 57, 105, 106
Wu T'ang, 46, 47, 52, 59, 105
Wu Te-chang, 85
Wu Ts'an-ch'eng: and Li Hung-chang, 70–73, 83–84, 86, 91; and Foochow dockyard, 97, 101–102, 105–106
Wu T'ung-yün, 215n39
Wu Wei-yin, 228n18
Wu Wen-yung, 22
Wu Yung-fu, 177

Yalu River action, *see* Sino-Japanese War
Yang Ch'ang-jui, 137
Yang Fang, 25
Yang Lien-ch'en, 86
Yang Tse-che, 220n76
Yang Wei, 92, 147, 166; in Sino-French War, 110, 121–122; in Sino-Japanese War, 182, 185, 193
Yang Wu, 50, 54, 80, 81, 87, 97; in Sino-French War, 112, 113, 116, 119, 127
Yang Yung-lin, 183, 188, 190, 191, 196, 197
Yang Yüeh-pin, 29, 58, 121
Yeh Chih-ch'ao, 171, 172, 188
Yeh Fu, 59, 216n60
Yeh Ming-ch'en, 29
Yeh T'ing-ch'uan, 106
Yeh Tsu-kuei, 184, 189, 191, 195, 220n76
Yeh Wen-lan, 105, 106
Yen Tsung-kwang (Yen Fu), 88, 91, 157, 216n60, 220n76
Yi Ch'ang-hua, 20, 25
Yi-sun, 171
Ying-kuei, 45, 46
Ying Pao-shih, 41
Yoshino, 145, 168, 170, 171, 181, 182, 189, 193, 194
Yu An, 42
Yu Hsiung-fei, 135
Yu Hsün, 147
Yu-k'un, 18
Yu Pu-yun, 11, 12
Yuan Chia-san, 34
Yuan K'ai, 97, 126
Yung Pao, 51, 59, 78, 80, 116
Yung Wing, 38, 41, 89, 107
Yu-ch'ien, 20, 22
Yü Yuan, 70, 120, 121, 123, 124, 127
Yüan Shih-k'ai, 167, 195

HARVARD EAST ASIAN SERIES

1. *China's Early Industrialization: Sheng Hsuan-huai (1844–1916) and Mandarin Enterprise.* By Albert Feuerwerker.
2. *Intellectual Trends in the Ch'ing Period.* By Liang Ch'i-ch'ao. Translation by Immanuel C. Y. Hsü.
3. *Reform in Sung China: Wang An-shih (1021–1086) and his New Policies.* By James T. C. Liu.
4. *Studies on the Population of China, 1368–1953.* By Ping-ti Ho.
5. *China's Entrance into the Family of Nations: The Diplomatic Phase, 1858–1880.* By Immanuel C. Y. Hsü.
6. *The May Fourth Movement: Intellectual Revolution in Modern China.* By Chow Tse-tsung.
7. *Ch'ing Administrative Terms: A Translation of The Terminology of the Six Boards with Explanatory Notes.* Translated and edited by E-tu Zen Sun.
8. *Anglo-American Steamship Rivalry in China, 1862–1876.* By Kwang-Ching Liu.
9. *Local Government in China under the Ch'ing.* By T'ung-tsu Ch'ü.
10. *Communist China 1955–1959: Policy Documents with Analysis.* With a foreword by Robert R. Bowie and John K. Fairbank. (Prepared at Harvard University under the joint auspices of the Center for International Affairs and the East Asian Research Center.)
11. *China and Christianity: The Missionary Movement and the Growth of Chinese Antiforeignism, 1860–1870.* By Paul A. Cohen.
12. *China and the Helping Hand, 1937–1945.* By Arthur N. Young.
13. *Research Guide to the May Fourth Movement: Intellectual Revolution in Modern China, 1915–1924.* By Chow Tse-tsung.
14. *The United States and the Far Eastern Crises of 1933–1938: From the Manchurian Incident through the Initial Stage of the Undeclared Sino-Japanese War.* By Dorothy Borg.
15. *China and the West, 1858–1861: The Origins of the Tsungli Yamen.* By Masataka Banno.
16. *In Search of Wealth and Power: Yen Fu and the West.* By Benjamin Schwartz.
17. *The Origins of Entrepreneurship in Meiji Japan.* By Johannes Hirschmeier, S.V.D.
18. *Commissioner Lin and the Opium War.* By Hsin-pao Chang.
19. *Money and Monetary Policy in China, 1845–1895.* By Frank H. H. King.
20. *China's Wartime Finance and Inflation, 1937–1945.* By Arthur N. Young.
21. *Foreign Investment and Economic Development in China, 1840–1937.* By Chi-ming Hou.
22. *After Imperialism: The Search for a New Order in the Far East, 1921–1931.* By Akira Iriye.
23. *Foundations of Constitutional Government in Modern Japan, 1868–1900.* By George Akita.
24. *Political Thought in Early Meiji Japan, 1868–1889.* By Joseph Pittau, S.J.
25. *China's Struggle for Naval Development, 1839–1895.* By John L. Rawlinson.